D1458516

EAMON DeVALERA
1882-1975

IRISH CATHOLIC : VISIONARY

ANTHONY J. JORDAN

Edited by Fiona Jordan

Eamon DeValera, 1915.

ACKNOWLEDGEMENTS

I wish to thank the many Libraries and Archives where I was facilitated, including National Library of Ireland, National Archives, UCD Archives, Dublin Archdiocesan Archives, Irish College Rome, Royal Dublin Society, Royal Irish Academy, Dublin City Council's Gilbert Archive, Pembroke and Ringsend Public Libraries.

I would like to mention Gerard Whelan, Denise Arigho, (who enabled me to establish a relationship between DeValera and John MacBride) at the RDS; Mary Clarke at the Gilbert; Seamus Helferty at UCD; Noelle Dowling at Drumcondra; Brendan Keane and Dr. Pat McCarthy for reading the text, and conducting a seminar with me subsequently; Patrick Hugh Lynch for providing archival materials, and Judith Jordan for reading the Introduction. I would also like to thank Fr. Aidan Lehane CSSp and Father Seán Farragher CSSp, a fellow Mayo man, now in his 88th year, who gave me valuable information. Thanks are also due to David Lowe for his dedication to the production of this work.

ᗄᚗ ᚗᗄ

Copyright @ 2010, Anthony J. Jordan.

Published by: Westport Books, Dublin 4.

Email: westportbooks@yahoo.co.uk

ISBN: 9780952444794

ᗄᚗ ᚗᗄ

ᗄᚗ ᚗᗄ

Cover Design, Book Layout and Print Reproduction, David Lowe.

Printed in Ireland by ColourBooks Ltd, Baldoyle, Dublin 13.

Dedication

For

Mary, Antonia, Judith, Stephen, Fiona, Murphy

and

Lily Antonia Moran.

CONTENTS

Eamon DeValera, Taoiseach, 1958.

INTRODUCTION

Eamon DeValera's long life and political career were mediated by his brand of Irish Catholicism. He maintained a close life-long association with Blackrock College, which for him was as much a second home as an *alma mater*. He participated in all its activities, educational, sporting, cultural and religious, forming important friendships, lay and clerical. He believed profoundly that he had a religious vocation to the priesthood but was thwarted in this by successive institutions. He was happy to continue to live in the College as an adult, for as long as proved possible. He absorbed its Catholic ethos and way of life becoming and remaining, a devoutly committed Catholic, adept in the practice of mental reservation, as the occasion demanded. The most important event of his life, a vision of Jesus Christ, occurred there.

Eamon DeValera developed into a leader of men and was promoted quickly in the Volunteers and emerged as the major survivor of the 1916 Revolution, which, as we shall see, was steeped in Catholic devotion. The Treaty and Civil War cut short his leadership as erstwhile colleagues, some of whom who had been longer in the field than he, established the new Irish Free State. The founding of Fianna Fáil in 1926 led to Dev assuming power in 1932. He instituted radical constitutional changes and was successful in keeping Ireland out of the Second World War. He lost power in 1948 to a Coalition Government, which almost immediately declared a Republic. Dev regained political power in 1951 and later served for two terms as President.

All those who have written about or studied aspects of the long life of Eamon DeValera agree on one thing at least, that he was a most complex man.

From the earliest years of apparent rejection by his own mother, the escape from the drudgery of life at Bruree to the hallowed walks of Blackrock College, he continued to develop an independent mind-set, which gradually led him to veritable certainties. He remained most comfortable in clerical company, remaining loyal to the Catholic Church, on his own terms, even when enduring bouts of Episcopal condemnation. His long periods in jail and living abroad, offered him security in dangerous times, and opportunities for introspection, which bolstered his self-belief and certainty of action.

He had no hesitation in speaking of his vision of Jesus Christ, which occurred at Blackrock College in 1928[1]. In later life he contemplated becoming a lay Holy Ghost brother and did become a lay member of the Carmelites. He wrote, *"Every instinct of mine would indicate that that I was meant to be a dyed-in-the-wool Tory, or even a bishop rather than the leader of a Revolution"*[2]. He was very pleased to receive the Supreme Order of Christ, which was reserved for Heads of State professing the Catholic faith, from the saintly Pope John XXIII.

Speaking on RTE in December 2007, Professor John A Murphy recounted being brought into the presence of Dev while he was campaigning in Cork in 1933. Murphy said, *"My mother brought me into the house where Dev was being received. He was sitting in an armchair and I think I actually genuflected before him. It seemed to be no different between the exposition of the Blessed Sacrament and Dev"*[3]. Dev's Church policy on attaining office was one way he reassured people who were afraid of his accession to power, while conveying the impression that he and his followers were somehow more independent of the Church. Dev represented the political tradition in Ireland, thought most capable of standing up to the Church; the tradition of Irish Republicanism, the Fenian tradition. His style conveyed this more than the substance, though he did stand up to the Church when he thought it was wrong. But on issues like divorce, contraception, obscene literature, he did not, because he was a traditional rural Catholic and agreed with the Church on such issues.

Yet this man who always had 'another world' air about him, was involved in violent revolution, civil war, bitter political enmity and infighting. To some he was a noble figure, a hero, prepared to sacrifice himself for the freedom of Ireland, while to others he was a self-seeker who looked after himself and his family, while preaching frugal comfort to the masses. In a very real way he was to combine the roles of Lords Spiritual and Lords Temporal in his own person, as far as his many followers were concerned.

Dev founded Fianna Fáil, the most successful political party in Ireland, which has remained in almost permanent government since 1932. He was able as Diarmaid Ferriter writes, *"to reap the benefits of the significant achievements of the Cumann na nGaedheal governments of the 1920's"* in reinforcing the sovereignty of Ireland during the Second World War [4]. His later years in government proved difficult as the economy was stagnant and emigration became the norm for huge sections of Irish people. He clung to an old fashioned vision of a simple rural life where people would be happy and Gaelic speaking. He never came to terms with Northern Unionists and was unable to get any movement on Partition. When John A Costello declared the Republic, Dev was sorry that he had not taken that historic step. Late in life he reluctantly moved aside to allow men with new economic ideas to take the helm in Fianna Fáil. His long and full life had been dedicated to the service of Ireland. He was among that band of heroes who risked their lives for its freedom and will forever be honoured for that patriotic offering.

Dev was keenly aware of the fact that the writing of history was dependent on available documentation. From a very early stage of his career he took (obsessive) steps to ensure that his papers would be preserved and released only under the most careful circumstances. It is only in the early years of the 21st century that his papers have been deposited to University College Dublin's Archives, which has a reputation for being fastidious in its release of documentation. Dev participated in the exercise of vindicating himself with several accommodating historians. These were admirers of his and their work can be seen as an extension of his own[5]. Thomas O'Neill, who initially began as Dev's sole biographer, left his post in the National Library and transferred to Áras an Uachtaráin to write the book in 1963.

He had to sign an agreement that the contract for the book was 'contingent' on compliance with conditions laid down by Dev. Among those were that Dev had to approve of each chapter prior to O'Neill getting access to the next traunch of papers. The book was finished in 1965 but the publishers were dissatisfied with it. Lord Longford was brought in as co-author in 1965 and a new contract signed.[6]

The official biography of Dev by Longford and O'Neill was published in 1970, during Dev's second tenure as President. The authors were given complete freedom to Dev's own papers and this was useful on many areas that had not previously been written about, from his point of view. Dev did allow the authors to rely on documentation where it was in conflict with his own recollection. They wrote in their 'Introduction' that this rarely occurred. But their book was too subservient in almost all aspects of Dev's long and controversial career, to be taken at face value. T. Ryle Dwyer wrote, *"Their hagiographical account was like a case for DeValera's canonisation to crown off his presidency"*[7]. John Bowman regarded this book as akin to autobiography[8.]

Dev was reacting to the historical works that had already been written from the Irish Free State point of view. These would have included Piaras O'Beaslai's book on Michael Collins, Padraig Colum's *Arthur Griffith, The Great Betrayal by* PS O'Hegarty, Terence de Vere White's *Kevin O'Higgins* and later Donal O'Sullivan's. *The Irish Free State*. Frank Pakenham's *Peace by Ordeal* in 1935 was the first major effort to rehabilitate Dev. Dorothy Macardle spent ten years, working closely with her subject, to produce the documentary *The Irish Republic* in 1937. Frank O'Connor's *The Big Fellow* of the same year was a counter to Pakenham's and Macardles' works. After reviewing these texts in his *Judging Dev* book Diarmaid Ferriter argues *"DeValera's historical policing did not occur in an obsessive' vacuum as Patrick Murray suggests"* in his critique of Dev in his Royal Irish Academy paper[9].

In 1936 Dev proposed a Commission to study his early record. It could engage legal and historical experts, with 3 Fianna Fáil and 3 Cumann na nGaedheal politicians as members. If they could not agree on an independent Chair, Dev proposed that a bishop be agreed. He said he was prepared to give evidence to the Commission. He would face questioning from accusers like WT Cosgrave and Miss Mary MacSweeney, "if they choose". The whole of the government archives could be made available[10]. Dev, instrumental in setting up the Bureau of Military History Project, never made a statement to it himself, nor did most of those associated with him.

Though Dev was thwarted in becoming a priest, he remained a fervent Catholic throughout his entire long life, despite suffering the embarrassment of being excommunicated with all the republicans during the Civil War. (His official biographers state that he was not excommunicated). His religion represented the very core of his being and he drew his ultimate strength from it. Because of his familiarity with clergy, they did not overawe him, as John Charles McQuaid was to discover on several occasions.

While he was happy to consult the clergy, he generally remained his own man in State affairs and had no hesitation in publicly distancing himself from the Knights of St. Columbanus. Though utterly confident in his religion, he was no evangelist. Many remarked on the sense of other-worldliness about him and this was a reflection of his clerical manner. The incident that contributed to that sense of him being close to the person of Jesus Christ occurred in 1928 and could only have served to reinforce this ethereal quality of his.

His vision of Christ was linked to a mystic and psychic priest named Fr. Leen, who of all the members of the Holy Ghost Order, made the greatest impression on Dev. This remained so though their temperaments were very different. Fr. Leen ridiculed the value of mathematics as a preparation for dealing with human affairs, adding that mathematicians and scientists should leave the affairs of man to philosophers. Despite this, the two men who had played rugby together for Rockwell, had a deep spiritual affinity. In 1928 Dev had still not been reconstituted as a public visitor to Blackrock College. Fr. Seán Farragher CCSp. writes that on one private visit to Fr. Leen, Dev was in conversation with Fr. Leen in the boarders' recreation ground, when for one moment instead of Fr. Leen he saw superimposed on him the figure of Our Lord. Dev added that he frequently felt that he was never as close to Christ and His Mother as in the presence of Fr. Leen.

That experience, however one might try to interpret it, left such an abiding impression on Dev, that on the last occasion he visited the College, some months before his death, he asked to be alerted as the car drove past the exact spot which he had clearly indicated. Fr. Farragher adds, *"Lest the reader should think that the present writer imagined he heard Dev say all of this, he was not the only one to whom Dev mentioned the incident"*[11]. The other person to whom Dev spoke of this experience to was his own son Eamon. Dev's astute secretary Kathleen O'Connell also knew of it and felt that it would be wiser not to publicise the event.

JUBILEE PILGRIMAGE TO ROME

In 1933 Dev demonstrated his fervent Catholicism by attending the centenary celebrations of the Society of St. Vincent De Paul in Paris, with Seán T. O'Kelly. He also made a Holy Year pilgrimage to Rome. His hand-written account of his Roman pilgrimage dated 27 May 1933 reads:

"I have been here now for a few days and have more than half the Jubilee Devotions done. On arrival on Wednesday a large body of young clerics were enthusiastic in their greeting, met me at the station. On Thursday I went to Confession and Holy Communion in the American Paulist Church St. Susanna. Later we went to St. John Latern where we assisted at High Mass with the Pope presiding. Later we went to see the excavations of the ancient port of Rome 'Ostia'.

Yesterday I had an audience with the Pope. His Holiness, though now an old man, 76 we think, is strong and apparently quite alert in mind. Later I saw Cardinal Pacelli who is simple and most likeable. I would put him at under 60. He gave me the Sash and 'Grand Cross' of the Order of Pius IX, a decoration from the Pope. It was taken for granted that I would like it and I didn't get the opportunity of having it commuted to something else for Ireland. I think the Rector of the Irish College (Michael Curran) was responsible for the suggestion. His view was that as my predecessor had been decorated, I should also. We did the Jubilee in St. Mary Majors and St Peters yesterday.

Sunday 7.45 a.m. I am about to go to the Catacombs of St. Callixtus and Sebastian to hear Mass – possibly serve it. Later I shall be at St. Isadores and in the evening at St. Peter's for the beatification of Catherine Laboure of the Sisters of Charity of St. Vincent de Paul.

Mon. 29. I laid a wreath to Unknown Soldier – visited the Pantheon- lunched at the Irish College and visited Mussolini.

Tues. 30. Mass at St. Agnes, visited Catacombs; visited San Clemente (Irish Dominicans), St. Patricio (Augustinians) Christian Brothers who gave Irish Exhibition.

Wed. 31. Went to Church of St. Cecilia for Mass. The martyr's body is under high altar but no mass there. Went then to St. Mary of the Angels and went to Mass there. Later I went to Fascist Exhibition and gave lunch at the legation to Cardinals Lauer, Mgs Luzio, Pizani, Bernadini, and the heads of the Irish College and religious houses there.

In the evening I called on Cardinal (blank) doyen of the College of Cardinals[12].

"AM I A JEW?"

During a debate on the *Wearing of Uniforms Bill* in 1934 Dev declared in an astonishingly embarrassing way: *"there is not, as far as I know, a single drop of Jewish blood in my veins. I know that originally they were God's people, that they turned against Him and that the punishment, which their turning against God brought them, made even Christ Himself weep. In disclaiming that there is no Jewish blood in me I do not want it to be interpreted as an attack upon the Jews. I am not one of those who attack the Jews or want to make any use out of the popular dislike of them. But as there has been even from that bench over there, this dirty innuendo and suggestion carried, as I have said formally to God's Altar, I say on both sides I come from Catholic stock. My father and mother were married in a Catholic church on 19 September 1881. I was born in October 1882. I was baptised in a Catholic church. I was brought up here in a Catholic home. I have lived among the Irish people and loved them, and loved every blade of grass that grew in this land. I do not care who says or who tries to pretend that I am not Irish. I say that I have been known to be Irish and that I have given everything in me to the Irish nation"*[13].

DeValera family residence 1936, 'Bellevue', on Cross Avenue Booterstown, Co. Dublin.

*DeValera at the funeral of his son Brian who died in February 1936, aged 21 years,
with his sons L to R: Vivion, Rory, and Eamon Jr.*

A CATHOLIC NATION

Dev made a St. Patrick's Day broadcast to the USA in 1935 saying, *"Since the coming of St. Patrick, fifteen hundred years ago, Ireland has been a Christian and a Catholic nation. All the ruthless attempts made through the centuries to force her from this allegiance have not shaken her faith. She remains a Catholic nation"*[14]. Conor Cruise O'Brien mediates this statement by saying that Dev was not forgetting the Protestant patriots – Tone, McCracken, Emmet, Davis, Mitchell, and Parnell – when he made this statement. Rather, O'Brien writes in a logic worthy of Dev himself, *"The nation is felt to be the Catholic nation, Catholic by religion. Protestants are welcome to join this nation. If they do, they may or may not retain their religious profession, but they become, as it were, Catholic by nationality"*[14a]. Heather K. Crawford finds, in a study published in 2010, that Protestants are still excluded from "Irishness" because of the link between Irish identity and Catholicism and Gaelic cultural principles[14b]. Dev respected other religious faiths, as he was to demonstrate so clearly against some contrary pressures, in his 1937 Constitution.

DEATH OF BRIAN DeVALERA

One of Dev's sons, Brian, was a keen horseman and rode regularly in the Fifteen Acres of the Phoenix Park under the tutelage of an experienced horseman, his cousin, Lar Flanagan. His mother wrote that horse riding "was the joy of his life". Brian wished to become a jockey but his parents "laughed and would not hear of it". On Sunday 9 February 1936 he went riding as usual with Lar Flanagan. His regular horse was unavailable and he rode a strange one. During the ride the horse became disturbed and bolted. As the horse ran through the trees, Brian was hit on the head by a branch and severally injured. He died at the Mater Private Hospital that same afternoon aged twenty-one years. The family then lived at Bellevue on Cross Avenue and the funeral took place from Booterstown Church to Glasnevin. Sinéad never visited her son's grave though his father did so every Sunday morning. Dev had a simple granite cross placed over the grave and always stressed that he himself wished for a similar memorial. By tradition, those of the family who are buried in this plot have only their name, date of birth, and their date of death, engraved on the memorial stone.[15]

RELICS

During the crucial Anglo-Irish Trade negotiations in 1938, Dev carried "a first-class relic" of St. Therese (The Little Flower), and indeed did so during the course of the Second World War. Seán Farragher also states that though Dev had to adopt an intellectual approach to the strict boundaries between religious dogma and the lines of social legislation, he was known to have the approach of the simple Christian in his attachment to certain private manifestations of piety; especially in the matter of reverence for relics of saints and the making of pilgrimages to noted shrines[16].

DeValera's 'Alma Mater', Blackrock College, Co. Dublin.

DeValera's letter on display in the Carmelite Church Whitefrair Street Dublin, with instructions re his laying out, after his death, in the Order's robes.

BECOMING A HOLY GHOST BROTHER AT 80?

As Dev approached eighty years of age, his wife Sinéad, who was four years older than he, appeared to be in failing health. He decided that if she should pre-decease him and he was still President, he would resign and seek to join the Blackrock Community. Dr. O'Rahilly who was a very late ordained to the priesthood, and who happily joined the Blackrock Community, influenced him. Dev did not wish to be ordained but rather would prefer to be accepted as a lay Brother of the Society. It appears that while Dev had many close friends among the priests at Blackrock, there were others he did not admire. That was not so with the Brothers, whom he found to a man, to be worthy Christians. His attitude to his own increasing blindness was that "It is a small cross to have to carry for Christ".[17]

Despite being rejected in his early attempts to become a priest, Dev did become a lay member of the Carmelites. He wrote a letter on 21 September 1972, indicating his wish on his death to be buried in the habit of that Order. The following letter hangs in the entrance to the Carmelite Church on Whitefriars St. Church in Dublin. It reads;

Uachtarán na hÉireann

President of Ireland

Baile Atha Cliath,

Dublin 8.

To whom it concerns,

I want it to be known that it is my wish that when I die, I be laid out in the habit of the Carmelite Order (Calced). I have already made my wish known to my friend Dr. Donald O'Callaghan, O Carm. 29th St. New York, and to the present Fr. Provincial, Very Rev. J. Ryan, O. Carm.

Eamon DeValera,

21 Mean Fómhair, 1972.

Dev had long been a daily communicant. He visited the oratory in Áras an Uachtaráin five times daily and prayed before the Blessed Sacrament. He kept the keys of the tabernacle in his own desk and loved reading the Gospels. His absorption in the life and teaching of Jesus might have qualified him as an amateur Christologist. Religious discussion with selected clergy had a strong appeal for him. He was docile to the Church in matters of faith and morals and was proud to have been received by four Popes and to have attended three papal coronations. One of his regrets in life was that while on a visit to the Holy Land in the Holy Year of 1950, he was not able to visit Nazareth[18]. He did not fear death, telling his son Eamon, *"You know, dying will be a wonderful adventure"*[19].

John Cooney writes, *"DeValera's move to the presidency enhanced the Irish Republic's outward appearance as a solidly unchanging Catholic State. The general perception of DeValera as Cardinal Spellman of New York articulated, was 'Father of the Nation'. President DeValera conceived himself as a Catholic lay statesman and utilised the facilities of Áras an Uachtaráin as a spiritual guesthouse, especially for visiting Church dignitaries. As President, DeValera was able to combine the lifestyle of a Tory grandee with that of a bishop manqué... both McQuaid and (Cardinal) d'Alton must have felt that the Irish nation had acquired a third prelate"*[20].

The official biographers of Dev pay particular attention to the fact that Dev *"submitted all his actions to a criterion which was at once intellectual and moral"*[21]. He examined his conscience and always ensured that a powerful argument could be constructed and presented for the course he chose. The authors say that such an approach leads itself easily to accusations of casuistry, with possibly his attitude to taking the Oath of Allegiance an example of *"his more ingenious and controversial conclusions"*. The authors find that Dev *"stands out as a Christian, rather than a peculiarly, Catholic statesman"*. The book then surprisingly uses Frank Aiken as a guide to establish the role of Dev as a democratic constitutionalist.

Conor Cruise O'Brien said that Dev's independence of the hierarchy was *"rooted in the fact that he knew he was right. His cold certitude on this point was at least the equal of that possessed by an Irish Archbishop. The bishops knew this characteristic and had a certain grudging respect for it. They were no more anxious than he was, to provoke a confrontation"*. O'Brien quoted Maxim Gorky's epigram on Tolstoy; *'With God he maintains very suspicious relations. They are like two bears in one den'*[22]. Ryle Dwyer adds, *"In fact, his personal certitude was more akin to that of papal infallablity"*[23].

Lord Longford asked Dev if the Pope had confirmed that in fact he had been excommunicated during the Civil War, how would he have reacted. Dev replied, *"I should have considered that His Holiness was misinformed"*[24].

CHAPTER 1

THE EARLY LIFE OF EAMON DeVALERA

THE REJECTED ONE

A study of the life of the young Eamon DeValera, or Eddie Coll as he was known around his home at Knockmore/Bruree in County Limerick, evokes sympathy and a vast amount of admiration for one who had to make his own way through early life. He was born on 14 October 1882 at the New York Nursery & Children's Hospital on Lexington Avenue to a young strong-willed emigrant girl, Catherine or Kate Coll. The baby was registered as George de Valero on 10 November. His parents had been married on 19 September 1881 in New York City with a Fr. Hennessy officiating. The bridesmaid and best man were Kitty Brady and Frederick Hamilton. The baby boy was baptised in St Agnes Church on 3 December 1882. The godparents were Mary Shine and John Hennessy, both friends of the mother[1].

The baby's 'reputed father' was the elusive Vivion Juan deValero[2]. Eamon O'Cuiv, grandson of Dev has said of Kate Coll, *"she married this man DeValera. He was from Cuba, but he wasn't Cuban. He was a Spaniard. But I think his family had a sugar plantation in Cuba. He was living in New York and Eamon was born. His father died. Then they had to decide what would happen to the child"*[3]. On the same TG4 programme Jim Duffy said, *"Independent experts cannot find a record of the marriage or even of Juan DeValera existing"*. According to Fr Farragher, Juan died prematurely in Denver when the boy was only three[4]. His mother felt unable to raise the boy herself, and sent him back to her own mother in Knockmore in the company of her young brother Ned, who was returning home on medical advice. Dev himself has said, *"I can remember my journey here to Ireland when I was two and a half"*[5].

Terry DeValera, the youngest son of Dev, writes, *"One writer in particular has circulated a theory that my father's parents were not married at the time of his birth. To support this theory he relies on gossip, rumour, hearsay and wild speculation. It should be noted that some of the rumours stem from black propaganda circulated by my father's opponents following the Rising, the War of Independence, the Civil War and in later periods of his political career"*[6].

The Coll's home had been a one-roomed cottage but they were almost immediately to occupy a new three roomed slate roofed cottage surrounded by a small piece of land. The boy would share a bed with his Grandmother and later his Uncle Patrick. His Aunt Hannie went to America in 1886. A year later his mother Kate returned home for a holiday. She returned to New York however, without her son and soon married an English Protestant named Charles Wheelwright. This probably put paid to any possibility of Kate's first born ever re-joining his mother, as she gave birth to a new family.

STATE OF NEW YORK.   9352241

County of New York.   City of New York.

BIRTH RETURN.   352241

(In full where possible.)

1. Name of Child George De Valero
2. Sex M   Color or Race, if other than the White,   Date of Birth Oct. 14, 1882
3. Place of Birth (Street and Number) Nursery & Child's Hospital   (out of wedlock and name not given, write O.W.)
4. Name of Father Vivion De Valero
5. Full Name of Mother Kate De Valero
6. Maiden Name of Mother "   Coll
7. Birthplace (Country or State) of Mother Ireland   Age 24
8. "   "   of Father Spain   Age 28   Occupation Artist
9. Number of Child of Mother (whether 1, 2, 3, &c.) 1   How many of them now living 1
10. Name and address of Medical Attendant or other Authorized person, in own handwriting Charles L. Murray M.D. Nursery Child's Hospital
11. Date of this Return Nov. 10 '82

APPLICATION APPROVED BY COMMISSIONER OF HEALTH. JUN 30 1910

1 B—2814 P 05902

Wm A. Guilfoy M.D. No. of Certificate.

THE CITY OF NEW YORK.   STATE OF NEW YORK. REGISTRAR 35 2241
DEPARTMENT OF HEALTH.   CERTIFICATE AND RECORD OF BIRTH

CORRECTED CERTIFICATE

Name of Child Edward de Valera   352241

Sex	male	Father's Occupation	Artist
Color	white	Mother's Name	Kate or Catherine de Valera
Date of Birth	Oct 14-1882	Mother's Name before Marriage	Coll
Place of Birth, Street and No.	Nursery & Childs Hospital	Mother's Residence	61 East 41st Street
Father's Name	Vivion de Valera	Mother's Birthplace	Ireland
Father's Residence	61 East 41st Street	Mother's Age	24
Father's Birthplace	Spain	Number of previous Children	none, First Child
Father's Age	28	How many now living (in all)	

I, the undersigned, hereby certify that I attended professionally at the above birth and I am personally cognizant thereof; and that all the facts stated in said certificate and report of birth are true to the best of my knowledge, information and belief.

Signature Catherine Wheelwright
Residence 18 Brighton St Rochester N.Y.

DATE OF EXPORT.   19

DeValera's birth certificates of 1882.

Eddie walked the mile to Bruree primary school with an older neighbour's son, Jamsie MacEniry on 7 May 1888, for his first day at school, at the age of six. Though his name inscribed on the school roll was Eddie DeValera, he was still known as Eddie Coll. He spent six years there and though he was a very bright pupil, his attendance was not perfect. His Uncle Pat beat him on occasion as he mitched from school[7]. Some of his frequent absences from school, were often due to being kept at home to work for his Uncle Pat, who was a local notable, serving three three-year terms on the Board of Guardians at Killmallock. Among the pastimes Eddie indulged in were 'digging for springs' and fowl shooting. He became so accustomed to and loved handling guns that he remarked once, "I'm afraid I shall be a soldier". Irish history was not taught in the primary school, so Eddie relied on the local priest, the famous Fr. Sheehy of Land League fame, for regular sermons on the injustices put upon the Irish people by their English rulers. In May 1961 as Conor Cruise O'Brien was preparing to go to the Congo as United Nations Representative in Katanga, he was invited to visit President DeValera at Áras an Uachtaráin. As a good luck memento, Dev gave him a 19th century *daguerreotype* of Conor's great uncle, Father Sheehy. Dev had written on the picture, "He taught me patriotism"[8].

Dev's Aunt Hannie had to return from New York to nurse her ailing mother in the family home. Granny Coll doted on her Grandson and had hopes that he might become a priest. Hannie and Eddie got on well. After the death of Granny Coll on 31 July 1895, Hannie returned to America and Eddie's Uncle Pat planned to marry. This prospect had a huge isolating effect on the position of the young boy, who rated his prospects as becoming a farm labourer or at best a school monitor. Eddie had learned from other boys at school that the only way he could ever hope to get on in the world was by going to a secondary school and winning scholarships to further his education. He did not want to spend all his life as a school monitor or a farm labourer[9]. There was a Christian Brothers Secondary school in Charleville, some seven miles away, but his Uncle Pat was not very supportive of his going there. In some desperation and cunning, Eddie wrote to Hannie, demanding that his mother either send him the money to join her in New York or else arrange that he be allowed to go the CBS in Charleville[10]. His plan worked and he enrolled with the CBS on 2 November 1896. Uncle Pat could not afford to buy him a bicycle so Eddie walked the round trip of fourteen miles each day, though Dev himself was adamant that, "I didn't walk to school. I went on the train. But I would often walk home. Now and again I'd get a lift"[11].

Eddie was a good student and soon won an Exhibition Scholarship worth £20 for three years, to attend further education. He applied to the prestigious Jesuit schools of St. Munchin's and Mungret College in Limerick but did not gain admission.

Fate was to play an important part during that summer of 1898, as the boy feared that all his work and walking were to be in vain. His local curate, Fr. James Liston, happened to meet the President of Blackrock College, Fr. Larry Healy, in Lisdoonvarna. He told Healy about the young scholar and his current difficulty.

Fr. Liston must have alluded to the fact that it was believed that Eddie had a religious vocation. Fr Healy soon wrote to Fr. Liston confirming what he had earlier told him, that he would accept the young scholar in Blackrock. He wrote:

Blackrock College,

County Dublin.

31/8/1898

Dear Fr. Liston,

I send you the Prospectus of our Junior Scholasticate, and also that of our lay College. If your young friend on reading carefully the Prospectus feels drawn to the work of sacrifice, which the Missions entail, let him write a line to Fr. Kearney at the College, expressing his desires. But as our Scholasticate is very crowded, I would suggest that Master DeValera enter our lay college for a year and study his vocation *. I would accept in lieu of pension, his Junior Grade Exhibition when he gets it. And our arrangement for subsequent years would be as favourable for the boy. If his application is equal to his proved talents he ought to have a pretty brilliant career both in the Intermediate and at the Royal University.*

Yours sincerely,

L. Healy...[12].

Blackrock College was a Catholic institution managed by the Holy Ghost Order, which functioned as a boys' boarding school, an undergraduate preparatory department for examinations conducted by the Royal University and also as a seminary for those pursuing religious vocations. The Scholasticate was the Department within the college for students going on to become Holy Ghost priests. It had its own quarters and imposed a stricter regime than on the lay students[13].

The normal fee in the college was £40 per annum, but Fr. Healy was willing to accept the £20 Exhibition money in lieu. A problem arose when Uncle Pat Coll sought £5 out of the £20. This was reasonable in the circumstances, as he had to incur expenses in providing Eddie with the necessary accoutrements to attend Blackrock. These included a trunk and a new suit costing sixteen shillings[14].

Though Eddie was late arriving for the start of term and was consequently initially isolated among the students, who found his name very strange, he soon acclimatised himself to and loved the community ambience of college life. He recalled hearing a fellow student crying at night, because he was away from home. Dev felt the exact opposite, relieved to get away from manual work on the farm. He had a rather fraught relationship with the Latin teacher, who regularly sent him to the Dean of Studies. Eddie and the Dean came to a mutual understanding, which eased the problem satisfactorily.[15] In a rather sad recognition of the state of affairs of his early life, he decided that though all his fellow students went home for the Xmas holidays, he would remain in the College. His companions, with whom he felt totally at ease, were the clerical students who were not allowed home at Xmas.

Eddie applied himself so well to college life that he was nominated Student of the Year. He made some life-lasting friendships early on in Blackrock and learned that one of the main attributes of attending a 'high class school' was the opportunity it gave for meeting people, who would be useful and important in later life. Among them was Frank Hughes from Kiltimagh in County Mayo, with whose family he was to spend the Xmas holidays of 1899, and John d'Alton of Claremorris, the future Cardinal d'Alton. D'Alton later described Eddie as 'a good, very serious student, good at mathematics but not outstanding otherwise'. Eddie was a strong-willed young man who did not always accept discipline willingly. When he eventually got the opportunity of speaking with Fr. Healy about his vocation to the priesthood, he was strangely disabused of the idea. Another fellow student, Michael Smithwick, encouraged him to play rugby and study mathematics. He was subsequently to win a reputation of being something of a mastermind at mathematics. Eddie continued to win scholarships each year. At Xmas 1900, a Conference of the St. Vincent De Paul Society was set up in the College. Eddie was Secretary the first year and President the next year.[16]

In April of 1900, aged 18, Eddie witnessed the ordination of Joseph Shanahan at Blackrock. He wrote to his half-brother Thomas Wheelwright and later to his mother, saying that he thought he had a vocation also. His aim then was to become a clerical student in Clonliffe College and become a diocesan priest in Dublin. He wrote that he would have to work hard to secure the necessary scholarship to enter Clonliffe[17].

A section of Blackrock College also functioned as a University College and Eddie lived and studied there for a B.A. from 1900-1903, winning Exhibitions from First and Second Arts. In 1902 a competition among the university students at the College on Catholic Apologetics was held and the winner of first prize, a bible, was Eddie DeValera. He was also an outstanding debater and got into the mould of working assiduously for success and being awarded with leadership roles. He spoke on a variety of motions expressing opinions such as, constitutional monarchy as a form of government is preferable to republicanism, claiming that "constant elections disturbed the nation and are not conducive to the prosperity of the people'.[18] He did not attend the Irish language classes available in the college and showed no sign of being interested in the language revival.

As his final degree year arrived, Eddie was thrown in a quandary. He never had much money, though he managed to act in the fashion of most students. Now he was offered the option of a job teaching mathematics and physics at Rockwell College through Fr. Downey, the Dean at Blackrock. This offered the chance of earning some decent money. He had intended to devote himself to full-time study for his degree, but went to Rockwell and spent two of the happiest years of his life there. He had money; he joined in all the aspects of college life; he was a 'Professor' and the object of female affection from Mary Stewart from Cashel. Thomas MacDonagh, the poet, was also on the staff at the time.

During his first year at Rockwell, Eddie had become friendly with many of the Prefects there. Several of these then went on to a novitiate at Priory Park in Bath with a Fr. Murphy from Rockwell. He envied them, particularly when he got letters from them describing their outward journey and reception in Bath. A fellow teacher, Tom O'Donnell, gave him the nickname of 'Dev' at this time.

Eddie paid a very high price for his decision to teach at Rockwell for that year, when he was not awarded honours in his B.A. degree. This would hinder his attempts to become an academic. The Royal University of Ireland was a purely examining body, with its examining professors all from the Queens Colleges. Catholics like Eddie were in the invidious position that none of their own teachers were involved in the examinations.

He was still drawn to community life and during the summer after his first year at Rockwell, he decided to try out his vocation again. He went on a weekend retreat with the Jesuits at Rathfarnham Castle in the summer of 1904. When he spoke with his spiritual mentor there, he had difficulty keeping the priest's attention on the purpose of his mission. The priest was more intent in discussing other topics. In exasperation Dev asked, but "what about my vocation?" "Oh the priest replied, "your vocation. You have what is known as an incipient vocation". Dev laughed saying, "If that is all I have had after all these years, it is time I forgot about it"[19]. So he returned again to Rockwell for another year. But in spite of that, Fr. Farragher writes, Dev did not in fact, forget about his vocation.

Despite his enjoyable two years at Rockwell, which included playing at fullback on the college rugby team that reached the final of the Munster Cup, Eddie's ambitions were far greater than could be provided in a relatively undemanding country school. Once again the capital city was where he felt opportunity would be greater. He returned to Dublin in 1905, carrying a glowing reference from the College President, confident of getting a job in Blackrock College itself. This did not materialise and he faced a period of insecurity as he endeavoured to gain employment. He made an abortive attempt to get a job in Liverpool, visiting that city briefly. He then however got a temporary part-time job in Belvedere College with the Jesuits, where he also coached the college rugby team.

Dev had digs in several places around Gardiner Street and it was at the Thomond Hotel on Gardiner Place that he first got to know Major John MacBride[19a]. During that summer Dev played cricket for Blackrock. This led indirectly to him hearing from Fr. Baldwin, whom he had known at Rockwell, and was then confessor to the nuns at Carysfort, that there was a vacancy at Carysfort for a part–time mathematics teacher. His application was successful. He held this position, which entailed classes from nine to eleven daily, from September 1906 to October 1912. He became a conduit there for romantic letters from the girls to the boys in Blackrock and vice versa. He had been sharing digs with Frank Hughes on the northside but thanks to his friend Fr. Downey, he was allowed to return to live at Blackrock in the restored Castle, where he paid fifteen shillings for his weekly board. He impressed everybody by attending early morning Mass every day. He also captained the club's Second rugby team.

He later got some work at Clonliffe College, where on 7 January 1906 he again raised the question of his vocation with the College President. The President's diary note reads, *"DeValera consults on entering Eccl. State"*. Three days later the President records, *"Another interview with DeValera. Advised him not to come in now. To give up Trinity scholarship, to read for Th. And RNI (religious knowledge instruction) and to read what may be useful to begin TH. (Theology) Study next year"*[20].

It would have been very normal for a person like Eddie to consider that he might have a vocation and he would appear to have been an outstanding candidate. The obvious question arises as to why various clerics were so resistant to such a person with a serious long-term intent and desire of becoming a priest? One possible answer may lie in the judgemental arena of a practice of the Catholic Church, that anyone, whose paternity was in any way unclear, should not be accepted for the priesthood.

During 1907 when Eddie was twenty-five, his mother and her second son Thomas visited Ireland. Thomas was then studying to become a Redemptorist priest and would be ordained in June 1916. Kate thought that Eddie might return to America with them but he, as a self made man, had his own plans made for a career in education within Ireland. He continued to study mathematics intensely, though surprisingly, he never succeeded in gaining any post-graduate qualification. He did apply for teaching posts in UCC and UCG in 1912 and 1913, but the absence of an MA or PhD ensured, to his great disappointment, that a university teaching career was effectively ruled out for him.

During all these years he was never offered a teaching post in Blackrock, despite his dedication to the College in so many ways[21]. Fr. Seán Farragher surmises that this might simply be due to the fact that none became available to suit his qualifications. He adds however that one cannot help feeling that if Fr. Downey, for example, had his way, some position would have been found for him.

His wide variety of part-time teaching jobs continued and reached its highest point in 1912 when he got a temporary post, at St Patrick's College Maynooth as head of the department of mathematics and mathematical physics.

He had to invest in a motorcycle to get there. The President Dr. Daniel Mannix, who had also been a pupil at Charleville CBS, and was soon to go to Australia as Archbishop of Melbourne, invited him to apply for the post. John d'Alton was then a professor of Classics at Maynooth and assisted the mathematics teacher to become acquainted with clerics, who would become major players in the Catholic Church in Ireland and abroad. An Italian priest named Salvatore Luzio, who would meet DeValera in most dramatic circumstances during the Civil War, had just vacated the post of professor of Canon Law at Maynooth and returned to Rome.

Dev's education together with his teaching posts brought him into personal contact with the well-off middle class Catholics, who would duly take their places at the helm of clerical, political, educational, and social and business life in the emerging Ireland. He and his own family would become an integral part of that class.

Dr. Daniel Mannix, Archbishop of Melbourne, Australia.

CHAPTER 2

CONVERTING TO A GAELIC IRELAND

One of the most momentous decisions of Eddie DeValera's life occurred in 1908 when he decided to learn Irish. This decision arose as a result of the founding of the National University of Ireland in 1908, and Irish becoming an essential subject for matriculation. This led to his immersion in Irish culture, removing him from whatever Spanish background he might have had and giving him a new identity. As was usual for him, once he made his decision, he applied himself totally to the project in hand. Soon Eamon DeValera, Gaelgeoir, became more Irish than the Irish themselves, with the zeal that only a convert brings to a new faith. He had moved out of the Castle in Blackrock, probably due to a power struggle at the College between his mentor Fr. Downey and the College president[1] He took lodgings at Merrion View Avenue with a Mrs Russell from Mayo, and a native Irish speaker. She spoke Irish to the lodger and provided the real determining influence on Dev to learn Irish. His old friend from Blackrock, Michael Smithwick, then involved with Padraig Pearse and Tom MacDonagh in setting up St Enda's College, recommended that since Mrs Russell spoke Connacht Irish, Eamon should enrol at Colaiste Laighean, which specialised in Connacht Irish[2].

His teacher there was Sinéad Flanagan, a native of Balbriggan, Co. Dublin. Her family had moved into the Clonliffe road area of the city when she was seven and she attended the local Francis Xavier School. She trained as a primary teacher at the Baggot St Training College and became a language enthusiast and actor. For Xmas 1908 she received a "nice plant" from 'O chara'(!). She was unsure if it was from Dev, though she thought so, but was afraid to thank him. They continued to meet in class and at a few Céilidhs.

A romance soon developed between the rather tall pupil and his mu   smaller teacher, who was four years older than he. It soon became evident that their   'ionship was serious. When she planned to go to Touramakeady during the followi   ummer to teach Irish there, Eamon decided to accompany her. At Claremorris sta   he had arranged to meet his Kiltimagh friend Frank Hughes. When he saw Hu;   on the platform he asked Sinéad to wait apart for a moment, while he spoke to I.._ .s. The latter was so full of his own news about his pending wedding, that when Dev managed to ask what he thought of the lady standing apart, Hughes answered unthinkingly "not much"[3]. Dev was taken aback, but Hughes and Sinéad became life-long friends. They got engaged the next June and their engagement was so short that Sinéad said that they hardly knew each other, but Dev wanted to marry. A friend of Dev's, Jack Barrett advised against rushing into marriage.

Sinéad Flanagan (DeValera)   *Eddie Coll (Eamon DeValera)*

Roger Casement   *John Redmond*

This 'precipitate' entry into marriage was not unusual for a man who had actually attended a seminary for the priesthood, but later 'discovered' for whatever reason, that he had no vocation. Though Dev had not actually been accepted in any seminary, it was not for the want of trying. Having been turned down on several occasions, when he wanted to 'test' his vocation, he would have been in a similar state of mind to one who had been exposed to such an experience. The next natural step was to get married, and as so often happened in such circumstances, the 'spoiled priest' married the first woman who accepted his proposal and proceeded to start a family.

Sinéad noted that in small matters, Dev weighed up everything carefully but in major steps he went "boldly forward"[4]. The couple married at St. Paul's Church at Arran Quay in Dublin on 8 January 1910, with Frank Hughes as Best Man. While engrossed in shopping for the wedding, at Gill's Bookshop on O'Connell Street, Eamon had his valuable bicycle stolen. He and Sinéad moved into a flat at 38 Morehampton Terrace in Donnybrook. He joined the Gaelic League and acquired a teaching diploma. He later said, *"It was in the Gaelic League that I realised best what our nation was and what had to be done to get the freedom that was necessary"*. He became involved with committees of the Gaelic League and soon found himself put forward for membership of the executive committee. He was not elected and suspected that it was Arthur Griffith's Sinn Féin, which had opposed him. He was not pleased and decided that he would never join Sinn Féin. Up to then he had not got involved in politics, leaving that to John Redmond and the Irish Parliamentary Party, to whose policy he gave general support. This would have been natural for a man of his education and acquired social standing[5]. He never let his name go forward again for executive membership of the Gaelic League. He did not realise that it was the IRB, which thwarted his successful election as it moved to gain control in the Gaelic League[6]. The aim of the revival of the Irish language later became an official cultural imperative, with the first President of the Irish Free State, WT Cosgrave, stating, "The possession of a cultivated national language is known by every people who have it, to be a secure guarantee of their national future"[7]. Dev himself went a lot further as he told the *Times Educational Supplement,* "It is my opinion that Ireland with its language and without its freedom is preferable to Ireland with freedom and without its language"[8].

Eamon acted as Director of an Irish Summer School in 1912 at Tawin, a little island off the Galway coast. Roger Casement visited the school and was so impressed with the course that he presented Eamon with £5 worth of prizes for the sports day. That same year Sinéad's first child, Vivion, was born. Their daughter Mairin was born the following year. Sinéad was not able to accompany her husband to the Irish summer School due to a lack of suitable accommodation there. He missed his wife and babies as he wrote to Sinéad;

"I am very lonely without my own sweetheart and her babies. I'll never be a cross husband again. I feel empty, joyless without you… I love you a million, a billion times more now than when we were in Touramakeady"[9].

Two letters of advice Dev wrote to his Mayo friend, Frank Hughes, bear noting. In one concerning family property Dev wrote:

"Make all arrangements strong and binding, leave nothing to promises, and place no dependence on expressions of goodwill etc.- however genuine now".

Dev later advised Frank on his priest brother's reaction to stern clerical authority. He advised:

"You seem to be too sensitive about the opinion of the world. I am far too much that way myself, but I am not I think quite as bad as you are. It spoils ones peace of mind more than anything else I know. Get out of that if you can. We two are too fond of trying to look at things as we expect other people will look at them and generally go wrong in our estimate. Let what the world and your neighbour think be damned. Did you ever see a man who tried his best to be popular ever succeed except in a paltry measure – the old man and his ass just occurs to me? Aesop knew what I mean Here's to the sunshine when the thunder is over!" [10].

On a visit to the west of Ireland, 1912.

CHAPTER 3

CONVERT TO ADVANCED NATIONALISM

THE VOLUNTEERS

Home Rule for all of Ireland was passed in the House of Commons in 1913 but rejected by the House of Lords, so that it could not become law until the summer of 1914. Ulster Unionists armed themselves to fight this eventuality with the Ulster Volunteers staging a massive arms importation at Larne in 1913, without any opposition from the authorities. Instead they received open support from the Conservative Party for their stance. Eoin MacNeill, of Gaelic League fame, wrote an article for *An Claidheamh Solais*, the paper of the Gaelic League, in November 1913, which considered the possibility of another Irish armed force being necessary, in counterpoint to the Ulster Volunteers. Eamon read this carefully and was impressed by MacNeill's argument. The rule of Parliament had to be secured.

Later that month, he saw a notice for a meeting in the Rotunda to set up such a force. Eamon attended and though doubtful, decided to complete a membership form. Among others attending were Thomas Ashe, WT Cosgrave, Cathal Brugha, Diarmaid O'Hegarty, Diarmaid Lynch, and Michael Staines. A photo of these times shows Dev and WT Cosgrave side by side[1]. Dev's third child was then just six weeks old.

Two weeks later, the Volunteers from Pembroke and Rathmines assembled for the first occasion. As so often with Eamon, once he made up his mind on a course of action, he went at it wholeheartedly. Another conversion was enveloping him, which like the previous one was to take over his entire life, shutting out almost all else, except family. He soon gained recognition for his diligence and leadership qualities, as he became totally committed to the cause, though on occasion insisting on his own conditions. He drilled every week and also attended Saturday afternoon sessions for those who intended to become officers in the organisation. He attended Wednesday night lectures on military theory.

His membership card, which entailed a three-penny weekly contribution, put him at number 46 and named as 'Emin Dilvara'[2]. He was soon promoted from the ranks in successive stages to that of a second lieutenant, as his commitment and ability were rewarded. He was then elected Captain of the Donnybrook Company responsible for drilling, recruitment and collecting the membership fee. In 1915 he wrote his own manual for drilling, which emphasised that training in weaponry was vital and urgent. He paid £5 to the O'Rahilly for his own Mauser carbine.

Early in 1914, a provisional constitution contained three aims for the Volunteers:

To secure and maintain the rights and liberties common to all the people of Ireland.
To train, discipline, arm, and equip a body of Irish Volunteers for the above purpose.
To unite for this purpose Irishmen of every creed and of every party and class[2a].

The Catholic hierarchy, which was traditionally hostile to separatism, did not condemn the Volunteers, as unlike the IRB, it was not a secret society. Most of its members were Catholic and usually gathered after Mass for training. In the country many priests were active members of the Volunteers. In Dev's own area, Fr. Paddy Flanagan of Ringsend organised his own parish militia. Seán O'Shea reported, "He understood guerrilla warfare and passed on to us...He borrowed .22 rifles from all quarters so that we could march"[2b].

The Volunteers were involved in securing arms, ammunition and explosives from all kinds of sources. The most famous acquisition of arms came from the Erskine Childers inspired Howth Gun-running exercise, with the Asgard in June 1914. Eamon was among those officers who acted with ingenuity to protect the arms and have them spirited away safely. He used his own motorcycle and sidecar to get the arms for his Donnybrook Company taken to safety.

That same month saw John Redmond, the leader of the Irish Parliamentary Party; seek to take over the Volunteers. He succeeded in having twenty-five nominees appointed to the Executive. This caused some internal misgiving, but Eamon did not get involved. In September the Home Rule Bill was put on the Statute Book but suspended until the end of the war. Redmond exhorted the Volunteers to join the war effort on behalf of Britain. A split occurred in the Executive and down through the ranks. Eamon was forced to allow the issue be decided in his own Donnybrook Company. To his surprise and dismay, most of the men agreed with Redmond. Eamon and the minority had to withdraw from the Redmondite Hall, as he shouted back, "You will need us before you get Home Rule"[3].

On the anniversary of Parnell's death, there were separate commemorations at his grave in Glasnevin Cemetery by MacNeill's Volunteers and by Redmond's. The former paraded first and reassembled at Parnell Square afterwards for a public meeting. Eoin MacNeill, Bulmer Hobson, Denis McCullagh and the O'Rahilly addressed it. Then Jim Larkin made an attempt to get up on the platform, comprising of a pony-less trap, but was rebuffed. A hiatus developed and the crowd, which by then also included Redmonds' Volunteers returning from Glasnevin, grew restive. Dev was nearby with his Donnybrook group. Suddenly Dev heard Major John MacBride, who was standing beside him, tell him to get up on the trap and address the crowd. Dev did so and gave his first public address[4].

Eamon did not allow the setback of the Volunteer split upset his plans. He redoubled his efforts and advertised under the slogan, "Wanted: Eyes and Ears for the South City Battalions".

He introduced scout training, bayonet and musketry onto the activities at the new headquarters at Pearse's School at Oakley Road in Ranelagh. Eamon was soon to participate in military lectures with Thomas MacDonagh and James Connolly. In March a major reorganisation took place with Bulmer Hobson, the O'Rahilly, Pearse and Joseph Plunkett appointed Commandants at headquarters.

Four Commandants were also appointed to city battalions; these were Edward Daly, Thomas MacDonagh, Eamon Ceannt and Eamon DeValera. The latter's area consisted of Dublin South East. This was the high point of his career to date. He had been recognised and accepted for his worth. He would not falter. Prior to his appointment, Pearse had questioned DeValera on his attitude to a Rising. He replied that he would obey orders. Pearse then gave him his formal letter of appointment.

The Irish Volunteers, 41 Kildare St., Dublin, 11ᵗʰ March 1915.

A chara,

At last night's meeting of the Executive you were formally appointed Commandant of the 3ʳᵈ Battalion, with Capt. Fitzgibbon as Vice-Commandant and Capt. Begley as Adjutant. I have mislaid the name of the Quartermaster but he was also approved of. Could you let me know his name and former rank by return (to St Enda's)?

Can you attend a meeting of the four Battalion commandants on Saturday evening next after the officers' lecture? There are several important matters that the Headquarters staff wants to discuss with the Commandants.

Sincerely yours,

P. H. Pearse[5].

On 13 March the Commandants met under Pearse, where a Rising was discussed for some months hence. Each Commandant was given a strategic role. Eamon's was to contain Beggars Bush Barracks. He felt that he was the only one among them all who felt that he would not survive a Rising.

Eamon was perturbed later to discover that despite his position in the Volunteers, some members of his own 3ʳᵈ Battalion knew more about the details of the planned Rising than himself. He took this up with MacDonagh, who was Brigade Commander with Eamon as his Adjutant. MacDonagh was quite open with Eamon, telling him that as he was not a member of the IRB, this placed him outside the loop with certain vital information. WT Cosgrave had experienced a similar situation and had declined to join the IRB. MacDonagh invited Dev to take the oath and become a member. Eamon was influenced by the Catholic Church's condemnation of secret societies.

He declined MacDonagh's invitation, saying that he was a member of the Volunteers, an open and public body and would not become subservient to a secret organisation. MacDonagh explained that the IRB already controlled the Volunteers' Executive. Eamon wrestled with his conscience and with some mental reservation, decided to take the oath, believing that the means justified the end. But he did so on his own terms, telling MacDonagh that he would attend no secret meetings, nor did he wish to know those members of the IRB who controlled the Volunteers. He also refused the request to sit on the executive of the Volunteers. Eamon spent many hours walking around his Dublin South East Battalion area, often in the company of his five year old son Vivion, surveying it from a military view. The Rising planned for that autumn did not materialise.

John Redmond inspects Irish Volunteers, 1915.

Uniformed Irish Volunteers on roadside drill, 1915.

CHAPTER FOUR

EASTER RISING

The Volunteers staged a huge exercise in Dublin city centre on St Patrick's Day 1916, occupying College Green for over two hours, where Eoin MacNeill took the salute. At one point, Dev insisted that a British army car accept his instructions and divert away from College Green. A violent incident so close to the date of the planned Rising could have had calamitous consequences. Dev's Vice-Commandant, Seán Fitzgibbon, who was a member of the Executive of the IRB, opposed and criticised his action in front of some Volunteers. Dev later complained and both the officer and the O'Rahilly were transferred by the IRB[1]. This was an early indication that for Dev, discipline and obedience to his legitimate authority were fundamental and he would insist on them, with the clerical fundamentalism, in which he had been formed.

As the date for the Rising approached, Dev made his will, leaving his meagre possessions to his again pregnant wife. He did not sleep at home on the Friday or Saturday nights before the Rising. One of his officers met him on Holy Saturday and was surprised to hear him say, *"We'll be alright, it's the women who will suffer. The worst they can do to us is kill us, but the women will have to remain behind to rear the children"*[1a]. DeValera like most of the Volunteers was confused by Eoin MacNeill's countermanding the start of the Rising, scheduled for that Easter Sunday. Dev himself received a letter from MacNeill on Easter Sunday, which illustrates the background manoeuvring, that had taken place between MacNeill and the hardcore of conspirators.

Easter Sunday

1.20 p.m.

Commandt.

Eamon De Bhailear,

As Commandt. MacDonagh is not accessible, I have to give you this order direct. Commandt. MacDonagh left me last night with the understanding that he would return or send me a message. He has done neither.

As Chief of Staff, I have ordered and hereby order that no movement whosoever of Irish Volunteers is to be made today. You will carry out this order in your own command and make it known to other commands.

Eoin MacNeill.[1b]

An incident occurred on that Sunday morning which informs us that even at that stage, the members of the Military Council, who planned the Rising, were very aware of the fastidiousness of Dev's character. They met in Liberty Hall at 12 noon on Easter Sunday to review the situation and agreed to cancel the planned mobilisation for that day. But knowing the stickler that Dev was for protocol, they were concerned that he might proceed with his 3rd Battalion in spite of the cancellation, unless formally ordered not to do so. They sent Michael Staines, Quartermaster General, and Seán Heuston to Dev's headquarters to tell him that the order came from Thomas MacDonagh, Officer Commanding of the Dublin Brigade. Dev's reaction was to appear to threaten to take Staines a prisoner as Seán Heuston was almost on the point of drawing his gun. Dev gave the two men 'no indication whether or not he was prepared to obey the order', before they were allowed to depart[1c].

Dev came to his home after midnight on Easter Sunday to say goodbye to his family. As he left Sinéad and his children, he decided not to tell them of the almost certainty that they would never see him again. The leaders then spent Sunday night in Liberty Hall. Later that Easter Monday morning Dev sent a messenger for his kit, which he asked to be wrapped in brown paper. Even then Sinéad did not realise what was happening.

One year later in a remarkable letter, which some might fail to empathise with or even comprehend, he sought to explain his feelings for her on that day:

"…*I know you will not think it was selfishness or callous indifference or senseless optimism that made me so calm when I was about to offer up you and the children as a sacrifice. If you could have seen my heart on that terrible day of anxiety for you, Easter Sunday, you would have known – when I called to see you and found that the strain had been too much for you. I only found what I had anticipated all the day long… when I stooped to give you that parting kiss I believed it was the last kiss I would give on earth*"[2].

When the Military Council decided to go ahead on Easter Monday, DeValera's orders were to thwart troop movement to and from Beggar's Bush Barracks. His 3rd Battalion was very depleted with only one hundred men instead of five hundred; because of the confusion they occupied several positions in the vicinity. Lieutenant Michael Malone's men occupied St. Stephen's Parochial Hall, the local school and the three storied Clanwiliam House at Mount Street Bridge. Dev set up his headquarters a little to the east, at Boland's Mill on the second main artery from Dunlaoire port into the city. He feared immediate attack from nearby Beggar's Bush Barracks and disabled several bakery vans on Grand Canal Bridge facing up Clanwilliam Place towards Mount Street Bridge. He had a gangway erected linking the bakery to the railway line to and from Dunlaoire, which was cut. When the various positions were secured, the men felt very confident. The next morning Dev took the opportunity to send all those under 18 years home, telling them that they had done their duty.

He said the peaceful part of the operation was ended and that a real war would soon commence. All but two obeyed him and left. He had earlier refused to have any women in the garrison, saying that he did not wish to add to his problems by employing unproven women warriors[4]. He had the Gas Works disabled to prevent an explosion, though that deprived large parts of the city of power. The nearby *Cats* and *Dogs Home* was instructed to release all the animals, as were all the horses used by the bakery.

Even at this stage Dev was hyperactive, feeling the pressure of the responsibility upon him to carry out his orders. He could not rest or relax. He planned an expedition to travel surreptitiously to the Royal College of Surgeons to relieve Michael Mallin, who was under pressure there. The twelve men chosen were thrilled with the prospect of getting a new rifle and 50 rounds of ammunition each. Dev went off ahead by himself towards Westland Row, but quickly changed his mind and retreated to tell the men that the plan was cancelled, as their numbers were too few and he could not risk losing them from Boland's Garrison. Though Dev was austere and distant from his men, they respected him as a learned man with good ideas. Max Caulfield wrote that his men *"gave full marks to their Commandant for his humanitarianism, and especially for his willingness to take great personal risks, his desire to avoid injuring the innocent or causing any unnecessary damage to property"*[5].

The British 'established a central axis of communication running from Kingsbridge to the North Wall and Trinity College, followed by the cordoning off of the main rebel positions'[5a]. Its main presence was at Trinity College in the city centre. On Wednesday, as they brought in reinforcements through Dunlaoire, the Sherwood Foresters were instructed by General Lowe to proceed to Beggars Bush via Mount Street Bridge. The small group of Volunteers there engaged them for over five hours. It was only when the British brought up machine guns and bombs, that they eventually forced a retreat from the burning Clanwilliam House by the few remaining Volunteers. The British casualties were 4 officers killed and 14 wounded, with 215 other ranks killed or wounded.

Though Dev could see and hear this daylong battle, he made no attempt to reinforce or assist the garrison there, probably feeling that Boland's would come under attack next. His headquarters was continuously under fire from Beggars Bush. The British forces could easily have ignored the positions around Mount Street Bridge and taken another route, but chose not to do so.

The garrison at Boland's was very nervous waiting for the all out attack that was never to materialise. They were up all night watching the fire from Clanwilliam House and wondering about the fate of their comrades there. Dev was affected more than most, as he was among the leaders of the Rising who had foreseen what the outcome would be. Max Caulfield wrote, *"None had been more conscious than he of the reckless and irresponsible nature of what Pearse and the IRB proposed doing, and of its only too inevitable end, an undertaking which appeared ever more reckless, irresponsible and inevitable because of the Aud's sinking and MacNeill's countermand"*[6]. The Volunteers became nervous of each other, as mistakes were made about passwords,

Representation of Bolands Mills at the time of the 1916 Rising.

British Army barricade in Dublin City Centre.

almost leading to mistaken shootings. Dev's officers tried to get him to rest, as he had no sleep for several days of expending nervous energy. Lieutenant Joseph Fitzgerald asked him to lie down. Dev responded that if he did so, he was afraid the men might desert or fall asleep. Fitzgerald promised to sit beside Dev and waken him if anything happened. Dev fell asleep quickly in the Grand Canal Dispensary, but he soon began to have nightmares, waking up, shouting that Westland Row Station must be set on fire. This exercise was begun before Captain John MacMahon "eventually persuaded DeValera to listen to reason and the fires were put out. DeValera soon recovered his composure"[7].

Eamon O'Cuiv, grandson of Dev, has said, *"In Westland Row he decided to sleep for a while in an empty carriage. When he woke up he looked at the ceiling"*. O'Cuiv then quotes Dev as saying, *"I thought I was in heaven. I saw all the Seraphim and angels over my head"*. O'Cuiv continued, *"He then wiped his eyes and looked up again. He saw that he had broken into the State Carriage owned by the King"*[8].

Simon Donnelly, who was Captain in Boland's Mills, contradicted Max Caulfield's version of events in a letter to the *Irish Press* on 5/4/'62[9]. Charles Townshend has however pointed out that Donnelly's own version of events, confirms Dev's erratic and dangerous behaviour under pressure[10]. Sam Irwin, who had been on guard outside the Dispensary where Dev had been resting, wrote an open letter to Donnelly, reminding him that *"it took a number of officers to restrain him, I don't know what he wanted to do, but I recall he was gesticulating and talking nonsense. I was only a boy of 18 then, and the whole incident wasn't very reassuring…you and I are the only ones now alive who were present when he woke"*[11].

Townshend writes that these reports of Dev's erratic behaviour were only made public around 1960, when he was President of the Republic of Ireland. It was natural that his loyal followers would dispute them, as Dev's political career was founded on his being the sole surviving Commandant of the Rising. There could be no blemish on that record, despite the understandable fact that Dev was not the only inexperienced Commandant who broke under pressure[12]. Whatever happened in Boland's Mills, or any of the other garrisons, does not negate or undermine in any way the extraordinary heroism of Dev and his comrades[13]. As with other garrisons around the city, Boland's Mills was cut off from Headquarters at the GPO. On Thursday MacDonagh received a despatch from DeValera at Ringsend, notifying that his garrison was well supplied with food, but that the supply of ammunition was running low. MacDonagh sent a party of fifteen cyclists to make a reconnoitring sortie at 6 a.m. on Saturday morning, but they could only get as far as Mount Street. They lost one man, John O'Grady, on their return journey to Jacob's[13a].

When Pearse's order to surrender was brought to Boland's Mills by Elizabeth O'Farrell, Dev was sceptical about its validity. O'Farrell was being driven around the city by Captain Wheeler of the British army. The latter had taken her down Tara Street as far as Butt Bridge and said she would have to go by herself on foot the rest of the way to Boland's Mills, as barricades blocked the road.

Eamon Ceannt

Elizabeth O'Farrell

Willie Pearse

James Connolly

She had difficulty in locating Dev and had to rely on an army escort to get her through the military lines towards the Volunteers, as heavy fire continued all around. Eventually she located him at the Grand Canal Street Dispensary. She wrote, *"The barricades had to be removed and I was lifted in through the window into a small room. Here DeValera came to me. At first, I think, he considered the thing a hoax, but by the time some of my Volunteer friends came in, he realised I was to be trusted"*. He then said, *"I will not take any orders except from my immediate superior officer, Com. MacDonagh". So after all my trouble in finding him I had to go off again"*. When O'Farrell reported this to Capt. Wheeler, he decided that they would then head for Jacob's Factory, where MacDonagh was. After the surrender by MacDonagh and Eamon Ceannt, O'Farrell wrote, *"By this time it was getting dusk and Capt. Wheeler drove to Trinity College to telephone General Lowe to know if it was too late to go back down to Boland's to Com. DeValera with the orders from Com. Pearse, which Com. MacDonagh had countersigned. Whatever information Capt. Wheeler received, he conveyed me up to Dublin Castle. It appears that in the meantime DeValera had surrendered"*[14.].

As was to happen in the South Dublin Union under Eamon Ceannt and at Jacobs under Thomas MacDonagh, many of the garrison at Boland's had been very reluctant to surrender. It was a plea that only an immediate surrender might save DeValera's life, which quelled the near revolt[15]. Dev took a British army cadet prisoner, G. F. Mackay, to witness his surrender at Ballsbridge Town Hall. Thus he avoided the danger of being executed summarily. The garrison were held at the RDS before being marched to Richmond Barracks on Monday.

On Wednesday, Pearse, Clarke and MacDonagh were executed. The next day saw Plunkett, Edward Daly, Michael O'Hanrahan and Willie Pearse executed. That same day saw the transfer of Major John MacBride and WT Cosgrave to Kilmainham for execution. MacBride alone was executed on Friday. The following Monday 8 May, saw Eamon Ceannt, Michael Mallin, Con Colbert and Seán Heuston shot. Capuchin Friars from Church Street Monastery ministered to those executed. They died courageously after receiving the sacraments. Their heroic deaths at Eastertide naturally had an added significance for Catholic Ireland.

On Thursday 4 May, Dev and Dermod Lynch had appeared in the gymnasium, at Richmond Barracks, where conditions were primitive and where the police sought to identify the prisoners, who slept on the floor with each man getting a blanket. Dev slept alongside William O'Brien, a trade unionist and future Labour Party TD. For breakfast they got a bucket of tea per twenty men and a tin of bully beef and three army biscuits. For lunch and dinner they got more tea and biscuits. The latter were piled onto the floor and a guard ensured that no prisoner took more than three. Drinking water came in three buckets for about sixty men. Dev suggested to William O'Brien, that since he was used to organising people he should organise the distribution of the water. O'Brien divided the men into three groups and got a container to go with each bucket. Though it was May, the weather was cold and with the windows broken, it was very difficult to get any sleep on the hard floor[16].

Eoin MacNeill

Patrick Pearse

John MacBride

Michael O'Hanrahan

The prisoners were later moved to another part of the barracks where conditions were better. Among the prisoners there were Dev, William O'Brien, Seán T. O'Kelly, Larry O'Neill, Batt O'Connor and Count Plunkett. The latter was worried about his son, unaware that he had been already executed. The prisoners kept this information from him and to cheer him up put on a mock drama, *The Pretender to the King of Dalkey Island*. Dev played *The Pretender* with Plunkett the *Judge*[17].

Dev's trial took place on 8 May, together with Thomas Ashe and Thomas Hunter. They were then removed to Kilmainham to await execution. Dev wrote farewell letters to friends but not to his wife or mother. General Maxwell had come under severe pressure from Prime Minister Asquith to stop the executions. Maxwell insisted that the remaining two signatories had to be executed. Thus on 12 May the last executions took place, that of James Connolly and Seán MacDiarmada. Roger Casement was hanged in Pentonville Jail London on 3 August 1916.

The MI5 file on Dev was very sparse. He had a lower profile than some of the other leaders. Knowledge of him appears to have relied on his name appearing in James Connolly's notebook, which was uncovered in a house search after the Rising. A reference to him was also discovered on The O'Rahilly's body and his appearance in a group photograph unearthed in a raid on Tom Clarke's shop[18]. DeValera and Ashe were the only Commandants to survive the Rising. According to WE Wylie, prosecuting lawyer, General Maxwell received a telegram from Asquith saying that death was only to be inflicted "on ringleaders and proved murderers".

Dev was then next on the execution list after Connolly. General Maxwell asked Wylie who was next on the list and, *"was he someone important?"* Wylie replied *"Somebody called DeValera, sir. He was in command of Boland's bakery in the Ringsend area"*. Maxwell asked *"I wonder would he be likely to make trouble in the future?"* Wylie replied, *"I wouldn't think so, sir. I don't think he is important enough. From all I can hear he is not one of the leaders"*. Maxwell replied, *"Alright stop now except for the public trials, and come and dine with me tonight. I have another job for you"*[18a]. Some doubt has been expressed as to whether in fact Dev was court-martialled, but it appears most likely that he was. Seán T. O'Kelly saw Dev being led off to Kilmainham after his trial and anticipated execution. Brian Barton writes that the official text of Dev's courtmartial has not been released, though he would have been entitled to request a copy during his lifetime. Barton also finds Wylie's explanation above 'less than convincing' on the basis that surely Maxwell would have known who was in command at the location where most British casualties occurred[18b].

Dev wrote several letters on 9 May to friends, in anticipation of his execution. He wrote to Sister Gonzaga in Carysfort College saying that he had just heard that he was to be shot for his part in the Rising. He requested her to ask the girls to pray for him. His letter to Mick Ryan at Rockwell used a sporting metaphor as he said that he had played his final game last week and was to be shot tomorrow. He asked for prayers for one who played fairly as usual, and not for himself[18c].

Thomas Clarke

Con Colbert

The O'Rahilly

Seán Hueston

His letter to Frank Hughes reads:

"My Dear Frank,

Just a line to say a last goodbye. I am to be shot for my part in the Rebellion. If you can give any advice to Sinéad and the little ones I know you'll try.

Remember me to your wife, Aunt Stan etc. Pray for my soul.

DeV".

Sinéad had feared that Dev would be executed. She had taken his American birth certificate to the American Consul in Dublin. In America, his stepbrother Fr. Wheelwright contacted the State Department and his local Senator. He only received a reply from the latter later in July, stating that Dev's American citizenship had no relevance to his legal situation. He furthermore said that he understood that Dev had got a fair trial; with his death sentence commuted to life imprisonment, The Senator concluded that there was no possibility of the State Department getting involved in the affairs of a friendly country like Great Britain

Fr. McCarthy from James' St. brought the news to Sinéad that Dev had been reprieved[19]. He was soon transferred to Mountjoy Jail, where Sinéad and his children visited him. She found him in good spirits and glad that he was still alive. She soon had to return to her family home in Munster Street and sell her husband's motorcycle to raise some money[20]. Dev himself later wrote, *"I have not the slightest doubt that my reprieve in 1916 was due to the fact that my court-martial and sentence came later…Only Connolly and MacDiarmada were executed after my court-martial…By the way, Thomas Ashe was court-martialled the same day as I was. He too, would have been executed, I have no doubt, had he been tried earlier because of the part he took in the battle of Ashbourne, where he was in charge…He was not an American citizen, and it could not be suggested, therefore, that it was on that account he was reprieved"*[21].

The speculation as to why precisely Dev escaped execution continues. The official transcripts of his trial have not been released. Charles Townshend trying to elucidate the reason for the individual executions writes, "Though four battalion Commandants were executed, one was not. Eamon DeValera, most famously, escaped death for reasons that are still not clear"[21a]. In 2009 John J. Turi put forward a theory of Dev becoming a British spy. Even as proven a critic of Dev as Tim Pat Coogan, discounted this possibility out of hand, on the *Pat Kenny Show* on RTE [21b]

After a week in Mountjoy, Dev was deported to Dartmoor. He continued to exercise his leadership abilities there, when he ordered reluctant Volunteers to salute their leader, Professor Eoin MacNeill of UCD. As the elected spokesman of the prisoners, he soon asserted his right to make decisions, threatening to resign if the men did not agree.

Joseph Mary Plunkett

Thomas MacDonagh

Seán MacDiarmada

Edward Daly

He went on hunger and thirst strike for four days, after the governor unjustly punished a prisoner. The Deputy Medical Officer at Dartmoor wrote a report in which he seems to have accurately assessed Dev's character. He wrote:

"The prisoner's demeanour in hospital is civil and pleasant, but he maintains the attitude of a father to his children, with reference to the other Irish prisoners (65 held in prison) e.g. it hurts him to hear the others ordered about by the warders etc.

Insisting that he is a prisoner-of-war like the Belgians and should be treated in exactly the same way that the Belgians have been treated by the Germans all through this war – his own words,

He threatens also that if he is again placed under punishment he will repeat his hunger strike. Forcible feeding he will consider as causing an injury to his health and that will be sufficient grounds for him to refuse all food in future...It would be war to the bitter end.

I consider the prisoner to be of a determined and fanatical temperament and I fully believe he will carry out his threats re hunger striking. Prisoner looks upon everything from the political point of view and believes apparently that every man woman and child of English origin is imbued with hatred for Ireland and is constantly endeavouring to injure her...He accused medical staff of grossly ill-treating the whole Irish faction but would give no particulars"[22].

A report dated August 1916 by the Governor of Dartmoor Prison indicates that the authorities were examining Dev's nationality. It states, "the prisoner gives New York as his place of birth. He states that he has asked his mother to find out whether his father – who was a Spaniard – became an American citizen. If so, he (prisoner) claims to be such. If not, he is Spanish. He further states that he did not become a British citizen if that had been possible"[23]. The prison governor was certainly responding to an approach by the American embassy on behalf of the State Department on 28 June 1916 to the War Office.

Dev was later transferred to Maidstone Prison and from there to Lewes Jail. Lewes became the home of many hardened prisoners, where Dev continued to be accepted as their leader, against the authorities. Some prisoners, including Michael Collins and Arthur Griffith, were released from other prisons at Xmas for political reasons.

Lloyd George, plotting with the Conservatives, took over as Prime Minister from Asquith, and formed a 'national' government.

Sinéad wrote to Frank Hughes in July from 34 Munster St Phibsborough to thank him for all the help he had given. She had moved there at the end of May. Her new baby was with her, but the three older children were with her sister in Balbriggan. She had one letter from Dev on 19 May. He would be allowed write again on 10 September.

The record in Blackrock College, where life went on as normal during the Rising, stated, "Mr. DeValera, past student and past professor, who was one of the leaders of the 'Sinn Féin Rising', was sentenced by court martial to transportation for life.

Dublin City Centre, 1916, the aftermath.

Mr. Willie Corrigan, another past student, was sentenced to five years imprisonment, for participation in the same Rising. Fionan Lynch had also participated"[24].

The Bureau of Military History began to assemble witness accounts of the Rising in 1947 from all surviving participants. This continued to 1957. All this material was then placed in government archives, where it remained unavailable to researchers. It was finally opened to the public in March 2003. Though Dev often promised to make a contribution to the Bureau of Military History Archive, on his memory of events around the Rising, he never did so, unlike WT Cosgrave, who made a very detailed account[25]. This is a great pity. There can be little doubt that he acted in an extraordinarily brave and heroic way in the circumstances. His rather late conversion to militant nationalism and his acceptance by the leaders as one of the Commandants for the Rising, encouraged and facilitated his fateful reply to Pearse, "I will obey orders". In the circumstances of leaving his pregnant wife and three young children behind, his action was extraordinary.

Ferghal McGarry, in his 2010 book, *The Rising, Ireland; Easter Rising 1916,* based on the statements made to the Bureau of Military History, writes that *"The ninetieth commemoration witnessed the largest and most popular commemoration since 1966…Throughout the long fall and rise of its legacy, the Easter Rising consistently evoked more affection among the general public than academics, intellectuals, and politiciams"*[26]

The Rising was almost entirely undertaken by Catholics. As McGarry has demonstrated, *"Volunteers were armed not only with guns but rosary beads, scapulars, and holy water. Confessions were heard, conditional absolution was granted, and the rosary recited"*[27]. In Boland's bakery, Father McMahon 'made a confessional in a four-wheel bread van. We said our penance in a nook in a huge stack of flour bags'[28]. One Protestant at Boland's bakery, Cathal McDowell, converted to Catholicism during the Rising;' he laid down his Howth rifle beside him and the priest baptised him'[29].

The public had thought the Rising a foolish and reckless event with the Irish newspapers particularly scathing against the rebels and backing the execution of the leaders. Some Catholic bishops also denounced the Rising. As early as 11 May, however, John Dillon of the Irish Parliamentary Party raged against the executions and declared in the House of Commons, his pride for the 'misguided' rebels 'whose conduct was beyond reproach as fighting men'[30] The view of the general public changed, as news of the executions became widely known. Arthur Griffith said, *"Something of the primitive man awoke in me. I clenched my fists with rage and I longed for vengeance"*[31.] Ernie O'Malley wrote, *"Four days after the surrender a brief announcement; three men had been shot at dawn- Padraig Pearse, Tom Clarke, Thomas MacDonagh"*. Next day four were executed and the following day one, Major John MacBride. I had felt resentment at the death of the others; now a strange rage replaced it. I had known MacBride. He had been to our house a week before the Rising and had laughed when I told him I would soon join the British army. He had patted my shoulder and said, *"No you won't*"[32]. The Protestant patriot Roger Casement converted to Catholicism before his execution in England. A proposal at the June meeting of the Catholic hierarchy to condemn the Rising was defeated[33].

Throughout the summer of 1916 it became common throughout the country to have requiem masses said for those executed. More and more people gradually attended these, as the dead were revered like Catholic martyrs.

Gradually the Rising came to be viewed as an iconic and almost sacred event and its leaders treated as the country's founding fathers. As the sole surviving leader, after the 1917 death of Thomas Ashe, Dev inherited much of this pious veneration as he assumed national leadership[34]. Towards the end of his career he said, *"I've always thought that the decision of the men who came out in 1916 was the biggest decision that has been made in Irish history, because they fully realised what the problem was and the difficulties. I suppose the fact that I was afterwards in a position in which I could carry on that work was the occasion for great happiness"*[35].

General Maxwell (centre) with some of his general staff, 1916.

CHAPTER 5

ELECTION VICTORIES 1917

Arthur Griffith, founder of the Sinn Féin movement, had for very long, advocated the policy that Irish parliamentarians should absent themselves from going to the House of Commons and once again set up an Irish Parliament in Dublin. This appeared most unlikely in the face of the well established Irish Parliamentary Party's policy of achieving Home Rule by parliamentary means at Westminster. Griffith's idea did attract some support, when in 1908 three sitting Irish Parliamentary Party MP's resigned their seats. One of them, Charles Dolan, an ex-clerical student at Maynooth, offered to run in the bye-election for Sinn Féin on an abstentionist ticket. Sinn Féin was not geared for electioneering, but this was a challenge Griffith could not possibly resist, if Sinn Féin was to retain any credibility[1]. Dolan was defeated by a margin of three to one. This made Griffith and others very wary of the idea of standing again on an abstentionist ticket. In January 1917, Count Plunkett, the father of the executed Joseph Mary, stood against the Irish Parliamentary Party in the famous bye-election in North Roscommon. As the British military had dubbed the Easter Rising a Sinn Féin Rising, they again mistakenly dubbed Plunkett's campaign, as that of a Sinn Féin candidate. Those Volunteers who had been released earlier were confused on procedure, but Michael Collins decided that they should support Plunkett, who won and only then declared, somewhat reluctantly, that he would abstain from Westminster.

America's entry into the war in April 1917 on the Allied side, gave great heart to Sinn Féin, given Woodrow Wilson's policy of national self-determination for a post-war settlement. In May, Collins proposed running a Lewes prisoner Joe McGuinnes in a bye election at Longford, Dev and most of the prisoners were against it, fearing a defeat, Dev thought it 'extremely dangerous from several points of view' and McGuinness though a member of the IRB was not keen. Their position was conditioned by negative experiences from the general public after the Rising. Thomas Ashe however, the only other surviving commander with Dev, and Tom Hunter, supported running McGuinness. Ashe, President of the Supreme Council of the IRB argued that this 'was not giving recognition to the British Parliament but giving the people an opportunity to support Irish freedom'. Ashe had close contacts with his IRB colleagues, who informed him that the tide of public opinion was changing. Collins ignored those opposed and went ahead, and Joe McGuinness won a stunning cliffhanger election by 37 votes. Later that month the prisoners went on a 'no work' strike, demanding prisoner of war status. They were later to destroy prison property. Dev was punished, but refused to comply with prison authorities and he was transferred to Maidstone. On 17 June the British announced the unconditional release of all the prisoners. Dev paraded the prisoners at Holyhead before embarking on the boat home.

Michael Collins

Arthur Griffith

W. T. Cosgrave

Thomas Ashe

The prisoners paradoxically returned home as conquering heroes to their people. Many factors had contributed to this massive change in public opinion. Among the most important was the 17 May letter of the elderly and conservative Bishop Dwyer of Limerick to General Maxwell. The Bishop described Maxwell's actions "as wantonly cruel and oppressive... you took care that no plea for mercy should interpose on behalf of the poor young fellows who surrendered to you in Dublin. The first information that we got of their fate was the announcement that they had been shot in cold blood. Personally I regard your action with horror and I believe that it has outraged the conscience of the country. Then the deporting of hundreds and even thousands of poor fellows without a trial of any kind seems to me an abuse of power, as fatuous as it is arbitrary and altogether your regime has been one of the worst chapters in the history of the misgovernment of the country"[2].

On the boat journey to Ireland, Dev stood on deck with Professor Eoin MacNeill and Dr. Patrick McCartan. As the prisoners stepped down the gangway of the *SS Munster* they sang *The Soldiers Song,* written by a 1916 prisoner Peadar Kearney. At the reception for the prisoners, the leading Volunteers signed a proclamation to President Wilson on the cause for Ireland's freedom.

For a time Dev considered seeking another teaching post, but a grant of £250 from the National Aid Fund, which was managed by Collins in a full time capacity, persuaded him otherwise[3]. Dev who had travelled far and quickly on the nationalist path soon accepted the opportunity to stand for the Clare by election offered by the National Aid Executive. Willie Redmond MP, brother of John Redmond, had been killed at Messines in Belgium. In getting the nomination Dev outmanoeuvred the possible candidature of Thomas Ashe, who had been as likely as Dev to be selected to run in Clare. The fact that Clare had been the scene of Daniel O'Connell's famous victory for Catholic Emancipation in 1828, added extra significance. Dev was clear that he should be at the epicentre of affairs. He insisted that Eoin MacNeill appear on his first election platform saying, "the clergy are with MacNeill". The militants like Mrs Kathleen Clarke opposed this unifying move. Bishop O'Dwyer's death was announced during the election campaign. Dev spoke of him, *"All Ireland owed a debt of gratitude to Dr. O'Dwyer and she will never forget that debt, and his name will live in history and will be a model for Irish bishops who wish to win the hearts of their flocks. As long as there are bishops such as Bishop O'Dwyer there never will be anti-clericalism in this land"*[3a]

Dev's election literature included the *Shan Van Vocht* poem, which described the Irish Party thus:

And their god is Saxon pay,

For four hundred pounds a year,

(And deny it over here),

Lies must choke their traitor's breath…

Won the course of Judas gain.

Dev got 5,010 votes to 2,035 for Patrick Lynch of the Irish Party. He wanted an Irish Republic, as the most likely form of government the Irish people would freely choose. That would place them in a favourable light with America and France at a post-war Peace Conference. His main credo however was not any form of doctrinaire republicanism. He said *"We want an Irish republic, because if Ireland had her freedom, it is, I believe the most likely form of government. But if the Irish people wanted to have another form of government, as long as it was an Irish government, I would not put a word against it"*. In his victory speech in Clare Dev said that Clare had 'set up a lasting monument to the dead. Let it be your dead bodies they will conscript'.

Dev's attitude to forms of government, possibly placed him potentially at odds with the policy of Griffith's Sinn Féin, which had long favoured a Hungarian type Dual Monarchy between Britain and Ireland. Dev's victory in Clare, in July, with 71% of the vote, symbolised the turning away from the old IPP to the new radical nationalism of Sinn Féin, which demanded total independence from Britain. The following month Dev stood alongside another 1916 veteran, WT Cosgrave, a pioneer Sinn Féin member of Dublin Corporation, as he was elected as an MP for Kilkenny. During that campaign he had advised, "If you cannot get arms get that old useful weapon at close quarters – the seven foot pike"[4]. The old Sinn Féin party, which had, for long been inactive was, through the stupidity of the British military handling of the 1916 Rising and its aftermath, suddenly transformed into a mass political party.

The British, again through their own ineptitude, handed the Volunteers their first martyr since 1916. Dev's Commandant colleague, Thomas Ashe was an attractive figure from Lispole in Kerry, who was a Principal Teacher in Lusk, county Dublin. He had been the most successful military figure, alongside Richard Mulcahy, in the Rising, at Ashbourne in county Meath. Townshend writes of him, "His poetry, most famously his patriotic prayer-poem *'Let me carry your cross for Ireland. Lord'*, marked him out as Pearse's most authentic successor"[5]. He had been released in August 1917 but was arrested within weeks for "speeches calculated to cause disaffection". He was sentenced to one year's imprisonment. He demanded prisoner of war status in Mountjoy. This was denied and he died of forcible feeding on 25 September.

The Volunteers determined that he would receive a military funeral. This became an occasion for an immense demonstration of public sympathy. The Volunteers intended that Ashe would lie in an open coffin at Dublin's City Hall prior to a mass funeral. The British army intended to prevent this, but the recently elected Sinn Féin MP for Kilkenny WT Cosgrave, who was also a senior Dublin City Councillor, took steps that prevented any confrontation[5a]. Dev, strangely, did not attend the lying-in-state despite the funeral being a massive manifestation of militant nationalism. As the glass hearse, pulled by four black horses, made its way through the city to Glasnevin, vast crowds lined the route. The up and coming Michael Collins was given the honour of speaking at the graveside. Instead of giving a powerful oration, as was expected by the mourners, Collins announced that there would be no oration.

He reclaimed Pearse's famous oration there for O'Donovan Rossa, by saying that: 'There's no more to be said. The shots over a martyrs' grave speak louder than words'. Immediately afterwards, the Volunteers staged a mass rally at Smithfield close to the city centre.

Brian Feeney writes *"the death of Ashe, a prominent republican, who had been elected President of the Supreme Council of the IRB after the Rising, seemed to have a galvanic effect on people. Not only did young people pour into Sinn Féin, but many also joined the Volunteers and began to participate in the sort of violent attacks which, in 1918, eventually brought large areas of the country into de facto rebellion"*[6.] The Archbishop of Cashel had refused to allow a Mass to celebrate the first anniversary of the Rising, but in September 1917, he himself said a Mass for Thomas Ashe and in 1918 voted for Sinn Féin.

The British, by their insistence that the Easter Rising was a Sinn Féin Rising, had put Griffith's organisation to the forefront of political developments. The Volunteers had no intention of allowing this to continue. Neither had Dev, who as the surviving Commandant saw himself as the rightful heir to the men of 1916. He persuaded Griffith to agree to a Sinn Féin policy of republicanism and once that was achieved, they could hold a referendum on which form of government the people wanted. He also persuaded Griffith to withdraw from the election to become President of Sinn Féin at the forthcoming Ard Fheis on 25 October 1917. Griffith was devoid of personal ambition, having much earlier been happy to act as 'second' to William Rooney, in their efforts to stir up a nationalist consciousness.

William O'Brien, who met Cathal Brugha shortly before the Convention, provides a backdrop to this episode. Brugha informed him that everything was settled about Griffith and the Republic. Brugha said that Griffith had to swallow the Republic or else"[7]. Brugha had confronted Griffith in his home in Rathmines, refusing to allow Griffith or anybody else to leave the house until he had got agreement on the matter. Griffith held his ground saying, *"Sinn Féin will not give up its name. I was elected President of Sinn Féin by a convention and I cannot give up the Presidency except to a convention of Sinn Féin"*[8]. Thomas Morrissey writes that the arrogance displayed by Brugha was misplaced, as the election of the executive saw Griffith's supporters top the poll with the IRB sponsored candidates in the bottom half of the election[9].

Ernie O'Malley who was on a mission in Liverpool in 1918 met Brugha and described him thus, *"He wore a double reefer-jacket; he looked at times like a seaman; of medium height with broad shoulders, steady grey-blue eyes and a determined chin. He wore a green tie. That to me typified the man. It seemed the symbol of his nationality in a hostile country. He might change his appearance, but the tie meant the cause to him. He was the most uncompressing of all the army officers. He was over on special work himself; if conscription was attempted in Ireland the first blow would be struck by shooting the British Cabinet from the Visitors' Gallery in the House of Commons...Men had come over from Ireland for the purpose and were waiting but they knew they would never leave the House"*[10].

The first Dáil.
Front row; DeValera centre. Michael Collins 2nd from left, W.T. Cosgrave, 2nd from right.

An unusually smiling DeValera with Countess Markievicz.

Griffith, who admired Dev greatly, proposed Dev as President of Sinn Féin at the Convention, emphasising that 'he had the mind and capacity that Ireland will need at the Peace Conference – the mind and capacity of a Statesman'. In response, Dev, in a *quid pro quo*, announced, *"We are not doctrinaire republicans. Sinn Féin aims at securing the international recognition of Ireland as an independent republic. Having achieved that status, the Irish people may, by referendum choose their own form of government"*[11]. While a monarchy remained theoretically a possibility, Dev stated that it would not necessarily be linked to the House of Windsor. Dev, in effect, had staged a *coup d'etat* in becoming President of Sinn Féin. The post carried a salary of £500, which enabled Dev to rent a home in Greystones[12]. Half of the seats on the Sinn Féin Council were allocated to members of the Volunteers. Thus two very disparate groups emerged within Sinn Féin.

During the Ard Fheis, Cathal Brugha, Countess Markievicz, Mrs Tom Clarke and Helena Maloney, criticised Eoin MacNeill, who was defended by Dev and Griffith and received the biggest vote to the executive. Dev knew that very many people, who were not out in 1916, trusted MacNeill, as did many Gaelic Leaguers.

The Volunteers held their own Convention the following day and Dev was elected President, with Cathal Brugha Chief of Staff. Ernie O'Malley later described Brugha, *"Brugha never talked much to me; always seemed to be holding himself in check. He showed little of his many wounds save round his mouth and eyes; his face was often grey. When he had to talk he spoke with directness and finality as if the matter had been thought out and was now finished. Mulcahy never said anything stronger than "bloody". He did not smoke or drink. Cathal Brugha neither cursed, smoked nor drank. Collins was adept at all three"*[13]. Leaders from the four provinces sat on the executive. Among those with specific areas of responsibility, which also included a seat on the executive were, Collins for Organisation, Ristard Mulcahy, who had organised the Ashe funeral, for Training, Diarmaid Lynch for Communications, Michael Staines for Supply, and Rory O'Connor for Engineering[14]. Dev had become the political and military leader of militant nationalist Ireland. Of course the real power within the Volunteers remained with the secret IRB and particularly Michael Collins. Neither Dev not Cathal Brugha wanted anything to do with the IRB. Dev advised Richard Mulcahy at this period, that if he was interested in going into politics he should study economics and read *The Prince*. Maire O'Kelly, Dev's secretary, later confirmed that Dev himself had read the book[15].

When the morality of the Rising was criticised by Archbishop Gilmartin of Tuam and Cardinal Logue of Armagh, Dev compared it to Belgium's stand for freedom and rejected any charge of immorality, though he did not want any rupture with the hierarchy[16]. During the Ard Fheis Dev had criticised the 'theologians' of the *Irish Times* and the *Freeman's Journal* who had denounced the morality of the 1916 Rising. He spoke as a Catholic when he said, *"I say in theology...of all subjects a little learning is a dangerous thing"*[16a].

Dev then became a paid official of Sinn Féin as national organiser. Earlier in 1917 on his first visit to Clare, he had gone to Limerick in full Volunteer uniform to meet with Bishop O'Dwyer to thank him for his letter condemning Maxwell. This was of course an astute political move as well as a genuine act by a devout Catholic. The people of Bruree came out *en masse* to welcome him home. Their adopted son had come a long way.

CONSCRIPTION

Sinn Féin faced an early crisis in 1918, when it lost three consecutive bye-elections, South Armagh, Waterford and East Tyrone to the IPP. Once again however British ineptitude came to the rescue of the militants, when the Government, on the advice of Lord French and against the advice of Sir Edward Carson, authorised the extension of conscription to Ireland. This undermined the IPP, which in protest, adopted Sinn Féin's policy of abstention and withdrew from Westminster. This united nationalist Ireland came together at a conference in Dublin's Mansion House on 16 April, where Dev and Griffith joined John Dillon and Joe Devlin of the IPP and others on a standing committee. Here again Dev emerged as an astute leader in convincing and cajoling the committee to agree to a declaration that, Ireland's separate and distinct nationhood derived their just powers, from the consent of the governed and denied the right of the British government or any external authority to impose compulsory service in Ireland, against the clearly expressed will of the Irish people. They declared on 18 April that the Conscription Act, which had been enacted two days earlier, was against the Irish nation, "that the government of nations derive their just powers from the consent of the governed" and "to impose compulsory service in Ireland against the expressed will of the Irish people" was wrong. Dev had taken the trouble earlier that same morning to visit Archbishop William Walsh of Dublin and get his approval of the text of his form of words. Walsh knew that Cardinal Logue's attitude of a vague passive resistance to conscription was not strong enough and that his influence had to be neutralised.

Dev also persuaded the Mansion House Committee to ask the Catholic hierarchy, which was meeting that same day, to discuss conscription. A delegation went to Maynooth to confer with the bishops. The latter had already agreed a statement which said, "conscription forced in this way upon Ireland is an oppressive and inhuman law, which the Irish people have a right to resist by all means that are consonant with the law of God"[17].

Many of the delegation, which included John Dillon, Joseph Devlin, Thomas Johnson, William O'Brien and Tim Healy, were very nervous at the prospect of meeting members of the hierarchy in a formal situation. As the arrogant TM Healy expressed his nervousness, Dev reassured them all saying, "Oh there's nothing in that. I have lived all my life among priests". Healy retorted, "Have you lived all your life among bishops?"[17a]. The clerical students received them with acclaim and the bishops were mostly friendly. Even Cardinal Logue, who was hostile to Sinn Féin, assented to a favourable statement after the meeting. Nevertheless, Dev obliged to tell Cardinal Logue that 'no matter whom decided anything, the Volunteers would fight if conscription was enforced, and they had no use for passive resistance'[18]. The bishops also decided that on the following Sunday, masses were said in every parish "to avert the scourge of conscription" and a collection would be taken up outside the church gates for the anti-conscription cause[19]. A one-day national strike cemented the entire country against conscription. Though the IPP and Sinn Féin were cooperating on the anti-conscription front, Dev and his men remained dedicated to obliterating the IPP. Dev refused IPP overtures from Dillon to agree a common candidate for the forthcoming East Cavan bye-election. The Maynooth meeting, which was in effect a merger of Catholicism and nationalism, had accepted the moral-political leadership of nationalist Ireland. Dev and Sinn Féin were victorious in Catholic eyes, despite the continuing opposition of Cardinal Logue.

GERMAN PLOT ARRESTS 1918

Lord French's ascent to the office of Lord Lieutenant on 5 May was on the basis that he did so, "as a military Viceroy at the head of a quasi-military government". On 16 May he issued a proclamation, which led to the arrest and deportation of about 200 leading Sinn Féiners in a so-called 'German Plot'. This resulted from the Germans putting one Joseph Dowling ashore in Galway Bay[20]. Those deported included Dev, arrested as he alighted from the train at Greystones with his bicycle, Griffith, W.T. Cosgrave, Count Plunkett, Countess Marckievicz, Kathleen Clarke and Maud Gonne[21]. By this action the British succeeded again, in handing power over to the militants, particularly to the person of Michael Collins, who avoided arrest and intended to pursue a violent path. Collins wrote in the autumn of 1918; *"The principal duty of the Executive is to put the Volunteers in a position to complete by force of arms the work begun by the men of Easter Week. The Volunteers are notified that the only orders they are to obey, are those of their own Executive"*[22]. Due to the military attitude of the Viceroy, Lord French, the Volunteers became the storm troopers of Sinn Féin.

The police called to Dev's house in Greystones to trawl through his papers and told Sinéad that her husband had just been arrested[23]. All the prisoners were held initially at Gloucester Jail. They held an athletics day where Dev won the mile race. He was transferred later to Lincoln Jail, where he continued to keep fit by playing handball and rounders and again coming first in a mile race. He wrote to his wife that he was not an old man yet. He organised study for himself and fellow prisoners and again negotiated with the prison governor on their behalf. The Sinn Féin bye-election victory cavalcade soon resumed, when the prisoner Arthur Griffith was elected in East Cavan. He told his fellow prisoners at Gloucester, "I have complete confidence in DeValera"[24]. Dev wrote from Lincoln to Sinéad in joy at this victory, avoiding the strict censorship. He wrote to his mother saying that he was serving all the prison masses and telling her that they said the rosary nightly[25]. As the war ended in November, Dev wrote to his mother from Lincoln Jail, "If America holds to the principles enunciated by her President during the war, she will have a noble place in the history of nations"[26].

Austin Stack

Liam Mellowes

Kathleen Clarke

Maude Gonne

1918 ELECTION – THE NEW ORDER

The General Election of 14 December 1918 again saw the IRB, through Michael Collins, Harry Boland and Diarmaid Hegarty, put forward many prisoners as Sinn Féin candidates, to win 73 seats to 26 Unionists and 6 for the once powerful IPP. The latter was so demoralised that it did not contest 25 seats that it had held already. Dev was unopposed in Clare. He was opposed in East Mayo by John Dillon whom he defeated very heavily. Dev however was defeated in West Belfast by Joe Devlin. As was to become commonplace, this election saw personation and intimidation operate on a wide scale. As late as 1938 Seán MacKeown admitted that the Volunteers "ballyragged the Irish Party from one end of the country to the other".

Among those who were absent due to being in jail were: Arthur Griffith, Desmond Fitzgerald, Joseph McGrath, Eamon DeValera, Brian O'Higgins, Padraig O'Keeffe, Liam Mellowes, Dr. Cusack, Frank Fahy, Fionan Lynch, Austin Stack, and Countess Markievicz. The tide had gone out on a party that had laboured long in the cause of moderate Irish nationalism. It had been destroyed to a great extent by the ineptitude of British governments, which exposed it as unable to influence policy on conscription and the implementation of the Home Rule Act 1914. Most Irish people soon forgot its work, as a new order arose from the embers of 1916 and its immediate aftermath. In the North, the Unionists had increased their number of seats from 18 to 26, while under the auspices of Cardinal Logue, Sinn Féin and the IIP shared eight seats, without contest.

The newly elected Sinn Féin T.D's, who were at liberty, came together in the Mansion House on 21 January 1919. Thirty-six elected Sinn Féin representatives were still in jail. Only two of the those present on that fateful day, had sat in Westminster. Three quarters were under 45 years of age. They constituted themselves as the parliament of Ireland – Dáil Éireann. In accordance with Griffith's original 1905 policy, the Dáil repudiated Westminster's right to govern Ireland. Cathal Brugha was elected President of the Dáil . The new parliament, which lasted to May 1921, had no legal standing and received no international recognition. It was suppressed by Britain in September 1919. Its Declaration of Independence saw itself as the National Parliament and ratified the establishment of the Irish Republic proclaimed in 1916. It sent a 'Message to the Free Nations of the World', saying *"Ireland today reasserts her historic nationhood, the more confidently before the new world emerging from the War, because she believes in freedom and justice as the fundamental principles of international law…calls upon every free nation to uphold her national claim to complete independence as an Irish Republic…and demands to be confronted publicly with England at the Congress of the Nations"*. As one of the victorious nations, it was most unlikely that Britain would be so challenged by its victorious allies.

On that same day a group of Volunteers, completely oblivious or disdainful to the political significance of what was happening in Dublin, ambushed a carload of gelignite and shot dead the two RIC men escorting it at Soloheadbeg in County Tipperary.

This is generally reckoned as the start of the Anglo-Irish War, though Cathal Brugha, Chairman of the Dáil and Richard Mulcahy, Chief of Staff and Minister for Defence, condemned the ambush. A more correct commencement of the war may be later in the autumn of 1919, when the Dáil was suppressed and the British forces harassed Deputies. The Dáil remained subordinate to the military campaign but did "establish the authentic credentials of Irish democracy" as Brian Farrell wrote[27].

Michael Collins decided to get Dev out of jail and gave him the task of drawing the contours of the prison key. Dev, who acted as mass server and sacristan, studied the key that hung from the prison chaplain's vestments, worn during Mass. After initial failure, a key was smuggled into the prison in an Xmas cake. Collins and Harry Boland were outside the jail on 3 February 1919, awaiting the escapees, Dev, the IRB President Seán McGarry and Sinn Féiner Seán Milroy. The trio were soon deposited in a safe house at Fallowfield in Manchester.

Dev then made the momentous decision that he was going to go to America. When this was announced to the Volunteer GHQ in Dublin, they were aghast. They insisted that he come to Dublin first. Cathal Brugha was sent to Manchester to ensure that. Dev was smuggled back to Dublin. Shemers Donoghue who was 2nd mate on the Cambria made his own cabin available, with Con Murray holding the key, as Dev arrived home on the *Cambria* on 20 February[28]. Dev's arranged safe house in Dublin was the gate lodge of the Archbishop's residence in Drumcondra.

On 1 April, Dev was elected President of Dáil Éireann. His cabinet consisted of: Collins at Finance, Griffith at Home Affairs, Brugha at Defence, WT Cosgrave at Local Government, Eoin MacNeill at Industry, Robert Barton at Agriculture and Markievicz at Labour and Lawrence Ginnell in Propaganda. Dr. McCartan was appointed to the Irish embassy in Washington, and Seán T. O'Kelly posted to Paris.

The T.D's did not receive a salary, but could claim up to £20 a month in expenses. They also received a third-class rail fare from their constituencies to Dublin and a nightly lodging allowance of 15 shillings. The Ministers were paid £350 initially and then £500, with the president getting £600. Directors of government departments got £400. The Dáil met on twenty occasions, but its very existence was what mattered. Many of the departments had only a shadow existence. One notable exception was WT Cosgrave's Local Government, which had the task of getting the various local councils to transfer allegiance to Dáil Éireann. This gradual erosion of British administration through the country weakened their resolve and standing. The Irish administration simply copied that of the British system. This meant that the Prime Minister and the Executive held all power. It was notable that Dev did not appoint a Minister for Education. He probably deferred to the bishops on the matter, who regarded their continuing control of education as vital for their own religious interests. Collins was authorised to float a national loan. Plans were set to takeover local government from the British and establish Sinn Féin Courts. Brugha continued to run his own business and deferred his salary to his assistant, Army Chief of Staff, Ristard Mulcahy[29.]

In theory the Volunteers should have come under the jurisdiction of the Minister of Defence and the Dáil. Mulcahy and Brugha worked towards that aim. In August 1919 Brugha tried to get Volunteers to swear an oath of loyalty to the Dáil but some opposed this. A Convention of Volunteers was never held to consider the matter.[30]. Some felt that Brugha's target was the IRB and Collins. Brugha resented the fact that Collins was foremost among that small revolutionary group that occupied military and political control during the War of Independence. Army GHQ issued an order that the Volunteers must take an individual oath to the Republic and to the Government of the Republic by August 1920. Thus the Volunteers became the Irish Republican Army. Despite this, the Volunteer Executive continued to exist and the Volunteers retained a spirit of independence, which came to the fore when the split over the Treaty occurred and has remained a part of Irish military history. Dev had explained the fluid situation on 19 April 1919 by saying, *"The Minister for Defence is of course, in close association with the voluntary military forces which are the foundation of the national army"*[31].

One of the most fundamental aims of the new government was to achieve international recognition. On 12 April, WT Cosgrave proposed a motion in the Dáil supporting President Wilson's principles enunciated at Washington's Tomb on 4 July 1918, and outlining Ireland's eagerness to join a World League of Nations, based on equality of rights between big nations and small. Collins seconded the motion. Dev, Plunkett and Griffith wrote to Clemenceau, President of the Paris Peace Conference, requesting the recognition of Ireland as an independent State. The Irish-American *Friends of Irish Freedom* lobbied President Wilson in Paris, to no avail. On 28 June the Versailles Treaty was signed with no reference to Ireland's claims to independence. Sinn Féin, as a political movement, appeared to be almost irrelevant, as the Dáil itself sought to set up its own structures and the Volunteers continued with its military role. Dev had decided that his own best role for Ireland as President of the Dáil, lay in America, where he could seek to mobilise public opinion in favour of Irish freedom as well as collecting much needed funds. Griffith told the Dáil that Dev had the unanimous approval of the cabinet for his American mission[32].

The failure to gain international recognition after the war was a bitter lesson for moderate opinion in Ireland. As thousands of Irish soldiers returned from the war, many were disillusioned and enlisted in the IRA. Collins berated the Sinn Féin executive for being over-cautious as he determined on military action.

☙❧ ❧☙

Arthur Griffith, Eamon DeValera, Laurence O'Neill, Michael Collins and Harry Boland, enjoy a hurling match at Croke Park Dublin, April 1919.

DeValera visits Newport, Rhode Island left, and happy with his supporters, both USA, 1919.

CHAPTER 6

DeVALERA IN AMERICA

Harry Boland, a veteran of 1916, had been in America for a month preparing for Dev's arrival. On 1 June 1919, Collins visited Dev at Greystones to tell him that there was an immediate opportunity available for him to begin his journey to America, in a fairly secure manner. Though that day was Sinéad's birthday her husband left almost immediately. He wrote to her the next day, trusting that she would not allow herself to be lonely. *"It will be but for a short time. I have only a minute or two. Kiss the children. Dev."* On the boat to Holyhead he met Fr. McCarthy, curate at James St Church, who had ministered to him and the Cosgrave brothers, in Richmond Barracks.

On 11 June Dev disembarked in New York from the *SS Lapland*, posing as a sailor, after a trying trans-Atlantic boat journey. The surprised Harry Boland and the Irish-American organiser, Joseph McGarrity soon arrived to greet him. McGarrity took him immediately to his own house. Dev later visited his mother and her husband in Rochester. She was in her 60's. His Aunt Hannie and her family lived nearby, so Dev had lots of people to meet. He travelled to Boston to meet his half-brother Fr. Thomas Wheelwright, who bore a remarkable likeness to him.

Dev's presence in America soon became well known in Irish circles. Preparations were made for him to be introduced to the press on 23 June at the Waldorf Astoria Hotel. He established his HQ at this prestigious and expensive hotel during his long American stay, which in itself called for a large expenditure.

The street was packed as Dev arrived at the hotel to be met by Judge Daniel Cohalan and John Devoy, two leading members of the diverse Irish American communities. Dev declared that he was the *"official head of the Republic established by the will of the Irish people"*. He wanted Ireland to be part of a real League of Nations. He expressed the belief that President Wilson was sincere in Paris, but said that he was now appealing directly to the people of America. If the people could be aroused, government action would follow. He said that he intended to travel to all the large cities to talk directly to the people.

Dev's initial comments caused immediate difficulty among Irish-American politicians. The latter were not a single group but reflected American politics, with some being republican, supporting the committed anglophile, President Wilson, and others democrats. There was also ill feeling between different leading personalities involved. Judge Cohalan and John Devoy were inimical to Dr. Patrick McCartan and Joe McGarrity. Cohalan and Devoy were against the idea of the League of Nations Covenant, whose policy accepted existing national boundaries.

This was regarded as being a contrivance of Britain and not in American or Irish interests. Dev wrote to Griffith saying, "The political situation here is obscure for the moment". The Irish-Americans also resisted Dev's view that he could speak for them. Cohalan told Dev that he acted in the first instance as an American and denied Dev the allegiance he sought from the Judge and from John Devoy's newspaper *The Gaelic American*[1]. Dev continued with his tour of the country and was well received by very large crowds. Liam Mellowes managed the logistics of this massive undertaking.

Both the *New York Times* and the *Los Angeles Times* remained hostile to Dev, due to his opposition and that of his colleagues, to joining the Allies in the Great War. He returned to Rochester and his mother for the Xmas, before resuming his continental travels in the New Year with Dr. McCartan. On 18 March the Senate passed a resolution in favour of Ireland. The previous day had seen Dev honoured by reviewing the St Patrick's Day parade in New York, together with the State Governor, City Mayor and the Archbishop.

BONDS

The Dáil Éireann cabinet had authorised floating a loan in America. At the Irish Race Convention held in Philadelphia in February 1919, an *Irish Victory Fund* was set up. Devoy and Cohalan thought $250,000 should be sufficient for Ireland's needs. When they now heard of Dev's intention to float a loan for millions of dollars, they saw it as an infringement on their own Irish-American work. The bonds could be redeemed when the Irish Republic came into being. Dev felt it necessary to proceed on the matter sooner than he had intended. He verified the legality of the process through solicitors Martin Conboy and Franklin D Roosevelt.

He hoped to get initial monies from the *Friends of Irish Freedom*. Difficulties arose with issuing the bond concerning when interest charges would occur. Dev consulted Collins on the matter, and James O'Mara, TD for South Kilkenny, and a former Irish Party MP, was sent to America by Arthur Griffith, to organise the practicalities of the loan, which he did with remarkable skill. O'Mara came from a wealthy Limerick family and had great expertise in dealings on the London Stock Exchange.

DEV SEEKS ASSURANCE FROM CABINET

On 17 February, Dev wrote from New York to Griffith and the Cabinet in Dublin, explaining in a most comprehensive fashion the complexities of the Irish-American situation. He refrained from naming those whom he regarded as jeopardising his mission in raising the Bond, least the letter be intercepted. He was adamant that he was not bound to consult any American as regards his policy. The letter illustrates how Dev would brook no opposition and wanted assurance that his cabinet understood and backed him.

The letter reads.

New York, 17 February 1920.

A Cháirde,

The necessity of preventing possible serious consequences from a movement now on foot here makes it necessary for me to risk sending Dr. McCartan to you. At this distance the enemy and mischief makers could create such trouble as would make it impossible to do effective work.

(1) I am presuming on this - that the moment the Cabinet or Dáil feel the slightest want of confidence in me they will let me know immediately. If I can, as I feel certain I can, count solidly on this, then I can go on with my work without fearing that malicious persons can stir up misunderstandings.

(2) To ease the mind of everybody I want you to know at all times that I never in public or private say or do anything here which is not thoroughly consistent with my attitude at home as you have known it. That will enable you to judge whether anything I may by newspapers be reported to have said is true or false. Never forget that the Press is an instrument used by the enemy - garbled statements, misleading headlines etc. You know the press and a word to the wise ought be enough...

It is a time for plain speaking now. A deadly attempt to ruin our chances for the bonds and for everything we came here to accomplish is being made. If I am asked for the ulterior motives I can only guess that they are -

(1) To drive me home - jealousy, envy, resentment of a rival - some devilish cause I do not know what prompts.

or

(2) To compel me to be a rubber stamp for somebody. The position I have held, (I was rapidly driven to assert it or surrender) is the following -

(1) No American has a right to dictate policy to the Irish people

(2) We are here with a definite objective - Americans banded under the trade name (the word will not be misunderstood) Friends of Irish Freedom - ought to help us to attain that objective if they are truly what the name implies.

This organisation F.O.I.F. owes its life to the idea that it is an organisation to work for Irish freedom. It is not its primary object to secure in American life a prominent place for our race here...

Consistent with this position I have insisted then that as regards Irish policy I am not bound to consult any American..

On questions of tactics to secure our objectives of course Americans must be consulted...

Fundamentally Irish Americans differ from us in this - they being Americans first would sacrifice Irish interests if need be to American interests - we, Irish first, would do the reverse...

It is not however from fundamentals like this the trouble arises. The trouble is purely one of personalities. I cannot feel confidence enough in a certain man to let him have implicit control of tactics here without consultation and agreement with me.,,

I never forget Ireland must mainly rely upon herself. I never forget that it is a question of forward more determinedly now than ever before - looking neither to right nor to left. Be assured of this and believe me as ever.

Eamon [2].

In cabinet, Brugha, Plunkett and Markievicz were hostile to Dev's views. Collins and Griffith argued on 11 March that Dev was their delegate and they should stand by him[3]. Dev was essentially a moderate, if not a conservative, as he would describe himself, and he knew that the hardliners would never allow him to undermine their 'republic'.

James O'Mara later wanted to return to Ireland and tendered his resignation to Dev. He was pressurised both in America and from Ireland to withdraw it, as it might undermine Dev's position viz Irish American opposition, as a split loomed within the Irish American society on allegiance to Dev. Dev told O'Mara that *"My entreaty is personal as well as official. You do not need to be reminded of the peculiar difficulties of the moment, you know the campaign that has been taking place underground. I had dreamed that we would see the end of this mission here together"*. After the intervention of Collins and Griffith, O'Mara put off until the autumn his return to his own business interests in Limerick.

THAT CUBAN SPEECH

Dev created great confusion when in March 1920, without consulting anyone, he compared the American-Cuban relationship to the British-Irish one and saw a *modus vivendi* there. This appeared a massive climb-down by Dev, on the idea of an Irish republic, as under the Monroe Doctrine, America had the right to intervene in Cuba and control part of it, should it deem that necessary. Dev declared *"The United States, by the Monroe Doctrine, made provision for its security without depriving the Southern Latin Republics of their independence and their life. The United States safeguarded itself from the possible use of the Cuban island as a base for attack by a foreign power, by stipulating that the 'Cuban Government shall never enter into any treaty with any foreign power or powers, to obtain by colonisation or for military or naval power or otherwise, a lodgement in or control over any parties of said island'. Why doesn't Britain do with Ireland as the United States did with Cuba? Why doesn't Britain declare a Monroe Doctrine for her neighbouring island? The people of Ireland, so far from objecting, would co-operate with their whole zeal"*[4].

Devoy editorialised in the *Gaelic American* that Dev was ready to capitulate to Britain. Dev had antagonised all the Irish-American supporters and entered into grim correspondence with Judge Cohalan, who was a judge of the New York Supreme Court. This episode demonstrated starkly that as he had earlier written to Griffith, Dev abrogated to himself the way forward for Ireland, without any consultation with Irish-America.

That Cuban Speech of Dev's continued to have repercussions. Maire Comerford later claimed that Dev "had led them on with his Cuban speech to the brink of compromise" and that, "the Pro-Treaty side knew that he only wanted a favourable compromise to jettison the Republic"[5]. After the Dáil had passed the Treaty, Dev pointed out that a Republican statement he had made was on the record of the Dáil. Arthur Griffith intervened to say: "So is your Cuban statement". Dev replied, "Oh you are mean! You are vilely mean! You know you said that those who attacked me on that occasion were mainly responsible for the record of terror in Ireland"[6]. The Ceann Comhairle intervened," I think this has gone far enough". Dev agreed adding, "I think it has".

As late as 1948, Dev was engaged in correcting the negative aspect of that 'Cuban Speech', when he organised the writing of a letter to the *Irish Press* by Mrs Kathleen O'Doherty, an admirer of his and also a friend of his secretary Kathleen O'Connell. The *Irish Times* had earlier refused to publish the letter. Mrs O'Doherty had been in America at the time Dev had made the speech.

In May 1920 WB Yeats, then in America, met Dev and wrote to Lady Gregory of "a living argument rather than a living man, all propaganda, no human life, but not bitter or hysterical or unjust. I judged him persistent, being both patient and energetic, but that he will fail through not having enough human life as to judge life in others. He will ask too much of everyone and will ask it without charm. He will be pushed aside by others "[7].

Harry Boland returned to Ireland in May and persuaded a reluctant Sinéad to leave her children and visit her exhausted husband in America[8]. Collins called for her at her home and carried her trunk out into the car. She travelled on a false passport, provided by Collins, arrived in August, and returned home in early November. The publicity and ceaseless activity in America had few attractions for Sinéad, who longed to return to the quiet of her Greystones home.

Sinéad regarded that trip as one of the greatest mistakes she ever made. Terry DeValera wrote, *"Father was greatly surprised to learn of Mother's arrival and the pair saw little of each other. Father was heavily engaged in serious strife with John Devoy and Judge Daniel Cohalan and had to attend a multitude of meetings"*[9]. Dev and Sinéad had not lived together as husband and wife since May 1918. Ryle Dwyer comments that, "organising Sinéad's visit would not therefore have been one of Collins's more helpful gestures in DeValera's eyes"[10].

During her unhappy stay in America, James O'Mara and his wife were her closest companions. Before Sinéad's departure, Dev took time off from his busy schedule to take her on a visit to his mother in Rochester. During Dev's time in America, Collins called every week to Sinéad in Greystones with money. They formed a close friendship.

The fact that ugly rumours were circulating and found their way into the press, that Dev and his secretary, Kathleen O'Connell (Dev's secretary from 1919-1956) were having an affair did not help matters. The 'clerical' part of Dev would have rendered him uncomprehending of such innuendo. The fact of the extensive friendly letter writing between Sinéad and Kathleen tends to rule out any basis for such rumours. In October 1952 when Dev was in a Utrecht hospital for an eye operation, realising that Kathleen had a life threatening illness; he wrote to her, *"You know how I wish you every happiness. We have had a third of a century now working together—no short spell. It is too much to hope that the partnership will not be severed before the half-century could come around. Our spells of life are usually not given for such long periods. We can rejoice at what we have seen done, at the heart of which you can feel that you have played no small part"*[11]. Four years later, as Kathleen died, Dev wrote, *"In my life I have had as co-workers some of the finest people that God has made—noble, devoted, loyal. I am writing this a few days after we have laid to rest one who has worked with me for more than a third of a century. One who has shared, I had almost said my most intimate thoughts, so far as they were concerned with public affairs"*[12].

DeValera with his mother Catherine Coll, USA 1920.

In May 1920, Dev reported to Griffith, "Expenses are awful here. Cost of collecting the bond subscriptions will I fear, be very high. There is no close unit of organisation here, as at home. The fund being collected by the *Friends of Irish Freedom* is a bit disconcerting"[13]. The appeal however was most successful with over $5 million from $10 to $10,000 bond certificates being purchased.

In early June 1920, the Republicans gathered in Chicago to select their candidate for the Presidency. Judge Cohalan had got Dev's agreement that he, Coughlan, would seek to have the Irish Republic recognised there. Dev however later decided that he himself would become directly involved in Chicago. This provoked a public dispute between the two 'Irish' camps and the Republicans omitted the Irish matter entirely from its platform. Dev then thought the best chance for Irish recognition rested with the Democratic Party.

In September, Dev drafted letters to the State Department and to President Wilson, setting out the case for recognition of an independent Ireland. America was due to elect a new President in 1920. Dev saw this as an opportunity to press the Irish cause. Irish-Americans were heavily involved in American party politics and resented Dev's attempt to insist that he should be the arbiter of how the Irish card should be played. Cohalan was a Republican whom the Democrats hated, as a turncoat. He loathed President Wilson who reciprocated that feeling. When it was discovered that the Dáil authorised Dev to spend a half a million dollars on the American Presidential election, this caused great anger[14].

After the debacle of Chicago, Dev called for a Convention to smooth Irish policy in America. Judge Cohalan refused to consider this until after the Presidential election in November. On 17 September in New York the *National Council of the Friends of Irish Freedom* met. Dev was unable to get his way there and led a walkout of his own supporters. He announced outside that he intended to found another organisation, which would not be under the control of people living in New York. He outlined his feeling that, "We from Ireland should be accepted as the interpreters of what the Irish people want-we are responsible to them; they can repudiate us if we represent them incorrectly". The *American Association for the Recognition of the Irish Republic* was set up in Washington DC on 16 November. Dev told the assembled throng; "I have called you here today in order that you may plan concerted action, so that this great current of sympathy and goodwill may be harnessed and made effective. This action on our part is, I know, long overdue". The *AARIR* soon outshone The *Friends of Irish Freedom* vastly in its membership. Bishop Michael Gallagher, president of the *FOIF* wrote; *"President DeValera deliberately split the Irish movement in America, and all the energy of his followers has been wasted in the struggle to destroy instead of being expended for Ireland's cause against the common enemy...Anybody who suggests that DeValera is not master of the people of Irish blood everywhere, or that, like ordinary mortals, he has never made a mistake in his whole life, is overwhelmed with billingsgate and foul abuse in the DeValera press"*[15].

The Republican candidate, Senator Warren Harding won the Presidential election. He had earlier outlined his views on the Irish question as, "I would not care to undertake to say to Great Britain what she must do any more than I would permit her to tell us what we must do with the Phillipines"[16]. Though Dev did not succeed in getting official America to back the Irish cause, he did gain massive publicity for that cause. He also created the political situation where the British Government were under pressure from a variety of international sources to settle the Irish Question. Dev decided to leave 60% of the $5 million collected in bonds, in America. He sought unsuccessfully to make his friend Joe McGarrity the sole trustee. On legal advice an agreement stating that the funds committed to their care by Dev and O'Mara "are the funds of the Irish Republican Government, and we pledge our honour to surrender on the joint requisition of these two gentlemen, or their substitutes duly appointed, in accordance with the decree of Dáil Éireann, by which they become Trustees such of these funds as may be in our keeping on the day of the aforesaid requisition". Dev, McGarrity, Jos Fawsit, and Harry Boland signed this convoluted procedure.

Meantime back in Ireland, tentative peace feelers were emanating from the British side, via Archbishop Clune of Perth, to Collins and the imprisoned Griffith. Dev decided that it was time for him to return home to be in position to deal with them. He paid a brief visit to Rochester to see his mother. On 10 December he had a last supper with McGarrity, Harry Boland and Seán Nunn (Clerk of Dáil Éireann and Dev's secretary) in room 228 of the Waldorf Astoria. Boland then escorted him to the White Star Line pier where he was smuggled aboard the *Celtic* bound for Liverpool. Dev undoubtedly learned much from the internecine civil war that developed among Irish Americans during his stay. He arrived back in Ireland on 21 December after an 18 month absence. Sinéad visited him the next day at his safe house[17].

The SS Celtic, used by the Volunteers to bring arms and DeValera from the USA.

CHAPTER 7

MEANWHILE BACK IN IRELAND

When Griffith was arrested in late 1920, Michael Collins took his place as Acting President. This together with his supreme role within the IRB made him the *de facto* nationalist leader within the country. Dev had left the politicians in charge when he had gone to America. Collins, however, decided to pursue an armed campaign against the British presence. Through his various roles in the government and the IRB, he had assumed an almost totally independent role for his 'terror squad', which assassinated a series of intelligence agents operating from Dublin Castle. Dev recognised great danger for his own leadership position in Ireland due to the rapid ascent of Collins, as he made immediate plans to return home.

On 10 May 1920 Lloyd George had written to Churchill, *"I am very anxious about Ireland and I want your help. We cannot leave things as they are. DeValera has practically challenged the British Empire and unless he is put down, the Empire will look silly. I know how difficult it is to spare men and materials, but it seems to me to be the most urgent problem for us"*[1]. The British responded with a dual policy of militarism and politics. The army believed, especially after it successfully identified Collins as the 'terror chief', through a double agent named 'Jameson', that they could defeat the threat of a terror force with the 'Black and Tans'. This force caused havoc around the country, committing very many atrocities, in response to IRA outrages. At the same time, through another Castle official, Andy Cope, they sought to make overtures to Griffith and Collins for a political settlement. Dublin was a very dangerous place, as political murder became commonplace in the spy war. This reached its zenith on Bloody Sunday 21 November, when Collins' men assassinated twelve newly arrived Army Intelligence Officers, (The so called *'Cairo Gang'*). The British responded by torturing and killing two captured IRA men, Peadar Clancy and Dick McKee. Later that same Sunday, the military attacked a crowd attending a football match in Croke Park, killing fourteen and wounding sixty. At that stage the British believed that the IRA was nearly defeated and cancelled plans to continue peace overtures.

Collins had arranged for Dev to base himself at Loughnabale on Strand Road in Sandymount. On hearing that the house was to be raided, Collins transferred Dev to Glenvar on Cross Avenue, with the main entrance off Merrion Avenue and a wicket gate leading to Cross Avenue. He moved there "with his three lady helpers" on 18 May 1921[2]. Dev appeared not to understand the nature and aim of the guerrilla war Collins was waging and decided that the campaign against the British was too intense. He told Mulcahy, *"You are going too fast. This odd shooting of a policeman here and there, is having a very bad effect, from the propaganda point of view, on us in America. What we want is, one good battle about once a month with about 500 men on each side"*.

*Photo said to be of some of the 'Cairo Gang', a group of British intelligence officers,
12 of whom were assassinated by some of Michael Collin's 'Squads' in November 1920.*

*Some members of one of Michael Collins' so called 'Squads',
L to R: Mick McDonnell, Tom Keogh, Vinnie Byrne, Paddy Daly, Jim Slattery.*

This became public knowledge, when Griffith raised it in the Dáil on 27 April 1922, during an altercation with Dev over the 'republic'. Griffith said, *"Mr. DeValera came back from America when I was in prison, and he advised the members of the Dáil to ease off the war"*, to which Michael Collins added, *"President Griffith is right"*.

PRESIDENT GRIFFITH

Dev agreed that as Brugha was Minister of Defence, he should be in control of military operations. Dev held several cabinet meetings within a short time of returning home, insistent in re-establishing his control of the cabinet, where deep divisions existed, especially between Brugha and Stack on one side and Collins on the other. Valulis writes that Brugha became "almost obsessive about Collins". She says that up to that, Brugha had little input into military affairs and adds, "It was also possible that the feud between Brugha and Collins impelled the Defence Minister to exert his authority more directly and thus try to undermine Collins' dominance"[3]. This placed Mulcahy, as Chief of Staff, in a difficult position and he reported the matter to Dev, who acknowledged Brugha's jealously of Collins, regretting that "a man with the qualities that Cathal undoubtedly has, can fall victim to such a dirty little vice"[4]. Dev then began to back Brugha and Austin Stack, who had been antagonised by Collins' criticisms of him as an incompetent Minister of Home Affairs. Dev realised that Brugha was "a bit slow" but "could be persuaded", while Stack "could not"[5]. Dev's manoeuvres back in Ireland had comparisons to the splits he had recently caused in Irish-America.

During this early period of 1921 after his return, Dev's closest personal friendship was with WT Cosgrave. When Dev had attended the Blackrock Past Pupils Union dinner in the Gresham Hotel in October 1917, his guest was WT Cosgrave[6]. Dev told Frank Gallagher that Cosgrave was "nearer to me in a personal sense than anybody in cabinet"[7]. Tim Pat Coogan writes "Cosgrave was the one who called at DeValera's office to take him to lunch and performed other small necessary services such as ensuring that he got his hair cut"[8]. Dev acknowledged this closeness on the occasion of Cosgrave's death when he said, "Before the division on the Treaty, we were very close friends and it has always been a regret of mine that political differences should have marred our personal friendship"[9].

Ernie O'Malley described Dev at this time, "He was tall, and his lean stringy build overemphasised his height. His face was drawn and pale as if he had little exercise or was recovering from serious illness. The lines running to his mouth edges made furrows, ridges stood out in relief. He looked worn. He smiled with his eyes. The lines on his face broke as if ice had cracked. His voice rumbled from the depths with a hard but not a harsh dryness. Dev, the Long Fellow or the Chief, had come back from the United States two months ago…At home he was looked upon with awe. There was a sense of sternness about him, dignity, a definite honesty, and a friendly way of making one feel at ease. He had lost personal contact during the year and a half he had been away...He had not the human qualities of Collins, the Big Fellow. Dev was more reserved, a scholarly type. He was controlled"[10].

Arthur Griffith arrives in style at Earlsforth Terrace Dublin, 1921.

Harry Boland, Michael Collins, and Eamon DeValera, share a light hearted moment.

On one occasion after Dev had questioned Mulcahy on logistics and then departed, O'Malley sat with Collins and Mulcahy. Collins asked O'Malley what he had thought of the interview. When O'Malley replied that Dev did not appear to know to much about the army in the south, both his companions laughed. This made O'Malley uncomfortable. For him Dev was the President and he resented their jokes at "the expense of the Long Fellow"[11].

Liam Mellowes had also returned from America and was appointed Director of Purchasing. Collins had been using IRB and Volunteer monies to buy arms. Brugha accused him of impropriety. Dev held an inquiry that cleared Collins but it served to emphasise that Dev was then in control[12]. Dev also tried to convince Collins that he should go to America and continue the work that he had done there. The members of the cabinet agreed to this, but Collins refused to agree to the plan, which he interpreted as a move by Dev to sideline him. Dev did his best to assuage Collins writing, *"I would be sorry to think that your feeling discontented and dissatisfied and fed up was due to anything more than natural physical reaction after the terrible strain you have been subjected to. It really is not fair to throw every task that comes along ultimately upon your shoulders, and it must stop...you have got enough things, God knows, to attend to"*[13]. When Desmond Fitzgerald, Director of Publicity, was arrested, Dev, to the annoyance of Griffith, appointed Erskine Childers to the post. Griffith had described Childers as a disgruntled Englishman. Dev later said that from April 1921, Collins *"did not seem to accept my view of things as he had done before and was inclined to give public expression to his own opinions, even when they were different from mine"*. Dev felt that in so doing, Collins was 'not acting loyally'[14]. Collins could be very destructive in cabinet dishing out personal criticism to Ministers he felt were not performing adequately, as he himself assembled a personal coterie outside government. Dev was a constitutionalist while Collins was fundamentally an IRB man protecting his own people and position[15].

In March 1921, a group of Irish Labour Party people, including Tom Johnson, Cathal O'Shannon and William O'Brien met Home Secretary, and a former Chief secretary in Ireland, Edward Short, in London. He told them that the British cabinet was prepared to offer Dominion status to the 26 counties, but that Ulster had to be allowed to make up its own mind on its constitutional future. When the group later met Dev, his response was, "They would have to come another bit". When a further communication was made to the group that Lloyd George was amenable to negotiations, O'Brien responded, as instructed by Dev, that contact should be through the Dáil [16].

Dev achieved one of his aims on the home front, when in May the Dublin Brigade of the IRA, in a gesture of the spectacular, destroyed the Custom House. They lost six men, with twelve wounded and seventy captured. This debacle rebounded to Dev's and Brugha's favour when as a result of these losses, it was decided that Collins' various groups should be amalgamated into the Dublin Brigade and come under the Minister of Defence. The spectacular may also have moved Lloyd George towards a truce[17].

On the diplomatic front Dev received a most unwelcome reminder of his Cuban Speech, from a most unexpected source.

The destruction of the Custom House Dublin, by the IRA, May 1921.

Mansion House debate post Truce, August 1921.

Within a few months of returning to Ireland Dev was greatly annoyed when Seán T. O'Kelly, the Envoy of the Republic in Paris, had the temerity to contemplate making a parallel proposal of Dev's Cuban Speech. Dev responded harshly on this matter as well as other issues, for which he chastised O'Kelly. The letter demonstrates several of Dev's characteristics, especially his insistence on proper protocol with himself at the centre, controlling matters. An extract reads:

Dublin, 28 April 1921.

A Chara,

Your reference to the so-called Cuban proposal proves to me that so far from understanding the 'full meaning' of it, you do not understand it at all…

If you have looked up the Cuban Treaty, will you please remember that my statement had reference to Article 1 only, and that the 'Westminster Gazette' interview was but a cabled fragment of a much larger article, in which there was no doubt that I referred to one part of the Treaty only. You had better not attempt to draw up this proposed parallel.

I might have known that cut off from home as you are, and with only misrepresentations of its meaning, on the one hand by the British and on the other by certain Americans - each for its own peculiar purpose, you could not be supposed to understand this question as it should be understood, before it could be appreciated or dealt with…

Our representatives abroad, whether they be members of the DÁIL or not, must regard themselves unequivocally the direct agents of the Department of Foreign Affairs, and must carry out the instructions of that Department, whether they personally agree with the Policy or not…

The Ministry is responsible to the DÁIL, and therefore its policy is ultimately DÁIL policy. When those of our representatives who are members of the DÁIL wish to communicate with the DÁIL, they must do so in an independent and separate communication, either through me or the Secretary of the DÁIL - not through the Foreign Affairs Department. I will see that it is duly brought forward and considered at our Sessions…

The Ministry has recently been taking stock of our finances, and the absence of a detailed statement of the expenditures of your establishment has caused considerable inconvenience. You will please not neglect furnishing such statements monthly in future, as required by the Minister of Finance.

Very sincerely yours,

Eamon DeValera

P.S. In a raid on the London Office despatches from you were captured unopened. I asked our Foreign Affairs Department to make inquiries from you as to their contents.

I am anxiously waiting for this information[18].

The British political mission continued to put out peace feelers, as the events of Bloody Sunday and the introduction of the Government of Ireland Act in December 1920, that was to Partition Ireland, had together led to the first tentative indication that Lloyd George might negotiate with Sinn Féin. Lord Derby, using the name of 'Mr. Edwards', travelled to Dublin, where he had a "long but inconclusive talk" with Dev on 21 April[19]. Derby had earlier met Cardinal Logue, who proved unsusceptible to Dev's suggestion that he tell Lord Derby that the Irish had their own elected representatives, who alone had the right to speak for them. Derby was an intermediary from Lloyd George who was under severe pressure from General Smuts of South Africa, among others, to do business with the Irish. In June, Dev wrote to Collins, "This particular 'peace business' has been on for some time. They have tried so many lines of approach that they are banking somewhat on it"[20].

In the North, Carson had resigned as Unionist leader in February 1921 to be succeeded by James Craig. The Unionists won 40 of the 52 seats in the May General Election, which was held under the Government of Ireland Act establishing a Parliament in the North. The 124 Sinn Féin candidates were returned unopposed, with four Unionists representing Trinity College, making a futile attempt to convene as the parliament of Southern Ireland.

On 18 May Dev received a letter from a close colleague, solicitor Seamus O' Concubair. The latter told him that he had received an invitation to the house of Lord Justice O'Connor. He was there about five minutes, when Andy Cope arrived. Cope asked him, *"If an offer of Independence within the Empire with complete fiscal control, the withdrawal of the armed forces and no reserve forces, no imperial contribution and control of the armed police, were made, would Sinn Féin accept it?"* O'Concubair added, *"The impression which Cope left upon me is that they are desperately anxious for a settlement, and desperately anxious to get us to say that we will take something less than the Republic, and also that they are anxious to save the face of Sir James Craig"*. Cope was also keen that Dev would agree to meet Craig[20a].

Craig courageously came to Howth to meet Dev, but they reached no agreement. Craig said he found Dev "impossible"[21]. Craig was willing to negotiate, but only on his own terms, that accepted Protestant rule in the Six Counties. He ruled the North in an anti-Catholic manner, bolstered by the Government in London with money and weapons. In 1922 he would introduce internment and a Special Powers Act, which gave him unlimited power[22]. Dev wrote to Lord Justice O'Connor on 4 June about his meeting with Craig in fundamentalist terms, which remained the basis of his life long, but futile attempts to end Partition. He believed that only by dealing directly with Great Britain, as the principle authority involved, would there be any success. He wrote, "If the sky fell we should catch larks, and such is the hope of securing the end of the struggle with England, through a prior agreement with the unionist minority. From my interview with Sir James Craig I am convinced that nothing is to be gained by a futile conference with him"[23].

The British government knew there were differences between Dev and Collins, both of whom they regarded as terrorists. They thought Collins to be the more hard-liner of the two and thought Dev the best person to negotiate with. They also understood that as Collins controlled the violence, it might be politic to meet him. At a joint cabinet, military and administrative meeting, in London, Andy Cope argued so strongly for a peace mission that Hamar Greenwood advised him to "curb his Sinn Féin tendencies"[24].

Lloyd George came under great pressure, about the draft statement the King would make on 22 June, opening the new Northern Ireland Parliament. The King, taking General Smuts advice and with Lloyd George's imprimatur, appealed *"to all Irishmen to pause, to stretch out the hand of forbearance and conciliation, to forgive and forget and to join in making for the land they love, a new era of peace and contentment and goodwill"*. Even Churchill was advising Lloyd George to *"quit murdering and start talking"*.

By a strange coincidence on that same day of 22 June, Dev was arrested with incriminating documents in an army raid at Glenvar, Merrion Avenue, Blackrock, where he and Kathleen O'Connell were living[25]. A Lancia open lorry with ten men of the Worcestershire Regiment arrived around nine o'clock in the evening. Dev had been working on army documents during the day and still had them on him. Had Dev a key for the wicket gate exit on to Cross Avenue, he could have escaped[26]. He was taken to the Bridewell, where he was roughly questioned and identified. Within a few hours, Andy Cope, Assistant Under-Secretary, arrived in his cell. It is unclear what transpired between them, but Dev was transferred to comfortable quarters at Portobello Barracks for the night. In the morning he witnessed the funeral of an army officer, who had been killed in an ambush in the Dublin Mountains. Dev was released later on that Friday morning of 23 June.

Though his official biographer writes that Dev then went to Greystones, Fr. Farragher writes, that in fact, he cycled back towards Glenvar and stopped at Blackrock College, where he got a meal. Fr. Farragher adds, "When it was discovered that Dev's aides were also released and were already back in Glenvar, the mystery deepened". Dev was invited to return to the College for Sunday Mass and lunch by Fr. Downey, the college President. He duly arrived along with Kathleen O'Connell[27].

Dev's official biographers write, *"Dev walked confusedly out of Portobello Barracks onto Rathmines Road. His release made nonsense of his arrest. There must be some political purpose behind it. What on earth was open to him now?"*[28]. He felt that his role in government could not continue. He immediately met Collins, Brugha and Stack, to brief them on his arrest and the discovery of secret documentation, which would put many lives in danger. Dev feared, not surprisingly, that he 'might be suspect to our own'[29]. His sudden release was bound to raise questions about why the British treated him so carefully and released him so quickly. Dev 'was very despondent' as to his future within the movement and considered joining up with Liam Lynch's Southern Division. He then left for his home to Greystones, feeling that his leadership role within Irish republicanism might be at an end.

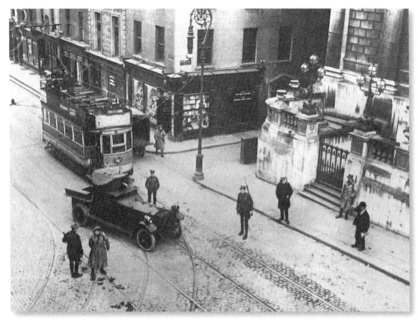

The 'Black and Tans' British auxillary force, caused havoc around Dublin and throughout the country, committing atrocities, in response in the main, to the many IRA outrages.

There is, however, no evidence that he was indeed ever suspected of doing any deal with the British, despite the sensational new book published in late 2009 in America, positing that Dev became a life-long British agent in 1916, as the price for not being executed. The American author claims that Dev's arrest at Glenvar was a ploy to enable Andy Cope to meet him. There is little doubt that the whole episode looks very strange, as Dev himself adverted to. If one wished to engage in conspiracy theories about Dev being 'turned' by the British, this arrest and subsequent fortuitous release and the immediate action of Lloyd George in cabinet, would be a better starting point than 1916. It is my own belief that the episode is an example of the twin approach of the British military and politicians being sometimes in conflict or even competition, rather than in tandem[29a]. There is little doubt that Collins, and others, would have checked out every eventuality.

Possibly arising directly from this debacle, Lloyd George on 24 June was able to tell his cabinet that, "in the course of the last three days we have received indications that DeValera is in a frame of mind to discuss a settlement, on a basis other than independence".[30..]

Two days later, Lloyd George issued his invitations to Dev and any colleagues he wished to bring with him, and also to James Craig, to a conference in London, "to explore to the utmost the possibility of a settlement".

London, 24 June 1921.

Sir,

The British Government are deeply anxious that, so far as they can assure it, the King's appeal for reconciliation in Ireland shall not have not been made in vain. Rather than allow yet another opportunity of settlement in Ireland to be cast aside, they felt it incumbent upon them to make a final appeal, in the spirit of the King's words, for a conference between themselves and the representatives of Southern and Northern Ireland.

I write, therefore, to convey the following invitation to you as the chosen leader of the great majority in Southern Ireland, and to Sir James Craig, the Premier of Northern Ireland:-

(1) That you should attend a conference here in London, in company with Sir James Craig, to explore to the utmost the possibility of a settlement.

(2) That you should bring with you for the purpose any colleagues whom you may select. The Government will, of course, give a safe conduct to all who may be chosen to participate in the conference.

We make this invitation with a fervent desire to end the ruinous conflict which has for centuries divided Ireland and embittered the relations of the peoples of these two islands, who ought to live in neighbourly harmony with each other, and whose co-operation would mean so much not only to the Empire but to humanity...

I am, Sir, Your obedient servant,

David Lloyd George.

Because his cover was blown by his arrest, Dev then set up a Headquarters at the Mansion House. He responded to Lloyd George's invitation on 28 June saying:

Mansion House, Dublin, 28 June 1921.

Sir,

I have received your letter. I am in consultation with such of the principal representatives of our nation as are available. We most earnestly desire to help in bringing about a lasting peace between the peoples of these two islands, but see no avenue by which it can be reached if you deny Ireland's essential unity and set aside the principle of national self-determination.

Before replying more fully to your letter, I am seeking a conference with certain representatives of the political minority in this country.

Eamon DeValera.

Dev issued an invitation to Irish Unionists that same day. Craig felt insulted, declaring that he was satisfied with what he had got in the North. The conference with southern Unionists opened in the Mansion House on 4 July. Lord Middleton said that if peace was to be considered, a truce was the first necessity. He undertook to see Lloyd George.

Tom Casement, a brother of Roger's, organised a meeting in Dublin between Smuts and Dev. Barton, Duggan, Griffith, MacNeill and Michael Staines were all released as a peace gesture for attendance at the meeting. Collins was not present at this meeting with Smuts. Dev told Smuts that he wanted a republic. Smuts responded, "Do you really think that the British people are ever likely to agree to such a republic?" Smuts explained that in the Transvaal, when the people got a chance to vote they voted for a free partnership within the Empire. Dev concluded the long meeting saying, "If the status of Dominion rule is offered, I will use all our machinery to get people to accept it"[31]. Smuts advised Dev to leave Craig out of the matter and accept Lloyd George's invitation. Smuts reported that he found Griffith the most sensible of those he met. Duggan and Barton said nothing. He said that DeValera was like a visionary; he spoke continually of generations of oppression and seemed to live in a world of dreams, fantasies and shadows[31a].

The Mansion House conference resumed on 8 July. Middleton reported that Lloyd George agreed to the need for a truce. Dev informed the Conference of his reply to Lloyd George, to explore on "what basis such a conference as that proposed can reasonably hope to achieve the object desired"[32]. He also told a disbelieving Middleton that he intended to go alone to meet the British PM. On Sunday 10 July Lloyd George asked Dev to nominate a date for their meeting.

On 11 July when General Macready came to the Mansion House to sign the Truce and deal with the practicalities, the assembled crowd cheered him. Eamon Duggan and Robert Barton were appointed to liaise with the British and Irish armies.

On 9 July Dev had issued a proclamation to the nation:

"During the period of the truce each individual soldier and citizen must regard himself as a custodian of the nation's honour. Your discipline must prove in the most convincing manner that this is the struggle of an organised nation. In the negotiations now initiated, your representatives will do their utmost to secure a just and peaceful termination of this struggle, but history, particularly our own history, and the character of the issue to be decided, are a warning against undue confidence. An unbending determination to endure all, may still be necessary, and fortitude such as you have shown in all your recent sufferings—these alone will lead you to the peace you desire. Should force be resumed against our nation, you must be ready on your part once more to resist. Thus alone will you secure the final abandonment of force, and the acceptance of justice and reason as the arbitrer"[33].

DEV MEETS LLOYD GEORGE

Dev arrived in London on a Thursday together with Griffith, Stack, Barton, Erskine Childers, his secretary Kathleen O'Connell and Dr Farnan TD with his wife. Collins was furious that he was not in the delegation and had spent several hours arguing with Dev on the matter[34]. The official delegation stayed at the Grosvenor Hotel. Dev, Kathleen O'Connell and the Farnans stayed in a private house[35].

Dev and Lloyd George initially met alone for two hours, at Downing St on 14 July, as a large Irish crowd waved green flags outside"[36]. Dev wrote to Collins that same evening.

"Lloyd George is developing a proposal that he wishes me to bring in my pocket as a proposal to the Irish people for its consideration. The meetings have been between us two alone as principals. You will be glad to know that I am not dissatisfied with the general situation. The proposal will be theirs — we will be free to consider it without prejudice. I hope to see you about the middle of the week"[37].

As the meetings went on, the question of Ulster loomed large with both Craig and Dev feeling that Lloyd George was playing one off against the other. After his meeting Lloyd George, Craig announced, "It now merely remains for Mr. DeValera and the British people to come to terms regarding the area outside of which I am Prime Minister"[38]. Craig would maintain this confident stance right throughout the year, in the knowledge that his powerful Conservative friends would support him. When Dev claimed to speak for the whole Irish nation, Craig refuted it publicly. Dev demanded that Lloyd George state publicly whether he supported Craig's position, or otherwise there was little point in going on with their talks. Lloyd George refused saying "I am neither responsible for Sir James Craig's statement to the press, to which you refer, nor for your statement to which Sir James purports to be a reply". Dev did not appear to consider the relatively weak position Lloyd George had in his cabinet where only three weeks previously, a plot against him was hatched by Birkenhead and Churchill[39].

Two of many delegations that accompanied DeValera to the Anglo-Irish negotiations.

Dev wrote immediately to Collins,

London, 19 July 1921.

Things may burst up here suddenly, so all should be prepared.
I intend adhering to our original plan as closely as possible, but the changes in the situation have to be met as they arise.

I expect to be back by the end of the week.

(initialled) E d V[40].

This came as no surprise to Collins, who was aware that the British military in Ireland were planning and prepared for such an eventuality. Collins also knew that the Irish were not prepared or able, for a long drawn out war. He wrote to Dev admonishing him, "In the final result it would be worth while stipulating that no matter how bad the terms are, they would be submitted to a full meeting". This would give the Irish the opportunity to prepare for the worst.

David Lloyd George to Eamon DeValera (London)

London, 20 July 1921.

Sir,

I send you herewith the proposals of the British Government, which I promised you by this evening. I fear that they will reach you rather late, but I have only just been able to submit them on behalf of the Cabinet to the King.

I shall expect you here to-morrow at 11.30 a.m., as arranged at our last meeting.

I am,

Your obedient servant,

David Lloyd George.

Enclosure

Proposals of the British Government for an Irish Settlement.

20th July, 1921.

The British Government are actuated by an earnest desire to end the unhappy divisions between Great Britain and Ireland which have produced so many conflicts in the past. They are convinced that the Irish people may find as worthy and as complete an expression of their political and spiritual ideals within the Empire as any of the numerous and varied nations united in allegiance to His Majesty's throne…

The free Nations which compose the British Empire are drawn from many races, with different histories, traditions, ideals…The British people cannot believe that where Canada and South Africa, with equal or even greater difficulties, have so signally succeeded, Ireland will fail;

The British Government will therefore leave Irishmen themselves to determine by negotiations between themselves whether the new powers which the Pact defines shall be taken over by Ireland as a whole and administered by a single Irish body, or be taken over separately by Southern and Northern Ireland, with or without a joint authority to harmonise their common interests. They will willingly assist in the negotiation of such a settlement, if Irishmen should so desire.

By these proposals the British Government sincerely believe that they will have shattered the foundations of that ancient hatred and distrust which have disfigured our common history for centuries past. The future of Ireland within the Commonwealth is for the Irish people to shape...

10 Downing Street, S.W.1,

July 20th, 1921[41].

The British proposals offered a form of Dominion rule for the 26 Counties, with Partition continuing for as long as the North wished. The British would defend the Irish coasts and their navy would have facilities in a number of Irish ports. The Irish army would be limited to a certain size and the Irish would pay a proportion of the British National Debt and free trade would remain between the two countries.

Dev consulted his colleagues before meeting Lloyd George. He told him that he rejected the proposals and would not recommend them to the cabinet or the Dáil. Lloyd George then said, "Do you realise that this means war?. Do you realise that the responsibility for it will rest on your shoulders alone?" Dev answered, "No Mr. Lloyd George. If you insist on attacking us it is you, not I will be responsible, because you will be the aggressor". The Prime Minster countered, "I could put a soldier in Ireland for every man woman and child in it" to which Dev replied, "very well. But you would have to keep them there". Dev left without taking the official document with him but sent a messenger for it later, before returning to Ireland.

Edward Carson and James Craig

The British cabinet record on 20 July reported that, "The Prime Minister informed the Cabinet that after three interviews with Mr. DeValera, he found it difficult to say exactly where the Irish leader stood. What he wanted was a Republic, but the Prime Minister said this was impossible, being inconsistent with the Monarchy. Mr DeValera did not admit the inconsistency".

Joe Lee writes, "Lloyd George succeeded in establishing, during a protracted bout of sparring with DeValera following the Truce, that the achievement of a Republic through negotiation was impossible"[42].

Back in Dublin, all the imprisoned Dáil Deputies were released to consider the British offer, except Commandant Seán MacEoin, who was under sentence of death. Collins insisted that Dev demand MacEoin's release as a precondition. This demand was reluctantly adhered to.

At a cabinet meeting on 25 July, Griffith and Cosgrave thought the British offer better than they had expected. MacNeill welcomed it and Collins thought it a step forward. Stack, Childers, Joseph MacDonagh and Brugha were very negative, with the latter ominously reminding Dev that a Republic had been declared in arms and that he should never deviate from that again. Dev is reported to have replied, "I think I can promise Cathal that you won't have to complain again"[43]. JJ O'Kelly and Countess Markievicz were both in favour of circulating the terms. Ernest Blythe appeared to agree with Griffith and Collins.

Dev worked on several replies to the British before getting general agreement on a form of 'external association' with the British Commonwealth, which satisfied Stack and Brugha. Barton and Duggan took the formal reply to London on 10 August. It said, *"A certain treaty of free association with the British Commonwealth group, as with a partial League of Nations, we would have been ready to recommend, and as a government to negotiate and to take responsibility for, had we an assurance that an entry of the nation as a whole into such association would secure for it the allegiance of the present dissenting minority, to meet whose sentiment alone this step could be contemplated"*. The new state could not derive its authority from the crown, but rather from the right of the Irish people to self-determination.

The British press headlined that Dev was prepared to drop the Republic. Fifteen communications were exchanged between Dev and Lloyd George throughout the summer. During that time the Volunteers, now called the IRA, prepared for a possible return to violence. The Dáil operated openly as an alternate government.

Lloyd George however, rejected the Irish claim to sovereignty, saying that Ireland could not secede from allegiance to the King. He said that the closeness of the two islands prevented such a possibility[44]. However the British did not issue any ultimatum about negotiations. The majority of the Irish people, including many of the Volunteers themselves, assumed that peace was assured.

David Lloyd George

Edward Carson

King George V

Erskine Childers

CHAPTER 8

TREATY NEGOTIATIONS

The Dáil met on 16, 17,18, 22, 23, 25 of August 1921. Dev demanded a totally free hand as 'President of the Republic'. He said, *"I am no longer to be looked on as a party leader. I am representing the nation and I shall represent the whole nation if I am elected to office, and I shall not be bound by any section whatever of the nation. I have one allegiance only to the people of Ireland, and that is to do the best we can for the people of Ireland as we conceive it... I would not like therefore, that anyone should propose me for election as President who would think that I had my mind definitely made up on any situation that may arise. I keep myself free to consider each question as it arises – I never bind myself in any other way"[1].*

Dev perturbed some of his closest allies by saying that the interpretation he put on the oath to the republic, was "that he should do the best for Ireland" and used the expression, that he was not a doctrinaire republican as such[2]. It is clear that in these statements, Dev foresaw great difficulties ahead with those who had taken the oath to the republic and would accept nothing less. It is also clear that he was planning strategies that might overcome such eventualities.

DeValera and the Dáil, while rejecting the British proposals, were willing to appoint representatives and to invest them with plenary powers, if the principle of "consent of the governed" was accepted as the basis for peace; "as our nation has formally declared its independence and recognised itself as a sovereign state" and "that it is only as representatives of that state we have any authority". Lloyd George read that as being disloyal to the King and Empire and refused such a basis for formal negotiations.

Dev protested, *"we have had no thought at any time of asking you to accept any conditions precedent to a conference".* He hoped that any conference would be free and "without prejudice". Lloyd George then issued the invitation to a conference, "to ascertain how the association of Ireland within the community of nations known as the British Empire, could best be reconciled with Irish national aspirations", to be held on Tuesday 11 October. There was no agreement that Ireland would acquiesce in remaining within the Empire, and no agreement that England would accept anything less[3]. The fact of agreement to enter into negotiations, presumed compromise. Britain had already established the Northern Parliament and then wished to achieve the best possible result in the South, for itself.

At the next day's cabinet meeting with Robert Barton, Brugha, Collins, Cosgrave, Griffith and Austin Stack, Dev announced that he did not intend to be one of the delegation going to London. He decided on the premise that if matters got too hot, the delegation could legitimately say that it had to consult him, before agreeing to anything.

This caused great unease and suspicion among some cabinet members. Collins, Cosgrave and Griffith rejected this line of thinking and demanded that Dev go to London for the negotiations. Dev argued that as President, he was the symbol of the Republic and as such he should not negotiate. Joe Lee writes, *"This sounds suspiciously like an anti-Collins rationalisation. The one thing that DeValera was, and that Collins was not, was President!. DeValera would have gained a more acute appreciation of the negotiating possibilities in London, where he could also presumably have exerted greater influence on the Irish delegates"*[4].

Barton, Brugha and Stack supported Dev's line. Griffith was appointed Chairman, with a most reluctant Collins as his deputy. Stack objected to Griffith and Collins, as both had expressed favourable views on the July proposals. Collins' colleagues in the IRB, "thought there was something sinister" in Dev's plan. He realised this, but was somewhat reassured by Dev's declaration to him that compromise would be necessary.

When the Dáil again met on 14 September, to ratify the appointment of the plenipotentiaries, WT Cosgrave, clearly indicating his personal dissatisfaction, and despite the earlier cabinet decision, proposed that Dev should lead the delegation. Cosgrave realised that the British would be putting forward their greatest diplomatic team. Cosgrave said that Dev had an extraordinary experience in negotiations. He also had the advantage of being in touch already. The head of government of England was Lloyd George and he expected that Dev would be one of the plenipotentiaries. The Irish were sending over a team and they were keeping their ablest player in reserve. The reserve would have to be used sometime and it struck him that now was the time he was required. Cosgrave's motion received little support[5].

Stephen Collins writes that at that stage, WT Cosgrave became very suspicious of DeValera, as he knew that Dev was working on his 'External Association' proposal[6]. This envisaged Irish sovereignty in internal affairs, without the oath of allegiance to the King, but Ireland would be associated with the Commonwealth for external affairs, of which the King was head. While Dev succeeded in getting Brugha and Stack to agree to this formula, there was no possibility of the die-hards like Rory O'Connor accepting it. Cosgrave felt that Dev was expecting that Griffith would move Lloyd George towards this position. He sought to warn Griffith that Dev might be creating a scapegoat. But Griffith knew what he was doing. Griffith was older than most of his colleagues. He had been an ardent Parnellite who had shaken Parnell's hand as he left the Broadstone station in September 1891 embarking on that fateful journey to the election in Creggs. Griffith had then attached his star to Willie Rooney and in 1917 to Eamon DeValera. But now he knew that he had to be his own man in a leadership role, even if it meant risking another split.

Griffith later told the Dáil, *"When I was going to London – when the Cabinet sent me to London with the other plenipotentiaries-I knew that neither I nor any other man could bring back a Republic, and he (Dev) admitted to me that it could not be done.*

DeValera made a speech in which he said, he took his oath in the sense of doing the best he could for the country, that he was not a doctrinaire Republican. And he said to me before I went to London, "Get me out of this strait-jacket of the Republic"[7].

Diarmaid Ferriter finds it 'puzzling' that Dev did not go to London and 'bears responsibility for allowing such confusion to develop'. His gamble (in not going) involved a serious underestimation of the pressure his colleagues were under, pressure he had directly contributed to by refusing to go to London. The British and Northern Irish prime ministers always represented themselves at such important Anglo-Irish negotiations, and Lloyd George too had Cabinet considerations. Joe Lee is probably correct in asserting that DeValera's choice in 1921 was less conspiracy than miscalculation"[8].

The decision of the Dáil to give the delegation plenipotentiary power meant that Dev's intention to exercise control over them through the cabinet and his own authority held no legal standing and was a mistake. Though Dev sent Childers as secretary to the plenipotentiaries, it was clear that Childers' job was to 'keep an eye' on them for Dev. Collins resented this and ensured that Childers played no part in discussions with the British.

The British and Irish delegations met for the first time on 11 October in London. There were no handshakes. The first major row occurred after Dev intervened in messages from the Pope to King George. On 19 October the Pope sent a telegram to King George V rejoicing at the Anglo-Irish negotiations, to which the King graciously replied. Dev telegrammed the Pope on 20 October, hoping that the "ambiguities in the reply sent in the name of the King will not mislead you into believing that the troubles are 'in' Ireland or that the people of Ireland owe allegiance to the British King.... the rulers of Britain have sought to impose their will upon Ireland and by brutal force have endeavoured to rob her people of the liberty which is her natural right and heritage"[9].

Lloyd George deemed Dev's words 'challenging, defiant and ill-conditioned'. Though Griffith, Collins and Duggan thought Dev's message inopportune, Griffith backed up Dev in reply to Lloyd George, saying, "Mr. DeValera only stated public facts. The trouble is not in Ireland, but is one between Ireland and Great Britain".

Lloyd George proposed that full delegation meetings were not productive and proposed meetings in sub-conference. This led to meetings between Griffith and Collins with Lloyd George and some of his colleagues.

Delegation led by DeValera, with Arthur Griffith, Austin Stack, R.C. Barton,
and two secretaries, Lily O'Brennan and Kathleen O'Connell, July 1921.

Treaty Delegation October 1921,
L to R: Gavin Duffy, Michael Collins, Arthur Griffith, R.C. Barton.

Griffith wrote a series of letters to Dev:

22 Hans Place, London, 25 October 1921.

A E.(amon), A Chara,

To-day M.C. and myself met Chamberlain and Hewart, the Attorney General in a sub-Conference on 'Ulster'.

They argued the ethics of Partition very little. The discussion on their side resolved itself practically into 'well, we are committed to the six-county area - what can we do ?'. 'The people must have at least freedom of choice' we replied. They did not deny the justice, but did the practicability of this. They made two suggestions - the whole province of Ulster to vote in or out. I said 'Yes', if the vote went by constituencies and those who voted out were a subordinate legislature. We were willing to confirm the existing powers of the six-county area, as a legislature subordinate to the Parliament of Ireland, provided the 1918 constituencies in the six-county area could vote directly into the Parliament.

They demurred. They wanted the province of Ulster to vote as an entity. I said we could not accept that. The Province was not an economic entity but an historic name. Michael easily knocked down their arguments. Eventually they suggested the six-county area remaining as at present, but coming into the All-Ireland Parliament. This was a new proposal and while we did not hold any hope out that it might be a basis, we, between ourselves, thought it might be a possible basis.

They declared they had no authority. They were merely discussing with us to see some solution. In the end I told them that no Irishman could even discuss with his countrymen or any Association with the British Crown unless the essential unity of Ireland was agreed to by the citizens. This should put them up against the Ulster Die-hards.

Mise, Do Chara,

(Initialled) E.(rskine) C.(hilders) for A.(rthur) G [10.]

Members of the delegation did not remain continuously in London but travelled home most weekends and attended cabinet meetings and informal meetings with colleagues, as well as sending written communications back and forth throughout.

The next row was again caused when Dev made another intervention. He had given the delegation a draft Treaty that included an external form of relationship with Britain, which could be raised at some time if necessary. This would automatically bring the matter of the Irish attitude to the King into play. As the negotiations proceeded the British sought an assurance that if they came to other agreements, the Irish would accept the Crown. Griffith wrote to Dev who replied that there could be no question of asking the Irish people to give any allegiance to the King.

The cabinet members in Dublin, Brugha, Cosgrave, O'Higgins and Stack supported this. Dev added in his reply to Griffith, "if war was the alternative, we can only face it". This apparent curtailment of their negotiating position, infuriated most of the delegation in London. Griffith replied in a letter signed by all the delegation:

Letter from the combined Irish Delegation to Eamon DeValera (Dublin).

London, 26 October 1921.

A. E.(amon) A Chara,

… The delegates regard the first paragraph of your letter as tying their hands in discussion and as inconsistent with the powers given them on their appointment and Nos. 1 and 2 of 'Instructions to Plenipotentiaries from Cabinet' dated 7th October. Obviously any form of association necessitates discussion of recognition in some form or other of the head of the association. Instruction 2 conferred this power of discussion but required before a decision was made reference to the members of the Cabinet in Dublin.

The powers were given by the Cabinet as a whole and can only be withdrawn or varied by the Cabinet as a whole. Having regard to the stage discussions have reached now, it is obvious that we could not continue any longer in the Conference and should return to Dublin immediately if the powers were withdrawn. We strongly resent the position in which we are placed, the interference with our powers. The responsibility, if this interference breaks the very slight possibility there is of settlement, will not and must not rest on the plenipotentiaries.

As to your coming to London, we think, if you can come without being known, it is most important you should do so immediately. But if you cannot come privately, do not come publicly, unless we send you a message that in our opinion it is essential.

Art O'Griobha,

Riobárd Bartún,

Seosamh Gabháin ui Dubhaigh,

E. J. O'Dugáin[11].

Dev expressed surprise at the way his warning had been taken and assured the delegation that "there can be no question of tying the hands of the plenipotentaries beyond the extent to which they were tied by their original instructions. These memos of mine, except I explicitly state otherwise, are nothing more than an attempt to keep you in touch with the views of the cabinet in Dublin". This row blew over.

Arthur Griffith to Eamon DeValera (Dublin).

22 Hans Place, London, 27 October1921.

A E.(amon), A Chara,

Enclosed document handed in to us to-day.

Michael and myself were at the same time requested to see Lloyd George and Lord Birkenhead before we sent the written answer.

We did so, and were with them for 1 1/2 hours. The conversation was general. The gist of it was that if we would accept the Crown, they would send for Craig, i.e. — force 'Ulster' in, as I understood.

We told them we had no power to do so. We might recommend some form of association if all other matters were satisfactory - above all Ireland unified.

We are to send them a reply to-morrow. I am writing in great haste. I deeply appreciate your letter.

Mise, Do Chara,

(Initialled) E.(rskine) C.(hilders) for A.(rthur) G.[12]

On 30 October, Griffith proposed to his delegates that he was prepared to send a letter on the Crown, free partnership with the Empire and naval facilities, to assist the Prime Minister, who was under pressure in the Commons from those opposed to the negotiations. In return Lloyd George promised that he would "go down to smite the Die-Hards and would fight on the Ulster matter to secure essential unity"[13].

When Griffith showed his letter to the delegates, Barton, Duffy and Childers objected until Griffith re-wrote his letter. Gavan Duffy went to Dublin at the request of Barton and Childers, to brief Dev on the sub-conferences and on the Crown matter. Childers visited Dublin later to see Dev, who indicated that he still retained confidence in Collins and Griffith.

Dev made contact with Harry Boland in Washington on 5 November, indicating clearly that he was quite prepared for a hard line response and resumption of the war, should negotiations fail, *"You must be careful whilst exposing the fraud that the British have offered Dominion rule for Ireland, not to make it appear that Ireland would accept Dominion Rule as a satisfaction of her claims. If there be a breakdown, we must take good care that we have not compromised our position, so that we could resume again on the old footing"*[14].

෨✿ ✿෨

Griffith again wrote to Dev on the ever evolving situation:

22 Hans Place, London, 8 November 1921.

A E(amon), a chara:

To-day M. C. and myself were asked, unofficially to see Jones, Lloyd George's secretary at Whitehall Gardens. We declined, but agreed to meet him at one of our Headquarters, the Grosvenor.

He told us that Craig is standing pat. Refuses to come under any all-Ireland Parliament. Refuses to change Six-County area. He said that L. G. is going to put up to the 'Ulster' Govt. on Thursday the proposal that they should accept the 6-County area under an Irish Parliament. If they refuse, he will go down to the House of Commons and announce his resignation.

Birkenhead and Chamberlain will probably resign along with him, but they will do nothing further (this is Jones' statement). Said they would not dissolve, giving various reasons, nor go into opposition. L. G. would retire altogether from public life. Bonar Law would probably form a Militarist Govt. against Ireland.

Said he had a scheme in his own mind - that L. G. should, as an alternative to the 'Ulster' refusal, offer to set up a Govt. for the 26 Counties with all the proposed powers, and appoint a Boundary Commission to delimit 'Ulster', confining this Ulster to its Partition Act powers. This would give us most of Tyrone, Fermanagh, and part of Armagh, Down, etc.

We did not give any definite opinion on the matter. It is their look-out for the moment. He is to see us again tomorrow. It is partly bluff, but not wholly. It is possible the Conference may end with this week. If so, all policy dictates it should end on the note of 'Ulster' being impossibilist, in order to throw the Dominions against her.

Do chara

Arthur[15].

CATHAL BRUGHA

When it appeared that the negotiations might break down, Cathal Brugha, as Minister of Defence, told William O'Brien that he was making plans, in the event of the negotiations breaking down, to resume activities in Britain. He wanted O'Brien to put him in touch with Labour people in Britain and leaders of the unemployed who were then engaged in demonstrations in Britain. O'Brien demurred saying that Labour would not get involved in anything like that. Then Brugha asked him to introduce him to some British communists. O'Brien did so and introduced Brugha to William Gallagher and Arthur McManus of the British Communistic Party at Liberty Hall.

Rory O'Connor accompanied Brugha, whom he told that O'Brien would be in charge of operations in Britain. Several more meetings were held between the parties. Brugha envisaged attacking British Ministers in the House of Commons. Brugha told O'Brien that the Dáil cabinet had voted £5.000 for this special campaign. Brugha gave O'Brien £500 to put into his own bank account from which he "could pay on demand". All that was spent was £10 for printing inflammatory leaflets, which were stored in Liberty Hall. Later when the Dáil passed the Treaty, Brugha called in the balance from O'Brien[16]. Thomas Morrissey also reports Tom Clarke referring to Cathal Brugha *as a fine fellow but a crank, who could not agree with anybody"*.[17.]

A crucial cabinet meeting took place in Dublin on 25 November, as end game approached in the negotiations in London. It was Griffith's first time to meet Dev since the start of negotiations.

The cabinet approved *"Ireland shall agree to be associated with the British Commonwealth for the purposes of common concern such as defence, peace and war; and she shall recognise the British Crown as head of the association. Her legislative and executive authority shall be derived exclusively from her elected representatives"*[18]. On 28 Nov Griffith and Eamon Duggan met Lloyd George, Birkenhead and the Chancellor of the Exchequer at Chequers. Lloyd George said the Irish document was impossible. *"Any British government that attempted to propose to the British people the abrogation of the Crown would be smashed to atoms"*[19]. Griffith replied placidly that they had no authority to deal on any other basis than the exclusion of the Crown from purely Irish affairs. As the discussion went on, Griffith and Duggan were very surprised to hear Lloyd George say that he was willing to include in a treaty that the Crown would have no more authority in Ireland than in Canada or any other Dominion, and agreed to a modification of the oath, if that was helpful. This was a major concession and added to the attraction of Dominion Status. The elective head of the Irish government would be the Premier. The nominal head, the King's representative, would only be appointed in consultation with the Irish ministry. No one would be appointed to whom the Irish ministry offered any objection. They guaranteed that he would have no power, be in fact merely a symbol[20]. Frank Pakenham terms this breakthrough, *"Sterilisation of the Crown! Modification of the Oath! The collapse of the argument hitherto most relied on against Dominion Status, assumed subsidiary proportions"*[21].

The next day, Tuesday 29 November, the Irish delegation consisting of Griffith, Collins and Duggan met the British side, which reaffirmed formally what had been said the previous night. While the Irish rejected a new oath there was no sense of deadlock as drafts of a possible treaty began to be worked on by both sides. The British undertook to send their final proposals, by 6 December, to the delegation and to Craig.

Barton and Duffy were being sidelined on recent delegations and together with Childers, were regarded as close to Dev. At this very juncture Dev, presumably acting on information received from 'his men' in London, wrote a letter to Harry Boland in Washington, preparing him for Dev's rejection of what was to be offered. Dev also stated that he was confident that there would be a majority in cabinet for his stance.

This letter may bolster the theory that Dev had plotted to make scapegoats of Griffith/Collins from the start and have them sidelined, leaving himself as the 'Great Leader'.

Dublin, 29 November 1921.

My dear Harry:-

As things stand to-day it means war. The British ultimatum is allegiance to their King. We will never recommend that such allegiance be rendered.

You know how fully I appreciate all that WAR means to our people, and what my misgivings are as to the outcome of war. Without explanation you will understand then that if I appear with those who choose war, it is only because the alternative is impossible without dishonour. For us to recommend that our people should subscribe with their lips to an allegiance which they could not render in their hearts, would be to recommend to them subscription to a living lie, and the abandonment of the supreme issue in the struggle through all the centuries.

As far as I am concerned, it is now - External Association, YES. - Internal Association involving Allegiance, NO.

I am writing before the final recommendation of our plenipotentiaries is made, and so am speaking solely for myself, but it is likely that my view will be that of the Cabinet as a whole[22].

Eamon DeValera to Harry Boland (Washington).

The delegation returned to Dublin on 2 December with the final British proposals, for an immediate cabinet meeting at the Mansion House. Barton and Duffy were reluctant to travel but Griffith insisted that the entire delegation was under instruction to consult the cabinet "before a grave decision was made". Their interrupted travel arrangements meant that they only arrived at Kingstown at 10.30 in the morning. As Frank Pakenham writes, "They were a desperately tired and haggard little party when they arrived at the Mansion House"[23]. This meeting turned out to be most acrimonious, with Brugha asserting that the British had "selected its men", referring to Collins and Griffith. Griffith alone was willing to accept the terms the British offered. These were Dominion status "in law and constitutional usage". There would be free trade and the British would defend the coast and occupy some ports. TD's would swear "allegiance to the Constitution of the Irish Free State, to the Community of Nations known as the British Empire and to the King as Head of the State and Empire". The North would have the choice of opting in or out and a Boundary Commission could be set up to draw boundaries, if necessary. Dev would not accept the oath. WT Cosgrave said likewise. Dev could understand accepting Dominion status if it covered the whole country. Barton asked him to come to London with them.

Eventually a confusing agreement was reached. The delegation would not sign the Treaty as it was, but seek amendments and return and submit it to the Dáil . Individual interpretations of what exactly was agreed inevitably arose from the hurried nature of the meeting, as the delegation was under severe time pressure to return immediately to London. The split in the delegation was obvious from their return travel arrangements as Barton, Childers and Gavan Duffy sailed from the North Wall, and Griffith, Collins and Duggan sailing from Kingstown. As Michael Collins later said, *"We went away with a document which none of us would sign. It must have been obvious, that in the meantime, a document arose which we thought we could sign"*[24].

Meantime Dev, Brugha and Mulcahy resumed a tour of the country seeking to bolster the Volunteers, least military activities resumed. The presence of the Boundary Commission in the Treaty, which Lloyd George had convinced the plenipotentiaries would make a six county state unviable, meant that they and their cabinet colleagues in Dublin did not then see the North as a breaking point in the negotiations.

Back in London, Griffith, in a compromise move to his 'Republican' opponents in the delegation agreed to lead the delegation and to press the Irish proposals on the British delegation, who rejected them as a rehash of earlier proposals. Collins had refused to participate in the meeting at all. The British said they had offered Ireland the chance to become a willing member of the Empire, like the Boers, who had fought with equal gallantry, but the amendments consisted of a refusal to enter the Empire and accept the common bond of the Crown. The British offered "to immediately call Parliament together and pass the ratifying Act before Xmas. They would hand over Dublin Castle and withdraw their troops from the country" if the Irish signed the Treaty. A breakdown seemed imminent but further negotiations went on over Ulster and the Empire.

Then on 6 December the British met the Irish delegation of Griffith, Collins, and Barton. Detailed discussions took place, especially on the North, the Oath, Finance and Defence. There was a major concession of full fiscal autonomy and the possibility of an agreeable oath. The British then withdrew. The Irish decided that if the British insisted on an immediate reply, they would break off the negotiations or reject the terms pending a decision on the North from Craig. Whatever was proposed, Griffith intended to demand reference to the Dominion Premiers.

The British reappeared slowly minus Lloyd George, who was searching for the letter Griffith had earlier written accepting the Crown, if Ulster and other matters were acceptable. The British realised that Griffith's strategy had been to break on Ulster. When Lloyd George returned he recalled Griffith's earlier pledge to him that Griffith would not break on Ulster if a Boundary Commission was agreed. Griffith replied that he would stick to his promise and accept that position, but asked for a week's grace to get back to the Dáil. The Prime Minister then said that Dominion status like that of Canada was on offer, with a Boundary Commission to decide on Ulster. Then, according to Winston Churchill, Lloyd George delivered his ultimatum, *"The Irish must settle now. They must sign the Agreement or quit…and both sides would be free to resume whatever warfare they could wage against each other"*[25].

The state of the political situation in the House of Commons was that if the Prime Minister retreated from that threat, the uncompromising Bonar Law would have replaced him[26]. Griffith later wrote to Dev that he replied to Lloyd George "Provided we came to an agreement on other points, I would accept inclusion in the Empire on the basis of the Free State. They then asked whether I spoke for the Delegation or myself. I said I spoke for myself"[27]. Collins knew better than anybody that if the British put all their resources into the war, his side did not have the arms to resist.

The Irish withdrew for a few hours to their headquarters at Hans Place to consider their options. All of the delegation was of the same view, that arising from the putting of the draft Treaty before the cabinet on the previous weekend, they were fully entitled by their mandate to sign the amended Treaty if they so wished. There was furious discussion among the delegates. Griffith tried to break the impasse by declaring that he would sign. Collins and Duggan also agreed. Barton came under severe pressure to agree to sign. He resisted and a breakdown appeared likely. An emotional appeal by Duggan to Barton, not to throw away this chance, for which many young men had been hanged in Mountjoy, finally succeeded in changing Barton's mind. He agreed to sign and then Duffy would not stand-alone against signing. Amid anger, tears and confusion, the delegation had agreed and returned to Downing St. Griffith announced, "Mr Prime Minister, the delegation is willing to sign the agreement". "Then we accept", the Prime Minister replied[28].

The Union between Great Britain and Ireland, which powerful British parties thought of as sacrosanct, the Union which Daniel O'Connell had vainly tried to repeal and Charles Stewart Parnell to modify, the Union under which all through the nineteenth century, Ireland had lost population, industry, commerce, morale and status, was set aside by the Treaty. Arthur Griffith's wife, Maud, had joined him in London for the few weeks previously. Griffith described Lloyd George to her that night as "like a benevolent old gentleman, with white hair and a smooth face showing no lines on it, and having no conscience". Maude Griffith described her husband's reaction later that night as he walked the floor of their room for hours: I knew Arthur Griffith from the time I was a little girl and I never saw him excited before. He was in an expansive discursive mood, as he told her *"we have got the army. The North will come in. The business people will be with us. You can have your wish. I will leave politics. There is a great deal I have still to do, but in a few months all will be cleared up. I will leave politics in August"*[28a].

ଽଈ ଈଽ

DEV'S REACTION TO TREATY SIGNING

Dev was then in Limerick staying at the home of Stephen O'Mara, when a phone call from London, from Gearoid O'Sullivan of GHQ, to Mulcahy was received. The Treaty had been signed. Mulcahy told Dev that an agreement had been reached and invited him to come to the phone, but Dev declined saying, *"I didn't think they'd sign so soon."*[29] It took some hours for the details to become clear and they were not to Dev's liking. He travelled by train to Dublin the next day in the company of Brugha, while Mulcahy occupied another coach. There is no doubt what Brugha's advice to and expectation of his leader on the Treaty would be, but what transpired between the two men is unknown. Sinéad DeValera wrote that when Dev came home that night he asked her what she thought of the Treaty. She replied that everyone seemed pleased but that she did not like it[30].

The next day's newspapers carried detailed reports of the Treaty, which was welcomed around the world as "fitting terms for peace". The text was released and a summary said:

"The terms agreed last night by the British and Irish representatives at the Peace Conference were issued last night.

They provide for a Free State of Ireland, having Dominion status, and associated with the Commonwealth of Nations as the British Empire.

Northern Ireland is to have power within a month to enter the Free State or to remain outside it and retain its present position.

The Oath of Allegiance will be taken to the Free State of Ireland and to the King and his successors.

Provisions are made for Admiralty and other rights in Irish waters and for free trading facilities between England and Ireland.

Questions of finance are to be settled by a Commission, or, in the last resort by an arbitrator, who must be of British birth.

Parliament is to meet immediately to ratify the agreement.

The King, in a message to Mr. Lloyd George, states that he is overjoyed, at the splendid news of the agreement".

In Dublin a cabinet meeting was called for the next morning. All those who were not on the Treaty delegation were present. Dev made a crucial mistake in taking for granted that his friend and long-time colleague WT Cosgrave would automatically support him in cabinet. Dev announced that he was going to call for the resignation of Griffith, Collins and Barton. Cosgrave intervened "persistently" to say that he felt that they should be given a hearing, before such precipitate action was taken[31]. Cosgrave's stance surprised Dev, who then realised that he should be more cautious, as Cosgrave already had established his independent action, when he had insisted on proposing that Dev should go on the delegation to London.

Cosgrave was also in a position to cast the decisive vote in the seven-member cabinet. Dev issued a statement, *"In view of the nature of the proposed Treaty with Great Britain, President DeValera has sent an urgent summons to the members of the cabinet in London to report at once, so that a full Cabinet decision may be taken. The hour of the meeting is fixed for 12 o'clock noon tomorrow. A meeting of the Dáil will be summoned later"*. Desmond Fitzgerald, who had just returned from London, suggested to Dev that the statement appeared to indicate that he was against the Treaty and that it might be rephrased. Dev replied, *"That's the way I intend it to read. Publish it as it is"*. Fitzgerald commented to Stack, *"I did not think he was against this kind of settlement before we went to London"*. Stack responded, *"He's dead against it now anyway. That's enough"*[32].

Garret Fitzgerald writes, *"When on the evening of December 7th my father and Eamon Duggan handed DeValera the text of the Treaty just as he, as newly-elected Chancellor of the NUI, was about to attend a Dante Commemoration in the Mansion House, they recognised from his expression that he had already made up his mind to oppose it. It seemed to them, and to their pro-Treaty colleagues, to have been an irrational turnabout by a moderate – a turnabout they attributed to a weakness in DeValera's character, played upon by more extreme colleagues – and it led to their subsequent bitterness towards him. To the extent that he spent so much of his life thereafter, seeking to justify his actions at that time, he seems himself to have been uneasy about his own motivation"*[33]. Dev's party for the Dante Sexcentenary in the Mansion House that evening included, the Lord Mayor, Count Plunkett, Alderman Cosgrave, Austin Stack and Sir Thomas Esmonde. We can only speculate which of the pair, WT Cosgrave or Eamon DeValera felt under most pressure that evening.

The Treaty had 17 sections and an Annex. It gave Ireland the same Constitutional status as Canada, Australia, New Zealand and South Africa with a Parliament to make laws for good government. The Oath to be taken by members of Parliament stated "I…do solemnly swear true faith and allegiance to the Constitution of the Irish Free State and that I will be faithful to HM King George, his heirs and successors by law, in virtue of the common citizenship of Ireland with Great Britain and her adherence to and membership of the group of nations forming the British Commonwealth of Nations".

The crisis cabinet meeting parsed the Treaty clause by clause. Dev was angry that the delegation had not come back to him before signing, as he had understood the tactics. He argued that under the Treaty, Ireland would remain in the Empire and swear an oath of allegiance to the King. Barton blamed Dev for not coming to London with them as he had requested the previous week. As Dev had earlier feared, Cosgrave sided with Griffith, Collins and Barton to have the Dáil cast the decisive vote on the Treaty. Dev, Brugha and Stack voted against.

DeValera issued an explosive statement:

To The Irish People,

"My fellow Irishmen, you have seen in the public Press the text of the proposed Treaty with Great Britain. The terms of the agreement are in violent conflict with the wishes of the majority of the Nation, as expressed freely in successive elections, during the last three years. I feel it my duty to inform you immediately that I cannot recommend the acceptance of the treaty either to Dáil Éireann or the country. In this attitude the Ministers of Home Affairs and Defence support me. A public session of Dáil Éireann is being summoned for Wednesday next at 11 o'clock…the great test of our people has come. Let us face it worthily without bitterness and above all recriminations. There is a definite constitutional way of resolving our political differences…"

Before the Dáil met on 14 December to consider the Treaty, violent acts occurred around the country and TD's were intimidated as to how they should vote. Among the army there were very significant figures that were totally opposed to the Treaty. These included Liam Lynch, Ernie O'Malley, Rory O'Connor, Liam Mellowes, Seán Russell and Jim O'Donovan. Dev's stance gave an important political dimension to bolster their position and resolve. He argued *"the people have never a right to do wrong"*[34].

Dev wrote to Frank Pakenham in 1963 saying *"The reasons for the decision that I should not go to London were overwhelming…it was the signing of the Articles of Agreement, without reference to the cabinet in Dublin, that alone threw everything out of joint"*. Diarmaid Ferriter describes this statement as *"self-righteous"*, adding, *"DeValera should have gone to London and he knew it"*[35].

THE BRITISH VIEW IN PARLIAMENT

Winston Churchill had the task of selling the Treaty in the House of Commons. He did so in a remarkable speech, reminding the members of the "grim, grave, and in many cases, shocking realities" of the previous two years in Ireland. He insisted that while Sinn Féin sought an "independent sovereign republic for the whole of Ireland, including Ulster", his side had demanded allegiance to the Crown, membership of the Empire, facilities and securities for the Navy and a complete option on Ulster". He noted how in the House of Lords on the previous day, Lord Carson condemned Lord Curzon for signing the Treaty, just as DeValera had condemned Michael Collins for the same thing. He asked, *"Are we not getting a little tired of all this? These absolutely sincere, consistent, unswerving gentlemen, faithful in all circumstances to their implacable quarrels, seek to mount their respective war horses, in person or by proxy, and to drive at full tilt at one another, shattering and splintering down the lists, to the indescribable misery of the common people and to the utter confusion of our imperial affairs?"*[36].

Anti-Treaty members led by DeValera, walk out of Dáil 1922.

DeValera gets ready to address a meeting in Cork, 1922.

TREATY DEBATES

Although the Cabinet had voted in favour of the Treaty, Dev insisted that Griffith would have to propose the motion for ratification in the Dáil as Chairman of the delegation[37].

The Proposed Treaty of Association between Ireland and the British Commonwealth stated, in part: *In order to bring to an end the long and ruinous conflict between Great Britain and Ireland by a sure and lasting peace honourable to both nations, it is agreed:*

STATUS OF IRELAND

1. That the legislative, executive, and judicial authority of Ireland shall be derived solely from the people of Ireland.

TERMS OF ASSOCIATION

2. That, for purposes of common concern, Ireland shall be associated with the States of the British Commonwealth, viz.: the Kingdom of Great Britain, the Dominion of Canada, the Commonwealth of Australia, the Dominion of New Zealand, and the Union of South Africa.

3. That when acting as an associate, the rights, status and privileges of Ireland, shall be in no respect less than those enjoyed by any of the component States of the British Commonwealth...

5. That in virtue of this Association of Ireland with the States of the British Commonwealth, citizens of Ireland in any of these States shall not be subject to any disabilities which a citizen of one of the component States of the British Commonwealth would not be subject to, and reciprocally for citizens of these States in Ireland.

6. That, for purposes of the Association, Ireland shall recognise His Britannic Majesty as head of the Association.

RATIFICATION

7. That this instrument shall be submitted for ratification forthwith by His Britannic Majesty's Government to the Parliament at Westminster, and by the Cabinet of Dáil Éireann to a meeting of the members elected for the constituencies in Ireland set forth in the British Government of Ireland Act 1920, and when ratifications have been exchanged shall take immediate effect.

ADDENDUM. NORTH EAST ULSTER. RESOLVED:

That whilst refusing to admit the right of any part of Ireland to be excluded from the supreme authority of the Parliament of Ireland, or that the relations between the Parliament of Ireland and any subordinate legislature in Ireland can be a matter for treaty with a Government outside Ireland, nevertheless, in sincere regard for internal peace, and in order to make manifest our desire not to bring force or coercion to bear upon any substantial part of the province of Ulster, whose inhabitants may now be unwilling to accept the national authority, we are prepared to grant to that portion of

Ulster which is defined as Northern Ireland in the British Government of Ireland Act of 1920, privileges and safeguards not less substantial than those provided for in the 'Articles of Agreement for a Treaty' between Great Britain and Ireland signed in London on December 6th, 1921[38].

The Treaty Debates were held in public and private sessions at UCD on Earlsfort Terrace and lasted from 14 December 1921 to 7 January 1922. Dev was the major figure during the debates, speaking no less than 250 times. He was recognised by all as the 'Great Leader', with Collins and Griffith particularly appealing to him to accept the Treaty as a stepping-stone. On 19 December he spoke saying, *"I think it would be scarcely in accordance with Standing Orders of the Dáil if I were to move directly the rejection of this Treaty...I am against this Treaty, not because I am a man of war, but a man of peace"*. Dev's early strategy was to present an alternative to the Treaty. This plan was named Document No. Two and was based on external association of the Republic with the Commonwealth. This found no favour from those for the Treaty and served to confuse the anti-Treaty TD's, especially on where exactly Dev stood on the Oath[39]. Dev realised that while Griffith was the main speaker for the Treaty, Collins had the backing of the IRB, which Dev had no time for as a secret organisation and not answerable to the people. WT Cosgrave, who like Griffith had been in the national movement for a very long time, challenged Dev on several occasions.

Cosgrave said *"The loss of the President to the Irish Free State, should this instrument be approved, would be a terrible loss. I believe the loss of the Minister for Home Affairs and the Minister for Finance would be equally irreparable"*. As the debates went on it became clear that the majority of the people, the Church, many army officers and business leaders and significantly Irish-America, were for it. As the Dáil moved to the decisive vote, counter measures were attempted by the anti-Treaty TD's to circumvent the vote on the Treaty, by taking a motion to have Dev re-elected as President.

The Dáil adjourned for the Xmas without taking the decisive vote on the Treaty or Dev's Document Number Two. The Labour Party leadership sought to work out a compromise between the two sides. It proposed a formula, which would see the Dáil remain as the supreme legislative body which would ratify the Treaty, but in the context "that the legislative, executive, and judicial authority in Ireland is, and shall be, derived solely from the people of Ireland". The oath in the Treaty would then imply "allegiance to the Constitution of the Irish Free State as by law established-such law to be established by Dáil Éireann. The Constitution will be framed by the Dáil, and subject to its approval". The Provisional Government would be subject to the decisions of the Dáil, which remains in power, and retains power over the army, the present organisation and command continuing". The Labour Group met Collins, Griffith, Mulcahy, and subsequently Dev. The official Labour report said, "Their reception by Messers. Collins and Griffith led us to hope that a basis of agreement had been found, but this hope was shattered at the interview with Mr DeValera, and the proceedings at the resumed dates in the Dáil confirmed our disappointment"[40].

On 7 January 1922 at 8 p.m. the Dáil approved the Treaty as signed on 6 December 1921 by 64 votes for to 57 votes against.

Dev immediately set up a new grouping of those TD's who had voted against the Treaty, called Cumann na Poblachta. On 9 January he offered his resignation as President of the Dáil, with the idea that his new group would attempt to have him re-elected. Thus he would sack all the pro-Treaty cabinet members and sabotage the Treaty. He spoke tacticly:

"What I do formally is to lay before the House my resignation, definitely as Chief Executive Authority. I resign and with it goes the cabinet...This House has got my Document Number Two. The new cabinet that will be formed if I am re-elected will put it before the House. We will put that document. It will be submitted to the House".

Cosgrave objected vehemently to the motion to discuss Dev's tactics and it was withdrawn. Cosgrave deemed it:

"The latest interpretation of constitutional practice is that a minority in an assembly, is to form the government and carry out the various functions of the government in the country".

DeValera: *"Remember I am only putting myself at your disposal and at the disposal of the nation. I do not want office at all. Go and elect your President and all the rest of it. You have sixty-five. I do not want office at all. Select your President".*

Cosgrave: *"The President dictates to the House. The minority is to regulate whether a decision of this House is to be put or not".*

DeValera: *"This is a deliberate misrepresentation and you know it".*

Cosgrave: *"Let us have the exact representation".*

DeValera: *"I resigned...the majority can go and take over the machinery of the Republic. I do not ask you to elect me. I am quite glad and anxious to get back to private life".*

Cosgrave: *"As an ordinary man who has been in public life and who has generally managed to understand what people have said in public, it is this way, The President does not want to be in this position, where his advisors want to put him".*

DeValera: *"I said I was not consulting anybody".*

Cosgrave: *"It may be my own stupidity in the difficulty of understanding this. But the position appears- that the advisers to the President seek to take advantage of his personal popularity and the respect on which the people of this Assembly hold him- they desire to establish an autocracy...The people who do not want this Treaty, desire to have the resources of the Republic and the Army and the finances - that and they can blaze away... I submit that the resolution to re-elect the President is out of order... Under the Treaty the Irish people are Irish citizens and not British subjects".*

The motion on the re-election of Dev as President was put to a vote and lost by 60 votes to 58. After this the following exchange took place.

Arthur Griffith: *"I want the Deputies to know and all Ireland to know that this vote is not to be taken as against President DeValera. It is a vote to help the Treaty and I want to say now that there is scarcely a man I have ever met in my life that I have more love and respect for than President DeValera".*

Griffith had been ready, since at least 1917, as he had earlier been with William Rooney, to treat Dev as his avatar, but Dev was taking another turning on the road.

DeValera: *"Now I think the right thing has been done, that the people who are responsible have done the right thing. I hope that nobody will talk of fratricidal strife. That is all nonsense. We have got a nation that knows how to conduct itself...I tell you now, you will need us yet".*

Collins: *"We want you now".*

DeValera: *"I am against you on principle and I believe that you will get the best out of that Treaty; you will need us in a solid compact body. We will not interfere with you, except when we find you going to do something that will definitely injure the Irish nation... I would like my last word here to be this: we have had a glorious record for four years; it has been four years of magnificent discipline in our nation. The world is looking at us now".*

Dev then broke down and wept [41].

Document No. 2 involved the key principle of excluding Britain from the internal affairs of the Irish State, jettisoning Dominion status and the oath, in favour of a statement that Ireland's association with the Commonwealth would be strictly limited to defence, peace, war and political treaties. For some, it was not republican enough, and for the British an unacceptable alteration of the Treaty terms.

Dev held that the Dáil brought into being by the 1918 Election and the Republic as voted for by the people in May 1921, must be preserved until the people voted again.

When he resigned as President on 9 January, he was replaced by Arthur Griffith with George Gavan Duffy becoming Minister for Foreign Affairs. Griffith was elected President of the Dáil on 10 January and Dev and his anti-Treaty TD's walked out in protest. Dev said:

"As a protest against the election as President of the Irish Republic of the Chairman of the delegation, who is bound by the Treaty conditions to set up a State which is to subvert the Republic and who, in the interim period instead of using the office as it should be used to support the Republic, will of necessity, have to be taking action which will lead to its destruction, I, while this vote is being taken, am going to leave the House".

As Dev and his followers walked out, Collins shouted after them;

"Deserters all. We will now call on the Irish people to rally to us. Deserters all".

Dev claimed outside that he had a perfect right to resist, by every means in his power, the authority imposed on "this country from outside"[42.]

T Ryle Dwyer writes, *"On learning of the details of the Anglo-Irish Treaty DeValera announced it was a matter for the cabinet, and when the cabinet approved the agreement, he said it was a matter for the Dáil. And when the Dáil approved, he contended that the Treaty could only be ratified by the Irish people"*[43].

The Provisional Government of the Irish Free State was formed on 14 January 1922, with Michael Collins as Chairman.

George Russell (AE) wrote to WB Yeats on 16 January, *"Griffith is proving himself a competent chief I think. His speech winding up Dáil debate was astonishing from him. He is generally cold and ineffective. There his voice was resonant, his thinking clear, his sentences incisive, and that dear, woolly-minded DeValera appeared a sheep beside an exceedingly clever and yet not too wicked goat. Ireland is intensely interesting, more so than I have found since I was a boy. The young men are full of possibilities, and I watch them and study their mind, and I am full of hope not of an ever peaceful country, but for a country with a great many fine possibilities"*[44].

The same day as the Dáil walkout, a meeting of senior army officers in the Mansion House occurred. Liam Mellowes, Rory O'Connor, Cathal Brugha, and Ernie O'Malley did not attend. The new Minister of Defence and head of the army, Ristard Mulcahy, invited Dev to attend. Dev urged the army to hold together and support Mulcahy[45]. But the reality was that the Volunteers, from which the army had developed, were also split on the Treaty. The very next day Mulcahy received a request for a Volunteer Convention to consider a motion that would place the army under an Army Convention and entirely outside civilian control[46]. Mulcahy and Collins procrastinated on the request.

On 12 January Dev wrote to Monsignor John Hagan in terms, which defined where he then stood and where he would conscientiously remain. He said:

"A party set out to cross a desert, to reach a certain fertile country beyond – where they intended to settle down. As they were coming to the end of their journey and about to emerge from the desert, they came upon a broad oasis. Those who were weary said, 'Why go further – let us settle down here and rest, and be content'. But the hardier spirits would not, and decided to face the further hardships and travel on. They then divided- sorrowfully, but without recriminations"[47].

⋙ ⋘

Though many individual clerical friends continued to support Dev, the Hierarchy supported the Treaty and Pope Benedict XV sent a telegram of congratulations to the Dáil[48]. Later that same year of 1922 the bishops issued a Pastoral condemning the militant anti-Treatyites for *"wrecking Ireland from end to end. And in spite of all this sin and crime, they claim to be good Catholics and demand at the hands of the church her most sacred privileges like the Sacraments, reserved for worthy members alone"*[49]. Dev wrote to Dr. Mannix describing the pastoral as *"most unfortunate; never was charity of judgement so necessary and apparently so disastrously absent. Ireland and the church will, I fear, suffer in consequence"*[50].

The annual Sinn Féin Ard Fheis took place on 22 February before 3,000 delegates, a majority of them anti-Treaty. It appeared that a formal split would occur over the Treaty, with Griffith proposing a substantive amendment to Dev's anti-Treaty motion. A compromise ensued, which postponed the Ard Fheis and the General Election for three months, to consider the new Constitution and the Treaty. In the meantime the Dáil would meet regularly and continue to function in all its departments as before.

Despite the initial walkout from the Dáil, Dev returned later on, to participate in an adjournment debate. Griffith, while still referring to Dev as 'President', requested an adjournment for about one month, to allow the Provisional Government to establish itself. *"Give us a chance. We cannot work as it is,"* he said. Dev replied, *"We ought, I think, to take that as reasonable. The only thing we are anxious about is the army…"*

The Dáil had re-assembled on 28 February with a full attendance. It met and conducted business on fifteen occasions up to the 8 June, when it adjourned to 30 June after the planned General Election.

Dev, still styling himself as 'President of the Republic' embarked on a countrywide series of meetings during March, assailing the Treaty. His language contrasted greatly to what he had written to Hagan. In Dungarvan he said he was "against the Treaty because it bars the way to independence with the blood of fellow Irishmen. It is only by civil war after this that they can get independence"[51]. The very next day at Thurles he said that if the Volunteers of the future try to complete the work, "they will have to complete it, not over the bodies of foreign soldiers, but over the dead bodies of their own countrymen. They will have to wade through Irish blood, through the blood of the soldiers of the Irish Government and through, perhaps, the blood of some members of the Government to get Irish freedom". Dev's statements were condemned in editorials both in the *Irish Independent* and the *Irish Times*. Dev wrote to the *Irish Independent* accusing it of distorting the meaning of his words. Alongside his published letter the editor of the paper wrote, "We think we made no attempt to distort the plain meaning of Mr. DeValera's speeches…we dealt with his language as reported in at least three speeches..."[52]. Kevin O'Higgins challenged Dev on these statements some two months later in the Dáil. Dev denied them, saying that the reports were a misrepresentation of what he had said. O'Higgins accepted Dev's denial[53].

As the British began to hand over barracks around the country, it became evident that pro and anti-Treaty military forces were vying with each other to take over these military bases. The Provisional Government forces established their GHQ at Beggars Bush Barracks and prohibited the holding of an Army Convention, as the anti-Treaty forces operated all over the country stockpiling arms. Tim Healy was sent to meet Dev to seek his support in opposing the Army Convention. Dev said that army matters were not his business[54]. The Convention went ahead on 26 March. Liam Lynch was appointed Chief of Staff with Rory O'Connor, and Liam Mellowes, Joe McKelvey, Ernie O'Malley, Seamus Robinson and Peadar O'Donnell on the Army Council. The original motion sent to Mulcahy, putting the Army outside control of the Dáil or GHQ, was adopted.

Law and order broke down all over the country. The Volunteers had split into the Army under the Provisional Government, and those loyal to the anti Treaty officers. Rory O'Connor had an office in the same building as Dev on Suffolk St. in Dublin's city centre. Dev's official biography describes this fact as *"a painful embarrassment for Dev"*[55]. It was still by no means clear whether they were *ad idem* on how Dev as a politician and O'Connor as a soldier would operate. O'Connor said after the Convention, "Some of us are no more prepared to stand for DeValera than for the Treaty"[56]. This placed Dev in a quandary as events moved swiftly. Could he continue to operate from a political base or would the militarists cast him aside and seek to establish a military dictatorship?. He had to be steadfast, brave and tacticly astute to survive politically. On 6 April Dev said, *"When Dáil Éireann took its rightful place as the Government of the nation, then they would have a stable Government, but if they attempted to do what they legally could not do, to set up a Provisional Government as the Government of the country, that government would not be obeyed"*[57]. Dev subsequently confirmed that his own political aims were the same as those of the anti-Treaty forces, though he reiterated that his political grouping was separate from those Army forces[58].

FOUR COURTS DEBACLE

The IRA as the anti-Treaty army forces were being called, took a major military initiative on 13 April by occupying a series of public buildings in Dublin, including the symbolic Four Courts. Their terms for talks would have repudiated the Treaty, Dáil, official army and police force. This repudiation of the Dáil placed Dev "in an appalling situation" as it was the natural forum in which he wanted to participate[59]. Rory O'Connor, while still adamant that he was under no civilian control added, "I am safe in saying that if the Army were ever to follow a political leader, Mr. DeValera is the man"[60]. Dev issued an Easter Proclamation appealing to *"young men and young women of Ireland, the goal is at last in sight - steady, all together forward, Ireland is yours for the taking. Take it"*[61].

DÁIL ÉIREANN 27 APRIL 1922

In the Dáil on 27 April, Dev complained that British troops were not evacuating the six counties because of the Boundary Commission. He said that it was the policy of that minority of Ireland, who were a majority in that area, or part of that area, to maintain those six counties by force, despite any decision that the Boundary Commission may arrive at. He blamed the Provisional Government, which purported to come into existence as a consequence of the Treaty, for that. He claimed that it was not in the power of the Assembly to ratify that Treaty and therefore the Provisional Government, as a Government, could not come into existence as such. He declared that the Assembly had no power to give away the Government of the Country. His thinking was that every member of the Assembly, including those on the minority side, was part of the Government of Ireland, and not just the Cabinet. No section could give away the sovereign rights to any other body. Everything in the Articles of Agreement, that would be consistent with the maintenance of the sovereign authority of the Assembly, could be done. But anything that would be inconsistent with that could not be done and was illegal. Every time the Provisional Government acted as a Government, it was usurpation.

This was too much for President Griffith, who said that the Cabinet and the Dáil accepted the Treaty. He asserted that Dev was quite prepared to accept other than a Republic. Griffith then quoted occasions when Dev acted as a moderate and a realist abjuring doctrinaire republicanism. He said that Dev's External Association involved, *"agreement to accept the King of England, and the payment to the Government of England and Association with the King of England, for defence and treaties"*. Griffith added that they were sent to London *"to arrange how best the aspirations of Ireland could be reconciled with the community of nations that is known as the British Commonwealth; not an Irish Republic. Every night from Hans Place a special courier was sent to Mr. DeValera. He knew everything that was going on. Why didn't he send Lloyd George in July 1921 a simple statement that we would negotiate on no other basis but the recognition of the Republic? Why did he withdraw that basis and send us there? We went there, and fought there, and we won there. And when I was going to London Mr. DeValera said to me, 'there may have to be scapegoats'... I said I was willing to be a scapegoat to save him from some of his present supporters' criticism and Mr. Collins and myself were willing to be scapegoats as long as Mr. DeValera's face was saved. That is the inner history of what happened. And the reason I am referring to it is, because in the last two weeks an attempt was made on the life of my colleague Michael Collins... Some gentlemen laughed here when I referred to the attempted assassination of Michael Collins. When recent incitements were made about 'wading through blood', we were told they meant nothing. We know what they mean, and we are not going to let gentlemen ride off on this thing, when they inspire dupes and young and impetuous boys to do, what they want done. I think that is a deliberate incitement to the assassination of the plenipotentiaries."*

Dev replied to Griffiths' allegations:

"When the President of Dáil Éireann makes charges such as he has made, I think it is only fair that an opportunity should be afforded, first of all, to this assembly itself and, secondly to the Irish people to get to the bottom and get to the truth of this matter. Griffith responded, *"Hear! hear!".*

Mr. DeValera: *"I am to-day defending the sovereign rights of the Irish people—the sovereignty of the Irish nation…the word Republic denotes not merely sovereignty but independence…I deny that I have treated the members of the delegation in the manner that has been suggested. I have said here in Dáil Éireann definitely that my position was that if there was something which I thought the Irish people should take under the circumstances—while I personally could not be myself the sponsor of anything less than that for which my comrades had died, with which I associated isolation to a large extent, as well as the sovereignty of the country—if there was something less than that, whilst I myself could not take it, yet I would never do anything to stand in the way of the Irish people accepting it. But I am now in this particular case standing against this Treaty because I don't believe the Irish people should accept it".*

Mr. Milroy: *"Let them judge for themselves".*

Mr. DeValera: *"Exactly! Give them an opportunity of judging for themselves. I stood for that position and I will be consistent with it the whole time. I have been accused of not standing up for the sovereignty of Dáil Éireann. The record of every meeting here is a testimony to the fact that I stood up for the sovereignty of this assembly".*

Mr. M. Collins: *"Even when you walked out".*

Mr. DeValera: *"I walked out as a legitimate protest against the election as President of Dáil Éireann of a man who should uphold the Republic, but a man whose policy it was to destroy it".*

President Griffith; *"You know that to be a falsehood. Document No. 2 was the thing that let down any chance of a Republic".*

Mr. DeValera: *"The reference with which I am dealing is my going out. It was the only protest that I could make against the election as President of one who was subverting the Republic. I wanted to maintain the Republic until the time the people were entitled to speak on this question. That was the only protest I could make against the election of a Minister whose policy it was to destroy it, and I made that protest. My statement is on record".*

President Griffith: *"So is your Cuban speech".*

Mr. DeValera: *"Oh! You are mean! You are vilely mean! You know you said those who attacked me on that occasion were mainly responsible for the record of terror in Ireland".*

An Ceann Comhairle: *"I think this has gone far enough".*

Mr. DeValera: *"I think it has".*

MANSION HOUSE CONFERENCE

Dev, Brugha, Collins, Griffith, William O'Brien and Cathal O'Shannon, of the Labour Party delegates attended a conference in The Mansion House called by Archbishop Byrne of Dublin on 29 April. Collins and Griffith would not tolerate the presence of representatives of the Army Council. The meeting proved futile as both side's minds were on the forthcoming election. William O'Brien reported that *"neither side had any faith in the honour or honesty of its opponents"* as vengeful language passed between them[62]. Brugha accused Collins and Griffith of being "agents of the British Government" and confirmed that both were two of the ministers he had in mind when he said their blood was to be waded through. When Dev sought to explain his position, Griffith interjected, *"Was that your attitude? If so a penny post card would have been sufficient to inform the British Government without going to the trouble of sending us over"*. As Dev continued Griffth again interjected, *"did you not ask me to get you out of the straight-jacket of the Republic?"*. Archbishop Byrne then tried to calm matters saying, *"Oh, now gentlemen, this won't do any good"*. The Labour members then saw each side separately and the meeting broke up[63].

Dev issued a statement saying, *"Republicans maintain that there are rights which a minority may justly uphold, even by arms, against a majority"*. He told the *Chicago Tribune* that in the USA, their Senate required a two-thirds majority to pass a Treaty, adding that in Ireland, *"the Army sees in itself the only brake at the present time and is using its strength as such"*[64].

ELECTION PACT WITH COLLINS

Collins was desperate to avoid internal military conflict. Winston Churchill was watching these manoeuvres with trepidation. The Provisional Government intended to have a General election to seek approval from the electorate for the Treaty. It felt that this was their only way to establish legitimacy. Churchill urged the early holding of this election. General Macready had written to Churchill as early as 14 February saying that if Dev won the election on his republican claim, then he Macready would declare martial law. He added that if DeValera staged a *coup d'etat* before the election, he would also declare martial law[65]. As the security situation in Ireland deteriorated, Churchill wrote directly to Collins. He said, *"The wealth of Ireland is undergoing a woeful shrinkage. There is no doubt that capital is taking flight. Credits are shutting up, railways are slowing down, and business and enterprise are baffled. Up to a point no doubt, these facts may have the beneficial effect of rousing all classes to defend their own material interests, and Mr. DeValera may gradually come to personify not a case, but a catastrophe"*[66]. When the Government postponed the election, Churchill told the Commons on 16 May, *"We had a right to be disappointed with the Provisional Government. We thought we were dealing with plenipotentiaries and that we should have an election. But DeValera, recognising that this would have gone against him, has succeeded in delaying it"*[67].

On 17 May in the Dáil, Dev said that he would confer with Collins on the basis that he and his Deputies were not committed to the Treaty and that 'the people should not be asked to commit themselves to the Treaty'. On 20 May, Dev and Collins agreed the 'Pact Election', to the consternation of the pro-Treaty people. When the Cabinet met to consider the pact, the decisive voice was that of Arthur Griffith, who after remaining silent for some minutes, and repeatedly taking off his glasses and wiping them, said, "I agree"[67a].

All election candidates would be from the one Sinn Féin panel and the result would provide a national coalition for the Third Dáil and postpone a vote on the Treaty. The Minister of Defence would be representative of the two wings of the army and the other ministers would be proportionate to the current Dáil numbers. Collins agreed to the pact for a variety of reasons but primarily because he knew that an election could not be held without it. Stephen Collins has pointed out that this plan was impossible under proportional representation on which the election would take place[68].

The British were outraged and threatened war as the Provisional Government ministers were summoned to London to agree the draft Constitution, which was made public just prior to the election. Churchill compared Collins and Dev to Lenin and Trotsky saying, *"The Irish terrorists are naturally drawn to imitate Lenin and Trotsky"*[69]. In London, he told Collins and Griffith that events in Ireland were under "fierce scrutiny", adding *"You will find that we are just as tenacious on essential points – the Crown, the British Commonwealth, no Republic – as DeValera and Rory O'Connor, and we intend to fight for our points"*.

Mulcahy and Liam Lynch met to agree the sharing of a new Army Council on 7 June[70]. The IRA executive rejected this agreement with only Lynch, Liam Deasy and Seán Moylan voting in favour.

On 8 June 1922 at the last meeting of the Dáil before the forthcoming Pact Election, Cathal Brugha introduced a motion of condemnation of President Arthur Griffith, who was not present. This concerned Griffith's criticism of various Deputies in the Dáil, especially Erskine Childers. Griffith has referred to him as "the damned Englishman" and refused to answer his questions. Brugha said, *"It is most undignified for the first man in Ireland, the President of the Republic, to refer to members in such a way"*. He instanced Childers' great work for Ireland, which Griffith was well acquainted with. Brugha then asked the Dáil to condemn Griffith.

Childers himself then spoke, saying that Griffith's criticisms implied that as an English born intelligence officer in the British Army, he might have been a secret agent in Irish affairs. He said his mother was Irish and his home was in Glendalough. He acknowledged that he had fought in the British army in the South African War, like many thousands of Irishmen. He said he was sorry that he did so, but he could not re-live his life. His path came from Unionism to Nationalism into Republicanism. In 1914 he brought in arms for the Volunteers. He re-joined the British army for the Great War.

After demobilisation he devoted himself entirely to Irish Republicanism, working for Griffith himself on occasion. After the arrest of Desmond Fitzgerald he published *The Bulletin* for six months. In May 1921 he was elected to the Dáil. He became secretary to the Delegation in London and did his duty honestly. It was only after the Treaty split that he came under any attack as a foreigner, an alien and worse. He said that personal vendettas had no place in public life and regretted President Griffith was not present. Dev then spoke saying that he agreed that the motion should be put, affording Childers the opportunity to speak. He however did not wish the motion to be pressed, adding that when he returned from America, it was Collins who introduced him to Childers. Collins retorted *"God forgive me"*. Dev then agreed with the details given by Brugha and Childers. When Collins said that he would have to reply to the motion, Dev asked formally, *"I wish to ask Deputy Cathal Brugha to withdraw that motion"*.

Michael Collins said that as three speeches had been made on one side, he was obliged to speak. If the matter had been withdrawn graciously at the outset, he would have reciprocated in the same spirit. He had more vitriol poured on himself over the past days than any other member of the Assembly and there were no generous gestures from the other side then. They were on the eve of an election and were asked to treat the matter as if it had not been raised. If the resolution was pressed, his side would support President Griffith. He concluded that the Dáil should meet again on 30 June and again on 1 July when the new Parliament should be summoned. Dev again called for Brugha to withdraw the motion, suggesting that if the changed circumstances of Griffith's illness had been known, it might not have been put. Brugha acceded to Dev's request and withdrew the motion[71].

The General Election in the South resulted in a clear mandate for the Treaty with 58 TD's for, 35 against and 35 others, who were also for the Treaty. The Constitution, still containing the oath, had only been published on the morning of the election. Dev had expected to become Minister of Defence in the new cabinet and had planned to oppose the new Constitution. He was outraged at the failure to implement his pact with Collins. Harry Boland, who waited for a call from Collins on the Pact, wrote to Joe McGarrity, *"As you know I was the liaison or medium acting between our party and Collins. I expected a call from Mick as to the men on our side that would be required to fill the posts in Cabinet in accordance with the agreement. No word came"*[72].

The divergence from the hitherto all-embracing Sinn Féin movement into pro and anti-Treaty parties left Sinn Féin as a party in limbo, as both sides would wish to claim its nomenclature. Since it was not in a position to have campaigned as a political party in the recent election, what future did it have? Thanks to Griffith's insistence on the promotion of women within the movement, the current treasurer was the formidable Jennie Wyse-Power. On 26 July 1921 she closed the party's HQ in Harcourt Street and the secretary Paidin O'Keeffe removed all party records. Later in January 1922 the Standing Committee wound itself up and two years later its cash balance of £8,610 was lodged with the chancery division of the High Court[73]. These actions would later cause problems for Dev.

CHAPTER 9

CIVIL WAR

The occupation of the Four Courts was entirely exasperated by the assassination in London on 22 June of Field Marshall Sir Henry Wilson. He had been Chief of the Imperial Staff and was then security advisor to the Unionist Government as well as being a Unionist M.P. He was a bigoted anti-Nationalist. The British Government demanded the immediate expulsion of those occupying the Four Courts, whom it decided were to blame for the assassination, or else they would deem the Treaty violated. Dev said *"I do not know who they were who shot Sir Henry Wilson, or why they shot him. I know that life has been made a hell for the Nationalist minority in Belfast and its neighbourhood for the past couple of years. I do not approve, but I must not pretend to misunderstand"*[1].

The Four Courts garrison, with whom Collins had earlier been in negotiation, captured Ginger O'Connell, Deputy Chief of Staff for the Provisional Government. Collins then believed that he had to issue an ultimatum for the evacuation of the Four Courts or else face the wrath of the British army. When this was refused, he had the buildings shelled and those within arrested. The Civil War that all the politicians had not wanted, began. The Republicans regarded the move as a *coup d'etat* by the Provisional Government. Eamon O'Cuiv has said that when Dev arrived in the city from his home in Greystones, the Civil War had started at the Four Courts[2].

Dev issued a statement, which clearly sided with the Four Courts garrison. He said that:-

"At the bidding of the English, Irishmen are today shooting down on the streets of our capital, brother Irishmen - old comrades in arms, companions in the recent struggle for Ireland's independence and its embodiment - the Republic - the men who have refused to foreswear their allegiance to the Republic, who have refused to sacrifice honour for expediency and sell their country to a foreign King. In Rory O'Connor and his comrades lives the unbought indominitable soul of Ireland. Irish citizens! Give them support! Irish soldiers! Bring them aid!"[3].

As the fighting spread, Dev enlisted in his old battalion, the 3rd Dublin Battalion, as a private, and swore the Volunteer oath of allegiance to the Republic. He was assigned to the Hamman Hotel in O'Connell Street, where Barton, Brugha, Austin Stack and Oscar Traynor OC of the Dublin Brigade, were also based. F. Honan of Vernon Avenue Clontarf, a member of the St. John's Ambulance Brigade, found himself acting as an intermediary between the belligerents, on behalf of Fr. Albert; a member of the Capuchin Friary on Church Street.

Civil War. Battle for the Four Courts Dublin, July 1922.

Fr. Albert had heard the confessions of some members of a 1916 battalion. He had then told one of them afterwards to *"Go forth now my child and if necessary die for Ireland as Christ died for mankind"*[3a]. Over a few days, at great risk to himself, Honan met Dev and Collins several times. He met Collins at the 'offices of the Provisional Government' on Saturday 1 July. Collins agreed to allow those under arms to *"march out and go to their homes unmolested, if they will deposit their arms in the National armoury. I do not use the word surrender"*. The next day Honan met Dev, who said that he had no power to stop the hostilities, blaming the Government for starting it at the behest of the British, but that 'he would be prepared to recommend to the insurgents, and was confident he could get them to agree, to go home, each man carrying his weapon with him". On the Monday, Collins rejected this proposal as *"unreasonable and on several grounds inadvisable"*. Collins said that his policy would be one of leniency. Honan thought there might still be some common ground between Collins and Dev. He went to the Hamman Hotel hoping to meet Dev, who was not there. Cathal Brugha met him and he passed on Collin's position to him. Brugha then questioned Honan carefully as to 'What exactly did Mr DeValera propose?' When told, Brugha responded, *"He could not carry the fighting men with him in that; the most they would agree to would be to leave this place with their arms and go and join our men fighting elsewhere. And for my part - I would oppose even that. You are wasting your time. We are here to fight to the death"*. On Wednesday Honan returned to the Hamman Hotel seeking out Dev with a new set of proposals. The hotel was partially ablaze. Heavy fire was proceeding from Government troops in Cathedral Street and from their two machine guns at Cahill's corner of Talbot and Marlborough Streets, and from the insurgents machine gun further up the Lane. Honan later discovered that Cathal Brugha operated this gun personally. Fr. Flanagan told Honan that Dev had evacuated the hotel with the rest and gone 'on the run'[4]. Dev's family home was raided that night and on several subsequent occasions. Sinéad would only speak in Irish to the soldiers. She later moved from Greystones to 10 Claremont Road in Sandymount[5]. Brugha, who rejected all talk of negotiations, was shot dead near a barricade at the Hamman Hotel, defending the Republic to the end.

Dev and the 'irregulars' escaped from Dublin and moved south to Clonmel, where Liam Lynch had set up his GHQ. Dev was appointed adjutant to Seán Moylan who had the title of Director of Operations. They controlled Cork and installed Frank Gallagher as Editor of the *Examiner*. Dev himself got involved in propaganda with Erskine Childers, Robert Brennan and the ever-close Kathleen O'Connell. He brought down his son Vivion, to live nearby[6]. One military operation Dev was involved in was the controversial destruction of the Ten Arch Bridge, which carried the railway line over the Blackwater[7].

Michael Collins then became Commander in Chief of the Army with WT Cosgrave taking over Collins' governmental duties. The army began to pressurise the 'Irregulars', who had to resort to guerrilla warfare from an early stage. Atrocities occurred on both sides.

Harry Boland

Liam Lynch

Rory O'Connor

General Sir Henry Wilson

The Labour Party continued to seek peace. On 2 July they had a fruitless meeting with Liam Mellowes, Rory O'Connor and Joe McKelvey in Mountjoy Jail[8]. Their attempt to reconvene a Mansion House meeting ended when the anti-Treaty side refused to attend[9]. On 6 August they met with Dev, Seán T. O'Kelly and Harry Boland, without any progress[10].

Very soon, deaths of prominent personalities occurred. Harry Boland, confidant to Collins and DeValera, at different times, was shot dead and buried in Skerries Co. Dublin, on 5 August. This was a severe personal blow for Dev, who was living at Fermoy Barracks at the time. He referred to Boland as the "dearest friend I had on earth"[11]. Kathleen O'Connell wrote in her diary for 4 August 1922, *"Kathy (a sister of Kevin Barry) told him of H's death. He felt it terribly – crushed and broken. He lost his most faithful friend. We travelled in silence all the way to Clonmel"*[12]. Dev felt that it was his duty to plan peace moves as he realised that the opposing forces were vastly superior. He also realised that he had little power over those carrying out the guerrilla war. He also feared that if perchance, Collins and Lynch made peace, he might once again be left out of the loop[13].

Arthur Griffith collapsed and died of a brain haemorrhage at St Vincent's Nursing Home in Dublin on 12 August. His premature death was an incalculable loss to the country. It deprived the country of a man who might have come up with a clear-sighted economic vision to set before the people, drawing on a philosophy of national renaissance, which laid equal stress on industrial and rural development. He had for long been an integral part of the national struggle, having published a series of articles on Dual Monarchy in Hungary as far back as 1904, and linking it to the Irish Constitution of 1782. Griffith had played a key role as a moderating realist. His friend and admirer Oliver St. John Gogarty wrote;

He fought as many fights as Conn the Fighter;

And all alone he fought

Without a friend to make his sword arm lighter,

Unblindable, unbought.

He held his shield until the waves resounded,

The men of Ireland woke.

He made the loud tyrannical foe dumb-founded

And to relax his yoke.

෯෴ ෴෯

Michael Collins went on a tour of the South on 20 August. He visited Limerick and reached Cork city by nightfall. On the morning of 22 August he left for a tour of his constituency stopping at Clonakilty and Bandon. The return journey to Cork lay between Bandon and Macroom, with Béal na Bláth in between. The 'Irregulars' decided to set up an ambush at Béal na Bláth. Peter Hart writes that the ambush was not set up specifically to ambush Collins and that many involved were sorry to have done so after his death[13a].

Tim Pat Coogan writes that the ambushers knew that Collins was visiting his local area in west Cork and had passed through Béal na Bláth. They set up an ambush least he return by the same route. Dev, who was in the area, opposed this, arguing that they would be most likely to get better terms for surrender from Collins, in his own native county, than from those in Dublin. Dev, went to Ballyvourney where a high level meeting of the IRA had been taking place. There he was told that his own rank did not carry any weight with the 'Irregulars' and the directive on guerrilla warfare issued by Liam Lynch was to be followed. He was also told that his rank of a staff officer carried little weight. He left the area in anger and on hearing later that night of the shooting dead of Collins, he was "furious and visibly upset". Dev also knew that his own life was in great danger, as his presence nearby was publicised, with the inference that he might indeed have been responsible for the ambush. It was decided to evacuate him by foot from Fethard in County Tipperary, to Callan in Kilkenny, with a large armed escort. He was in a terrible psychological state during that journey[14].

Joe Lee compares Collins to DeValera, *"His performance as a political tactician was at least as able as DeValera's in this traumatic period, and DeValera himself could hardly rival the popular electoral appeal of the finest of crowd psychologists laying hands on the mood of the people"*[15].

An annual commemoration of the death of Collins takes place at Béal na Bláth. On 27 June 1957 Seán Collins, a brother of Michael's, wrote to Taoiseach Eamon DeValera with a "dying request" from the organiser, Col Coughlan, to permit Army participation in the annual commemoration. Seán Collins also wrote to President Seán T. O'Kelly, saying, *"Apart from Mick being my brother, I believe that such a gesture from the President and the Government, would be the means of healing the sores of the Civil War and again uniting in the field of national endeavour, men who have ever since the unfortunate split caused thereby, given their best efforts to the work of the nation"*. In his reply Dev said he had given the matter "the most careful consideration" and spoken to other members of the Government, but they all felt they should adhere to the decision taken some years earlier, to designate Easter Sunday for the commemoration of all who took part in the struggle for independence. Later, after he was elected President, Dev attended the annual Mass for Michael Collins at Dublin Castle on 7 July 1968[16].

Garret Fitzgerald has written that when he was campaigning for election to the Senate in the 1960's, he met Dev, who was most friendly and spoke of Garret's father. He spoke most intently that he did not have any responsibility for the Civil War[17].

After the deaths of Griffith and Collins, Winston Churchill immediately feared that the Provisional Government might make peace with Dev. He telegraphed Andy Cope in Dublin.

"For your guidance; the danger to be avoided is a sloppy accommodation with a quasi-repentant DeValera. It may well be that he will take advantage of the present situation to try and get back, from the position of a hunted rebel to that of a political negotiator. You should do everything in your power to frustrate this"[18].

Terry DeValera writes about his mother's relationship with Michael Collins thus:

"I heard her tell a story about an event which took place shortly before Collins' death. She had received a message from him, which said 'Send my love to Mrs Dev'. When Mother spoke of Michael Collins, which she often did, she did so with a feeling of gratitude and affection and always acknowledged his daring and supreme courage"[19]. Sinéad wrote, "As a girl I had a great admiration for Griffith. Mick, too, was a friend of mine. All war is bad but civil war is dreadful"[20].

Diarmaid Ferriter writes, *"Michael Collins always consistently outclassed and outperformed DeValera after the signing of the Treaty...one of the main characteristics of Collins was his sheer decisiveness, once a decision had been made. The same could not be said for DeValera during this period; it is likely that the reason he kept returning to the subject of the Treaty and the Civil War was to reimpose a retrospective decisiveness on his actions that was simply not in accordance with the sequence of events as they unfolded"[21].*

POLITICIAN BACK IN DUBLIN

Eventually after a fortnight travelling through rough southern terrain, Dev got back to Dublin, where the postponed meeting of the new Dáil had been scheduled for 9 September. He realised that as a politician, this might afford him some opportunity of exercising his influence. Dermot Keogh writes that Dev possibly considered entering the Dáil at this juncture and taking the required oath[22]. Dev sought a meeting with Ristard Mulcahy who had succeeded Collins as army chief and Minister of Defence in WT Cosgrave's cabinet. Mulcahy took a calculated risk by agreeing to meet Dev without informing his cabinet colleagues, who had agreed only on 5 September that it was essential for them all to accept the principle of collective cabinet responsibility[23]. Monsignor Ryan of San Francisco had appealed to Mulcahy to meet Dev[24]. The meeting was not productive to either party. Mulcahy held that the Treaty had to be adhered to. Dev wanted a revision of terms towards his 'external association'[25]. Dev wrote to McGarrity about the meeting, *"I met Mulcahy the other evening. Rather amusing. We gave mutual safe conducts to each other for the meeting. We got nowhere in discussion, however"[26].* Mulcahy's colleagues were not amused when told of this meeting. O'Higgins was furious being adamant that civilian control was the way forward, unlike the *modus operandi* of Collins' time.

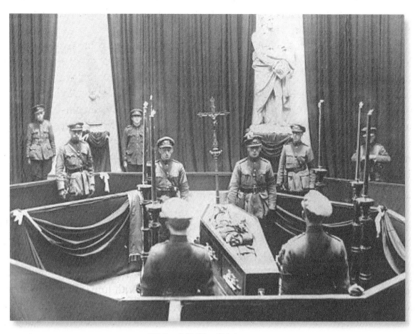

Michael Collins lies in state.

Michael Collins funeral.

Though Dev termed the meeting 'Amusing' to Joseph McGarrity, Mulcahy concluded that Dev was totally committed to the 'Irregulars' and there was no *via media* for the survival of the burgeoning State, except a military solution using Emergency Powers to defeat the enemy within. The Government introduced harsh military courts with powers of summary execution for a large series of offences. After that meeting, Mulcahy became obsessive about Dev's responsibility for the Civil War. He believed that the Civil War assumed the scale it did because DeValera persuaded Liam Lynch, with his tremendous influence in the Southern division, to go against the Treaty[27]. Valulis writes, *"an obsession which obscured from him the fact that, despite a degree of complicity on the part of DeValera, a section of the army was determined to revolt"*[28]. By the same token, of all those who had taken the pro-Treaty side, Dev found it most difficult to forgive Richard Mulcahy and Ernest Blythe[29].

Dev had been trying to exercise his influence on the 'Irregulars' for some time, but without much success. He had written several times to Liam Lynch without acknowledgement. Eventually Lynch told him in a rather demeaning tone that if Dev wished to send him his views "they will have my earnest consideration". Dev then began to threaten his resignation as a public representative, if the militarists continued to ignore the politicians. On 13 September he wrote to Cumann Na Poblacht and the Executive of the IRA, demanding the IRA share power with him. On 17 October the Executive of the IRA met at Mrs Nugent's house, Poulatar, Ballybacon, and agreed to issue Dev's suggested statement, *"We, on behalf of the soldiers of the Republic in concert with such faithful members of Dáil Éireann as are at liberty, have called upon the former President Eamon DeValera to resume the Presidency and to form a government, which shall preserve inviolate the sacred trust of National sovereignty and Independence"*[30]. On 25 September Dev held a meeting in Dublin of the "2nd Dáil" and nominated a cabinet 'in aspiration'[31], with Stack in Finance, Barton in Economics, Mellowes in Defence, Seán T. O'Kelly in Local Government, and PJ Ruttledge in Home Affairs. Mellowes was then in Mountjoy jail, so Dev and Liam Lynch as Chief of Staff, agreed to co-sign all Departmental documents.

Dev wrote to Colm O Murchadha that he could not advise his Deputies to enter the new Dáil, as it would appear a betrayal of those fighting for the Republic and he would not take the Oath. He also alluded however to a future time when "a course other than non-attendance should seem wise". Dev wrote a remarkable forward-looking letter to his friend McGarrity;

"The Provisional Government feel that they are strong enough now to throw away all camouflage and reveal themselves as creatures of a British institution. This is all to the good, for the deceptions of Republicans by Michael Collins, especially the men in the army, was what secured the acceptance of the Treaty at all. There cannot be deception any longer. The personnel of the Provisional Government is very weak. Cosgrave is a ninny. He will however be egged on by the church. Were it not for Mick's lead, there is no doubt in my mind that Mulcahys' policy would have been 'unity against the enemy', as the primary consideration".

Erskine Childers in Boer War uniform. DeValera said of him,
"He died the Prince that he was. Of all the men I ever met, I would say he was the noblest"

People being led to safety by a priest in Dublin during the Civil War.

Dev's idea for a way forward was:

"If the Free State should become operative and the present physical resistance fails, I see no programme by which we can secure independence but by a revival of the Sinn Féin idea in a new form. Ignoring England. Acting in Ireland as if there were no such person as the English king, no Governor General, no Treaty, no oath of Allegiance. In fact acting as if Document No. 2 were the Treaty. Later on we could act more independently still. Whilst the Free State was in supposed existence would be the best time to secure the unity of the country. If we can get a single State for the whole country, then the future is safe".

Dev also told McGarrity, *"If the army thinks I am too moderate, well let them get a better President and go ahead...I would make peace under present conditions, or any condition that I think likely to prevail in the immediate future, on the basis of that document and I do not want the young fellows who are fighting for the Republic to think otherwise"[32].*

This appears a remarkably similar policy as that of the pro-Treaty people![33]. In the same letter to McGarrity, Dev also wrote about protecting the funds he had collected in America from the clutches of the Provisional Government.

On 10 October the Catholic bishops issued a pastoral letter, which condemned and excommunicated the Republicans in no uncertain terms. It said, *"They carry on what they call a war, but which in the absence of any legitimate authority to justify it, is morally a system of murder and assassination of the National forces".* Dev was very disappointed by the pastoral writing to Archbishop Mannix that, *"Never was charity of judgement so necessary, and apparently so disastrously absent. Ireland and the church will, I fear, suffer in consequence"* [34].

On 17 November the first executions took place under the emergency legislation. Four young IRA men who had been found with arms, were executed in Dublin. That same day Erskine Childers, who had come from Cork at Dev's request, was tried for having a small pistol, given him by Collins. Childers had become a despised figure for some members of the Provisional Government. To the consternation of all the anti-Treaty people, he was executed a week later. Dev was heartbroken. He wrote to McGarrity; *"He died the Prince that he was. Of all the men I ever met, I would say he was the noblest"[35].*

When his body was due to be released to his widow Molly Childers, she wrote to the Catholic Archbishop of Dublin, requesting that his body be received at Whitefriars St Church as she believed he had all the intentions of becoming a Catholic[36].

Dev said of Childers after the execution, *"If it is not the people's will that a faithful and loyal servant should be sacrificed to any of Churchill's hate, then within an hour, you will rise up and fling from the positions they have usurped and dishonoured, those who would dare so to blacken forever the fair name of this nation"[37].*

Liam Lynch responded to the executions by ordering his Dublin Brigades to execute nine members of the Provisional Government. Dev acquiesced in this writing: *"The efficacy of reprisals is open to doubt, but as I see no other way to protect our men, I cannot disapprove"[38]*. On 30 November three more IRA men were executed. As a reprisal two Government TD's were attacked and one of them, Seán Hales, killed. In reprisal four prisoners, Rory O'Connor, Liam Mellowes, Dick Barrett and Joe McKelvey, who had been captured at the fall of the Four Courts, were summarily executed in Mountjoy Jail.

In the Dáil, the shootings were criticised by Tom Johnston, leader of the Labour Party and by Gavan Duffy in powerful speeches[39]. Cosgrave defended the summary executions, saying, *"There is an elementary law in this case. The people who have challenged the very existence of society, have put themselves outside the Constitution and only at the last moment, not thinking there was such infamy in this country, we safeguarded this Dáil and the Government and the people of Ireland, from being at the mercy of these people…There is only one way to crush it and show them that terror will be struck into them"[40]*. The Dáil voted approval by 39 votes to 14.

These executions set off a terrible series of outrages throughout the country, including shootings and house-burnings. Kevin O'Higgins' father was shot dead in his home. One house burning claimed the death of Seán McGarry's young son. Dev was appalled by this mayhem. He wrote to Liam Lynch confirming his agreement and acceptance of such burnings, but he deemed the burning of McGarry's house *"badly executed. and looks mean and petty. Terrorist methods may silence those of our opponents, who are cowards, but many of them are very far from being cowards, and attempts at terrorism will only stiffen the bold men amongst them. I am against such methods on principle, and believe we will never win in this war unless we attach the people to our government by contrast to others. The recent burnings were in my opinion, puerile and futile from a military or any other point of view"[41]*.

Dev however, while urging restraint on Lynch, also assured him that he understood that the Republicans had to be ruthless against that of the Free State forces. He quoted *Macbeth*, *"…I am in blood, Steep'd in so far that, should I wade no more, Returning were as tedious as go o'er"[42]*.

When the Free State came into official being on 6 December 1922, Cosgrave acknowledged the honourable manner in which the British had dealt with the Provisional Government, since the signing of the Treaty. He knew that the Northern Parliament was to meet soon. He invited it to opt into the Free State, as it had the right to do under the Treaty. He added:

"On the other hand, should they decide to cut themselves off from all contact with us, we will regret very much such a decision. We will consider it both inopportune and unwise, believing, as we do, that it is bound to have disastrous reactions on the northern enterprise. Nevertheless, as they are perfectly entitled to take this course under the Treaty, we are bound to respect such a decision in the event of it coming to pass"[43].

COSGRAVE TALKS TOUGH

In late January 1923, Cosgrave contacted Mulcahy with a document from the Government law officer, on the matter of '*Revolt Against the Constitutional Authority*'[44]. Cosgrave told a neutral IRA group led by Donal Hannigan and MJ Burke on 27 Feb. *"I am coming to the conclusion that if we are to exercise clemency at any time – it can only be of use to us when the irregulars crave it "*[45]. He added, *"I am not going to hesitate if the country is going to live, and if we have to exterminate ten thousand Republicans, the three million of our people is greater than this ten thousand"*. He was of the view, as was Mulcahy, that the civil war was provoked by DeValera. He added that the civil war had meant that there was almost no hope that the North would come into the Free State[46].

Liam Lynch's second in command, Liam Deasy, had come to the conclusion that the Civil War was futile and should cease. He was captured by the Free State forces, tried and sentenced to death. He requested an opportunity to address his colleagues on his views. He addressed an open letter to leading Republicans, "E. DeValera, F. Aiken, O. Ruttledge, F. Barrett, A. Stack, T Barry, N. Oliver, S. McSweeney, D. O'Callaghan, Seamus Robinson, Liam Lynch, Humphrey Murphy, Conn Moloney, Seamus O'Donovan, T. Derrig, and Frank Carty, to accept and aid in an immediate unconditional surrender of all arms and men"[47].

His letter appeared in the papers on 13 February together with an offer by the Government offering an amnesty to those who complied by 18 February. Dev did not respond to Deasy's plea but persuaded Lynch to reject it. Dev wrote to Lynch on 9 February, *"Were we to lose all the lives that have been lost and get nothing of national value, it would be awful"*. He wrote to Miss Edith Ellis in London, *"I have been condemned to view the tragedy here for the last year as through a wall of glass, powerless to intervene effectively, I have, however, still the hope than an opportunity may come my way"*[48].

The official biographers, Longford and O'Neill, acknowledge that as the Free State Government was then fighting for its own existence, there was little use arguing who fired the first shot. Several attempts were made to bring peace. Frank Fahy approached Austin Stack in December 1922, hoping to arrange a truce.

Dev replied after consulting Lynch, "It is useless to ask Republicans to abandon ideals, which I know they will surrender only with their lives", while asserting, "I believe I know what is and what is not possible, as far as Britain is concerned"[49]. He always believed that his controversial Document No. 2 could be the basis for a peace agreement, but had to be very careful to keep Lynch on side or else lose the little influence he had with the militarists. He also had to be wary of some TD's like Mary MacSweeney, who was totally uncompromising and whom he termed a 'diehard'.

DeValera gives salute to Volunteers, Clare 1922.

Leaving for home. The British Army vacate a barracks.

He wrote an astonishing, almost 'confessional' letter to her saying:

"Reason rather than faith has been my master…I have felt for some time that this doctrine of mine ill-fitted me to be leader of the Republican Party…..Nature never fashioned me to be a partisan leader in any case, and I am sorry that I did not insist on Cathal's assuming the leadership when the party was being formed. For the sake of the cause I allowed myself to be put into a position which is impossible for one of my outlook and personal bias to fill with effect for the party…every instinct of mine would indicate that I was meant to be a dyed-in-the-wool Tory, or even a bishop, rather than the leader of a revolution… and now having made such a lengthy confession, it would be natural to look for absolution, but…[50].

WT Cosgrave realised that Dev was manoeuvring towards a peace agreement on his own terms. Cosgrave declared, *"DeValera hopes to bring about negotiations which will enable him to make a dignified withdrawal from his present position, but we are not going to help anybody in that way"*[51]. Kevin O'Higgins said *"This is not going to be a draw with a reply in the autumn"*[52].

On 23 March the IRA Executive met in the Comeragh Mountains in Waterford. Dev was determined to be there, realising that it might be an opportunity for him to exercise some direction on the civil war. He travelled *incognito* under severe constraints. When the meeting began he was not admitted and had to wait in another room, while the Executive decided whether he should be heard. Eventually he was allowed to attend but denied a vote in the proceedings. The meeting broke up on several occasions and reassembled at different locations in the mountains, to keep one step ahead of the Free State forces, who were in the immediate area. This process went on for nearly a week as the Executive tried to come to agreement. Dev supported a resolution, proposed by Tom Barry, which said *"that in the opinion of the Executive, further armed resistance and operations against the Free State Government, will not further the cause of independence of the country"*. This was defeated by six to five votes on the vote of the Chairman Liam Lynch. The majority had hopes that more substantial gun-power might become available to their side to challenge the National Army.

Dev was authorised to return to Dublin and explore whether peace might be available on his terms. Another meeting of the Executive was scheduled for 10 April. On the return journey, much of which was made overland away from roads, Free State soldiers at Paulstown stopped Dev and his group. Dev wore a heavy beard and was not recognised, and they were allowed continue their arduous journey[53a].

By 9 April Dev was telling both P.J. Ruttledge and Austin Stack that it was their duty to end the conflict without delay. He acknowledged that the phase begun in 1916 had run its course, and they had to take the decision to cease fire or else state the basis on which they would do so. On 10 April, the Free State forces in the Knockmealdown Mountains, fatally wounded Liam Lynch, who had been travelling to the meeting of the IRA Executive.

Dev told Ruttledge "This is our darkest hour". Realising that he had a cold way of putting things, Dev, argued that though his heart told him to fight on, his head and his conscience said otherwise. Despite this, Dev issued a rallying cry to Lynch's men telling them that it was better to die nobly, as their Chief had died, than live a slave. He assured them that *"Your cause is immortal... and the sacrifices you are making will ensure it ...and tomorrow will be forced to do you honour"*[53].

The IRA executive met on 20 April at Poulacappal. Frank Aiken was the new Chief of Staff. He realised that peace was the only option. This time they agreed to end the fighting. Soundings were sent to the Government about a cessation. However only an unconditional surrender was acceptable. Very gradually the National Army had broken up and defeated the IRA, imprisoning thousands. By 1 July 1923 there were 11,000 prisoners.

PEACE NEGOTIATIONS
MONSIGNOR LUZIO

In April of 1923, an unusual visitor to Ireland named Monsignor Salvatore Luzio, arrived. The purpose of his journey was to bring peace to the country. His mission arose through a variety of Vatican and anti-Treatyite Irish clergy in Rome. Monsignor Hagan, who became Rector of the Irish College there in 1919, and his deputy Fr. Cronin were very actively against the Treaty. Seán MacBride had worked as a secretary to DeValera for a period in the 1920's. Together they visited Rome to meet with supportive clergy. Hagan advised DeValera to set up a political party and seek political power[54]. He and others persuaded the Secretary of State, Cardinal Gaspari, to send a papal delegate to Ireland. The Vatican, which knew that the Free State was keen to establish international status, was also interested in exploring the possibility of a permanent Vatican delegate in Ireland. Cardinal MacRory had also requested Gaspari to send a delegate. Though Hagan was involved in the process he did not have a high opinion of Luzio, describing him to Dev as 'the best of a bad lot'. Hagan appears to have assisted Dev's family during these years as a letter from Sinéad DeValera to Hagan of 25 April 1926 indicates[54a].

Archbishop Byrne of Dublin, Cosgrave's close friend, did not favour the mission, believing that it might make the situation worse. When Luzio arrived, he went immediately to Armagh to see MacRory. He also met DeValera, who was sympathetic, but felt that it was "a bad time for us". Luzio met a Dublin Sinn Féin peace group and let it be known that he was willing to intervene in the interests of peace. This angered the Government. Cosgrave met him, but purely as a matter of courtesy and did not engage on any substantive talks. Luzio did not receive any assistance from the bishops, who resented his presence in the country. A *Freeman's Journal* editorial criticised him for not having produced any credentials. It then received a letter from MacRory, with a copy of Luzio's credentials signed by Cardinal Gaspari, dated 9 March 1923. The *Freeman* criticised the fact that Luzio had been in the country one month and the

Government had to wait to see his credentials in the newspaper. At that point, the Government had called on the Vatican to withdraw Luzio. He then sought an interview with Cosgrave, who through Desmond Fitzgerald asked was it an official or unofficial meeting, he requested. When Luzio replied that it was an unofficial one, Cosgrave refused to meet him. The Government saw him as too close to Dev and the Bishops resented his 'interference'[55].

This was an embarrassing episode all round. As DeValera had said at the outset, the mission was badly timed, as it was then clear to most people, that the Civil War was in its last days. He wrote, *"He came, unfortunately, at a bad time for us. The peacemaker has always an almost irresistible temptation to try to affect his object by bringing pressure on the weaker side to give in. What his ecclesiastical mission was I do not know but he seems to have received scant courtesy from the bishops…We are in sore need of the assistance of all our friends everywhere"*[55a]. Dev told Monsignor Luzio that their opponents wanted a military triumph and rejected his proposals as "not sincerely made". He criticised the bishops for failing to condemn the ill treatment, torture and murder of prisoners, and the inflammatory addresses of some of their members as "scarcely worthy of representatives of Him who is Charity"[56]. Dev requested Luzio to; *"Please give to the Holy Father my dutiful homage. Though nominally cut away from the body of Holy Church we are still spiritually and mystically of it, and we refuse to regard ourselves except as his children"*.

Cosgrave was very interested in the idea of establishing diplomatic relations with the Vatican, but he was acutely aware of the opposition of the bishops, and particularly Archbishop Byrne. Cosgrave would have to bide his time before he was able to move in that direction. Dermot Keogh says that Luzio reported that he had gone to Ireland to bring about peace with the help of the bishops, and found that he *"had to deal with twenty six Popes"*[57].

SENATORS JAMESON AND DOUGLAS

Around that same time, of 23 April, DeValera himself had been putting out peace feelers to Cosgrave. Senator James Douglas received messages that a very important man wished to meet him. Movement around Dublin could be quite dangerous, as the army was vigorously seeking to apprehend all anti-Treatyites, including DeValera. However Douglas decided to allow himself to be taken to this meeting at an unspecified location. He was not surprised to find DeValera waiting to see him. DeValera said that he and his colleagues thought that the Civil War should be ended and he wanted to meet Cosgrave to that end. He was not prepared to meet O'Higgins. Douglas said that he would need somebody else to join him in the mission. DeValera suggested Senator Andrew Jameson and this was agreed. However later in the conversation, DeValera appeared to change his mind and asked Douglas to forget all about their conversation and not to tell Cosgrave about it. Douglas said it was his duty to inform Cosgrave who latter was ill at home, and Douglas did not see him for some days.

In the meantime, Douglas received another message that DeValera wished to see him again. Douglas then sought to get a most reluctant Senator Jameson, to join him. Jameson assented, on condition that they sought Cosgrave's prior consent, and acted purely as intermediaries. Cosgrave told the Senators he could not guarantee that they would not be followed, or vouch for their safety or immunity to arrest.

On Monday 30 April, Senators Douglas and Jameson received letters marked 'confidential' from DeValera. He asked them to meet him to discuss moves to an immediate end of the war. They replied that they could not discuss matters with him, but would act as intermediaries. Dev replied that that was his intention. Next evening, as they arrived at the nominated address, and were being welcomed by Dev, an army lorry pulled up outside. Dev went pale and said he realised that they were not responsible. While the three men waited apprehensively, a soldier emerged from the lorry and went into the house next door. He came out within a few minutes and got into the lorry and it drove away. Dev requested a conference with Government members. He would attend alone, or with other colleagues to discuss the proclamation published on 28 April, after a two day meeting of 'the Government and Army Council', which had given permission to make peace with the Free State authorities. The Senators reported to Cosgrave on Wednesday 2 May. Cosgrave said he would consult the Executive Council. On the Thursday Jameson met with Cosgrave and two other ministers. Jameson and Douglas were authorised to meet with DeValera and tell him that personal negotiations were inadvisable. They were also to inform him that the Government would not then negotiate on the Oath in the Constitution, with the British Government. Jameson also received a document from Cosgrave for DeValera, indicating the fundamental conditions for any agreement, which were:

All political action within the country should be based on a recognition by every party in the State of the following principles of order: —

(a) That all political issues whether now existing or in the future arising, shall be decided by the majority vote of the elected representatives of the people:

(b) As a corollary to (a) that the people are entitled to have all lethal weapons within the country, in the effective custody or control of the Executive Government, responsible to the people through their representatives.

The acceptance of these principles and practical compliance with (b) by the surrender of arms to be the preliminary condition for the release of prisoners, who shall be required to subscribe individually to (a) and (b).

Signed in acceptance of the foregoing principles this...............day of May, 1923.

....

Witness..............................

The Senators were instructed to tell DeValera that:

(1) Military action against him and his followers would cease, when the arms held by them were delivered into the effectual custody of the Free State Executive authorities. The arrangements for the delivery of the arms and the place of their deposit would be made with as much consideration as possible for the feelings of those concerned.

(2) Prisoners to be released on the satisfactory fulfillment of (1) and the signature of each prisoner before release to the conditions of the document above mentioned.

(3) The Free State Government would keep a clear field for Mr. DeValera and his followers, to enable them to canvass for the votes of the people at the next election, provided they undertook to adhere strictly to constitutional action.

The Government also wanted to know the names of the leaders for whom he could speak and what proportion of rank and file, and prisoners, would follow his instructions.

The Senators saw DeValera again that same evening Thursday 3 May and conveyed their messages. He undertook to come back to them in a few days. Douglas met DeValera on the Saturday and promised to have a written reply for the government on the Monday. Both Senators met him on the Monday. The document he produced was a lengthy one and he undertook to redraft it and deliver it to the Bank of Ireland the next morning. This arrived, but remained a lengthy document, which is published in Dorothy McArdle's volume[58].

The Government considered it and replied to Jameson on 8 May.

It found DeValera's document long and wordy, inviting debate where none was possible, as they were preparing for an early election. The Government insisted that they must control all arms and had made generous arrangements for their delivery. Once that was done, prisoners would be released. They reiterated that their conditions, already specified, could not and would not be departed from. No further communication with DeValera would be entertained except for his acceptance of the terms stated. The letter was signed, Liam MacCosgair.

The Senators wrote immediately to DeValera. He replied next day, 9 May, terminating matters, saying that, *"I have received your letter and Mr. Cosgrave's reply, which has disappointed me not a little...I have been met by rigid insistence on a condition in a form which is well known by everyone conversant with the situation to be unrealisable"[59].*

The IRA army council and Dev's Republican government met at Santry Dublin on 13/14 May. They decided to refuse Cosgrave's terms and to simply dump arms and cease action. It was agreed that Aiken would issue the order. Dev endured severe criticism both from the pro Treaty people and especially from the Republican die-hards, who blamed him. He told Monsignor Hagan, Rector of the Irish College in Rome, that the moral leaders had allowed themselves to be so entangled in the conflict that they were then useless[60].

DeValera issued his own statement to the IRA:

"Soldiers of the Republic, Legion of the Rearguard; The Republic can no longer be defended successfully by your arms. Further sacrifice of life would now be in vain...Military victory must be allowed to rest for the moment with those who have destroyed the Republic...May God guard every one of you and give to our country in all times of need sons who will love her as dearly and devotedly as you"[61].

Cardinal Logue wrote, *"We have comparative quiet here now. There is no real peace by consent. DeValera is keeping up his Republican claim as stubbornly as ever, but the republican leaders and most of the rank and file are in prison; so it is peace by exhaustion on one side"*[62]. Dev had earlier written to Hagan, *"as far as public opinion goes the people would probably vote against both sides"*[63]. Dev realised that the view of most of the hierarchy was that he as a political leader had failed to exercise control over the militarists on the anti-Treaty side. Nevertheless there continued to be plenty of clergy who retained faith in him, as the one who would win out in the end.

Liam Cosgrave, son of WT Cosgrave wrote of this period, *"Regarding the Executions, no civilised Government likes to have to do these things, but a Government's first duty is to govern by vindicating and asserting the will of the people. The Irregulars opposed the will of the people by every means, and the Government after having shown considerable restraint, eventually enforced the law. The Government considered the Executions shortened the Civil War and saved more innocent persons being killed by the Irregulars. My father accepted responsibility for the action of the Government"*[64].

Crowds gather in Dublin City Centre during the Civil War.

CHAPTER 10

FIANNA FÁIL FOUNDED

DeValera's fundamental position remained to ignore any aspect of the Treaty inconsistent with independence, such as the office of the Governor General. This would of course break the Treaty and the Oath, forcing Britain to tolerate it, or seek a revision, which would lead towards his own 'External Association' ideas in his Document No. Two. He continued to be liable to summary arrest and had to be careful. On 28 June 1923 he announced that Sinn Féin candidates would contest the next General Election, to give the people an opportunity to put on record by their first preference votes, their detestation of allegiance to a foreign king, their repudiation of Partition, and their desire for a government which would really be obedient to their own will and not an instrument of British domination.

The Government feared that the IRA would resume its war later and introduced a Public Safety Bill on 2 July and an Indemnity Bill to safeguard its forces from being sued by republicans. Thousands of republicans were still in jail and the army kept up its arrests and harassment. To counteract this fear, Dev declared that it was not the intention of the Republican Government or Army Executive to renew the war in the autumn. He said, *"The war, so far as we are concerned is finished. If there was a free election and if we were elected on a majority, our policy would be to govern the country on Sinn Féin lines as in 1919, refusing to cooperate with the English in any way, until England was able to make with us such an arrangement as would make a stable peace possible"*[1].

Dev decided it was vital for his political future, to run for Clare in the forthcoming election and despite the obvious danger, travelled to Ennis in great secrecy. Kathleen O'Connell also made her way there. Huge crowds had gathered to witness what would happen when he appeared on the election platform. Mayhem developed as the army moved to arrest him. Shots were fired and Dev felt an intense pain on his shinbone as a ricochet bullet hit him. He was held in Limerick Jail that night and transferred to Arbour Hill the next day. He was confident that he would not be executed, now that the civil war was over[2]. He spent two months there before being transferred to Kilmainham. He was kept in solitary confinement, and a soldier cut the name 'Mick Collins' over his cell door with his bayonet.

There had been great misgiving about Dev in some Republican circles, particularly in ending the Civil War. His appearance in Clare and subsequent treatment by the Free State solidified his reputation. T. Ryle Dwyer writes, *"He was arrested just in time to escape oblivion"*[3].

Sinéad DeValera was allowed to visit her husband on 23 August. She wrote *afterwards to Kathleen O'Connell, "For goodness sake don't let anyone take dangerous risks for D's sake. Write again if you cannot call. I know your poor heart is broken. I, too, am anxious but keep on at the prayers"[4].*

The election was a rough and dangerous exercise, with many candidates still in jail. The results were:

Cumann Na nGaedheal	62
Sinn Féin	44
Farmers' Party	15
Labour	14
Independents	17

This was a result, which clearly indicated that those against the Treaty retained the backing of a large section of the electorate, despite the strife of the Civil War. The Government was shocked by the result, which would have placed it in a minority position had the anti-Treaty TD's entered the Dáil. It is ironic that proportional representation, introduced by the British to protect Unionist representation, probably assisted the anti-treatites and Labour to such successful electoral positions.[5.]

Dev was allowed to write two letters per week. Sinéad and Kathleen O'Connell were regular recipients. He asked the Kathleen to send in a series of mathematical books, writing, *"If you want to make me happy, send me all of them books. It will be living life over again going through them and picking out what is of use. It will be like making the acquaintance of old friends again and what I have forgotten will come back through them more quickly than in any other way...I am afraid Sinéad has grown cynical about my relation to books, and will think this only another of my whims. The privilege of being in jail is that one can ask to be indulged in whims of this sort. I'll be shut off as completely as if I were on another planet and these books, old or new, the only friends at hand"[6].*

In jail, Dev had time to think about the future and as Diarmaid Ferriter writes, "to perhaps question his own arrogance", but also to ponder how his role in national affairs would be written about. He wrote to Kathleen O'Connell on 19 January 1924, outlining his considered view about how he intended to prepare for that historical future. He quoted the French historian Charles Seignobos, writing, *"History is made with documents. Documents are the imprints left of the thoughts and the deeds of the men of former times. For nothing can take the place of documents. No documents, no history".* He admonished O'Connell to collect and store every document towards writing about him in the future. He thought that she might be the one to do the writing, but her busy life as his secretary made that impossible[7]. Dev's obsessive insistence on preserving his documentation with an eye towards history compares with another contemporary, one who was also conscious of his singular gifts in another sphere and whose path would cross that of Dev's, WB Yeats.

Though Dev was in a position to police his own papers and in time choose friendly historians to write about him. WB Yeats did not live long enough to do that, but his son Michael Yeats performed a similar exercise for his father.

In America, Dev's mother agitated for his release, which came on 16 July 1924. This evinced an extraordinary outpouring of joyous congratulations from Dev's supporters around the world. Scores of telegrams arrived addressed to 'President DeValera, Suffolk Street, Dublin'. Poems and songs were written marking the occasion. Many of the messages from abroad, came from diocesan clergy as well as religious orders including Jesuits, Augustinians and Redemptorists. In Ireland a message was received from an organisation of 'republican priests'[7a].

Though many republican prisoners had earlier gone on hunger strike, Dev wisely did not join them, but kept himself fit by playing handball and tennis, as Austin Stack recounted in his diary[8]. The night after his release he joined Seán MacBride, an acknowledged senior member of the IRA, in a protest about the release of IRA men.

Brian Feeney writes of this episode, *"Dev had managed to extricate himself from the dilemma of whether to participate in Leinster House by the expedient of getting himself arrested, while addressing a meeting in Ennis ten days before the election"*[9]. The recently elected Republican TD's and those who had been elected to the Second Dáil met on 7-8 August 1924. They accepted Dev's suggestion that the Second Dáil be recognised as the *de jure* government and legislature, but that the whole body of elected members old and new, should act as the Council of State and be the actual Government of the country. Their aim was to preserve the mythical Republic in the face of the *de facto* Free State. The Cabinet included Dev as President, Stack at Home Affairs and Finance, and Aiken at Defence. PJ Ruttledge and Robert Barton were ministers without portfolios. Dev was then the supreme leader of the anti-treaty side, with all the other potential leaders dead[10].

Dev's first public appearance, in a series of appearances since his arrest, took place in Ennis on the anniversary of his arrest there. He later visited Dundalk and crossed the border as elected member for Down, despite being legally prohibited from doing so. As he attended a meeting in Newry on 24 October, he was arrested by the RUC and put across the border the next day. He soon recrossed the border in Derry, but was arrested again and brought to Belfast. On 1 November he was charged with contravening an order prohibiting him from crossing the border. When the Magistrate told him that he could not make political speeches in the court, Dev replied, *"In that case I have only to say that I do not recognise the court"*. He was imprisoned for one month and held in solitary confinement under constant surveillance. He was released on 28 November and put on a train southwards[11].

Nine by-elections were scheduled for the same day in March 1925, arising from the resignation of Joe McGrath's 'National Party' from the Dáil. Dev had hoped that the people might exercise their vote to repudiate the government.

This did not happen, with Cumann Na nGaedheal winning seven of the nine seats. A majority of the people were firmly behind Cosgrave's Government. Dev's reaction was an example of how he could interpret any eventuality to suit his own way of thinking. His view was that:

"Recently an opportunity was given in the elections to the people to declare their will. They did not declare that will as we know it to be their will…It is a shame that it should be so…So far as he could see, it was really because of the teaching of the last three years. He would be sorry to think that it was cowardice. There was no use in looking to one or other small body of men. It was only by the people that the people could be righted and it remained for the people to right the wrong they had done a couple of years ago, and apparently had been doing since"[12].

Seán Lemass' reaction to these defeats, was to berate the Catholic Church, whose clergy had been behind the Government for several years. He wanted to break the political power of the church, which he claimed in true Fenian fashion, had always been used against the "aspiration of Irish nationality. That political power must be destroyed if our national victory is ever to be won…if we succeed in destroying that influence, we will have done good work for Ireland and, I believe, for the Catholic religion in Ireland"[13]. Dev of course was more astute, realising that in a theological way that he and his people were the church and that their role was to 'capture' its clerical officers. He was close to some senior officers and knew that many of the juniors would rally to him, when circumstances permitted. He would prove to be as Catholic as even WT Cosgrave, whom he once described as *"a ninny, who would do anything the bishops ask"*. Despite the difficulties involved and the excommunications issued against his people, Dev never doubted his course of action, or his ability to succeed. He had right on his side. He had his God on his side.

Dev realised that he had to eventually enter the Dáil and challenge the *de facto* Government. The oath of allegiance was his major obstacle, and as usual he had to deal with the more extreme elements within the Republican family. Mary MacSweeney was representative of this group, which would under no circumstances consider such a move. He also had the 'army' against any recognition of the Free State. Dev and Frank Aiken, succeeded in making it clear that the army was subordinate to their Government. Aiken resigned as minister to work on this and Seán Lemass replaced him. An IRA Army Convention, repudiated all semblance of Government control against Aiken's wishes, in November 1925[14]. Dev realised that there were some whom he could never hope to bring with him, on his path to the new reality. His aim was to plan to take as many as possible with him. He needed some issue, which he hoped would stir the conscience of the people and allow him to move towards a political constitutional path.

இ✿✿இ

Early in 1925, DeValera travelled to Rome to meet with Monsignor John Hagan, Rector of the Irish College since 1919. Seán MacBride, who was acting as his interpreter/secretary at the time, accompanied Dev. According to MacBride, Hagan strongly advised Dev to enter Dáil Éireann. MacBride believed that such advice was what Dev wanted to hear. Later that year, Bishop Mannix came to Dublin carrying a document from Hagan, which gave an historical and theological vindication of how to enter the Dáil. Mannix himself backed the document[15]. At that time Seán T. O'Kelly, Gerry Boland and Seán Lemass were also pressurising Dev on entry to the Dáil[16].

The Labour party decided on a change of policy and began to oppose the Government, when it reduced the old age pension by one shilling and ended the dole. Labour also decided to try and persuade Dev to enter the Dáil and join in opposing the Government. On 13 January 1925, an 'Open Letter to Eamon DeValera' was published from 'A Labour TD'. It referred to Dev accepting the democratic programme of the Dáil in 1919, and suggested that the primary duty should be in seeking to implement that and disputes about forms of government should take second place. Dev was not quite ready to move in that direction. A very fruitful meeting took place between Labour and Dev on 7 December 1925, the results of which would become clear later[17].

BOUNDARY COMMISSION IMPELS DEV TO BREAK WITH SINN FÉIN

The terms of the Boundary Commission caused genuine shock among supporters of the Free State and the Republicans. All had assumed that this body would negate the existence of the border. Without the Boundary Commission there would have been no Treaty. Dev appealed to the Irish people saying, *"When Eoin MacNeill resigned (from the Boundary Commission) I had hoped that no Irishman, North or South, would be found prepared to put his hand to an instrument dismembering our country; but now that such Irishmen have been found, my only hope is that the people will not consent to it"*[17a]. A split occurred within Cumann na nGaedheal, when one of its Deputies, Professor Magennis, led a small break away group called the Clan na hÉireann. When eventually the Free State Government moved in the Dáil to accept the *status quo* along the border, Dev realised all too well that to have any political effect he and his followers had to take their seats. Austin Stack toyed about entering the Dáil oath or no oath and wrote to Dev on the possibility[18]. Despite Labour Party encouragement, Dev would not pay the price of taking the oath, though his presence might have made a decisive difference. All the Republican politicians could do was to make an ineffectual protest at a meeting in the Rotunda. Dev however was moving to cross his own Rubicon.

At the next Sinn Féin Ard Fheis in March 1926 Dev proposed:

"That once the admission oath of the twenty-six county and six-county assemblies are removed it becomes a question not of principle but of policy whether or not Republican representatives should attend these assemblies". Fr. Michael O'Flanagan moved an amendment; "That it is incompatible with the fundamental principle of Sinn Féin to send representatives into any usurping legislature set up by English law in Ireland".

The amendment, supported by Mary MacSweeney, was passed 223 votes to 218[19]. Dev's motion was then defeated by 179 votes to 177 with 85 abstentions. Fr. O'Flanagan tried to avoid a split by immediately proposing a motion, seconded by Mary MacSweeney, that Dev was the greatest Irishman for a century. This was carried unanimously[20]. Dev told the gathering, *"This is the opportune time, and I realise that the coming General Election is the time. I am from this moment a free man. My duty as President of this organisation is ended"*[20a].

Dev explained to Joe McGarrity, *"You perhaps will wonder why I did not wait longer. It is vital that the Free State be shaken at the next General Election, for if an opportunity be given it to consolidate itself as an institution – if the present Free State members are replaced by Farmers and Labourers and other class interests, the national interest as a whole will be submerged in the clashing of rival economic groups. It seems to be to be a case of now or never – at least in our time"*[21].

Dev resigned as President of Sinn Féin the very next day and took with him the bulk of the able, ambitious young men. Another parting of the ways had arrived.

Dev had anticipated his defeat within Sinn Féin and had made preparations for setting up a new party, his own party, which he would control. He had despatched Frank Aiken to America to his friend Joe McGarrity in January, to garner support there for the new departure and to fundraise. Within the very week of defeat at the Sinn Féin Ard Fheis, DeValera, Lemass, O'Kelly, Ryan, Boland, Ruttledge, Derrig, and MacEntee – later to be joined by Mrs Pearse, Madame Markievicz and Mrs Clarke, were meeting in DeValera's home in Dublin's Sandymount with the aim of launching a new Party"[22]. The new party Fianna Fáil was officially founded at the La Scala Theatre in Dublin on 16 May 1926. Branches were set up all over the country and it soon became a highly organised and professional national institution. Within a year of its establishment more than one thousand cumainn (branches) came into existence. Seán MacEntee said in 1974, *"For more than five years, hardly any of us were home for a single night or any weekend. Lemass bought up four or five second-hand Ford cars – bangers, and with them we toured every parish in the country founding Fianna Fáil branches on the solid basis of Old IRA and Sinn Féin members"*[23]. Early on the party gave its allegiance to the nation rather than the State.

Dev's aims for his new party were;

Securing the political independence of a united Ireland as a Republic.

The restoration of the Irish language and the development of an Irish culture.

The development of a social system in which, as far as possible, equal opportunity will be afforded to every Irish citizen to live a noble and useful Christian life.

The distribution of the land of Ireland, so as to get the greatest number of people possible of Irish families rooted in the soil of Ireland.

The making of Ireland as an economic unit, as self-contained and self-sufficient as possible - with a proper balance between agriculture and the other essential industries[24].

DeValera visited America in March 1926. His arrival at the Waldorf Astoria was major news as the media sought interviews. Members of his own family had to wait to see him, as his business came first. When he visited his mother she showed him a letter from Michael Collins. Frank Gallagher reports that the letter "moved Dev greatly, not in any sentimental way, but in appreciation of the finer things that were in Mick"[25]. As usual in America there were many disparate elements of Irish-American views and this time Dev's new party had added another complication. His old enemies remained, with some new ones added to, by his new policy and departure from Sinn Féin. He went on a major fundraising tour, which was so successful that it enabled Fianna Fáil to run 87 candidates compared to 15 for Sinn Féin, thereby making that party redundant before the election. Dev remained in America until 1 May.

One purpose of the American trip was to seek to get hold of some of the $3 million he had collected for the Irish cause, as President of the Dáil in 1919-1920. He had agreed with Collins at the time, that that money 'should not be used for party purposes'[26]. The right to this money had been contested between Cosgrave and DeValera for some years. In 1922 the Provisional Government secured an injunction preventing the banks from handing over the balance to Dev, Stephen O'Mara or anyone else acting for them. All this time, a crucial court case was finally in progress in New York, concerning the ownership of the money. The Free State Government had laid claim to it. Dev, as one of the Trustees, entered the witness box over three days to be cross-examined on Irish history. He said that the Free State was not the legitimate successor to the Republican Government, on whose behalf the money was given. When eventually the court decided that the vast amount of money should be returned to those who had subscribed it, Dev saw that as a victory[27]

In Ennis on 29 June Dev said, *"I stand for an Irish Republic, for the full freedom of Ireland as thoroughly today, as I stood nine years ago when I first came before you".*

Dev wrote to McGarrity, *"As to the hope of winning through elections, it is not a question of choice of methods at the moment. The acceptance of the 'Treaty' is a situation such as we never had in Irish history before. The essence of that situation is that we now appear to be governed by the wishes of the people, as determined by the majority. This is the barrier to freedom that I have been always been speaking about and until it is removed; the methods of physical force are bound to fail. You are not to conclude from this that I have any delusion as to the difficulty of winning an election"*[28].

The first Fianna Fáil Ard Fheis took place on 24 November 1926, where Dev rededicated himself to the republican struggle. He also reminded the delegates that that date, was the anniversary of the death of Erskine Childers. Some few weeks later he joined Seán MacBride on a platform protesting at the prison treatment of the IRA leader George Gilmore.

1927 ELECTION

As the scheduled June 1927 General Election approached, the IRA was anxious that some understanding should be made between Sinn Féin and Fianna Fáil. In January 1927 Dan Breen T. D. shocked many republicans by taking his seat in the Dáil, after taking the Oath. On 6 April in his maiden speech he sought to introduce a motion to abolish the Oath. Breen said, "My principal reason for introducing this Bill, is that I am convinced that you will have no prospect of unity amongst national forces, until such time as that Article, which debars a large number of elected representatives from entering this House is removed"[29]. Cosgrave opposed the move saying that it sought to remove a fundamental provision of the Treaty. He added, "That Treaty has been approved by the Dáil and endorsed by the people at two General Elections, as well as 17 out of 21 by-elections". The Bill was refused a First Reading by 47 votes to 17. Labour (11) Clann Éireann (1), Farmers (2), National League (1) and Independent Labour (2) voted for, with Cumann Na nGaedheal (34), Farmers (6), Independents (7) voting against.

The IRA sought to broker an agreement, whereby Sinn Féin and Fianna Fáil would run a joint panel of candidates. This foundered on the question of not taking the Oath, as this was a *sine qua non* for Sinn Féin. Despite this, Coogan writes that in certain parts of the country, "Fianna Fáil Cumainn by day, drilled as IRA columns by night"[30]. Fianna Fáil campaigned clearly on the notion that they were going into the Dáil, Oath or no Oath.

1927 GENERAL ELECTIONS

The result of the 1927 election was extraordinary, as Fianna Fáil succeeded in getting almost as many seat as Cumann Na nGaedheal, with Sinn Féin almost disappearing. The results were:

Cumann Na nGaedheal	47
Fianna Fáil	44
Labour	22
Independents	16
Farmers Party	11
National League	8
Sinn Féin	5

It was clear that if Dev entered the Dáil, the Government could be defeated, but the barrier of the Oath stood between Fianna Fáil and the Dáil chamber. Dev decided to seek a legal opinion on the validity of forcing elected Deputies to take the Oath, before allowing them to take their seats. This opinion, signed by Arthur Meredith, Albert Wood and George Gavan Duffy, held that there was no legal authority under the Constitution or the Treaty to exclude a Deputy from any part of the House, before the Dáil was constituted and the Speaker elected.

On 23 June after attending mass at Westland Row church, DeValera made an ostentatious entry to the Dáil precincts, where a huge crowd had assembled. The Captain of the Guard, Colonel Brennan, the Dáil Clerk, Colm O'Murchadha, and his assistant met him. They escorted the Fianna Fáil T.D's to a committee room, having already taken the precaution of locking the doors of the Dáil chamber. Despite this, both DeValera and Seán T. O'Kelly tried forcibly to proceed in the direction of the chamber, but were prevented from doing so. Back in the committee room, a discussion began on the matter of the Oath. O'Murchadha would not budge from the necessity of the Fianna Fáil T.D.'s taking the Oath, before they could be allowed entry to the chamber. The *Irish Independent* of 24 June reported that tense excitement permeated the city streets with a series of demonstrations, as the Fianna Fáil T.D.'s returned to their party rooms in Lower Abbey St.

On 1 July Fianna Fáil began collecting 75,000 signatures for a referendum to abolish the Oath in the Constitution. Such a referendum would be a certain winner and create a crisis for the Cosgrave Government.

O'HIGGINS MURDER

Kevin O'Higgins had been in Geneva, and when he returned on 9 July, his wife told him of a rumour that Cosgrave was going to be assassinated. He discounted the idea. On the following Sunday morning, as he walked alone to Mass on Booterstown Ave, he was shot by three men and fatally wounded. Eoin MacNeill was first on the scene. The Government presumed that it was the work of the IRA, and arrested all the leaders it could find. Dev, who was as outraged as most, moved immediately to distance himself and Fianna Fáil from the shooting. He issued a statement saying, *"The assassination of Mr. O'Higgins is murder and is inexcusable from any standpoint. I am confident that no Republican organisation was responsible for it or would give it any countenance"*. He hoped that this was true but could only wait and hope.

In fact it transpired very much later that one of the gunmen was Timothy Coughlan, a member of Fianna Fáil. The other two were Archie Doyle and Bill Gannon. All three were IRA members. Later in 1928, Coughlan was killed while attempting to murder a police informer. Large numbers of Fianna Fáil TD's attended Coughlan's funeral. A branch of the Party was named after him and Seán McEntee declared the *"the murder of Timothy Coughlan would not go unpunished"*[31].

The Government reacted by introducing a Public Safety Bill. It also introduced two other Bills, which were clearly directed towards forcing Fianna Fáil to take their seats in the Dáil, thus facilitating Dev in bringing any doubtful Deputies with him on that fateful step. Patrick Belton entered the Dáil in July and was expelled from Fianna Fáil. One Bill provided that every candidate for election had to sign an affidavit that if elected, he would take his seat and the oath. The other Bill proposed to remove the clause from the Constitution giving citizens the right to call a referendum.

Cosgrave spoke in the Dáil on 12 July about the murder of O'Higgins:

"Private individuals have not committed this crime against Kevin O'Higgins. It is the political assassination of a pillar of the State. It is the fruit of the steady, persistent attack against the State and its fundamental institutions. On the heads of those who have devoted their energies to the direction of that attack, lay the bloodguilt What shall I say of the crime against the home, the wife, the infant children, the mother and brothers and sisters of our murdered colleague? There are some things too sacred for debate in a public assembly, and I dare not intrude upon that sorrow and drag it into the public view".

The Labour Party's Tom Johnson met Cosgrave on 18 July and offered an all-party coalition. Cosgrave told him of the impending new legislation. He said that he proposed an election to fill the fifty-one seats of the abstentionists and offered a deal to split them with Labour. Johnson refused the offer and conveyed the information to DeValera. This only increased the urgency on him to enter the Dáil, and quickly. Cosgrave was so used to having Labour as the opposition party, that he never appeared to make a concerted effort to meet their political needs and gain their support[32]. It was at this point that Seán Lemass tried to contact Archbishop Byrne on the matter of the Oath of Allegiance. He wrote to Archbishop's House from Rokeby, Terenure on 19 July 1927 indicating that he wished to contact the Archbishop. He wrote, "I did not consult any political colleagues of my intention to ask his advice with reference to the Oath of Allegiance"[33].

L to R: Countess Markievicz, Eamon DeValera, Mrs Tom Clarke, 1926.

Dev knew what he had to do and he set about choreographing the movements. On 5 August he spoke at a national executive meeting of his party and said that they had to enter the Dáil or quit politics. As Cosgrave continued to back Dev into a corner, that sinuously scholastic mind at last saw the logic of the 'empty political formula' approach to the Oath[34]. Dev raised the possibility that there might be a way of avoiding taking it, through mental reservation, on the basis that it was not being administered as an Oath in the usual sense or form.

Dev held extensive talks with Tom Johnson of the Labour Party the very next day. Labour was very keen to form an alliance with Fianna Fáil in the Dáil. Dev said that to take the Oath "would be an act of national apostasy that would never be forgotten or forgiven". Dev's two colleagues, Gerald Boland and Seán T. O'Kelly, did not appear unduly influenced by Dev's words, as various eventualities were explored. Dev insisted that he would not form a Government but would support Labour if they did.

Negotiations between the two parties continued and resulted in a memorandum to withdraw the promised Government legislation that Dáil candidates had to take the oath or be disqualified from standing, and the abolition of the Oath by negotiation with the British or by referendum. The leader of the National Party in the Dáil, Captain Redmond, promised Fianna Fáil that he would recommend his party agree to the memorandum. The prospects for a Government defeat heightened.

The next day, 10 August, Dev proposed that the Fianna Fáil Deputies go to Leinster House and test the procedure. The executive agreed by forty-four votes to seven. All the Deputies signed a declaration. Fianna Fáil issued a statement: *"The legislation now being passed through the Free State Parliament created a national emergency which might imperil the general peace and which disenfranchised all republicans, who will not acknowledge that any allegiance is due to the English Crown. The required declaration is not an oath, that the signing of it implies no contractual obligation, and that it has no binding significance in law; that in short, it is merely an empty political formula which deputies could conscientiously sign, without becoming involved in obligations of loyalty to the English Crown"*.

DeValera and Jim Larkin proposed a conference of opposition groups to discuss an alternative government, which Labour ignored[35]. On 11 August Labour voted to form a coalition government with Fianna Fáil.[36] .

Kevin O'Higgins

Seán Lemass

Jim Larkin

Seán T. O'Kelly

CHAPTER 11

FIANNA FÁIL INTO DÁIL

The next day, 12 August 1927, the Fianna Fáil TD's, led by DeValera, attended the Dáil. Dev told the Clerk of the Dáil, *"I am not prepared to take the oath. I am not going to take the oath. I am prepared to put my name to this book in order to get permission to go into the Dáil. It has no other significance"*[1]. When he was presented with the register containing the Oath and the Bible, Dev removed the Bible, covered the words containing the Oath and signed the Declaration which read: *"I, Eamon DeValera, do solemnly swear true faith and allegiance to the constitution of the Irish Free State as by law established and that I will be faithful to HM King George V, his heirs and successors by law, in virtue of the common citizenship of Ireland with Great Britain and her adherences to and membership of the group of nations forming the British Commonwealth of Nations"*. All his TD's then duly signed the book in the office of the Clerk as required. Dev had signed with Jim Ryan and Frank Aiken as witnesses. Dev was not happy about it and wrestled with his conscience, but he did what he felt he had to do in the circumstances, making the best out of an impossible situation, as any self respecting Catholic would be capable of doing. He threatened that one day he would burn the same book containing his signature[2]. On 26 September Patrick Cardinal O'Donnell wrote, *"It is an oath. But as the deputies believe that duress exists, it is for them to say that they take the oath under duress and say no more except perhaps a word on what the duress is"*[2a].

In far away Melbourne, Archbishop Mannix recognised the Catholic-clerical mind of Dev operating and gave it his imprimatur, by proclaiming that the Fianna Fáil TD's who took the Oath (didn't take the Oath) 'no more told a falsehood than I would if I sent down word to an unfortunate visitor that I was not at home'[3]. This decision by Fianna Fáil was also a vindication of John Hagan's policy of backing Dev and encouraging him to enter the Dáil.

Michael J. Browne, Professor of moral theology at Maynooth, and later Bishop of Galway, wrote to Dev, *"Fear does not invalidate an oath, It does however justify the swearer in taking the Oath in a qualified or restricted sense, that will make it compatible with his rights, provided the reservation is not purely mental...If the swearer makes public the sense in which he takes the oath and is allowed to swear, then there is no question at all, that he is bound only in this sense and to its extent"*[4].

Joe Lee wrote of the event, *"seeing no Oath, hearing no Oath, speaking no Oath, signing no Oath, the Soldiers of Destiny shuffled into Dáil Éireann"*[5].

The Clerk then informed the Dáil that the Fianna Fáil deputies "had complied with the provisions of Article 17 of the Constitution". Dev was tempted to rise to deny that they had taken the oath but accepted the Clerk's announcement in silence.

Dev gave an interview to a Swedish newspaper on 27 October. The reporter said, "In Sweden they think that when you entered the Free State Parliament recently it meant that you had accepted the Treaty and were prepared to abide by it". Dev replied, "Your countrymen are mistaken". The reporter countered, "But so far you have consented to the oath?" Dev replied, *"We have consented to nothing. We have expressly stated in advance that we would conform to the act of putting our names in a certain book as a formality but that we did not intend that be an oath or to have significance whatsoever. From the national standpoint it would have been better had this action of ours not been necessary"*[5a].

This whole episode is reminiscent of the 'Mental Reservation', practised by some leading members of the Catholic Hierarchy, as outlined in the *Murphy Report* into the Archdiocese of Dublin in November 2009.

Dermot Keogh writes that *"While DeValera must take credit for carrying the most politically significant section of Sinn Féin with him into the Dáil, Cosgrave made it possible for entry into Leinster House without too much bruising of republican consciences. This was an episode in Irish history, which reflected the statesman-qualities of both political opponents. It is probable that Cosgrave had difficulty persuading some Cumann Na nGaedheal ministers of the wisdom of the gesture"*[6]. Robert W. White wrote of Dev's action, "This decision haunts his place in history"[7].

Four days later Tom Johnson, having already agreed on the composition of his Government, proposed a vote of no confidence in the Government. On paper, the combined Opposition had a majority of one and the defeat of the Government appeared a matter of course. WT Cosgrave was very calm about the situation, feeling that his policy of adhering to the terms of the Treaty had been vindicated. He said;

"...Well, after five years of office, and they were fairly strenuous years, I am sleeping well. I wish I had more of it... The eyes of the people of this country are on this Parliament to day, looking for that constructive effort, looking for some appreciation of the responsibility, which is on us, and we are not offered a solution by the motion that is before the House. We stand for one Army, one armed force in this country under this Parliament, no other, no matter what sacrifices may be entailed by nailing that on our mast.... We told this Parliament within the last two or three weeks, that we wanted 152 seats filled in this Dáil. Within the past week I have seen the vindication of that policy, and I am glad of it. Do not think for a moment that we are upset by any change that may take place on these benches"[8].

After Captain Redmond, leader of the National League Party, announced that his seven members had unanimously decided to support the Opposition, everyone was prepared to see the motion carried. Four Independent TD's, who were expected to oppose the government, did not do so. Whether Fianna Fáil would have participated in a new government with Labour and others remains open to speculation.

When the division took place however, one of the National League deputies, John Jinks an ex-Mayor of Sligo, did not vote. Desmond Fitzgerald had gone against medical advice to attend and vote. This resulted in a tie of 71 for each side. The Ceann Comhairle then intervened to say, "It devolves on me in pursuance of Article 22 of the Constitution and Standing Order 68 to give a casting vote…I vote against the motion". The *Irish Times* of 17 August reported, "It was a crestfallen party that Mr. DeValera led from the chamber at a few minutes past eight tonight, when the House adjourned".

John Jinks arrived back in Sligo that night by train where a crowd of about 150 met him with cries of 'Here's the missing Deputy'. On his return to Dublin the next day, Mr Jinks asserted to the *Irish Times,* that he had not been inveigled out of the Dáil in any way. Jink's added, "There is no truth in that; I acted purely on my own initiative…I felt that I could never have anything to do with Mr DeValera…I have been and remain a constitutional nationalist". However the accepted version is that Jinks was plied with drink and put on the train to Sligo by another Sligo man, RM Smyllie of the *Irish Times*. Cosgrave was always interested in horses and at his suggestion a thoroughbred horse was named after Jinks. *Mr. Jinks* won the *Two Thousand Guineas* in England in 1929 but failed dramatically in the Derby[9].

SECOND ELECTION 1927

There were two by-elections pending, to fill the seats of Countess Marckievz who died prematurely of peritonitis in June 1927, and the murdered Kevin O'Higgins. Cosgrave undertook to recall the Dáil, if the Government did not win both. It won both, and on 25 August, he called another General Election for 15 September 1927.

A short bitter campaign followed, with DeValera seeking to appeal to enlist support from moderates, by emphasising that his party would act as a responsible constitutional government, acknowledging that all power comes from the sovereign people, who were entitled to be taken into the fullest consultation.[10.] He said at Blackrock, *"I want to reply to the suggestion now being put forward, that out purpose in entering the Free State Dáil, is to destroy it. That is a falsehood. Our purpose is not to destroy but to broaden and widen the Free State assembly. I, for my part, accept the principle of one government and one army. I made those proposals in April 1923"*[10a]. He assured public servants that there would be no dismissals and replacement by Fianna Fáil supporters. There was little money available for the campaign and as a result, only 261 candidates stood, as against 383 in June.

The results of the 15 September 1927 General Election were:

Party	% Vote	Seats Won
Cumann Na nGaedheal	39	61
Fianna Fáil	35	57
Labour	9	13

Farmers	6	4
National League	2	2
Communists	1	1
Independents	8	12

It was a famous and remarkable victory for Dev, who could surely look forward to going into Government sooner rather than later. The smaller parties did poorly, with the Labour Party doing particularly so, and losing its leader Tom Johnson. Dev had always maintained that Fianna Fáil, and not Labour, was the party of the working class. He often invoked the rhetoric of James Connolly for that purpose.

Cosgrave's party formed a Government on 11 October 1927, with the assistance of the Farmers Party and Independents. Dev's first speech in the Dáil was in Irish, on the election of the Ceann Comhairle. President WT Cosgrave, following precedent, proposed Micheal O hAodha. Cosgrave emphasised that the Chair of the Dáil was above Party. TJ O'Connell of the Labour Party seconded, noting the rulings of the Chair, were so wise that they were always accepted without question. He said that all the members had an interest in seeing that the rulings of the Chair were accepted and respected.

Eamon DeValera on right, together with PJ Ruttledge, middle,
help carry the coffin of Countess Markievicz.

Dev spoke briefly in Irish saying that his Party would not oppose the proposal. He however made it clear to everyone that they were not satisfied to pay over a thousand pounds to the Ceann Comhairle, nor to a Minister or any officer of the Oireachtas, as long as the people of Ireland were in poor circumstances. He said that they would endeavour when the time came, to deduct £700 from the salary of the Ceann Comhairle. The Fianna Fáil parliamentary party only agreed by a majority vote and after long discussion that no Minister be paid more than £1,000[11]. That sum would be equivalent to *circa* €40,000 in today's currency.

The election of the Leas-Cheann Chomhairle took place on 27 October. TJ O'Connell nominated Patrick Hogan of Clare. Dev opposed the motion, speaking again in Irish. He said that while a salary of £1,000 went with the post, his Party's position was that the post should not be filled. He felt it should be an honorary position without salary. There was more work attached to the position of Chairman of County Councils, which were not salaried. He made it clear that their opposition was not to the person nominated, but to the principle of a salaried position. TJ O'Connell explained that the matter of salary did not arise at the moment as it was fixed by Parliament. The vote resulted in 90 votes for and 58 against.

On the nomination of WT Cosgrave as President of the executive Council on 11 Oct 1927, his erstwhile Sinn Féin colleague from Dublin Corporation, Seán T. O'Kelly, intervened, saying bitterly, *"the political history of the last five years made the Deputy unfitted for the office"*. O'Kelly referred to the sorrows that the policy pursued by Cosgrave brought on Ireland, and of the anguish of mind that he and his policy brought into so many homes. He said that he did not want to evoke these things, saying, *"I do not want to start on a bitter note, though God knows I could, and God knows I would have justification, in thinking of those who lie in cold graves — 77 of my comrades who lie in cold graves to-day —and the fathers and mothers, and the sons and daughters of these people expect us and look to us to vindicate them in some way. The gentleman who has been nominated came into public life pledged to work for and to devote his life to achieve an Ireland free and independent. That is my recollection of the political gospel he preached when I used to stand on platforms with him — thanks be to God, I do not now. Deputy Cosgrave brought Partition into full and complete operation for the first time in the history of our country"*.

The Ceann Comhairle then moved to the vote on Cosgrave's nomination as President of the Executive Council. Cosgrave proposed to adjourn proceedings to the next day, until he had advised the Governor General and received his appointment accordingly. Dev acquiesced saying that it did not matter to him.

From 1927 onwards, Fianna Fáil nationalism, in reaction to the Government favouring the maintenance of existing political and economic links with Britain, matured into a critique of dependency with a pronounced working-class appeal, which had a negative effect on Labour.

The nomination of the Ministers of the Executive Council saw Dev's first important intervention in the Dáil. He realised that all his supporters were expecting him to make an immediate impression. Cosgrave informed the Dáil on the following day of his nominations for ministerial office. He invited the Dáil to agree, but controversy arose when Mr Morrissey took exception to one nomination. He was adamantly against the nomination of Paddy McGilligan at Industry and Commerce. Morrissey was outraged that McGilligan had stated that it was not the function of his Department to find work for the unemployed. He wanted the opportunity to vote against McGilligan's nomination. When the Ceann Comhairle said that the nominations were to be taken as a bloc, Dev saw his opportunity to intervene. Speaking in Irish, he asked why this should be so. The Ceann Comhairle said that the Executive Council proposed by the President, had collective responsibility, and that, the practice had been to take the vote as one. Dev wanted to know when a decision was taken on the matter. He said that the Constitution's intention was to give the House the right of veto over any individual that might be nominated. He regretted to say that his Deputies objected to the ruling. The Ceann Comhairle said that while the Constitution did allow for it, the matter was one of parliamentary practice. Dev asked had his side any redress in the matter and was told, not so. Dev declared the practice unfair and not in line with the Constitution. He said that if there was another individual in the Chair the ruling might be different. He added that his Party intended to object on every occasion that this came up and to take what action they could to change the procedure. He said, "We do not agree that parliamentary practice can over ride the Constitution".

Dev's first major attack on Cosgrave's Government occurred that same month of November, when Fianna Fáil sought to remove the Public Safety Laws introduced after the murder of the Minister of Justice. His declared aim was to remove the Bill because in itself it was unconstitutional and a source of public danger. He said there were enough powers available to deal with criminals. He quoted the critical view of the Act by the *Irish Independent*, describing it as an organ certainly unlikely to favour the views of Republicans. He also quoted the *London Times* as saying; *"Mr Cosgrave has plumped for a good thumping Coercion Act, which would have brought a blush to the cheek of "Buckshot" Forster or "Blood" Balfour"*. Dev then acknowledged that insofar as any part of the Constitution could be regarded as having been freely accepted by the people, he accepted it. However he opposed the parts of the Constitution that were imposed and he hoped to change those Articles. He acknowledged that many Articles in the Constitution were admirable, though he claimed that this Act was superseding the Constitution and becoming the fundamental law. These powers were too dangerous to be given to any Executive.

The Ceann Comhairle intervened to state that the Act was the law and that Dev was trying to repeal it. He reminded him that the Act was there for any Executive to use and the debate was not on the merits of the present Executive. Dev said that those who make and those who receive arbitrary powers, are both criminal. He posed what would happen if they found themselves in a civil war situation again under this legislation?.

The Ceann Comhairle said that what Dev was doing was giving his own view, as veracious history since 1922. He pointed out that others would have a different view. Such debate now was pointless. Different Executives had existed since 1922. Dev said that he did not want to go back to 1922 and rake up everything, if he could avoid it. He felt he had to demonstrate why this Act was not necessary then. The Ceann Comhairle said that if they had a debate on matters since 1922, it would not be a debate but a wrangle. He would allow it if the House wished it. TJ O'Connell of the Labour Party intervened to support Dev, saying that since Fianna Fáil had come into the Dáil a new atmosphere had been created there, and also in the country. He wanted Dev to be allowed to continue without going into all the bitterness and wrongs, which all now regretted. He believed that Dev could make a sound argument for the repeal of the Act, which his Party would support.

Dev agreed that bitterness was futile, but asserted that history could repeat itself and the Executive should not have the powers available in the Act. He asked when is this matter ever going to be settled? He said the Act gave the Executive the power to declare any organisation whatsoever, which in their opinion is treasonable, unlawful. It can deport any person within 24 to 48 hours. Any citizen can be arrested by the police and held for 7 days, extended to two months. He adverted to the fact that the police were set up when it was clear they would be supporters of a particular party. He did not blame the police for that. He charged the Executive for seeking to identify itself with the State, and the police did the same. He said that behind the State was a nation that the Executive was supposed to minister to. Mr Ruttedge formally seconded Dev's motion.

Ernest Blythe, the Minister of Finance responded at length. The Executive did not want to change the Constitution. Blythe tried to deal with the technicalities, but eventually spoke about the dangers members of the Executive had faced and continued to face. He reminded Dev that the passage of the Act arose entirely from the assassination of the late Minister of Justice, Kevin O'Higgins. He declared that those who murdered O'Higgins were not oblivious of political considerations. He acknowledged that nothing disastrous happened after his death, but the assassination of Ministers could not go on without the possibility of the country falling back into the abyss. He said the Executive felt it necessary to ensure that there could be no repetition of the assassination of a single Minister, with the great danger of the country going back into barbarism. The Act stood.

The advent of Fianna Fáil to the Dáil might have been expected to lead to a normalising of politics in the Chamber and the State, but this did not happen. Though they had aspired to an immediate ascent to form a Government, Fianna Fáil was far from ready to form an administration, even in a technical role. During their early months in the Dáil, it became clear, not unnaturally, that they were not *au fait* with a vast array of procedures of government. In a real way, Fianna Fáil was fortunate that it did not gain power in 1927, and was afforded an apprenticeship of five years, during which the Cosgrave administration had established an international political platform, from which it could safely pursue its constitutional programme.

Seán Lemass would later admit that, *"perhaps it was good for us we had not succeeded in getting any responsibility for government at that time"*[12]. Gerry Boland expressed thanks, saying, *"I was glad we were beaten in that effort against the Government. At that time we knew nothing about parliamentary procedure or the science of government"*. He appreciated the five years apprenticeship that followed[13].

But even within the narrow local politics of the Dáil and country, Fianna Fáil did not act as a normal political party. Dev had become Leader of the Opposition in the Dáil. But in a very real way he also represented those who remained in Sinn Féin and the IRA, and continued to oppose Government measures against them. He continued this dual, if not paradoxical role even when the IRA renewed its violent activity against the Free State. Fianna Fáil representatives continued to refuse to attend with Free State representatives on formal or social occasions. This included a reception for the newly appointed Apostolic Nuncio Paschal Robinson in 1929.

That same year Dev was very embarrassed to find himself being arrested in Northern Ireland. He had travelled by train in February for the opening of Aonach Na nGaedheal. He was taken off the train at Goraghwood by the RUC, brought to Belfast, and charged with breaking the exclusion order made against him in 1924. He was sentenced to a month in jail amid protests in the South.

The duality of Fianna Fáil's stance was made brutally clear both by Dev and by Seán Lemass in the Dáil during 1928 and 1929. Speaking in the Dáil on 21 March 1928, Lemass declared that *"Fianna Fáil is a slightly constitutional party…. before anything we are a Republican party. We adapted the methods of political agitation to achieve our end because we believe in the present circumstances, that method is best in the interest of the nation and for the Republican movement and for no other reason. Five years ago the methods we adopted were not the methods we adopted now. Our aim is to establish a Republican Government in Ireland…If that can be done by the present methods we have, we will be very pleased, but if not, we would not confine ourselves to them"*.

Fianna Fáil refused, in the Dáil on 28 March 1928, to give any assurance that its members would cooperate with the Gardai in apprehending the murderers of O'Higgins. On 6 June 1928 Dev questioned the Minister of Justice on the numbers of persons arrested and the numbers sentenced under a series of Public Safety Acts. Mr Fitzgerald-Kenny replied that 356 had been arrested, 124 had been sentenced and that 8 were still in prison, two of which were women, Sheila McInerney and Florence McCarthy. Seán T. O'Kelly referred to the Minister for Defence as "the so-called Minister for Defence" on 27 February 1929, in the Dáil .

Dev himself gave his views in an extraordinary statement in the Dáil, on 14 March 1929. He regarded the Dáil as illegitimate and did not necessarily feel bound by majority rule. He was prepared to return to force again, if necessary. He recognised the legitimate continuity of Sinn Féin and by inference of the IRA, as the legitimate army.

DeValera accused the Executive of using force. He said: *"I still hold that our right to be regarded as the legitimate government of this country is faulty, that this House itself is faulty. You have secured a de facto position…you brought off a coup d'etat in the summer of 1922…there is a moral handicap in your case…we had to come in here, if there was to be a majority at all of the people's representatives in any one assembly…As a practical rule, and not because there is anything sacred in it, I am prepared to accept majority rule, as settling matters of national policy"*[13a].

As late as the summer of 1931 Dev and Fianna Fáil attended the Wolfe Tone commemoration with the IRA, after Cosgrave's government had banned the event.

DUNBAR-HARRISON CONTROVERSY

A local row in Mayo over the appointment of a librarian, gave a good example of the operation of Dev in parish politics. The Mayo Library Committee, consisting of one Catholic bishop, five priests, a Christian Brother, a Protestant Rector and four laymen refused to approve the appointment of a Trinity College Protestant graduate, Miss Letitia Dunbar Harrison, to their library in Castlebar, by ten votes to two[14]. The row had national implications, as the appointment had been via the process of the Local Appointments Board, which was set up by Cosgrave to seek to remove jobbery from local politics. This was greatly resented by local interests, which had previously controlled all local appointments. It also had clear religious overtones with the Catholic clergy and hierarchy acting in a blatantly sectarian manner. Among these were Geoffrey Prendergast of Castlebar and Dean d'Alton of Tuam, who was of course well known to Dev from his Blackrock College student days. WT Cosgrave got directly involved as he assured the Dáil that he had reviewed the file and that the whole process of appointment had been properly adjudicated.

Dev saw an opportunity to find favour with the local Catholics. He became directly involved and made a lengthy speech on the issue at Irishtown in Mayo in early January 1931. He said that, *"the whole question hinged on the duties of a librarian…if the whole idea behind the scheme was that the Librarian should go into the homes of the people, and into the schools, the position was an entirely different one."* His speech was an excellent example of the political astuteness of the man, in the run-up to a General Election, where Mayo was politically marginal. He covered all angles in such a way, that all sides could take support from his words. He appealed to local pride by questioning the notion of having a Local Appointments Commission in Dublin deciding on local matters. He acknowledged that Mayo was a Gaeltacht area and Irish was very important. He felt that as it was reasonable for majority religious areas to be concerned about their own ethos, then the same would have to hold for minorities, and they would also be entitled to have similar facilities provided out of public funds. He alluded to the Six Counties, where the rights of minorities were not being catered for and added, "but they did not propose to follow in their footsteps and ignore the rights of minorities here".

Cosgrave was annoyed by DeValera's intervention and said of him: *"That man is a type of mental arrested development – or perhaps a new type of administrator – who is prepared to spend public money to meet every contingency that may arise – Republican Police, Republican Attorney General, Republican Judge to try Republicans-Labour ditto for Labour prisoners and so on"*[15].

Dermot Keogh writes of Dev's speech, *"It was one of the most consciously Socratic speeches he was ever to deliver…. the 'Republican' dimension of Fianna Fáil ideology …did not enjoy a major philosophical advance"*[16]. Diarmaid Ferriter writes rather demurely, *"DeValera unwisely backed the campaign to insist that a Catholic librarian be appointed in Mayo…"*[17]. Dev's intervention was rewarded politically however, as in the next election, when Fianna Fáil gained an extra seat in Mayo[18].

Cosgrave investigated the appointment himself and decided it was valid. The Government dissolved Mayo County Council and replaced it by a Commissioner. Cosgrave then negotiated with Archbishop Gilmartin of Tuam who was quite intransigent. One proposal was that library posts should be made on the same basis as teachers, giving autonomy to the local religious interests. Cosgrave, when isolated in cabinet on this point, threatened resignation. He told Gilmartin that to agree to such a proposal "would be to repudiate some of the fundamental principles on which this State is founded". Miss Dunbar Harrison took up her position in Castlebar but there was an understanding, that another suitable position would materialise in due course. The *Irish Independent* reported on 4 January 1932, that Miss Dunbar Harrison had resigned to take up an important librarian post in the Department of Defence in Dublin[19].

Letitia Dunbar Harrison

CHAPTER 12

DIPLOMATIC ADVANCES BY FREE STATE

DeValera recognised the diplomatic advances made by the Free State, when speaking in the Senate in June 1932, on the motion to abolish the oath of allegiance. In reply to Senator Milroy, when speaking of Commonwealth Conferences, he said:

"I thought for one, at any rate, that the Twenty-six Counties here, as a result of the 1926 and 1930 Conferences, had practically got into the position—with the sole exception that instead of being a Republic it was a monarchy—that I was aiming at in 1921 for the whole of Ireland. I am quite willing to give to Senator Milroy or anybody else, any credit that can be got for the policy they aimed at, and I am prepared to confess that there have been advances made, that I did not believe would be made at the time. I am quite willing to confess it"[1].

The Free State Government had set about energetically demonstrating that the Treaty could be used as 'stepping stones' to full independence, in Collins' words. As the earliest Provisional Government had done, it paid great attention to international affairs, gaining admission to international organisations to assert an increasing level of independence from Britain. In this goal it was immensely successful.

The Dáil had bitter memory of the failure of the post war Peace Conference to give it a hearing. It also knew that the League of Nations gave no support to Sinn Féin's claims for international recognition for Ireland as an independent entity. The fact that successive governments had a portfolio of External Affairs indicated how important they viewed the matter of international relations. The British were ready to support Ireland's membership of the League, once a new Constitution was in force. WT Cosgrave had been told during 1921 that any application to the League would be referred to the British Government for adjudication on the State's status, as defined under Article 1 of the Covenant of the League.

In early1923, Cosgrave told Desmond Fitzgerald Minister for External Affairs that, "this question of our entry to the League of Nations ought to be definitely decided. Unless the state of war interferes or prejudices our application, we ought to apply in my opinion"[2]. The Irish Free State joined the League and set up a permanent presence in Geneva. It was the first Dominion country to do so, with Canada following in 1924.

In general, Ireland and Canada were keen to establish their international freedom of movement, independent from Great Britain. Cosgrave led the eight man Irish delegation to its first meeting of the League in September 1923. He addressed the assembly, first in Irish, to inform his audience that Ireland had its own language. He spoke at length about Ireland's heritage and her historical links as a European country.

Cosgrave concluded by saying, *"...Ireland comes amongst you as an independent Nation, and as a co-equal member of the Community of Nations known as the British Commonwealth, resolved to play her part in making much of this great institution for peace as complete and efficient as possible"*[3].

Ireland gave a new impetus to the League, as in 1923 the Dominions were an unknown factor in international law[4]. The Irish Times said in an editorial: *"In the interval between the election of 1922 and that of this year, President Cosgrave and his colleagues had, under difficulties such as rarely confronted any new government, to face the task of establishing peace and order and ensuring security for life and property. They not only succeeded in accomplishing that work but they also carried through many legislative reforms. The crowning achievement was the admission of the Free State as a member of the League of Nations. This is a demonstration to the other nations of the world of the independent status, which the Free State enjoys under the Anglo-Irish Treaty"*[5]. Ireland appointed a High Commissioner in London in 1923, and in 1924 one to the United States. Gradually, appointments were made to Tokyo, Paris, Geneva, Ottawa, Berlin and the Vatican. Ireland attended its first Imperial Conference in 1923, as a newcomer and observer. On 11 July 1924 it registered the Anglo-Irish Treaty with the League of Nations Treaty Bureau. This led to an objection from the British, who regarded the Treaty as an inter Commonwealth agreement, and not amenable to be so registered, under Article 18 of the League. For Ireland, the precedent of registration implied sovereignty from Britain, on the basis of an international Treaty and copper fastened the legitimacy of the Irish Free State at home and abroad. On June 1924 Cosgrave received a letter from Alfred O'Rahilly in Geneva, urging the immediate registration of the Treaty. Michael Kennedy writes, "Cosgrave took the decision to go ahead on his own initiative"[6]. Over the next two years Ireland joined Canada and South Africa in developing the Commonwealth into an association of equals. The Imperial Conference of 1926 laid down principles in the Balfour Declaration, which allowed a development to remove all restrictions remaining on the absolute co-equality of the member states of the British Commonwealth with Great Britain[7]. At the League of Nations Council in March 1927, Austen Chamberlain sought to claw back some British prestige by implying that only Britain could represent the Dominions on the Council. Ireland played a major role in organising the election of Canada to the Council in September[8].

RENUNCIATION OF WAR PACT

DeValera objected to the *'Renunciation of War Pact'*, on the basis that he was suspicious of the intentions of the British and unhappy that the matter was not fully debated in the Dáil. In the Dáil on 30 May 1928, he questioned the Minister of External Affairs about the *Kellogg Treaty for the Renunciation of War* and whether the Executive Council had received the terms of the British reply to the United States on the matter. Dev was very suspicious of the British stance, feeling that it sought to speak for and about the Free State.

Dev outlined the British view as stating, that it accepted the Treaty on the clear understanding that it did not prejudice its freedom of action in respect of certain regions of the world, which constituted a special and vital interest for their peace and safety, and that interference with those regions would not be tolerated. Their protection against attack was to the British Empire, a measure of self-defence. Mr. McGilligan told Dev that the Government had accepted an invitation from the USA to become one of the original parties to the proposed multilateral Treaty. He added that the British view had been communicated to his Government, before being issued. He said that Dev would see that the British note expressed its own Government's view, and did not purport to represent the views of the government of Saorstat Éireann. Dev sought to have the matter discussed in the Dáil, but was told that the Irish response had already been issued. He was unhappy about this and said he would raise the matter again.

WT Cosgrave signed the *Renunciation of War Pact* on 27 August 1928 as an "international instrument of very considerable importance". Fianna Fáil voted against the measure but it was passed by 84 votes to 60[9].

In 1929 the Free State became a signatory to submitting disputes to the Permanent Court of International Justice at Geneva. In September 1930 the State was elected to a non-permanent seat on the Council of the League of Nations in succession to Canada, and through the good offices of Australia[10].

STATUTE OF WESTMINSTER

The biggest breakthrough diplomatically, which lent credence to the Treaty being a stepping stone to greater independence from Britain, came on 11 December 1931, when Ireland was to the fore in having the *Statute of Westminster* enacted. This decreed that no law passed by the Parliament in Great Britain, could apply to any of the Dominions, without their requesting and agreeing to it. The Colonial Laws Validity Act of 1856 was thus repealed in its application to the Dominions.

The Cosgrave Government could possibly have made more of this major political advance, were it not for the fact that it did not wish to unduly upset its Unionist minded citizens. The reality then was that the Irish Free State emerged, in constitutional theory, as well as in actual practice, as a completely autonomous nation; and the sole link between it and Great Britain was the King. But the King was to function entirely, so far as Irish affairs were concerned, at the will of the Irish Government[11]. However, once more, Fianna Fáil opposed the measure in the Dáil.

The fundamental nature of this Act in relation to Ireland was highlighted, when on 20 November 1931, Winston Churchill opposed it on the Second Reading debate in the Commons, where it referred to Ireland. He had resigned from Stanley Baldwin's Shadow Cabinet earlier, on the issue of giving Dominion Status to India. In 1931 Baldwin and Ramsay MacDonald had combined to form a national Government, in which there was no office for Churchill. Churchill sought in 1931 to have the Irish Free State omitted from the Statute, "*as this Bill confers upon the Irish Free State, full legal power to abolish the Irish Treaty...It would be open to the Dáil ...to repudiate the Oath of Allegiance...they could repudiate the right of the Imperial Government to utilize for instance, the harbour facilities at Berehaven and Queenstown".* He sought to introduce an amendment to the Bill saying, *"nothing in this Act shall be deemed to authorise the Legislature of the Irish Free State to repeal, or alter the Irish Free State Agreement Act 1922, or so much of the Government of Ireland Act 1920, as continues to be in force in Northern Ireland".* Mr. Leo Amery, who had been first Lord of the Admiralty and Secretary of State for the Dominions, explained that he had extended to his colleagues from the Irish Free State the same complete confidence, loyalty, and whole-hearted welcome that he had extended to any other statesmen of any other Dominion. He added, *"If you give, you must give generously, and without looking back"*[12].

After the debate, Austen Chamberlain understood Churchill had been reassured that Cosgrave would give a declaration about future action. Two days later, however, Churchill wrote to Chamberlain saying that he did not think that an assurance by Cosgrave would be any substitute for the amendment he proposed. He continued, again indicating his detestation and distrust of DeValera, *"It is at best even money, that DeValera will have control of the Irish government very soon, and the mere fact that Cosgrave made this declaration, would only spur him on all the more to stultify it. Pray, therefore, do not assume me placable by any such assurances"*[13].

Cosgrave wrote to Stanley Baldwin after the Second Reading. Baldwin read the letter to the Commons. It said, *"I need scarcely impress upon you that the maintenance of the happy relations which now exist between our two countries, is absolutely dependent upon the continued acceptance by each of us of the good faith of the other. The situation has been constantly present to our minds, and we have reiterated time and again, that the Treaty is an agreement, which can only be altered by consent. I maintain this particularly, because there seems to be a mistaken view in some quarters, that the solemnity of this instrument in our eyes could derive any additional strength from a parliamentary law. So far from this being the case, any attempt to erect a Statute of the British Parliament into a safeguard of the Treaty, would have quite the opposite effect here, and would rather tend to give rise in the minds of our people to a doubt, as to the sanctity of this instrument"*[14]. Cosgrave added that the Statute was an agreement between all the Governments of the Commonwealth, which had been considered at great length by the Irish representatives at the Imperial Conference and endorsed as it stood, by Dáil and Senate. He declared that any amendment of the nature then suggested, would be a departure from the terms of the Imperial Conference Report and would be wholly unacceptable to them. *"The interests of the peoples of the Commonwealth as a whole, must be put before the prejudices of the small reactionary elements in these islands"*, he said. Baldwin rejected Churchill's attempt, saying, *"any restrictive clause would offend not only the Irish Free State, not only Irishmen all over the world, but other Dominions as well. The Statute of Westminster has to be an act of faith, or it was nothing".*

The Statute became law on 11 December 1931. It included the "Governments of the United Kingdom, Canada, Australia, New Zealand, South Africa, Irish Free State and Newfoundland. Each was to be completely self governing, but united by allegiances to the monarchy, the succession to which, each Dominion would have a say". The Commons passed the Bill by 360 votes to 50.

Desmond Fitzgerald wrote, *"Knowing the history of these last few years, as I do, I am amazed at the way we have changed the situation… By accepting the Treaty we certainly are getting all that the most fervid supporters were claiming for it – and more"*[15]. Michael Collins' prophetic words on the Treaty as providing stepping stones, were realised first by the Cosgrave Government, then by the DeValera Government, and later by the First Inter-Party Government. As Frank Pakenham said in *Peace by Ordeal*, "from the Statute onwards, it would be hard to name a single respect in which *qua* Dominion, she was prevented from enjoying full practical autonomy"[16]. Diarmaid Ferriter acknowledges *"the Cumann na nGaedheal's creative diplomatic action within the terms of the Treaty and developments within the Commonwealth through the Statute of Westminster, which had secured sovereign independence for the Dominions"*[17].

REMOVE THE OATH OR DeVALERA WILL…

Two parts of the Treaty still caused major problems for Cosgrave's Government and were seen by him as hostages to fortune and Fianna Fáil. These were the Appeal to the judicial committee of the Privy Council and the Oath. Cosgrave had been pressing the British privately to remove the Oath. He sent the Assistant secretary at External Affairs, Seán Murphy, to London to tell them that "Either remove the Oath or DeValera will win the next election. It has become a burning issue in Ireland and a major weapon in the Fianna Fáil armoury". The British were unsympathetic and the Oath remained, as Cosgrave was insistent on using only diplomacy in his negotiations with the British. Speaking in the Senate in 1932, on a Bill to scrap the Oath of Allegiance, Dev declared, *"I do not want to see these advances which I think have been made, beyond what would be reasonably expected at the time, lost; that I am anxious that no retrograde steps should be taken at the moment. Let us stand on this. If we do go to Ottawa and meet there British representatives, and if there is a Council, representative of the other States, and this question is discussed, I believe that every one of them will realise that we are fighting the common fight, in standing up for this principle in this case, and that it is a common fight and that there are common interests involved there"*. He challenged the legally minded Senators to demonstrate that the Bill was against the Treaty. He argued that the Treaty was *"forced on the people but such a Treaty has to be submitted to"*, but he added that you do your best to change it. He said that his earlier External Association policy for the whole island as a Republic would have been compatible with allegiance. But the Conference decisions of 1926 and 1930 changed matters. If those declarations meant anything they meant that Ireland like Canada, was entitled to remove the Oath, if the people wished[18].

Austen Chamberlain

Ramsay MacDonald

Stanley Baldwin

Winston Churchill

CHAPTER 13

SECURITY SITUATION

THE RED SCARE, THE IRISH PRESS

When Fianna Fáil entered the Dáil, the IRA felt that it had to protect its flank from losing out to the politicians. A political wing became a constant topic for debate, as Sinn Féin became almost moribund. Many within the IRA, however, were hostile to any tendency towards politics. Gradually though, the idea got support and in 1931, Seán MacBride officially launched a new organisation, called *Saor Éire*. It had a distinctly communistic flavour. Its subtitle was "An Organisation of Workers and Working Farmers"[1].

The Government had become so concerned with *Saor Éire*, that it sought its condemnation from the Church. Cosgrave briefed Cardinal MacRory, telling him that he had delayed as long as possible in adding to the Cardinal's many anxieties. But the facts made it imperative that the head of the Church in the country, should be given the fullest information about a situation, which threatened the whole fabric of both Church and State.

Not to be outflanked, Dev, who was shown the Cosgrave memoranda to the bishops, by one of the bishops, sought a meeting with the Cardinal. This took place in Maynooth. It was a cordial discussion. The Cardinal wrote, "I had a long talk with him at Maynooth"[2]. It is probable that Dev met other bishops at that time in Maynooth, as they were gathered there for a regular meeting. Though some of his critics among the hierarchy had died, there were some like Bishop Fogarty who remained an unforgiving critic. Dev was nonplussed by this, feeling and acting quite at home at Maynooth among the Church leaders, with whom he had so much in common.

Some few days later, however, Dev experienced the danger of his party being associated with the Communistic mantle, when one of his chief lieutenants, Frank Aiken, called in the Dáil, on 16 October, for all-party talks with Saor Éire[3].

Activities outside the Dáil were to mirror the above sentiments, with law and order a moveable feast for republicans. Murders continued and intimidation of juries became commonplace. The Government had earlier felt forced to introduce a *Juries Protection Bill* on 1 May 1929, which envisaged the secret empanelling of juries, majority verdicts of nine out of twelve, penalties for the intimidation of jurors and imprisonment for refusal to recognise the courts. But violence continued. During 1931, the IRA executed two of its members for giving information to the police. A garda was shot dead in Tipperary. One hundred men were found drilling in Laois. An arms dump was discovered at the Hell Fire Club in the Dublin Mountains, and Prison warders were attacked.

Frank Ryan, an IRA leader, stated in an interview in *An Phoblacht* in August 1931 that shootings, drilling, and intimidation were all IRA policies and that they would be escalated. The Government banned that summer's march to Wolfe Tone's grave at Bodenstown. But the IRA went ahead and was joined by Fianna Fáil[4]. As trial by jury proved impossible to secure, the government on 14 October 1931 inserted a new Article 2A into the Constitution which established military courts, to deal with political crime, from which there was no appeal. When Cosgrave enumerated, in the Dáil , the various outrages around the country, Dev decried Cosgrave's long list, describing them as 'incidents', and of creating unnecessary "excitement" in the Dáil and country. He accused Cosgrave of operating Black and Tan tactics, claiming "ordinary law" quite capable of dealing with the matter. He said that they should deal with the causes of the unrest, referring to the occasion when Mulcahy was demoted for activities in a secret society. There were political and economic problems, but there was no catastrophic situation imminent, as Cosgrave said. Dev declared that Fianna Fáil was against crime, saying, "If there is no authority in this House to rule, then there is no authority in any part of the Twenty Six Counties to rule". He then moved to distance himself from an earlier speech, which he claimed was misinterpreted by others, as suggesting that he did not subscribe to majority rule. Despite the fact that he was rowing back furiously, he could not resist again referring to the, "situation created by the Treaty and the *coup d'etat* by the gentlemen on the opposite benches", as he announced that he did accept majority rule.

Cosgrave accused DeValera of posing as a pacificator, a great man with great ideals who, when he used one sentence, followed it with another, which made it impossible for anybody to understand what he meant. He accused DeValera of pretending to show him respect, but who in reality, "dislikes me more and has greater hatred for me, than any other man in this country has for another"[5]. The new Bill became law on 17 October, resulting in leading IRA men leaving the country. The vote in the Dáil on 14 October was 82 for and 64 against. Three days later, the IRA, Saor Éire and ten other organisations were banned.

BISHOPS' PASTORAL

On 18 October, the Catholic hierarchy issued a pastoral letter, saying that no Catholic could belong to the IRA or Saor Éire[6]. The Government was disappointed that the pastoral was not stronger, but the bishops knew that their area was pastoral and not political. They remained strictly neutral between the Government and the opposition and refused an endorsement to the Public Safety Act. Like everyone else they knew that an election was imminent and the outcome uncertain. Dev, with the eager assistance of Seán T. O'Kelly, kept up strenuous efforts to let the bishops know that Fianna Fáil was made up of Catholics too. Dev's own tendency to stress spiritual rather than material values, helped those of his followers who were ardent Catholics, who might have seen him as a lay cardinal or even 'the new Jesus in a black coat', and regarded his pronouncements as indistinguishable from Episcopal pastorals, with a definite tinge of *ex-cathedra* about them[6a].

Frank Aiken wrote directly to Cardinal MacRory repeating his earlier embarrassing comments. He added, *"the excommunication of members of the IRA creates such a danger to the future of the church and to the people, that I am impelled as an Irishman, who wants to see the church stand as a bulwark to the faith and rights and liberties of the people, to appeal to you not to be content with condemnation of the results of evil, but to take active and fatherly steps to deal with the root cause…Immediate action on your part is important"*[7].

The Government, through the secretary of the Department of External Affairs, Joseph Walshe, tried foolishly to have the Papal Nuncio intervene with the bishops. When the Irish envoy to the Vatican, Charles Bewley sought to take soundings with the Nuncio, he was rebuffed with the information, "Seán MacBride was here with me yesterday. A nice fellow". Bewley asked in surprise, "Your Excellency did not find him a dangerous communist". "No, I didn't notice it", the Nuncio replied[8]. The gardai did not quite see it that way, as Seán MacBride had become public enemy number one, for the State security forces.

THE IRISH PRESS

DeValera had realised, during his experience in America, that it was essential to get friendly press coverage. He decided that since most of the press coverage of himself and his party was hostile, the best course of action was to set up his own newspaper. This would be read by his followers and portray him in a favourable light to the general public. Once again he went to America to collect the necessary funds. He travelled there in December 1927 for a three-month stay and again in November 1929, for six months. The fact of his long sojourns in America has often been remarked upon as suggesting that he felt that as America had rejected him as an infant, it owed him a great debt, which he continually drew upon. Another theory is that he liked to spend long periods there to make a similar point to his own family, which had also rejected him. He was an American and was immensely popular there. He succeeded in establishing an almost personalised relationship with his followers there. Of course there were some who remained inimical to him.

During his 1927 trip, he told his followers that his aim was to get one thousand people to invest $500 each in his newspaper enterprise. Within a few weeks he had collected $12,000. His associates were all men who had been active with him during the Troubles in Ireland, Frank Walsh, Martin Conboy, Garth Healy and Eugene Kincaid. A plan was devised to seek to divert some of the Republican Bond Millions, that the courts had decided earlier that year to redistribute back to the donors, towards Dev's new newspaper. He later organised a large bond issue in Ireland, which was well subscribed by his followers. Dev set up the *Irish Press Corporation* in Delaware in May 1931. It had two types of shares. The A shares had been bought by Irish-Americans and were non-voting shares. There were 200 hundred B shares which Dev himself acquired which were the sole shares with the voting rights.

The Irish Press, of Chicago USA, could have inspired DeValera to develop his own version.

DeValera tries his hand at hot metal typesetting at the Seattle Times newspaper, May 1930.

Dev's authorised biographers write that Dev, *"As trustee and representative of the American company, Irish Press Incorporated, on the board of directors, he had a controlling interest"*[9].

After much detailed planning with a hands-on approach by Dev himself, his *Irish Press* arrived on the streets on 5 September 1931. The first leading article said:

"Our services will be to the whole people. We are not the organ of an individual, or a group or a party. We are a national organ in all that the term conveys...in national affairs we stand for independence...our ideal culturally is an Irish Ireland".

The *Irish Press* turned out to be a very successful newspaper. It was bright and fresh, introducing several innovative journalistic features for children, such as *'Captain Mac'*, *'Roddy the Rover'* and *'Abairti an Lae'*. It made the *The Irish Independent* look staid and old fashioned. The *Press* introduced excellent coverage of GAA games, which made it especially popular with men. It introduced cartoons, a women's section and literary criticism. Of course it attacked the Cumann Na nGaedheal Government and used very negative adjectives to describe its leading figures. That same Government added to the popularity of the new newspaper, by taking a prosecution against its Editor for seditious libel before the Military Tribunal.

This five man Military Tribunal had been introduced three months earlier in the form of an amendment to the Constitution. The new Article 2A was concerned with political crime for which the death penalty could be handed down, without appeal.

The *Irish Press* editor, Frank Gallagher had printed material about prison conditions and how harshly the police had treated IRA suspects. Some police and jurors had been murdered. Gallagher was due to appear before the Tribunal on 5 February 1932 less than a fortnight before the General Election. Gallagher defended what he had written as the truth and many witnesses backed him up. As each day's proceedings was published at length in the *Irish Press*, its circulation catapulted from 70,00 to 115,00. This case proved to be like manna from heaven for the Fianna Fáil election campaign. The verdict, handed down the day after the election, was a £100 fine on the Editor and the newspaper[10].

෧❦ ❦෧

Seán Lemass and Cardinal Hayes, chat with Eamon DeValera 1932.

DeValera broadcast to the Irish in America after the 1932 election,
via a radio link from Dublin.

CHAPTER 14

TOWARDS 1932 ELECTION

October 1929 saw the *Wall Street Crash*, when the bottom fell out of the New York Stock Market, with 12 million shares sold in one day of total panic. Financial institutions around the world collapsed as America, the creditor nation to the world, called in its loans. An economic depression hit Europe, as countries sought to protect their interests by introducing tariff barriers. Unemployment rose as manufacturing industry collapsed. As food prices fell, the Irish economy saw its agricultural exports collapse from £36 million to £14 million within six years. Unemployment shot up by 30,000 in one year, as the lack of jobs in Britain and America put a hold on emigration. In 1930, 77,000 people were getting poor law assistance. The North fared just as bad.

The adjournment debate in the Dáil at the end of December 1931 was on unemployment. Fianna Fáil decried the attempts by the Government to improve economic life in the country. However, as was usual, bitter party politics always came to the fore. Fianna Fáil wanted to raise the treatment of political prisoners, which they termed, anybody sentenced by the Military Tribunal. When Seán Lemass offered to tell Cosgrave of his own personal experiences as a political prisoner, the latter retorted, *"You can tell them on the hustings"*.

Cosgrave, in closing the debate, ranged over many of the measures that the Government had taken to improve the economy of the country. He said that peace and good order were essentials. He said the main industry in the country was agriculture. He instanced various Acts which were passed to improve matters; the Live Stock Breeding, Butter, Eggs, Dead Meat, Sugar Beet Industry, Drainage, Forestation and the Electrification of the Shannon. He noted that Seán T. O'Kelly had practically charged him with responsibility for housing conditions in Dublin. He reminded O'Kelly that he had not been a member of the Dublin Corporation since May 1922, though O'Kelly was a current member. He said that over 6,000 houses were built in Dublin with the assistance of the Government.

At the end of Cosgrave's speech, Seán Lemass replied, *"If that is the President's election speech, he can bow himself out now"*. Cosgrave replied, *"If the Deputy likes to think so, he is welcome"*[1].

Around that same time, Paddy McGilligan and the Irish High Commissioner in London, John Dulanty, met King George in Sandringham. The King expressed admiration for the way Cosgrave had fought so well, through such troubled times in Ireland. He hoped Cosgrave would be returned to power, casting doubt on whether DeValera could even be classified as an Irishman[2].

The prerogative of dissolving the Dáil, which did not have to occur until October 1932, rested with Cosgrave. As in most elections, tactics are very important and correct timing vital. The budgetary outlook for 1932 was poor, with cutbacks the order of the day. Despite the fact that the Government was bound to gain great popular kudos out of the forthcoming Eucharistic Congress, Cosgrave decided that it was better to go for the election early, rather than later. Indeed the advent of the Congress may have been a factor on his part, as he would not have wished that occasion to be marked by divisive politicking. The Eucharistic Congress was awarded to a different capital city every three years. Cosgrave had put a lot of personal effort into its awarding to Dublin, and the Government had spent a very large amount of time and energy preparing for it. It would have been the crowning occasion for Cosgrave's association with the church. However, as it transpired, it was to be DeValera who gained from the massive event.

On 29 January, Cosgrave dissolved the Dáil and announced 16 February as the election date, with 6 March the date for the new Dáil to meet. The cabinet announced that the expected reduction of 5% in garda pay would not take place. A meeting was held at the Mansion House that night, to launch the Government election campaign. Thousands cheered Cosgrave from the street into the famous Round Room. Alfie Byrne chaired proceedings and spoke first. Cosgrave then addressed the packed hall. He addressed many of the issues; no discrimination, respect for State institutions, the Government record, good relations with Britain Ireland's best customer, emergence from chaos, ability to take decisions. He played great emphasis on doctrines, which were "subversive of religion, home and country". A Fianna Fáil victory would introduce *"a field for the cultivation of those doctrines of materialism and Communism which can so effectively poison the wells of religion and national traditions...Our place in the community of nations, the recognition we have received from the Holy Father and the principle powers of the world through the establishment of legations in our capital, will disappear with the destruction of the state!"*[3]. Cosgrave did not seek to make use of the great progress the State had made in the field of international relations, probably believing that that could be used by Dev as a tool with which to beat him with, in many ways. Dev was to display his ability to read the mind of the electorate expertly by issuing his election manifesto, which appealed to a great many people. He also had not alone the tacit assistance of the IRA, but their full logistical operation during the rough campaign and their active impersonating of emigrant, sick and deceased electors.

Dev campaigned on the abolition of the Oath and the withholding of the land annuities paid to Britain under the Treaty. These annuities were payments, relating to the handing over of land to farmers under earlier Land Acts. Lemass concentrated on social and economic policies and unemployment. He said that it was the duty of the State to provide work. They would reduce higher public salaries but maintain lower ones. Seán T. O'Kelly, who was well versed in Catholic social doctrine, made use of Papal encyclicals to emphasise that Fianna Fáil was *ad idem* with church doctrine. As Dev was speaking in county Clare, the Angelus bell rang, he immediately stopped his speech and quietly recited the Angelus, as his audience did likewise[4]. He denied his party had any communistic leanings, as might have been suggested by the Catholic hierarchy's pastoral letter some months earlier. Of course Dev was able to appeal to a wide variety of voters, as he made speeches, which could promise social radicalism, while pledging that private property would be safeguarded as well by a Fianna Fáil Government, as by a Cumann na nGaedhael Government. At the same time, he maintained that the State had the right to intervene if private property was being used contrary to the interests of the community.[4a]

The *New York Times* found Cosgrave, *"cold and unromantic, with no attraction for Irish youth"*, compared with the DeValera campaign which it found *"arousing emotions and enthusiasm, strangely like those Adolph Hitler is spreading through Germany. Only those with first hand knowledge of Cosgrave's difficulties can appreciate the greatness of this little tawny-headed man who has been in office longer than any other Prime Minister in Europe"*[5]. The election overall, passed off fairly peacefully. The IRA, while having their differences with Fianna Fáil, had no choice but to back DeValera. Their slogan was, *"Put Cosgrave Out"*[6]. It was also very much on the defensive from the effects on it of Article 2A. If it ran an abstentionist campaign, it risked returning Cosgrave to power. The Army Council of the IRA changed its policy and allowed its members to participate in the Free State election, while emphasising to them that, "our objects cannot be achieved by the methods of politicians of the parties seeking election"[7]. According to Bowyer Bell, *"IRA men participated in the time honoured fashion of multiple voting of emigrants, corpses and the poor man, who is slow to reach the booth"*, all on behalf of Fianna Fáil, which provided it with the necessary voting lists. He states that some Volunteers voted as many as fifty times[8]. After the election, Seán Lemass thanked the IRA for its support[9].

DeValera, being the cunning politician that he was, cut his cloth to suit his measure in the election campaign. Though he would abolish the Oath, there was no mention of the Republic or any thought of constitutional changes, without an additional mandate. He would abolish the land annuities and promote self-sufficiency on the land, through the promotion of tillage. He would protect Irish industry by establishing tariffs on imports. The result was not in any sense overwhelming in the circumstances, but it did offer the opportunity to *"Put Cosgrave Out"*, by a little temporary manoeuvring with the Labour Party. The *Irish Times* had little doubt as to which party, it wished to win the election, editorialising on Election Day: *"...The fact that today the Free State can be numbered among the most prosperous countries in Europe, is a tribute to the devoted work that has been done against heavy odds by President Cosgrave and his colleagues"*. It spoke about the great diplomatic advances that had been made in recent years. Then it dealt with Fianna Fáil, saying, *"The party that is offering itself as an alternative, advances a policy of sheer negation...only constructive plank is high tariffs which will impoverish the country...there can only be one choice for an intelligent voter. Fianna Fáil has an efficient organisation and will poll every available vote. Its policy appeals to younger and irresponsible elements"*.

By 18 February some results were in, with the figures for some leading personalities being compared with the two previous elections:

Name	1932	9/1927	6/1927
Cosgrave	18,125	7,395	-
DeValera	12,507	13,903	13,025
Blythe	7,524	7,171	5,532
Redmond	7,276	6,633	7,687
Byrne, Alfie	18,117	11,844	17,781
O'Kelly, Seán T.	9,176	6,968	6,040
Lemass	10,426	11,240	8,582

The final result was:

Cumann Na nGaedheal	57
Fianna Fáil	72
Labour	13
Independents	7
Farmers	4

The *Irish Independent* headline reported a, "Complex Political Situation",

"Seeking Compromise to avoid effect of election Deadlock",

"Mr. DeValera plans for Government".

The indecisiveness of the Fianna Fáil victory, assisted in calming the transitional period, between the election and the formation of the new government.

Shortly before the take-over of power, Fianna Fáil, in the persons of DeValera and Seán T. O'Kelly, met with Archbishop Byrne to ensure his good offices for the transition. Some of the party had opposed this meeting, on the basis that the bishops had been no friends of Fianna Fáil. But DeValera proved to be as keen as Cosgrave to have the hierarchy on side, and offer them full government consultation.

James Dillon, who voted for Dev in the Dáil, has left a vivid description of that day in 1932; *"The feeling in Dáil Éireann when I first arrived in it in 1932 was quite extraordinary. A very considerable number of the Fianna Fáil party arrived in the Dáil on the day that Mr DeValera was first elected, armed to the teeth. They thought there was going to be a putsch; that if Mr. DeValera was elected, Mr. Cosgrave wouldn't hand over the Government. They had a completely illusory notion of the standards and character of Mr. Cosgrave, who of course, had brought – indeed forced – Fianna Fáil into the Dáil Éireann in order to establish normal political functioning in the coutry"*[10].

WT Cosgrave and his Ministers decided that their role would be in opposition. Cosgrave proposed to let Fianna Fáil and Labour, who had been attacking his politics for the previous ten years, work for prosperity and better prices. He promised to assist them in every way he could and if they succeeded, he would take off his cap to them. He appeared completely unperturbed, and rather in high spirits by the situation. He hoped that the Government would proceed in a regular way, if it desired to remove the Oath, and negotiate with Great Britain on the matter. He offered to assist in every way, in anything that would be of value to the people.

Arrangements for the setting up of a new Government appeared to be running smoothly, with Labour and Fianna Fáil negotiating an understanding. Labour would support Fianna Fáil outside the Government. Seán T. O'Kelly and Gerard Boland accompanied Dev in the negotiations. Labour had Tom Johnson, William Norton and William Davin. Johnson himself had lost his seat in the election.

The two parties agreed a programme for:

A maintenance scheme for 80,000 unemployed.

Building of 40,000 houses.

A pension scheme for widows and orphans[11].

COUP D'ETAT?

On 10 February at Wynn's Hotel in Dublin, a meeting had taken place to organise an ex-army officers association. One week later a formal *Army Comrades Association* was formed[12]. On the morning of 26 February, the *Irish Press* newspaper caused consternation, by editorialising on measures in hand by disaffected groups, to stage a *coup d'etat*, preventing Fianna Fáil forming a government. The paper said:

"On Wednesday, commenting on the announcement that the members of the Government definitely intend to go into opposition, we expressed the hope that the decision would allay the rumour which has been in circulation about the activities of certain members of the outgoing government Ministry. Our hope has not been realised and are arousing considerable anxiety among a section of the public in Dublin. They are to the effect that two Ministers, a well-known member of the Cumann an nGaedheal party and some others, are engaged in a movement to obstruct the transfer of government to Fianna Fáil. They are alleged to have formed a secret organisation for this purpose among Free State army pensioners, to whom they appeal, it is said, on the grounds that a Fianna Fáil government would be committed to the revision of army pensions".

WT Cosgrave reacted immediately to the editorial deeming the suggestion, *"grossly untrue…and clearly mischievous. Its origin can only be explained by a disordered imagination or a guilty conscience. The Ministers and army pensioners have given the best years of their lives to vindicating the right of the people of Ireland to choose the Government".* Mr. Blythe called the editorial *"utterly absurd and untrue".*

During the resumed election campaign in Leitrim-Sligo, which had been postponed due to the sudden death of a candidate, Mr. Hogan, Minister of Agriculture assured the electorate that undertakings had been given to Fianna Fáil, that the Army, Civic Guard and ex-servicemen would be obedient servants of the established government.

It would indeed have been surprising, if the possibility of an attempt to prevent Fianna Fáil coming to power had not occurred to some people, who had reason to fear such an eventuality. Britain certainly could not have welcomed the advent of their *bete noir* to power[13].

Dev met General O'Duffy, head of the Gardai, and David Neligan head of Special Branch, and assured them that they had nothing to fear, as long as they operated in a professional manner. David Neligan reported in 1970 that the unreliable Eoin O'Duffy had planned a coup in late 1931[14]. John Regan explores the possibility of certain officers and civil servants, who might have had personal reasons for fearing a Fianna Fáil government, being involved in taking soundings about a coup[15]. But if so, there were few takers and an orderly transfer of power went ahead smoothly.

Gerry Boland had no doubt but that a coup was mooted by army and ex-servicemen and reported Fianna Fáil men being armed in the Dáil[16]. Seán Lemass said about the guns, *"That is all nonsense"*. Lemass however was certain that there was a strong effort by a number of army officers, to prevent Fianna Fáil taking over. He said circulars went around with officers names attached, urging action. Lemass then said that, *"Mr. Cosgrave must have known of these circulars and before we became ministers, we were given armed guards to protect us...It is a tribute to WT Cosgrave and to those associated with him, because there were some ministers who were mixed up with this idea of preventing a takeover, and they would have nothing to do with it. I suppose it is a remarkable thing, that ten years after the Civil War that the Party that lost the war, had by peaceful process, acquired political power and became the government of the State"*[17].

John Horgan writes that when some few years earlier Lemass was being criticised for his mode of public speaking, he adopted Cosgrave's style, clipped and direct without long rambling sentences[18].

Cosgrave told the *New York Times* during the interregnum, that he would have preferred as President one of DeValera's lieutenants, like Seán Lemass, whom he regarded as a practical politician, rather than DeValera, whom he looked upon as an impractical dreamer and a coiner of dangerous phrases[19]. Joe Lee has written, *"And Cosgrave would do the ship of state one final service, by the manner in which he quietly left the bridge and handed over the wheel to the rival captain. Bitter though it was in party terms – indeed precisely because it was so bitter in party terms - it was his finest hour"*[20]. Diarmaid Ferriter, unsurprisingly, appears to disagree, writing that Lee *"seems to imply that Cosgrave should be applauded for not staging a coup to prevent Fianna Fáil from taking power in 1932"*[21].

On the morning of the new Dáil meeting, Dev attended the votive mass at the Pro Cathedral. He made his way to the Dáil in the afternoon, fearful that after what he had considered a *coup d'etat* in 1922, there might not be a peaceful transfer of power[22]. Though he was unarmed, his son Vivion, who accompanied him, was armed.

According to Seán Farragher, the revolver, which Vivion carried, had belonged to Cathal Brugha and was stored in secret at Blackrock College[23].

On 9 March Dev was nominated as President of the Executive Council by Michael Kilroy, who said, *"the people had chosen him as their spokesman. Deputy DeValera was the leader of the national advance since 1916 and the people have decided to go forward again under his guidance. I pray that God will give him health and strength to carry out the programme he has for so long and so valiantly fought for, and that he may bring to our people freedom and happiness, prosperity and unity"*. Oscar Traynor seconded.

A vote was called when WT Cosgrave challenged the nomination. It resulted in 81 for and 68 against. Labour, two Farmer T.D's and one Independent, James Dillon, supported the election of DeValera as President. James Dillon, who represented Donegal, said that the people had chosen Dev as their leader and he voted accordingly[24].

The Governor General, James MacNeill, knowing Dev's aversion to his official role in the proceedings, made the journey to Leinster House, to spare Dev the embarrassment of going to the Viceregal Lodge, and appointed him.

The new President named his Cabinet:

The President, Department of External Affairs.

Deputy Seán T. O'Kelly, Vice-President, Department of Local Government and Public Health.

Deputy Thomas Derrig, Department of Education.

Deputy Patrick J. Ruttledge, Department of Lands and Fisheries.

Deputy James Geoghegan, Department of Justice.

Deputy Seán F. Lemass, Department of Industry and Commerce.

Deputy Seán MacEntee, Department of Finance.

Deputy James Ryan, Department of Agriculture.

Deputy Frank Aiken, Department of Defence.

Dev said, *"We heard of frightful things that would happen the moment the Fianna Fáil Government came into power. We have no evidence of those things...We have had a peaceful change of Government"*[25]. The next day Dev saw all the secretaries of the departments and assured them that he intended to make no major changes. He did transfer Maurice Moynihan from Finance to act as his own Private Secretary. He reinstated his personal secretary Kathleen O'Connell as a civil servant.

DeValera broadcast to the USA, reiterating his intention to remove the Oath and withhold land annuities. He said, *"Our annual payments to England are heavier upon us than a payment annually of £330 million would be on Britain, and that is a sum ten times as great as Britain's annual debt payments to the United States. My desire has been to bring about the friendliest relations between Britain and Ireland, but I know that the only sure foundation for such relations and for a lasting peace is justice and the recognition of the right of our people to be free. That is what I strove for from 1919 to 1921, when President of the Republic and that is what I intend now to strive for"*[26].

One of the most pleasant aspects of becoming legitimate and on the cusp of attaining power, for Dev on a personal basis, was that he could resume official attendance at functions at Blackrock College, after an absence of almost ten years. Fianna Fáil had undertaken a policy of not fraternising with members of the Free State Government, if at all possible. WT Cosgrave had become the regular guest of honour at Blackrock during his tenure of office. The press reports of the College Sports in 1931 included his name, though the person most specially welcomed there by the President Dr. John Charles McQuaid, was General Eoin O'Duffy[27].

The new Government sent a message of 'respectful homage and good wishes' to Pope Pius IX, assuring him of *"our intention to maintain with the Holy See that intimate and cordial relationship, which has become the tradition of Irish people"*[28]. Dev was intent on demonstrating that he and his people were no less filial to the Catholic Church than the outgoing Government. His motives were both religious and political. Mary Bromage described her icon at this time: *"With his religion went a puritanical morality which made him indifferent to taunts for airing his views in Leinster House. A bar was connected with the members' dining room. He questioned whether they could be separated or the bar abolished altogether. He himself, it was said, neither drank nor smoked...His strictures extended beyond the evils of drink to the evils of jazz, the evils of betting on the races, the dangers from indecent books"*[29].

IRA PRISONERS RELEASED

One of the first actions taken by the new Government was the immediate release of twenty prisoners from Mountjoy Jail. Frank Aiken with the Minister for Justice, James Geoghegan, a former Cumann na nGaedheal supporter, went to Arbour Hill prison to consult with IRA leaders. Those released included Frank Ryan and George Gilmore. Within a few days, for the first time in many years, several battalions of IRA men marched through Dublin to a large demonstration at College Green, to welcome home the prisoners. Leaders of both the IRA and Saor Éire addressed the large crowd [30]. Towards the end of the proceedings, Seán MacBride, who was on the platform party with his mother, Maud Gonne MacBride, cautioned against the euphoria of the occasion, saying, *"We must remember that while the day of coercion has passed for a time, the task we have set ourselves has not yet been achieved"*.

Dev had hoped that he could cajole the IRA to agree to a gradual dismantling of the provisions of the Treaty. But this proved impossible as he gradually and painfully discovered in talks with Seán Russell and later George Gilmore. Dev soon made it clear in the Dáil that there would only be one army in the State and he expected the IRA to obey that law. He announced plans to end the Oath, end the payment of land annuities and revoke Article 2A. He declared that the country was too small for Partition to remain. Membership of the IRA suddenly became fashionable as it was inundated with new recruits. Many felt that it would be incorporated into the national army. Frank Aiken offered Seán MacBride a commission in the army. MacBride felt insulted and rejected the offer immediately. However he soon accepted a job as sub editor in the *Irish Press*[31]. Maude Gonne soon felt that DeValera was reneging on his promises, spying and arresting members of the IRA. She reinstated her street activities, protesting against the holding of political prisoners, in her *Women's Prisoners Protection League*.

The IRA made a lot of the early running in inter-party rivalry during 1932, when essentially, as Frank Ryan declared their attitude to Cumann na nGaedheal as, *"No matter what anyone says to the contrary, while we have fists, and boots to use and guns, if necessary, we will not allow free speech to traitors"*. In May 1932, WT Cosgrave was shouted down at a meeting of his election workers in Cork. Patrick Lindsay writes, *"If it had not been for the presence and support of the Blueshirts, public meetings organised by Cumann na nGaedheal and the Centre Party could not have been held in 1932 and 1933, such was the ferocity of the organised conspiracy against these meetings. The supporters of Fianna Fáil and the IRA, many of the latter just recently released from jail, some of whom had been convicted of very serious offences, set out deliberately and with malice to smash up these meetings, to howl down men like WT Cosgrave, Paddy McGilligan and Patrick Hogan, who had given the best years of their lives to establishing a strong democracy in this country. DeValera, like the Pontius Pilate he could be, made no attempt to stop this happening"*[32]. Dev took several important measures to weaken the IRA. He introduced pensions for those who fought on the Anti-Treaty side in the civil war. He set up a new uniformed Army Volunteer Reserve that ex-IRA members could join. He also introduced about 600 ex-IRA men as non-uniformed members of the Gardai. These were known as Broy Harriers, after their commander Eamon Broy.

ଵଈ ଈଵ

IRA leader Frank Ryan. *IRA man to Garda Commander, Eamon Broy.*

DeValera addresses League of Nations.

CHAPTER 15

DeVALERA IN GOVERNMENT

DeValera wasted little time in tackling the issues that he had long campaigned on. As early as 12 March 1932 the cabinet minute reports, "It was decided that the Attorney General should submit heads of a Bill having the subject the removal of the obligation on members of the Oireachtas to take and subscribe to the Oath, specifically in Article 17 of the Constitution. It was agreed that it was not necessary that any intimation should be made to the British Government[1]. Dev laid out quite clearly his aims for the country. He wanted, "Ireland United, Ireland Free, Ireland Self-supporting and Self-reliant, Ireland speaking her own tongue, giving to the world her ancient Christian Gaelic culture. These are the ideals to which enthusiastic young Irish people are devoting their energies"[2].

He introduced a Bill to abolish the oath of allegiance on 20 April. Cosgrave described the Bill as one of the greatest pieces of political chicanery in history, saying that the Treaty was based on the confidence of mutual respect in each other's good faith, *"Two of the greatest Irishmen who ever lived, signed it and never believed that their signatures would be repudiated"*. Cosgrave added that the presence on the opposite benches of over 70 T.D's, was ample proof for him personally, and the late administration that their persuasive methods bore fruit. He acknowledged that it had been open to his government to enact this measure unilaterally, but though it would have been legal, it would have been dishonourable and a breech of faith. Cosgrave declared that the British Commonwealth of Nations was as far removed from the British Empire of his boyhood, as they were from the battle of Waterloo. If he was offered the unity of the country, with even less powers than they currently had, or a Republic for the Free State, he would plank for the former. He believed that one could advance with a united State, however different the views politically may be; but if such a division was made, as would forever divide off a very important portion of our country, then what do Irish national aspirations mean?. He did not see that the economy of the country was going to be assisted by the measure. Britain purchased £30 million worth of goods annually and took 90% of exports. That trade was vulnerable. Britain provided a great market for tourism. In the election Fianna Fáil promised a plan and a solution for unemployment". Cosgrave said that all other governments, including that of Hindenburg, Hoover, Britain, France and even Signor Mussolini, the Duce, had failed to cure unemployment[3].

The Bill was passed on 19 May in the Dáil. The Senate exercised its constitutional prerogative and rejected it. The Bill was then delayed until the following year. Dev was not pleased and announced his intention of abolishing the Senate.

DEV AT LEAGUE OF NATIONS 1932-1938

The ground work done by Cosgrave's Government paved the way for Dev to be entitled to take the office of the Presidency of the 13th Assembly of the League of Nations at Geneva in September 1932, and thus increase his international standing. He recognised that this would also be politically advantageous at home. It was a difficult time for the League, as the Japanese were flouting the Covenant of the League by their invasion of Manchuria. Though he had opposed the League in America in 1919, Dev went to Geneva, where according to his authorised biography "there was no handclap to welcome him. The formal politeness customarily shown to any chairman was absent"[4]. He did not accept a script provided but prepared his own speech, which was very well received and reported around the world. He said:

"Out beyond the walls of this Assembly, there is the public opinion of the world, and if the League is to prosper, or even survive, it must retain the support and confidence of that public opinion as a whole. The one effective way of silencing criticism of the League is to show unmistakeably that the Covenant of the League is a solemn pact, the obligations of which no State great or small, will find it possible to ignore"[5]. He later showed his independence, when in 1934 he voted for the admission of Russia to the League, recognising that the absence of the major powers from the League diminished its authority. During the debate, Dev said, *"Christians believe that the one hope of securing peace among men is to be found in obedience to the primary Christian commandment, that men should love one another for God's sake. I urge the Russian Government to proclaim that the rights and liberty of conscience shall henceforth be the rights of the nationals of all countries residing in Russia and of the Russian people"[5a].*

After the Italian invasion of Abyssinia, despite that country offering important concessions to appease Mussolini, Dev told the League in September 1935, *"Peace is dependent on the will of the great states. All the small states can do, if the statesmen of the greater states fail in their duty, is resolutely to determine that they will not become the tools of any great power, and that they will resist with whatever strength they may possess, every attempt to force them into a war against their will"[6].* Dev supported economic sanctions against the aggressor and also suggested military sanctions. One year later at the League, he admitted that economic sanctions had failed saying, *"We must now confess publicly that we must abandon the victim to his fate. It is a sad confession, as well as a bitter one. It is the fulfillment of the worst predictions of all who decried the League and said it would not succeed"[7].*

Dev later changed tack and adopted appeasement as a viable policy. He favoured problems being solved by conciliation if possible and if not, by arbitration. He hoped that neutrality could protect small nations. He refused to see the Spanish civil war as a religious affair, and discouraged Irishmen from becoming involved, as General Eoin O'Duffy led an Irish Brigade to fight for Franco, while others fought for the opposite side.

On 12 September 1938 Dev was elected the 19th President of the League. It was a dangerous moment in European history as Germany threatened Czechoslovakia. He told the General Assembly, *"We have been unable to bend our wills to sacrifice selfish advantage even when it conflicts with justice to others. We have been unable, no matter on what side we are, to apply to others the law we insist in having applied to ourselves. All history tells us that, in the long run, to be just is to be truly wise. But we seem unable to apply the lessons"*[8].

Dev supported Neville Chamberlain's attempt to avoid war, but warned him that if he failed, he would be blamed. Dev had some sympathy with Hitler's claim to the lands of the Sudetan, forfeited in the Treaty of Versailles, saying, *"The circumstances of war are such that the settlements imposed by it are inevitably unjust"*. When Chamberlain made a desperate attempt to avoid war by going to meet Hitler, Dev broadcast from Geneva saying that Chamberlain was putting peace before pride. He said, *"Not always will we have someone do what Mr Chamberlain has done, that is to go to see Hitler at Berchtesgaden on 15 September and a week later on 22nd at Gosesburg, and we shall find that we shall have had one crisis too many"*[9].

As Chamberlain prepared to go to meet Hitler at Munich, Dev telegraphed, *"Let nothing daunt you or deflect you in your effort to secure peace. The tens of millions of innocent people on both sides, who have no cause against each other but who are in danger of being hurled against each other, with no alternative but mutual slaughter, are praying that your efforts may find a way of saving them from a terrible doom"*[10].

WB Yeats wrote to his friend Lady Wellesley on 21 September, *"I am in complete agreement with what DeValera said at Geneva yesterday. Except that I can see no hope in his remedy. The armed mobs of Europe will now tare (sic) each other into pieces and the innocent will perish in the scuffle (sic)"*[11].

As Chamberlain signed the 'Munich Agreement' on 30 September 1938, Dev described him at Geneva as a *"knight of peace who had attained the highest peak of human greatness and a glory greater than all of the conquerors"*. It appeared that war had been averted and in Dev's concluding speech to the League, he said that the League with all its acknowledged shortcomings could be a basis on which to raise a genuine international organisation for the future.

Of course Dev naturally hoped that his investment in Chamberlain might result in movement on the North. On his way home from Geneva, Dev called on Chamberlain who was then enjoying great popularity. Dev argued that the time to act on Partition was at hand and that it had to be a Conservative Government, which acted decisively. The Liberals and Labour would not make trouble. Chamberlain was not convinced. Back in Dublin Dev again launched a publicity offensive on Partition, saying, *"Irish Leaders will never be able to get the Irish people to co-operate with Great Britain while Partition remains. I wouldn't attempt it myself, for I know I should fail"*[12]. He told the North to Keep your local Parliament with its local powers, but treat the Nationalists fairly and transfer the powers currently reserved to an English Parliament to an All-Ireland Parliament.

Neville Chamberlain extreme left, meets with Dictators Hitler and Mussolini.

On campaign trail, 1932.   *Eucharistic Congress Dublin, 1932.*

Dev's regular exposure at the League in Geneva played an important domestic role in establishing himself and Ireland as important on the international stage, despite the ultimate failure of the League to prevent the outbreak of the second World War.

EUCHARISTIC CONGRESS

The Eucharistic Congress in June 1932, offered Dev a welcome opportunity to demonstrate his unflinching allegiance to the Catholic Church. It would allow him to resume his personal and public interaction with leading members of the Hierarchy, after so many years of being an 'outcast' from that milieu. It was a role that he genuinely relished from a political and personally religious point of view. The canopy-bearers in a procession of the Blessed Sacrament at the main ceremony were, President DeValera, Mr. S.T O'Kelly, (Vice-president), Mr. Frank Fahy (Ceann Comhairle), Mr. W.T. Cosgrave, the Chief Justice, Mr. T.W. Westropp-Bennett (Chairman of the Senate), Senator Seán Farren, Mr. A. Byrne TD. (Lord Mayor of Dublin); the Mayors of Limerick, Waterford, Drogheda, Kilkenny, Clonmel, Wexford and Sligo; Count John McCormack, Mr. J. Devlin M.P., Mr. Cahir Healy M.P., Senator Campbell K.C., Sir Joseph Glynn. Mr T. McLoughlin, Dr. Coffey and Mr. J.J. Shiel[13]. A lavish State reception was organised for the dignitaries[14]. The Congress was a major diplomatic, social and political success for Dev[15]. All the months of planning by the Cosgrave Government played into the hands of their greatest enemy, as Irish Catholicism took centre stage. One million people attended Mass in the Phoenix Park and half a million attended Benediction on O'Connell Bridge.

Dev always remained friendly with the religious he had encountered during his earlier career. These included Jesuits, Dominicans and Carmelites. He spent a week every year at Mount Mellary with the Cistercian monks. But of course it was with the Holy Ghost Fathers that he was most friendly after his days at Blackrock. At Maynooth he was a friend of Michael Browne who became Bishop of Galway in 1937. Seán MacEntee's Dominican brother in law, Michael Browne, became a Cardinal, thus giving Dev another powerful insider advocate to the Church, which added to his confidence in dealing with it. He even felt confident enough to oppose the Knights of St. Columbanus, which had been set up in Belfast in 1915 and moved to Dublin in 1922. Dev dissuaded members of Fianna Fáil from joining the Knights, re-emphasising his dislike of secret organisations[16].

UPWARD MOBILITY

When the DeValeras left Greystones, they lived at 18 Claremount Road in Sandymount. In 1925 they moved a short distance to Elm Villa, a mock castle structure between Sandymount Avenue and Serpentine Avenue. Dev's son Terry writes of "fog-ridden Sandymount and that awful house which I am convinced was haunted"[17]. On 12 March 1930 they moved to Springville on Cross Avenue in Blackrock. Dev moved again in September 1933 to another house on Cross Avenue, called Bellevue.

It had been the home of the Countess of Brandon and was a large house with long corridors and huge bedrooms. It was surrounded by some four to five acres, with a long walk around the perimeter[18]. It bordered on Willow Park School and Dunamace, which had been the home of Kevin O'Higgins[19]. The family made one more move in 1940 to another house on Cross Avenue, called Herberton. In the 2007 RTE radio series on *Judging Dev*, Finola Kennedy, who was familiar with Dev's three homes on Cross Avenue, recounted that "Dev double crossed Cross Avenue over the years as he moved three times to ever more impressive houses. They were all absolutely magnificent".

The programme appeared to suggest that while Dev preached frugality for the masses, he himself lived in very comfortable and elegant surroundings, accepting a social hierarchy with reciprocal obligations downwards[20.]. He did little entertaining at home. His main visitors were close political friends such as Jim Ryan, Frank Aiken and Gerry Boland[21].

EYE OPERATION MARCH 1933

Even at the early stage of 1933, Dev's eyesight gave major cause for concern as he went to Switzerland for treatment. It was around that time that Malcolm MacDonald sent him a hand-written letter of good wishes:

Dear Mr. DeValera,

This is just a note to say how glad I am to hear that your eye operation is safely over. I do hope that you will make a steady recovery from it, and that the result will soon see a great improvement in your eyesight.

Of course do not bother to acknowledge this. It is just a note of sincere relief and good wishes.

Yours sincerely,

Malcolm MacDonald

(Secretary of State Dominions)[22].

THE ECONOMIC WAR

On 22 March 1932 DeValera introduced a Bill to remove the Annuities. These were financial agreements with the British Treasury, which bound the Irish Government to transfer the full amount of land purchases under the Land Acts, which bought out landlords and transferred their lands to tenant farmers. The agreements were signed in February 1923 and March 1926. The agreement was not published until April 1932, when Dev had assumed power. He repudiated their validity, saying that the British Parliament never approved them nor did Dáil Éireann. He added, "In justice, Ireland is under no debt to Great Britain"[22a]. Dev had been buoyed in his action by a legal opinion from a former Unionist and Senior Counsel, Arthur Meridith[23].

DeValera had been determined to keep the removal of the Oath and the matter of the Land Annuities separate. On 6 June JH Thomas, the Parliamentary Secretary for the Dominions and very hostile to Dev, together with Lord Hailsham, Minister of War arrived in Dublin for discussions on the annuities. Two days later Dev and Seán T. O'Kelly went to London to meet the Prime Minister, Ramsay MacDonald and other Ministers, including Stanley Baldwin. Dev would brook no negotiations on the Oath. They discussed arbitration on the annuities. But they differed on the composition of the arbiters. On 1 July Dev defaulted on the land annuity payments.

Almost immediately Britain introduced an Irish Emergency Duties Bill imposing tariffs on Irish imports to Britain. Seán Lemass, Seán T. O'Kelly and James Ryan were then en route to Ottawa for an Imperial Conference. Lemass as Minister of Industry and Commerce wrote immediately that they should retaliate on British coal imports. Dev instructed the delegates not to attend the Imperial Conference. He retaliated with duties on British goods and the Economic War commenced. William Norton facilitated an early meeting between Dev and Ramsay MacDonald. They agreed that the matter had to be settled by arbitration or negotiation. In the meantime MacDonald demanded payment of the annuities then held in a suspense account. Dev refused. The land annuities were worth £4 in 1932.

A document sent by the Department of External Affairs to Seán Lester at Geneva for transmission to Sir Eric Drummond, Secretary General of the League of Nations on 12 August 1931, outlined the factual situation of Irish exports dependency on Britain. An extract reads:

"The geographical situation of the Irish Free State results in dependence to a marked degree on the British market for the absorption of its exports. Thus, in the year 1929 when exports and re-exports were valued at £47,870,000, goods to the value of £44,172,000 or 92% of the total export trade were exported to Great Britain and Northern Ireland. In 1930 these markets took goods to the value of £41,781,000 out of an export trade valued at £45,731,000 or 91% of the total. The bulk of the export trade consists of live cattle, pigs, sheep, and various classes of foodstuffs;. It is to be observed therefore that the effects of the world depression reaches the Irish Free State mainly through its principal market - Great Britain..."[24].

The Economic War was bound to have devastating affects on Irish people, but Dev believed that they were prepared to suffer for their national dignity. On 5 August he told the Dáil that the government was *"not expecting to have omelettes without cracking eggs"*[25]. Dev was correct, as many Irish people did support him for standing up to bullying from Britain. Seán Lemass, however, wrote ominously, *"I do not think it can be denied that we are facing a crisis as grave as that of 1847, and I feel strongly that our present efforts are totally inadequate to deal with it...a collapse of our economic position is in sight"*[26]. But Britain was also being affected by the situation and willing to negotiate.

DeValera addressed many countrywide meetings to explain the economic war with the UK.

Local anti-annuities agitation around the country, had occured earlier with 11% uncollected in 1931. By 1933 this had risen to 57% and 97% in 1934. Dev reacted by reducing the annuities by 50% and began to use the money collected for normal government usage. This eased Government finances and illustrated that Dev had no intention of giving way to Britain on the matter. The rigid financial control of WT Cosgrave's earlier governments in controlling the balance of payments had left the country with the unusual status of being a creditor country[27].

The British refused to see Dev's economic and political moves separately and treated his constitutional moves with his economic policy. Their Attorney General said, *"It is not money that stands in the way of peace. There is something bigger and deeper. Does Mr. DeValera want to be a partner in the Empire, or is he pursuing the will-of-the-wisp of a Republic?"*[28].

In presumably feigned exasperation, Dev wrote to JH Thomas in July saying, *"I am at a loss to understand the reasons for your insistence that the Treaty and the Irish Free State's membership of the British Commonwealth must be accepted as the basis for any discussion directed to the termination of the present deadlock, since these matters have not been at issue in the financial dispute between the two Governments"*[29].

As cattle exports to Britain were worst affected, Dev sought to create a national movement and get the farmers to grow more tillage to become more self-sufficient, thereby reducing the needs for imports. He travelled the country holding rallies to whip up enthusiasm. He also tried to get the British to agree meaningful arbitration or negotiation. He accused them of an artificial restriction on the selection of arbitrators and rejecting his agreement to deposit the annuities in a Bank for International Settlements, pending negotiation. JH Thomas had wanted Dev to agree that Britain would get this money, even if negotiations failed. It was clear that the British were playing hardball. Clare Willis writes, *"DeValera's trade and industry policies, and his decision to withhold the land annuities provoked a bitter economic war with Britain. But the widely felt sense of grievance at the economic state in which the country had been left by Britain, ensured that he continued to receive support for his strategy of setting Ireland free from the British market"*[30].

Though Dev had been at pains to demonstrate his Catholic bonafides with the clergy and hierarchy, he had to listen, in person, to severe criticism from Cardinal MacRory on 15 August 1932 at Slane. The Cardinal said it was 'a shame and a sin' to prosecute the economic war with Britain without attempting to negotiate a settlement[31]. Other bishops too criticised him but the majority did not. Many people felt that it was economic suicide to play hard and fast against one of the strongest economies in the world. Dev had little interest in seeking a financial end to the economic war because for him the essence of the problem was political. A jaundiced British view of Dev was, *"As long as this obstinate fanatic remains in power, the chances of a settlement being reached are negligible...his exploits during the Irish rebellion have given him the character of a saint in the eyes of many Irishmen, and added to this, is the Irish love of a fight and enjoyment of martyrdom"*[32].

GOVERNOR GENERAL

Meantime, despite the Governor General's desire to be tactful with the new Government, problems continued to arise, which made him feel snubbed by Ministers. These came to a head before and during the Eucharistic Congress, when he as representative of the King was sidelined. He requested permission to send out invitations for the Congress and when this was not forthcoming, he proceeded against direct advice. Governor General MacNeill's correspondence with the Government was published creating a crisis. The Secretary of the External Affairs, JP Walshe, wrote that the Governor refused to resign and that he intended to send a letter to the King and was considering going to see the King[33]. Dev decided that he had to be removed from office. He requested the King to end MacNeill's appointment as the King's representative in the Irish Free State and be replaced by Hugh Kennedy the Chief Justice.

In the meantime, Ramsay MacDonald outlined his frustration with Dev in a letter to the Archbishop of York on 13 September, as he wrote that DeValera had a *"mentality, which simply baffles one in its lack of reason. Whatever he may have said to one or two people who have gone to him strenuously desiring peace, the position is that where we have tried to get him to face the real facts of the situation, he refuses to do so, and his generalities about goodwill have no existence in reality. His undisclosed actions, although some of them came out rather in unpleasant prominence during the Eucharistic Congress i.e. the MacNeill affair, really are the key to his mind. He will do nothing except what is a step to an Irish Republic and is unashamedly a complete prisoner to the Irish Republican Army...we are doing everything we can to get something done, but up to now, Dev does not budge"*[34].

It took some months for the King to comply with Dev's request, but he did so from 1 November. This created a problem as to who would give royal assent to Bills, or be involved in dissolution of parliament. Dev sought to get Hugh Kennedy the Chief Justice to act *pro tem* but he demurred saying that such a move could damage the judiciary. Eventually Kennedy recommended a strategy to Dev, which he adopted. When an Appropriations Bill had to be signed by 30 November, Dev advised the King to appoint a 1916 veteran named Domhnall O'Buachalla, which he did. The latter, a shopkeeper, never moved into the Vice Regal lodge and did not appear officially in public, as the office was allowed to fade away over the next four years. The salary paid to O'Buachalla fitted into Dev's attempts at public frugality, as the new man was paid £2,000 per annum in contrast to MacNeill's £24,000 and Dev's salary of £1,700[35]. One of DeValera's earliest decisions was to announce a reduction in salaries for the government personnel. His salary was reduced from £2,500 to £1,700 and that of his ministers from £1,700 to £1,000. The equivalent figures payable in the North were £3,200 and £2,000[36].

The Dominion office in London made it clear in October that the British were in no mood to accept Dev's constitutional or economic policies. It wanted Dev to recognise the validity of the Treaty, acceptance of various financial agreements, non-pursuance of the Oath Bill and suitable arrangements in accordance with the Treaty, when MacNeill relinquished his post of Governor General[37].

Dev felt under great pressure as he attacked the Opposition for tacitly supporting the British stance. He said in the Dáil that *"the present British Government, pressed forward as it is by certain anti-Irish feeling in Britain and supported by the attitude of a minority in this country, is not prepared to examine this position on its merits or to yield to claims of simple justice"*[38]. The ill feeling between the Opposition in the Dáil and the Government was palpable. Cosgrave felt that the Government might be brought down by the economic crisis and the British hoped for that outcome. Dev felt aggrieved by the political opposition, as he was achieving no success for his new policies with the British. He also however began to consider that he might come under attack from the Army Comrades Association (ACA), which was related to Cumann Na nGaedheal. Its new leader, a brother of the assassinated Kevin O'Higgins had said, *"Our objectives are peace. We are an army of peace. Policy may, however, not be able to control circumstances. If policy cannot control circumstances in the future, then policy in the future must be directed to some extent by circumstances"*[39]. Dev was fighting for his political life and used the dire situation to its utmost, as he told the Fianna Fáil Ard Fheis on 8 November 1932, *"If the British Government should succeed in beating us in this fight, then you would have no freedom, because at every step they could threaten you again and force you again to obey the British. What is involved is whether the Irish nation is going to be free or not"*. Dev's politics were about independence rather than economics. Campaigns against British produce were rife around the country, with the slogan, *"Burn everything British except their coal"* commonplace. The IRA hijacked a consignment of Bass at the docks in Dublin and dumped it into the Liffey. Frank Ryan declared that the IRA campaign of disrupting Cumann Na nGaedheal meetings was based on the principle that there would be, *"No free speech for traitors"*.

In December, France, Belgium and Hungary defaulted on war debt payments to the USA. Britain paid her debt of $95 million on time. To offset American public opinion, Dev announced that the Irish Free State would immediately repay the Republican loan, which he had raised in the USA in 1919. He also added that a 25% addition would also be paid. The loan was not supposed to be repaid until Ireland became an internationally recognised Republic.

WB Yeats prefaced an interview with the *New York Times Magazine* by stating, *"I am a Cosgrave man, but I believe that DeValera is dead right in his dispute with Great Britain. Cosgrave and DeValera do not disagree on objectives... Dev has a right aim, but whether Ireland can stand the racket or not is a ticklish question"*[40]. After Yeats met Dev about the Abbey Theatre, he wrote to Olivia Shakespeare on 9 March 1933, *"I was impressed by his simplicity and honesty, though we differed throughout". It was a curious experience, each recognised the other's point of view completely. I had gone there full of suspicion but my suspicion vanished at once"[41]*. Later in July 1933 Yeats diagnosed the difference between Fianna Fáil and Cumann na nGaedheal writing, *"what I have seen of the present Government, I get a sense of vigour and sincerity, very unlike the old Government party in the Senate, who left upon the mind an impression of something warm, damp and solid, middleclass democracy at its worst"[42]*.

In the Senate, Oliver St. John Gogarty, speaking on the Emergency Imposition of Duties Bill 1932, assailed Dev as *"the voice of a mathematical madhouse"*. He continued in typical overblown rhetoric; *"Since the betrayal of Kinsale by Don Juan Del Aquila there has never been a calamity comparable to the calamity that our Spaniard has brought on the country this month. The President ran the Irish treasureship on the rocks, in spite of many warnings from the Seánad and he wants it to be applauded because he gets away in the lifeboat with a quarter of beef and a lump of coal. He cost Ireland the blood of Collins, he broke the heart of Arthur Griffith and he has now broken the heart of Ireland itself"*.

James Dillon, who had supported Dev, now joined a National Centre Party with disaffected farmers, who only then realised that Dev's policy was not to abolish land annuities but rather to merely withhold them from Britain, while still collecting them for the Irish Exchequer. Before the new Centre Party could enter into negotiations with Cumann Na nGaedheal, Dev moved quickly towards an early election.

Eoin O'Duffy leader of the Blueshirts.

CHAPTER 16

ACA – BLUESHIRTS

Cumann na nGaedheal people had felt obliged to establish their own organisation to defend their supporters from IRA harassment. From the summer of 1932 they looked to the ACA, as the guardians of the people and every threat to their freedom, whether it took the form of mob-rule, Communistic tyranny, or a deValerian dictatorship. Conor Cruise O'Brien wrote, *"The respect for the democratic process shown by Mr. Cosgrave's Government was, in the circumstances, rather remarkable. It was, indeed, too remarkable to please many members of the fallen party, and some of these set about organising a para-military movement on the Fascist model, for the intimidation of their opponents and the recovery of power...Yeats took part in the launching of this movement and wrote songs for it"*[1].

1933 ELECTION

On 2 January 1933, DeValera stunned his own supporters, and the country, by dissolving the Dáil. He wanted a renewed mandate for his policies, which included the abolition of the Senate, and accused the Opposition of cavorting with the British to defeat him. Dev was dependent on Labour support in the Dáil. That party was growing restive as wage cuts on some public workers were mooted. Cosgrave undertook that if he were returned to power, he would cancel all arrears of the annuities and cancel any payment for 1934, while negotiating for reductions for the future. He undertook to enter into "courageous negotiations" with the British to end the economic war, sign a trade agreement and revise previous financial settlements. Tom Kelly, a stalwart of the national movement and a long-time colleague of WT Cosgrave, stood for Fianna Fáil on this occasion. As Sheila Carden writes, *"Kelly threw his weight behind DeValera in a very partisan way, saying on 17 May 1933 in the Dáil, that the instructions given to Fianna Fáil candidates were to vote early and often, and that he did not see anything wrong with impersonation"*. Kelly was successful and elected[2]. Dev's electoral strategy worked perfectly, as Fianna Fáil returned to the Dáil with the State's first overall majority, after getting most Labour transfers.

Results of 1933 election

	% Vote	Seats Won
Fianna Fáil	50	76
Cumann na nGaedheal	31	48
Centre Party	9	11
Labour Party	6	8
Independents	4	5

DISMISSAL OF EOIN O'DUFFY

The increasing conflict between the ACA and the IRA led to a worsening security situation. David Neligan, Collin's original spy in Dublin Castle, and now head of the Special Branch, was suspended in December 1932. Dev felt in a stronger position after his electoral success and on 19 February 1933, the deputy Head of the Special Branch EM O'Connell, was arrested together with an army colonel, Michael Hogan. The Garda Commissioner, Eoin O'Duffy was summarily dismissed by DeValera and Minister of Justice, P. Ruttledge on 22 February 1933. O'Duffy was offered an alternate position within the civil service at his current salary, but declined the offer. David Neligan accepted a similar offer and went to the Land Commission. Eamon Broy, who had worked closely with Michael Collins, succeeded Neligan and was now also made Garda Commissioner.

The *Irish Independent* headlined "A First Class Sensation was Sprung in the Dáil Last Night", when John A Costello asserted that the Section of the 1924 Act, under which the President had stated that General O'Duffy was removed from office, had been earlier repealed. A lively discussion ensued in the Dáil as the Ceann Comhairle, Frank Fahy, declared that it was not his job to rule on Statute Law. DeValera contributed several times, but no clarity was forthcoming. Eventually Frank Fahy disallowed any further questions on the matter and went on to the next business, which was Cosgrave's challenge to President DeValera to, "state the reasons for the removal" and indicate whether any charges were pending. Dev replied that "in the opinion of the Executive Council, a change of Commissioner was desirable in the public interest", but he refused to give any further explanation, though he did clarify that no charges were to be made against O'Duffy[3].

In March 1933, the Army Comrades Association adopted the wearing of the blue shirt and in May it adopted the stiff-arm salute. On 20 July 1933, O'Duffy became its leader and renamed it the National Guard. O'Duffy had a long pedigree in the national movement, as a man who got things done and would be capable of confronting the enemy. He called for a massive march on Leinster Lawn, where the Cenotaph commemorating Griffith, Collins and O'Higgins stood, to be held in August. For Dev, this was reminiscent of Mussolini's march on Rome. The IRA vowed to stop it by any means. Terry DeValera, who dubs that Sunday, *Blue Shirt Sunday,* writes that his father believed from intelligence that a *coup d'etat* was then expected. Dev banned the march and banned the National Guard[4]. He mobilised the Broy Harriers to protect Government Buildings. The march did not happen. Dev then ironically reintroduced Cosgrave's Military Tribunals to deal with the situation.

Dev had sanctioned the swearing-in of hundreds of former anti-Treaty IRA men as armed plain clothes Gardai in 1933. They were named after the Garda Commissioner Eamon Broy. They were Fianna Fáil supporters who had fought against O'Duffy in the Civil War. They received little induction into the Gardai but were competent with arms. Their employment was one attempt by Dev to wean men away from the IRA. Dev also launched an ostensibly Republican reserve of the army in 1934, which again drastically reduced support for the IRA[5].

During 1933 Cumann na nGeadheal amalgamated with the Centre Party, which was essentially the old Farmer's Party, and the ACA to form a United Ireland Party or Fine Gael, with O'Duffy as leader. After two General Election defeats, WT Cosgrave was no longer seen as an electoral asset. Cosgrave nominated Costello, Mulcahy and Blythe to the new party's National Executive. Costello became a frontbencher for the party. The Cumann na nGael element of the new party felt that it needed a strong man to survive. Very soon, however, O'Duffy proved to be too attracted by strong-arm tactics for their sensibilities, and as Brian Girvin writes *"Cosgrave effectively neutralized O'Duffy and forced him out of Fine Gael, on the grounds that democratic institutions and practices must be protected"*[6]. There was much confrontation at political rallies and renewed talk of *coup d'etats* from either side. O'Duffy was then arrested at a rally in Westport amid civil disorder. Costello, Paddy McGilligan and Vincent Rice immediately made an application, at the home of Mr. Justice Johnson, for an order of *habeas corpus:* they were given permission to apply to the Supreme Court for a writ. O'Duffy was moved to Mountjoy Jail the next day. The Supreme Court case lasted two days and ordered his release, finding "no reason mentioned in the Act under Section 13/Article 2A" on which he could be shown to have transgressed[7].

Fine Gael greeted news of O'Duffy's release with elation. The Bishop of Achonry sent O'Duffy a telegram, which read, *"Congratulations on victory of justice over shameless partisanship and contemptible tyranny"*[8]. In early February serious clashes had occurred between the IRA and the Blueshirts in Dundalk and Drogheda. Within a short time the Minister of Justice, Patrick Ruttledge, introduced the 'Wearing of Uniforms –(Restriction) Bill 1934'. This essentially was about banning the wearing of the Blueshirt at public rallies. It ignored the fact that the IRA was at least as culpable for the ongoing violence.

When this was debated in the Dáil on 2 & 3 March 1934, it evoked many bitter and recriminatory speeches. When Dr. O'Higgins claimed that some Fianna Fáil TD's appeared to be laughing at the murder of a Blueshirt in Cork, Seán MacEntee replied, "Any Deputy with the name O'Higgins has no right to talk about murder". John A Costello claimed that for several months, the police were preventing people from exercising their constitutional rights by wearing blue shirts at meetings. He suggested that the police realised their actions were foolish but feared summary dismissal, for any reluctance to take action. He claimed that such laws brought the law itself into disrepute. He referred to the recent debacle of the illegal arrest of O'Duffy and his release by the Supreme Court under *habeas corpus* proceedings, which found against the Government action. He claimed Fianna Fáil was "blinded by their own hatred against him". He noted that the Government had not sought to use the Military Tribunal or the Public Safety Act, if it was so concerned about public disorder.

Costello explained the tactical basis for wearing the blue shirt, saying, *"We wear a blue shirt, or those of us who happen to be members of the League of Youth, wear a blue shirt, and the girls wear blue blouses, not for the purpose of creating disorder, as the Minister of Justice would have us believe, but for the purpose of showing their*

Eoin O'Duffy (centre) and supporters. W.T. Cosgrave can be seen behind his left shoulder. Dublin Lord Mayor Alfie Byrne, is also on his left.

Female Blueshirts salute their cause.

comradeship and to indicate the decent people who are present at meetings and not the rowdies who are really the cause of disturbance at public meetings. The wearing of a uniform, so far from being provocative or unlawful, is adopted by our people so that we will be able to know that we have decent people, and so that, when there are disturbances in the crowd, the people who are creating the disturbance may be distinctly seen, and no one can say that it is the Blueshirts that are causing the disturbances at meetings".

Then Costello referred to the continental experience of wearing recognisable shirts, adding comments that he would later regret. He said, *"The Minister gave extracts from various laws on the Continent, but he carefully refrained from drawing attention to the fact that the Blackshirts were victorious in Italy and that the Hitler Shirts were victorious in Germany, as, assuredly, in spite of this Bill and in spite of the Public Safety Act, the Blueshirts will also be victorious in the Irish Free State"*[9]. Dev participated at great length in the debate on both days. He said that his government was up against the possibility of another Civil War. He said that the Cosgrave governments had used coercive methods, which had not solved the fundamental problems. With the removal of the Oath, all sections of the population had the opportunity of putting their programme, Republican or anything else, before the electorate. He had been patient, though the aggressors had deemed it cowardice.

Dev declared that he believed in patience, not in combat, in persuading the people to do what is right, if he could. He realised that he could use the forces of the State if necessary and the Opposition sought to push him into such a policy, which had failed them. He foresaw this might be required when he founded Fianna Fáil and was ready at all times to comply. Deputy Mulcahy had complained of being shouted down at election meetings. Dev made an unusually conciliatory offer for the time, that *"if they quit this tomfoolery of blue-shirting, which is provocative here as it was in Belgium and in Holland, and all those other countries on the Continent, and if we cannot get by the ordinary forces of the law, the existing forces of the law, fair-play at political meetings, freedom of speech at political meetings, we will get a joint composite force, a national force, and we will preserve order"*[10].

Dev had been reading government files and he was gracious enough to make an important acknowledgement, saying, *"Not very long ago I read a dispatch which Mr. Lloyd George sent over here in the summer of 1922, and I read the reply which the Executive of that day made, having Irish interests at heart as I will admit on seeing it. Trying to put off a conflict, they were temporising, when a spark out there in the streets, set fire to the powder magazine and we had a Civil War in which we were on both sides involved. Do we want that again? Are we going with our eyes open back into a situation like that? I appeal to every decent Irishman, to every Deputy here, to everyone through the country, not to play the game of the enemies of our country by allowing that to happen"*[11].

WT Cosgrave picked up immediately on Dev's reference to Lloyd George in 1922 and the efforts of the Provisional Government to avoid Civil War. He advised Dev not to be so introspective and thin skinned. He said that he should be mindful of what others had to endure. Cosgrave said that when Fianna Fáil was formed its members had left the Republic. He asked what the name 'Fianna Fáil' meant. Would it too, as 'soldiers of Ireland', be banned under the Bill? He claimed that they had then left their life of political sin and asserted that the Civil War had never happened and that they had no responsibility for it. For a few years afterwards they went on with such play-acting. He declared that he spoke without bitterness when he said, that when he was in power he could not allow people into the service of the State, whose loyalty to the State could not be depended upon. He had stood for majority rule since 1922. He instanced occasions when his Party members were attacked and left undefended in carrying out their public duties. He asked was he to be disbarred from supporting and organising a body of men such as the Blueshirts, to preserve order? The Government failed in their duty of protection and then declared this organisation illegal.

Dev asserted that he hated the taste of coercion and was bringing in the Bill with reluctance. He referred to Cosgrave's question as to whether he would be associated with any movement that might overthrow the political institutions. Dev replied by saying that Cosgrave's assurances might not be enough, as he had been moved aside by O'Duffy. He disputed ex-Attorney General Costello's statements saying that the Police Act allowed the Executive to sack the Commissioner without explanation. He added that if people wanted a reason for O'Duffy's sacking, his action since had provided it. Dev said that he liked the colour blue and had chosen that colour for the dress uniform of the cavalry at the Eucharistic Congress. He took the opportunity to say, though they were the defeated side in the Civil War, when elected by the people, the servants of the State, civil servants, police and army had all taken their orders from them without reserve[12].

Conor Cruise O'Brien writes perceptively, *"The existence of the Blueshirts cast Eamon DeValera in the role of defender of democracy. Although hardly anything in his past career seemed to qualify him for this role, he played it with genius. Paradoxically, the need to (real or apparent) defend democracy against the Blueshirts, helped him to move against what was for him and his colleagues (and the country) the far greater danger; their allies in the IRA. In moving against both extremes, DeValera now appeared as a sober father-figure, meeting out even-handed justice, defending the citizens against all the wild men, whether in trench coats or coloured shirts"*[13].

When Eoin O'Duffy died in December 1944, he was granted a state funeral, which was attended by Dev and most of the cabinet. The burial in Glasnevin, close to his mentor Michael Collins, was representative of every phase of Irish life. Ferghal McGarry quotes the *Walsh Memoir*, *"The Garda Siochana which he loved and served so well were a striking body as led by their Commissioner, the officers and men drawn from all over the country marched in the funeral procession"*. McGarry adds, *"The surprising gesture of a state funeral may have reflected his contribution to the struggle for independence, the conciliatory atmosphere of the emergency or DeValera's regret that a life that promised so much potential had ended in such ignominy"*[14].

During the debate on the *Wearing of Uniforms Bill,* Dev became very personal as he alluded to gossip about himself and Kathleen O'Connell, at the time of his wife's visit to America, and having to come into the House to speak on this "filthy propaganda". He then referred to the *Cork Examiner* and continuing speculation about his own ancestry being Jewish, as outlined in the Introduction[15]. This did not stop a later attack on him, and others in the Dáil, by the People's National Party headed by a former Blueshirt, George Griffin. According to the secret service G2, Griffin attacked the Jewish presence in the Dáil at his party's founding meeting, *"An Taoiseach's father was a Portuguese Jew. Erskine Childers' grandmother was a Jewess. Mr. Ruttledge has Jewish connections by marriage - and 'Jew' was written all over the face of Seán Lemass!. Practically all Fianna Fáil TDs are in the clutches of the Jews!"*[16].

At the conclusion of the debate, Dev suggested that all illegal arms should be used to make a cross, such as that of Christ in the Andes. He then added that it would be a glorious day for Ireland to see the monstrosity outside Leinster House removed, and in its place put up a monument as a pledge that brothers who fought each other in the past, would never again be led away to fight each other.

As so often with Dev, no matter how we might admire him, one shudders at his insensitivity or obduracy as he apparently made a proposal, which made some sense, but was couched in language guaranteed to insult and anger those whom he might have wished to influence. The monument on Leinster Lawn was the Cenotaph in memory of Michael Collins, Arthur Griffith and Kevin O'Higgins. It is quite possible though that Dev was merely referring to the current dilapidated state of the Cenotaph[17].

The Bill was guillotined in the Dáil on 14 March 1934. However to the consternation of the Government, the Senate refused it a Second Reading and it thus could not become law for 18 months. In fury DeValera on the very next day, declared his intention to abolish the Senate. On 22 March 1934, Dev introduced a Bill to amend Article 12 of the Constitution to abolish the Senate. As it was presently constituted, the Senate was in Dev's view, *"an absolute menace to this country. The Second Chamber had thwarted a decision of the majority of the elected representatives here that the wearing of political uniforms should be forbidden. It acted in a most partisan way and has to go".* Senator MacDermott characterised the decision as a "very discreditable piece of bad temper". After a very acrimonious debate, the Dáil passed the Bill and sent it to the Senate in December 1935. On 28 May 1936 Dev submitted a motion to the Dáil to the effect that, since the Senate had not passed the Bill within the period allowed by the Constitution, the Bill should then be deemed to have been passed by both Houses. He also announced that a new Constitution was to be introduced and invited proposals for a new Second Chamber, in some modified form[17a].

FIANNA FÁIL AND IRA DIVERGE

DeValera tried to talk the IRA into accepting his way forward, as an acceptable one. Seán MacBride, a future Chief-of-Staff of the IRA and a one time secretary to Dev, met him on a few occasions but commented, *"He is a very hard person to argue with. He spent a tremendous amount of time reiterating his position and justifying his actions in 1921-22-23 and '27 and I found it extremely hard to get him to consider anything except his own point of view"*. Dev refused to consider removing senior civil servants, whom MacBride described as "merely British secret service agents". Dev said that *"the only policy that I can see for abolishing Partition, is for us in this part of Ireland, to use such freedom as we can secure, to get the people in this part of Ireland such conditions as will make the people in the other part of Ireland wish to belong to this part"*. When MacBride reminded Dev of his earlier statement on how the majority had no right to do wrong, Dev lost his temper and echoing WT Cosgrave, *"got excited and said that he would maintain law and order, even if it cost him his life and no matter what he did to maintain it"*[18].

Dev had also sought the intervention of his good friend Joe McGarrity to influence the IRA[19]. In 1932 Dev was shocked to find McGarrity agreeing with the IRA and demanding Dev join forces with them and turn a blind eye to their violence against the British. Dev began to blame WT Cosgrave for his troubles with the IRA, asserting to McGarrity that if Cosgrave had accepted his terms to end the Civil War in 1923, that would have been the end of the violence. He said that the reason Cosgrave would not accept those terms was due to personal spite and in order to destroy him politically. Now Dev was offering similar terms to the IRA and they would not accept them[20]. He wrote in some anger to McGarrity, *"you talk of coming to an understanding with the IRA…It has taken ten long years of patient effort to get the Irish nation on the march again after a devastating Civil War. Are we to abandon all this, in order to satisfy a group who have not given the slightest evidence of any ability to lead our people anywhere, except back into the morass? We desire unity, but desire will get us nowhere unless we can get some accepted basis for determining what that national policy shall be and where leadership shall lie…Those who are barring our path now are doing exactly what Cohalan and Co did in 1919 to 1921"*[21]. Dev made a last attempt to get the IRA on side by meeting Seán Russell secretly in April 1935. But this was unsuccessful. McGarrity himself met Dev during Xmas 1935, but realised that Dev's terms were to be the only basis for discussions, on which he did not want to engage.

The final split came in late 1936, when a young IRA man named Seán Glynn, who was arrested while commandeering a lorry to go to the Wolfe Tone Commemoration, hanged himself in Arbour Hill prison. McGarrity criticised Dev publicly as, "selling out his former friends and repressing all freedom of thought in Ireland, with the ruthlessness of a dictator"[22]. McGarrity wrote to a friend, *"Dev! His very name makes me sick. What has he not done in reverse of everything he taught? We made him a little god here, and I now believe, and have thought for some time, that after Easter Week he was through with any physical contest against England"*[23].

Thus the long and fruitful association between the two men ended, with McGarrity soon dying of throat cancer and Dev settling into a road of realism, trodden earlier by another of his erstwhile friends, WT Cosgrave.

When the IRA proposed to march to Bodenstown in 1936 to commemorate Wolfe Tone, Dev banned the IRA as an illegal organisation. Its leader Maurice Toomey was arrested and sentenced to three years in jail for membership of the IRA. Gerald Boland said in the Dáil, *"the fact that murders have occurred makes it clear that stern action must be taken...I now give definite notice to all concerned that the so-called IRA, or any organisation which promotes or advocates the use of arms for the attainment of its objectives, will not be tolerated.....we smashed them (Blueshirts) and now we are going to smash the others (IRA)"*[24].

Mary MacSweeney wrote to Dev on 11 May 1936, *"You govern the Free State as it was when Cosgrave had your office"*. She reminded him that he had denounced Cosgrave for asserting that there should be only one army and one government. He replied on 22 June, remonstrating with her about recent murders of defenceless citizens in Cork and Waterford, asking had the prevention of crime to wait until the community is satisfied with its political status? She replied on 30 June, *"You are a fool – a criminal fool. You will go down in the time to come, as the greatest failure in Irish history has ever known. And you might have been so great!!"*[25].

James Dillon, whose father John Dillon had preferred DeValera to Cosgrave in the 1920's, and whom Dev himself had encouraged to join Fianna Fáil and who had voted for Dev in 1932, was another who had come to a very critical view of him by 1935. He made several critical references to Dev in the Dáil over these years. Dillon had little sympathy when the IRA turned against Fianna Fáil, and Dev and his ministers had to have intense police protection. He said, *"In the past the blackguard and the intimidation were clearly shown that they had the sympathy of the Government, so long as they confined their activities...It was not until the Minister of Defence was insulted on the streets of Tralee and until the President was insulted on the streets of Dublin that the Fianna Fáil Government began to sit up and take notice. Now you are reaping the whirlwind you yourselves sowed in the past few years"*[26]. Dillon was annoyed by the constant insinuation by Fianna Fáil that they were the only true patriots and that all those who opposed them were *"Judases, spies, informers, traitors"*[27].

Later in 1935, Dillon said, *"The President is and always has been, a close and scrupulous student of Nicolo Machiavelli. He will remember that Machiavelli recommended to him the stirring up of disturbance until he got into office, and to stir it up with all the exterior appearance of benignity, magnanimity, justice, truth and religion. He will remember that Nicolo Machiavelli further advised him, that having got into the saddle, to take mighty good care that he stayed there"*[28]. From September 1939 to June 1940, Dev held the office of Minister of Education.

In a debate to establish the *Dublin Institute of Advanced Studies* in April 1940, which contained two Schools – the School of Celtic Studies and the School of Theoretical Physics - Dillon supported the Institute but argued against the inclusion of mathematical physics as part of its remit. He said that that proposal was *"for one and one only silly childish purpose and that is to lend verisimilitude to the myth that the Taoiseach is a great mathematician, which he never was, and never will be. The myth has to be created...that we have a scholar prime minister...it is all cod"*[29].

REPENTANCE?

Dev was adamant that he had played a principled role in the Civil War. He had then come to the conclusion that the IRA could no longer claim exactly the same continuity that he had claimed up to 1925. When asked in a debate on Public Order in the Dáil on 23 June 1936, whether he regretted that previous policy he had held to, he replied, *"Do I regret that policy? If that policy has led in any way to the murder of individuals in this State I regret it. I cannot say whether it is that policy that has done it, but, if it has, I must regret it... We have taken these measures because we regard them as absolutely necessary unless great evils are to follow"*[30]. He challenged Cosgrave to accept setting up an historical commission to study the causes of the Civil War. Each of them would appoint three eminent people with a Bishop as chairman and let them have all necessary documentation. Cosgrave would have none of it.

Inspecting Old IRA veterans in O'Connell Street Dublin, 1936.

CHAPTER 17

CONSTITUTIONAL CHANGES

Despite the countrywide hardship caused by the Economic War, DeValera pressed ahead with his constitutional crusade and was most successful. He reintroduced the Bill to abolish the Oath of Allegiance in the new Dáil, where it passed easily, becoming law on 3 May 1933; the Oath was no more. He had embarked on the stepping-stone route to whittle away the Treaty. He introduced two Bills to curtail the power of the Governor General and another Bill to end the right of appeal to the judicial committee of the Privy Council. Both became law in November 1933. At that point JH Thomas, the Dominions Secretary, made an intervention in the House of Commons, stating that the Irish Free State, as a member of the British Commonwealth was free to order her own affairs. Dev used his reply to address his own political opponents and seek to justify his opposition to the Treaty, *"The Irish people have never sought membership of the British Commonwealth. The association with Great Britain and the Commonwealth has never been on their side a voluntary association. The Treaty of 1921 involved no fundamental change to their attitude. They submitted to the Treaty because they were presented with the alternative of immediate war. They did not accept it as a final settlement of their relations with Great Britain"*[1].

Dev kept up the momentum in 1934 with a *Citizens Bill* and an *Aliens Bill*, which described British subjects living in the Free State. A third Bill gave those British subjects similar rights as Irish citizens. By the end of 1934 the right of the Free State to abrogate the Treaty under the *Statute of Westminster*, was recognised by the British Privy Council. This served to change British constitutional thinking, though they warned that if the Irish weakened the link with the Crown, this would entail leaving the Commonwealth and a consequent loss of rights for Irish citizens in Britain and the Dominions.

The British had not been in any great hurry initially about the annuities, as they began to collect their equivalent through the tariffs they imposed. They soon realised, however, that their own economy was being exposed to potential damage by the Economic War. In 1934 both the *Manchester Guardian* and *The Economist* carried reports that the Irish might consider sourcing their supplies of coal from Germany and Poland. The British then offered to sign an agreement to increase their cattle quota by one third and in return the Irish increase their purchase of British coal. This agreement was signed in January 1935. During that same year Dev received an invitation to London for the silver jubilee celebrations of King George V. In a reply to Prime Minster Ramsay MacDonald, Dev declined the invitation due to the continuation of Partition and the Economic War.

ABDICATION CRISIS

EXTERNAL RELATIONS ACT 1936

In December 1936, a constitutional crisis arose in Britain with the abdication of Edward VIII. Dev saw this as an opportune moment to amend the existing Constitution by removing all references to the King and Governor General, as the British were occupied with their own crisis[2]. The abdication was scheduled for Thursday 10 December. Dev was informed that very day and intended to delay taking action, but the British wished all the Dominions to act in tandem on the day of the abdication. Malcolm MacDonald, Secretary of State for the Dominions, phoned Dev and requested him to comply[3]. Dev immediately agreed and the Dáil met on the next afternoon. Two Bills were introduced, followed by a guillotine, to complete all stages of the first Bill by 23.00 that night and all stages of the second Bill by 22.30 the following night.

The first Bill recognised the abdication of the King and proposed the deletion of all reference to the King and removing the Governor General from the Constitution. Dev acknowledged the new King's role, relating to the Irish Free State, was purely in relation to external affairs. This was intended to demonstrate that matters relating to the monarch's abdication and the precise role of his successor were properly an internal matter for the Irish Free State. In the Dáil, Dev explained that the King had no function in the internal affairs of the State, but was being retained for external purposes alone, "because he is recognised as the symbol of this particular cooperation with the States of the Commonwealth"[4].

On the following day, after dealing with the King's position, the External Relations Bill confining the King's role to external relations on the advice of the Government was taken. John A Costello deemed the Bill would produce "a political monstrosity, the like of which is unknown to political legal theory"[5]. He found that DeValera's assertion that the two Bills would not jeopardise Ireland's position in the Commonwealth to be unfounded. Costello said his mind was in a whirl and it capsized as he listened to DeValera's arguments. He could see no link between the abdication of the King and the removing of references to the King in the Bill. He thought DeValera to be saying that he laid claim to the constitutional advances made up to 1931, which Costello totally rejected. He said that DeValera's governments had made no constitutional advances. Costello claimed that in fact the guillotined Bill meant the State would have no Head of State for internal affairs but would have a foreign king for external affairs, a half Head of the State acting for us sometimes and not acting for us at other times, will make us "the laughing stock of international jurists throughout the world. What sort of State is that at all? This half Crown is now to be the symbol of our cooperation in the Commonwealth". Costello indicated how the leaders of all the Commonwealth countries including Canada, Australia, and South Africa, had backed the Free State in achieving its freedom. He said assuming that it is a mere trifle for us to so remove the King, whom millions of people in these Commonwealth countries had a deep attachment and loyalty to, was wrong; we owe a slight obligation, which costs very little to these countries who assisted us, but this measure dishonoured those slight obligations. These obligations were dishonoured by DeValera today, Costello said. He could understand being a full member of the Commonwealth or, interestingly in hindsight; he said he could understand a decent declaration of a Republic. However he did not know whether we were in the Commonwealth or whether we were now a Republic.

General Seán MacEoin said that DeValera had funked declaring a Republic. He said that DeValera should have put it to the British Government, that if they wanted us to remain in the Commonwealth then we would, but only as a Republic. He said that Fianna Fáil wanted to be able to say down in the Bog of Allen that they were republicans, and in Piccadilly, they wanted to say they were imperialists[6].

Dev responded saying, *"Quite clearly, what we have got to do is either to regularise the position or declare a Republic...I do not propose to use this situation to declare a Republic for the 26 Counties. Our people at any time will have their opportunity of doing that. We are putting no barrier of any sort in the way. They can do it if they want to do it at any time. If I was proposing that we should declare either a 26 County Republic or a 32 County Republic, an occasion like the present would not be the occasion to do it. Neither is the present occasion one on which we should introduce a permanent constitution here...So far as I can see on the face of this Bill, there is no change in regard to the title or anything of that sort. What I said I tried to make as explicit as I could. I said that we have taken all the internal functions away from the King. Is that clear?"*. He said the existing constitution had been introduced under threat of force. He thought that they could introduce a new constitution while retaining membership of the British Commonwealth of Nations[7].

Robert Brennan soon became aware of major disquiet within *The American Association for Recognition of the Irish Republic* (AARIR). He reported from Washington DC that some members felt that the voluntary recognition of George VI as head of the Commonwealth was an abandonment of the republican ideal and felt that they could no longer support Fianna Fáil or Dev himself. Brennan told Dev that he was seeking to ameliorate the situation[8].

Though it appeared fairly clear that the Free State might no longer be a member of the Commonwealth, the British cabinet committee on Ireland studied the matter carefully. It decided, possibly due to the crisis situation, that the new External Relations Act did not take the Free State outside the Commonwealth as Article 1 of the 1922 Constitution, which said the country was *"a co-equal member of the community of Nations forming the British Commonwealth of Nations"* had not been changed.

This External Relations Act was the first to be signed by the Chairman of the Dáil.

꒛꒜ ꒝꒞

1937 CONSTITUTION

DeValera had informed King Edward VIII on 8 June 1936, that he intended to replace the 1922 Constitution with one that would replace the office of the Governor General, create an office of the President elected by the people, and claim jurisdiction over the 32 counties. He had earlier, on 30 April 1935, instructed John Hearne, legal advisor to the Department of External Affairs, to prepare a draft of the heads of a new constitution for the State. He wanted a republican constitution removed from British law, which all conscientious objectors could give allegiance to[9]. Dev believed that the Irish people should have the opportunity to take ownership of their own Constitution. Despite understandable suspicions from the Opposition about Dev himself, and the trends among other European Catholic countries towards extreme right-wing tendencies, Dev was determined to avoid an authoritarian Constitution and in fact produced an exceptional document for the times.

On 9 June, Dev set up a Commission of 23 members to study the question of a second chamber, as he had earlier abolished the Senate under the 1922 Constitution[10]. The Committee was an all-party one consisting of among others, DeValera, Seán Lemass, John A Costello, Paddy McGilligan and William Norton. Dev's official biographers report that this Committee brought in two reports, the majority favouring representation from national interests and services. The minority report was in favour of vocational representation and the right of the Senate to refer legislation to the people. Having spoken to Seán MacEntee and Seán Moynihan, secretary to his Department, Dev favoured the minority report[11]. The result was that the Senate was to be under the thumb of the government of the day[12].

Dev consulted widely on the multitudinous aspects of the endeavour of a new constitution. All of the constitutional issues had been dealt with as Dev grappled with social principles to guide the State. He consulted John Charles McQuaid, CSSp of Blackrock College in detail on social clauses of his proposed new constitution, exchanging many drafts. This was a very complicated task in the 1930's with so many competing ideologies rife on the continent. Longford & O'Neill write, *"The subject left to last was one, that DeValera expected to present no trouble - religion. This, however, proved to be a delusion"*[13]. Even the mention of the special position of the Catholic Church in the Constitution presented great difficulty. Dev wanted the Constitution to be one suitable for the whole country and therefore wanted to recognise the other churches. An early draft had included the recognition that the "Church of Christ is the Catholic Church". The Apostolic Nuncio, the Cardinal and John Charles McQuaid were intimately involved in the debates. Cardinal MacRory wanted the inclusion of, *"the State reflecting the religious convictions of 93% of its citizens acknowledges the Catholic religion to be the religion established by Our Divine Lord Jesus Christ…"*. Dev was relieved when Archbishop Byrne of Dublin did not seek any particular mention of the status of the Catholic Church in the general article on religion.

Dev felt able to settle for the anodyne phrase which "recognises the special position" of the Holy Catholic Apostolic and Roman Church as the guardian of the faith professed by the great majority of its citizens. He also met the leaders of the other churches including, Dr. Massey of the Methodists, Dr. O'Neill of the Presbyterians, and the Church of Ireland Archbishop of Dublin, Dr. Gregg.

In the Dáil the main opposition to the Constitution came on the status of women and that of the powers of the President. Feminists objected to the notion of women being associated to such a degree with work in the home. A Joint Committee of Women's Societies, chaired by Mary Kettle argued that the draft Constitution would ensure that "no woman who works will have any security whatsoever". The *Irish Press* accused her of ignorance of drafting a Constitution and merely following the arguments of Fine Gael's John A Costello. Many prominent women including some devotees of Dev such as Dorothy Macardle condemned the Constitution. She wrote to Dev from London on 21 May 1937, "As the Constitution stands, I do not see how anyone holding advanced views on the rights of women can support it, and that it is a tragic dilemma for those who have been loyal and ardent workers in the national cause"[14]. Hanna Sheehy-Skeffington wrote in Maud Gonne's *Prison Bars,"never before have women been so united, as now when they are faced with Fascist proposals endangering their livelihood, cutting away their rights as human beings...Mr DeValera shows mawkish distrust of women which has always coloured his outlook...He has refused to restore 1916 Equal Rights and Equal Opportunities for women"*[15]. DeValera said, *"There is no distinction made in this Constitution, in regard to political rights, between men and women.... I believe that ninety nine per cent of women of this country will agree with every line of this...Women are mentioned in two articles. They are mentioned to give the protection, which, I think, is necessary as part of our social programme...we state here that mothers in their homes give to the State a support that is essential. Is there anybody who denies it?...Women ought not to be forced by economic necessity to go out and either supplement his wages or become the breadwinners themselves"*. The Constitution also referred to women in connection with social directives. Dev said, *"care should be taken by the State through its laws, that the inadequate strength of women and children shall not be abused. What is wrong about that?"*[15a]

John A Costello's main criticisms were;

1. *Women have not as of constitutional right any claim to the exercise of the franchise equally with men. He also opposed the ban on divorce.*

2. *While the Draft Amendment proposed that the State should recognise the special position of the Catholic Church, no such special position is accorded to it in any practical form.*

3. *The King will still act for us. Our constitutional status will be judged by the fact that our international relations are conducted through the institution of the Crown. Internationally we remain, will remain, and will be recognised as a member of the British Commonwealth of Nations.*

Joseph P Kennedy

Hanna Sheehy-Skeffington

John A Costello

John Charles McQuaid

4. *The powers and privileges proposed for the novelty of a new functionary called the President would appear to be entirely unjustifiable.*

5. *Under the Constitutional proposals, the Government sinks definitely into the background and the dominant personality and the person no doubt with the power is the Prime Minister.*

6. *The President may refer a Bill, at the public expense, in the teeth of the wishes of the Prime Minister and of the Dáil.*

7. *If the present proposals become law, we would never have more freedom that we have under the Constitution, made possible by the sacrifices of Griffith and Collins and the sacrifices and labours of O'Higgins and McGilligan[16].*

The Preamble to the Constitution read, *"We, the people of Éire, humbly acknowledge our obligations to Our Divine Lord Jesus Christ, Who sustained our fathers through centuries of trial.."* JH Whyte has said that this pointed the finger at Protestants and equated 'Irish' with 'Catholic'. Whyte adds that this is not so evident in the speeches of Mr. Cosgrave and his colleagues, in the preceding government[17]. An article in *Osservatore Romano* devoted high praise to the Constitution: *"It differs from other constitutions, because it is inspired by respect for the faith of the people, the dignity of the person, the sanctity of the family, of private property, and of social democracy. These principles are applied in a unique religious spirit, which animates the whole constitution"[18].* All the other churches in Ireland were pleased with the Constitution. The Jewish Rabbinate committee, *"noted with the greatest satisfaction and due appreciation that the Jewish congregation are included in the clause giving equal recognition to the religious bodies in Éire and they respectfully tender congratulations on the production of such a fair and just document"[19].*

In an article in *The Jurist* in 2005 the constitutional lawyer, Gerard Hogan, defends DeValera's Constitution from criticism from a variety of historians, including Professor Roy Foster. Hogan says that some criticism was due to hostility to Dev himself and the erroneous belief that he was the main draftsman rather than John Hearne. He also acknowledges that the absence of any detailed and legal commentary on the drafting of the Constitution has handicapped any fair historical evaluation. Hogan believes that the "vast corpus of law which has been generated since 1937" offers a favourable critique. He acknowledges that the Constitution had defects such as Articles 2 & 3, the ban on divorce, the 'special position of the Catholic Church' and the 'women in the home' section. On the positive side Hogan finds:

A clear articulation of the separation of powers.

Enhancement of the democratic process through special protection for electoral fairness and the referendum.

Recognition of general principles of international law.

Constitutional protection and judicial review of legislation and the articulation of important rights such as equality, life, the person, good name and property rights.

RESULTS OF REFERENDUM & ELECTION

The Dáil approved the Constitution on 14 June 1937 and that same day Dev announced a General Election and Referendum for 1 July. A cabinet committee on revising the constituencies set up after the 1933 election abolished the six-universitiy seats (Fine Gael had held four) and reduced the overall number of seats from 153 to 138. 685,105 votes were cast for and 526,945 against the Constitution. Thus it gained a relatively small majority of 56% being opposed vociferously by many women. It came into force on 29 December 1937.

Fianna Fáil did not do as well as expected in the General Election, losing eight seats. Fine Gael advertised itself in Dublin as putting forward 'Commonwealth Candidates'[20]. WT Cosgrave complained that the people had only 14 days to consider the new Constitution. James Dillon praised Cosgrave as the man who had *"saved the ship of State sixteen years ago, when about it were beating the winds of DeValera's Civil War. Today Mr. Cosgrave was the one man – the only man – who could save the State when about it was beating the winds of DeValera's Economic War"*[21]. Dev countered that they were bringing in the new Constitution in their own right, as expressed in the proclamation of Easter Week. He asserted that there was nothing in the Constitution which was derogatory to women. He defended his action on the annuities by saying that the Irish Parliament never was consulted about it, adding, *"If the Government was returned to office, they would not pay a single penny of those annuities. They belonged to the Irish Treasury"*[22].

The overall result of the election meant that Dev was again depending on Labour for support in a minority government. The results were:

Seats	won	previous
Fianna Fáil	6	77
Fine Gael	48	52
Labour	13	8
Independents	8	12

1938 ANGLO-IRISH AGREEMENT

There were still major outstanding issues to be settled with Britain. These included the constitutional position viz Commonwealth, Partition, trade, financial measures, defence, and the Treaty ports. The latter issue was of fundamental and rather immediate importance to Dev, who intended to keep Ireland out of the forthcoming European war. As Conor Cruise O'Brien has written, "Without the return of these ports, Ireland's neutrality in the coming war, which it was DeValera's policy to ensure, would scarcely have been practical politics"[23]. Dev had many meetings with the new Dominion Secretary Malcolm MacDonald, with whom he got on very well, unlike the previous incumbent, JH Thomas.

DeValera had taken the trouble to write a personal letter to MacDonald when he returned as Dominions Secretary, saying:

"I am very glad to learn that you had gone back to your old Department. Having done so much already to improve relations between these countries, I hope you will be able to see the task completed by the removal of the chief remaining obstacle – the Partition of Ireland. This is bound to assume more and more importance and become increasingly urgent as the months pass. I am sure you realise that the solution will not be made easier by delay and that time is very important in the matter"[24].

MacDonald would have been only too aware of Dev trying to influence him but one feels it necessary to question how in reality, did Dev think Partition was going to be ended by the British?

After many preliminary meetings, the two Governments finally met in formal session in London on 17 January 1938. Neville Chamberlain, Malcolm MacDonald together with the Chancellor of the Exchequer, the Home Secretary, Defence and Agriculture Ministers and the President of the Board of Trade represented Britain. Dev's team included Seán Lemass, Seán MacEntee and James Ryan. A notable omission was Frank Aiken Minister of Defence.

Dev's stated aims were, the unity of Ireland, the handing over of the Irish ports and the dropping of the British levies on Irish goods. Chamberlain found Dev a *"queer creature"*, adding, *"I shall be grievously disappointed if we don't get an all-round agreement on everything except Partition. That is the difference that cannot be bridged without the assent of Ulster"*. During the negotiations, Dev shocked John Cudahy, American Minister to Ireland, with his cold-blooded attitude to Chamberlain, admitting that men meant nothing to him. He said that Chamberlain, like himself, was merely the proponent of a cause[25].

The talks were interrupted for a short period when a General Election was called in Northern Ireland and the sudden resignation of Anthony Eden as Foreign Secretary, occurred. They resumed on 23 February. In the meantime Dev had launched an international media campaign on the Partition issue. He wrote to President Roosevelt on 25 January *"another great opportunity for a friendly ending to the quarrel of centuries between Great Britain and Ireland presents itself. The one remaining obstacle to be overcome is that of Partition."*. He asked the President to *"use your influence to get Great Britain to realize what would be gained by reconciliation and get them to move whilst there is time. In a short while, if the present negotiations fail, relations will be worsened"*[26]. President Roosevelt informed DeValera that he had instructed his new ambassador to Britain, Joseph P Kennedy, to inform Chamberlain that he was privately in favour of a settlement on Partition. The negotiations were to some extent reminiscent of the Treaty negotiations with the Irish delegation, led by Dev himself, returning to Dublin on several occasions. Unlike the Treaty negotiations however, the question of Partition was paramount. Dev pressurised the British at length, without any success. Dev was hoist to his own *petard* on Partition.

A nationalist delegation led by Cahir Healy told DeValera in London that; *"We would regard it as a betrayal of our interests if he ignored the problem of Partition by getting trade and defence agreements only"*. MacDonald reported Dev as saying that if Britain got involved in war, some in Ireland would see that as an opportunity for Ireland, but he was not of that view himself. He thought it very likely that the Irish Free State would be drawn in on our side"[27].

Dev informed President Roosevelt some days before the Agreement was officially concluded saying, *"An agreement between our two Governments has been reached… the Agreement will give satisfaction to both countries. Unfortunately – the ending of Partition – finds no place in the Agreement…"*[28].

After three long months the Agreement was officially reached on 25 April. The ports were to be returned to Ireland and Britain gave up any rights she might have demanded in time of war within the country. Ireland was to pay £10 million in settlement of the financial dispute. The respective trade tariffs were to be abandoned by both sides. There was no defence agreement and the British demand for access for goods from Northern Ireland to the South, was not conceded. Chamberlain accepted that *"we must face the fact that a Government without a majority in the Dáil could not get these particular provisions through"*[29]. The North too gained from the Agreement with benefits on agriculture subsidies and more manufacturing jobs for military equipment. It has been noted that during these lengthy negotiations, while Chamberlain went out of his way to be hospitable and friendly to Dev, he in turn, remained completely oblivious to the person of Chamberlain. Some might use this to criticise Dev, but others would regard it as sound negotiation. Garret Fitzgerald writes, *"Whatever one may think of DeValera's Economic War of the 1930's, one cannot but admire his extraordinarily skilful handling of the 1938 Anglo-Irish negotiation"*[30].

On his return journey to Ireland, Dev wrote a note aboard the Holyhead to Dun Laoghaire ferry, of what he would say to journalists. It reads: *"The Agreement which has just been signed between the representatives of the Irish and British peoples will I believe be universally received in the spirit in which it was concluded. It removes the existing and the more dangerous potential causes of quarrel between the two countries – all except one – "*. Then he referred to ongoing Partition, continuing, *"I repeat what I have been saying for nearly a quarter of a century. Great Britain has nothing to fear – nothing to lose but everything to gain from having as her neighbour, a completely independent and free Ireland"*[31].

The new Agreement was a triumph for DeValera who gave Chamberlain no praise. He wrote to Chamberlain, *"I have no doubt the happy ending of the disputes in question has begotten a new attitude of mind on the part of our people, and if we could only now succeed in solving the problem created by Partition, a happy future of mutual understanding and fruitful cooperation in matters of common concern lies ahead before our two peoples"*[32].

In the Dáil, Dev played down the Agreement as favouring Britain more than Ireland. Luckily for the country, there were other strong political personages who saw the pressing economic realities the country was in and insisted that a deal had to be cut. Dev had been pressurised into accepting it by Seán MacEntee, Oscar Traynor and Frank Aiken, who recognised that it was a great deal economically[33]. The absence of Lemass's name in MacEntee's Papers is indicative of the chasm between Lamass and MacEntee.

While Dev treated the Agreement in a low-key fashion, he used its success to call an election inside two months on 17 June 1938. Fianna Fáil got over 50% of the vote for the first time, returning to the Dáil with 77 seats, an overall majority that freed it from relying on Labour support. Dev had thus established Fianna Fáil as the natural party of government, drawing support from wide sections of the electorate and thereby representing various vested interests, which steered it into a middle of the road catch all party.

CHURCHILL CRITICISES HANDING OVER PORTS

The main criticism of the Agreement came from Winston Churchill, who was continually hostile to DeValera, whom he correctly saw as overthrowing the provisions of the Anglo-Irish Treaty. He said in the Commons; *"These ports are in fact, the sentinels of the Western approaches, by which the 65 million on this Island so enormously depend on foreign food for their daily bread, and by which they can carry on their trade, which is equally important to their existence...We give them up, unconditionally to an Irish Government led by men – I do not want to use hard words – whose rise to power has been proportionate to the animosity with which they have acted against this country, no doubt in pursuance of their own patriotic impulses, and whose position in power is based upon the violation of solemn Treaty engagements"*.

Churchill asked Chamberlain what would Britain do if in wartime the Irish refused access to the ports and declared neutrality. In November 1938 Churchill wrote, *"When the Prime Minister made a heart to heart settlements with Mr. DeValera and gave up to him those fortified ports on the south coast of Ireland, which are vital to our food supply in time of war, he led us to believe that henceforth Mr DeValera and the country now called Éire, were reconciled to us in friendship... But I warned him with my defective judgement, that if we got into any great danger, Mr DeValera would demand the surrender of Ulster as a price for any friendship or aid. This fell out exactly, for Mr DeValera has recently declared that he cannot give us any help or friendship, while any British troops remain to guard the Protestants of Northern Ireland"*[34]. As time went on Churchill's pronunciation of Dev's name came more and more to sound like Mr. 'Devil-Éire'.

In March 1939, Chamberlain defended his appeasement policy to Hitler from Churchill writing *"that was not the opinion of DeValera, who spent a couple of hours with me yesterday morning. He is strongly of the opinion that I have been right all through and am right now"*[35]. Dev favoured Chamberlain's appeasement policy over the German claim to the Czech Sudetenland, seeing a parallel between it and Northern Ireland, and having already benefited from appeasement by getting the Treaty Ports returned.

DEV IN CABINET

Within a few years of taking office, DeValera had attained the position of the Great Leader who took all the major decisions in cabinet, as John A Costello had said his Constitution would so enable him to do. The cabinets consisted of people who were devoted to Dev. He nevertheless encouraged each member to speak his mind freely. He did not believe in taking votes, rather would he allow debate to continue, gradually wearing down any opposition, until he himself would attempt to reach a consensus with which all could agree?. If that were not possible, rather than alienate any member, he would adjourn the matter for another occasion until such time as he got all to agree with his own view. Some decisions were his own prerogative *ex officio*, and these he guarded carefully, such as his decision to call the 1933 General Election[36]. Brian Farrell has said that Dev's relationship with Seán Lemass, who was dedicated to improving the economy, could not *"have survived without a considerable degree of conciliation and compromise and concession on both sides"*[37]. He was also careful to keep the Labour Party on-side, saying that he agreed with James Connolly that, *"to secure national freedom was the first step in order to get the workers of Ireland the living they were entitled to in their own country"*[38].

Dev found it difficult to delegate authority and often got involved in matters in which he had little expertise. His decision to retain the External Affairs portfolio for himself indicated that he felt that no one else could be trusted with such an important area. The most drastic changes he ever made in cabinet occurred at the outbreak of war in 1939. He created two new ministries, that of Minister of Supplies for Seán Lemass and Coordination of Defences for Frank Aiken. Seán T. O'Kelly went to Finance, Paddy Ruttledge to Local Government and Public Health, Oscar Traynor to Defence and Seán MacEntee to Industry and Commerce, while Gerry Boland got the challenging portfolio of Justice; Jim Ryan alone retained his position at Agriculture. PJ Little joined the Cabinet at Posts and Telegraphs. DeValera himself retained External Affairs and also Education for a time.

In general Dev told his cabinet colleagues very little. Maurice Moynihan, who was secretary for Dev's governments for 23 years, wrote of him, *"he was a very close man, he learned that as a revolutionary, but he was also a great strategist. He always had a plan. There was strategy behind every tactic. He was chess-like, some minor move here, then a big step forward. His thought was political"*[39].

Sean Lemass, speaking at the King's Inn on 18 February 1966, commemorating the 50th anniversary of the Easter Rising, explained the early absence of attention to 'economic and social aims'. There was a fear he said *"it might breed dissention in the national ranks or divert energies from the national struggle. James Connolly and Arthur Griffith had their own ideas about economic and social policy. Most of us thought freedom was an end in itself. It was quite some time before there was an awakening of the understanding of the need to use freedom for the national benefit in social and economic policy. We have moved a great distance and there is now a much wider understanding that the process will have no ending"*.

CHAPTER 18

VERSUS THE IRA IN WARTIME
NO SURRENDER ON LANGUAGE

While DeValera was achieving success in negotiating the Anglo-Irish Agreement of 1938, the IRA was favouring Seán Russell's plan of taking their war to Britain and starting a bombing campaign there. Some of the surviving members of the Second Dáil, which claimed to be the Government of the Republic of Ireland, gave its authority over to the Army Council of the IRA. This, in Republican purism, placed Russell on the same level as Dev had earlier claimed for himself as the guardian of the Republic. On 16 January 1939 a statement was issued to Lord Halifax, Britain's Foreign Minister, by the Army Council, "In the name of the unconquered dead and the faithful living", calling on Britain to withdraw from all of Ireland within four days. Very soon the bombing campaign was in progress[1].

On 7 February 1939, Dev addressed the Senate on his fundamental visions, of ending Partition and the restoration of Irish as the spoken language. Surprisingly, the latter aim was paramount.

He held Britain mainly responsible for Partition, accepting that their scheme was based on a minority, who did not wish to be a minority in the State. That minority had powerful friends in Britain and the British Parliament brought in Partition, as a "mere temporary affair", allegedly affecting a small area around Belfast, and as the best way of "bringing about ultimate unity". But Britain did not act logically, denying very many Nationalists the choice to join our State.

The British created Partition and they had the best chance of revoking it. DeValera saw little evidence that they wished to do so. He then described a large section of our people, as "entrapped in that territory and held there by force". He said it was important that his Government was candid in its view and so informs Britain and others, in every forum available. Dev said *"There is an injustice being done in our country, which I say would justify the use of force if it could be effective. I do not want, and I am not advocating force – and I hope that that is clear – because I do not think it would succeed. I do not want it. I do not think it would be right"*[2].

Critics of Dev pointed out that such language was inflammatory and that he never actually sought to have those same nationalist people join the southern State, and deemed his words as empty rhetoric and propaganda. He countered that such a movement would be a mere half measure and he thought, "The time has come to do the thing properly"[3]. The IRA could only have felt further empowered by such rhetoric, as Northern Unionists felt further threatened.

In the same debate DeValera had said, *"I would not to-morrow, for the sake of a united Ireland, give up the policy of trying to make this a really Irish Ireland—not by any means. If I were told to-morrow: you can have a united Ireland, if you give up your idea of restoring the national language to be the spoken language of the majority of the people, I would, for myself, say no. I do not know how many would agree with me. I would say no, and I would say it for this reason: I believe that as long as the language remains, you have a distinguishing characteristic of nationality, which will enable the nation to persist. If you lose the language, the danger is that there would be absorption. Much as I would desire to see unity—and I told you it was because of Partition I came into politics, I would not grasp it at the cost of losing the opportunity of restoring the language. Therefore, I would not pay that price"*[4].

DeValera has been severely criticised for this stance, as being completely oblivious to the feelings of the Protestant Unionist peoples in Northern Ireland, whom theoretically, he was trying to influence, if not woo. This together with the Catholic ethos of the Free State, reinforced Unionist beliefs that their best interests lay with Great Britain, despite the advent of war. The best that can be said of these utterances of Dev is that, at least, he was being candid and the Protestant Unionist people felt reinforced in their utter rejection of a united Ireland.

Dev's vision of a Gaelic speaking country was too idealistic. The Irish people in the 1830's had made a desperate bargain with a modernising economy by giving up their native language and culture for one, which offered the opportunity to improve itself economically. When Ireland became independent and mass emigration became continuous, the emigrants realised how lucky they were to have the English language in Britain, America and Australia. The cultural revival did not include for many, the restoration of the language as an absolute.

Dev introduced the Offences Against the State Act on 14 June, setting up military tribunals and internment. The IRA became an illegal organisation and seventy men were interned. The annual march to Wolfe Tone's grave was banned. The bombing campaign in England continued for over a year on various public facilities. On 23 August a bomb in Coventry killed five people. This was catastrophic from Dev's political strategy, particularly on the issue of Partition.

On 2 September 1939, the day after Germany invaded Poland, Dev introduced the First Amendment to the Constitution Bill and the Emergency Powers Bill. These defined 'time of war' to include an external armed conflict, in which the State was not a participant, but which created an 'emergency' for the State. This gave the Government control over all aspects of life such as transport, supplies, censorship, and army actions. In the Dáil, Dev said for the country to remain neutral, brings for the Government problems more delicate and much more difficult of solution that even arise for a belligerent. He said that it appeared that we are going to be faced with another terrible European War. The view of the Government is that the interests of the country would be best served by trying to keep the country out of it.

He adverted to the fact that Ireland was very near one of the belligerents and that normal trade arrangements with Britain had to be secured and would necessitate contact there. He then said that the fact of Partition made it impossible, whatever sympathies we might have, to take up any other position except neutrality. Sir John Keane, speaking in the Senate, was the only dissenting voice to this position.

Sir John claimed to speak for a substantial section of the population, when he said that though a sovereign State, Ireland must be in sympathy with the democracies. He said there was a thin line between national interests and national honour. He was uneasy that DeValera introduced the division of the country into the matter.

Gerard Boland became the new Minister for Justice on 8 September 1939 and the intelligences forces were reorganised. On 9 November Dev opposed a Labour Party motion seeking the release of an IRA hunger striker and veteran 1916 fighter, Patrick McGrath, who was near death. He said, *"The alternatives we are forced to face are the alternatives of two evils; one to see men die that we do not want to see die if we can save them; the other to permit them to bring the State and the community as a whole to disaster"*. McGrath, a veteran of the Anglo-Irish War, was later brought to hospital and survived. The official biography of DeValera says, *"Dev weakened. He allowed him to be removed to hospital and, despite the doctor's report, he recovered, and a nolle prosequi was entered in his case"*. In April 1940 two prisoners died in St. Bricin's Military Hospital in consequence of a hunger strike. In August, two detectives were shot dead in a house occupied by Patrick McGrath and another man, both of whom were tried, convicted of murder and executed. This tragic sequel was worse than DeValera feared and was to have a profound effect on his future course of action[5].

Judge Gavan Duffy on 11 December found the Offences Against the State Act unconstitutional and granted a *habeas corpus* to an IRA prisoner. The next day saw fifty more IRA men released. On 23 December the IRA entered the Magazine Fort in the Phoenix Park and made off with a million rounds of ammunition. On 3 January 1940, as a reaction to the IRA raiding the Magazine fort, the Dáil was recalled early as the Government introduced an Emergency Powers Bill. Dev had thought that the Government had the power of internment, but the *habeas corpus* case had ruled otherwise. Gerry Boland, Minister of Justice told the Dáil that the Government was absolutely convinced that it must have that power for the period of the emergency, telling WT Cosgrave that he had done similar things earlier.

Cosgrave preferred the Government would deal with the matter in a constitutional way and not give a propaganda tool to the IRA. He accused the Party in Government, of being responsible for deluding young people for the previous seventeen years, *"insofar as their participation in it has been a failure and a futility and that you are seeing the fruits of what you sowed yourselves"*. He said the country was a laughing stock all over the world as it allowed the IRA to take away one million rounds of ammunition in a raid over the Xmas. It should do the decent thing and retire.

Aftermath of IRA bomb in Coventry, England, August 1939.

*On 23 December 1939, the IRA entered the Magazine Fort in the Phoenix Park Dublin,
and made off with a million rounds of ammunition.*

John A Costello seconded Cosgrave's motion. He said that though the Bill deleted six words from a previous Act, its principle was to intern natural-born Irish citizens. That was a big principle, which they opposed. He feared that this method might lead to further insecurity and bring derision and scorn on succeeding Governments. He said the Government was using the war situation to mask what was a domestic problem, which existed before the war.

Dev spoke with urgency as he tried to be practical, after *"so much steam had been let off"*. He said in his view, internment was still constitutional despite the High Court ruling otherwise. The Supreme Court would later rule definitively. But meantime he could not wait for that outcome. A written constitution always offers the possibility of the Courts interpreting it in a different way to that intended by the framers. He would not change the Constitution until it was clear that was essential. He rejected the idea that this was a purely domestic situation and that the war did not effect the situation. He said that the Judiciary, the Executive and the Legislature, all have their proper functions working to a common end. He assumed that words would be taken in their ordinary commonsense intention. James Dillon suggested that the IRA would have to steal the "whole Curragh Camp before they bring that home to you".

President Douglas Hyde refused to sign the Bill, until the Supreme Court declared it constitutional on 9 February. Dev and his cabinet then showed no mercy to the IRA, as thousands were imprisoned and some hanged by an imported English executioner[6].

In England, two IRA men, Barnes and Richards had been condemned to death for their part in the Coventry bombings in 1939. DeValera pleaded unsuccessfully for a reprieve to Anthony Eden, the Dominion Secretary, writing on 29 January 1940, *"I know these men have been convicted of murder in accordance with law…Nevertheless I am convinced it will be a mistake if you let these considerations prevail…. The history of the relations between our two countries has already been stained with blood. Ought you not to make sure that you avoid doing likewise? The execution of these men will only give rise to new and bitter antagonisms between us. The moment Barnes and Richards are dead, they may well, in popular opinion, be enrolled in the long list of Irishmen who in varying conditions gave their lives in an effort to free their people"[7].*

DeValera then sent a personal letter to Chamberlain saying, *"I have received your decision with sorrow and dismay. The reprieve of these men would be regarded as an act of generosity, a thousand times more valuable to Britain than anything that can possibly be gained by their death…I hasten with a final entreaty that this execution be not permitted to take place".* The two men were hanged[8].

Though it had been Dev's erstwhile friend, Joe McGarrity who had assisted the English bombing campaign, Dev attended a memorial Mass for him on 12 August 1940 in Dublin.

The IRA again resorted to hunger strikes and soon some reached the door of death. Among them was a brother of Joseph Mary Plunkett, a signatory of the 1916 Proclamation and a son of the murdered Lord Mayor of Cork, Tomas MacCurtain. The first prisoner, Tony D'Arcy died on 19 April, as Dev remained steadfast. John Maguire writes the "prevailing mood in Dublin was remarkably subdued, as there was very little anger directed at the Government – a significant victory for Dev, undermining for the first time the power of hunger strikes"[9]. The hunger strike was later abandoned.

Dev contained the IRA during the war by meeting their violence head on, through harsh measures. Six Gardai were murdered and six IRA men were executed. It is ironic that when Dev considered appeals for the reprieve of these men, he acted as the British had done. Due to strict censorship, the Irish public only became aware of these executions after they had been carried out. Three had died on hunger strike; Jack McNeela, Tony D'Arcy and Seán McCaughey, and another three were shot by the Gardai. Hundreds of IRA men were interned during the war. In most of the internment camps they were allowed wear their own clothes. In Portlaoise, where the leaders were held, this was not allowed, so these men refused to wear prison clothes and were forerunners of Bobby Sands and the blanket-men of the 1980's in Long Kesh. From 1940 to 1943, ten men were held in solitary confinement in shocking conditions.

The Germans believed that the IRA was their natural ally during the war being so totally anti-British. They made abortive attempts to land the IRA leaders Seán Russell and Frank Ryan back into Ireland.

Garret Fitzgerald highlights that a factor of DeValera's policy during the war, was influenced by his realisation that the IRA might cause major complications for the country. He writes that Ireland's 'neutrality' is too strong a word to use, preferring non-belligerency; given the wide-ranging secret support Dev gave to Britain throughout the conflict. Fitzgerald also sees this policy as an assertion of Irish sovereignty but also the basis for avoiding another Civil War between, *"our three democratic parties, against an IRA probably bolstered with breakaway Fianna Fáil support, and externally supported by Nazi Germany"*[10].

ᏋᏋ ᏋᏋ

CHAPTER 19

DEFENDING NEUTRALITY 1939-1945

On 26 August 1939, Dr. Hempel, the German Minister in Ireland, informed his Foreign Ministry that Joseph Walshe Secretary of the Department of External Affairs, had told him, *"Ireland would definitely remain neutral except in the case of a definite attack, for example dropping bombs on Irish towns. He also expects Britain will, in view of the American-Irish, do everything to avoid violating Irish neutrality"*. Foreign Minister Ribbentrop told Hempel to call immediately on Dev and tell him Germany will, *"refrain from any hostile action against Irish territory and respect her integrity, provided that Ireland for her part maintains unimpeachable neutrality towards us in any conflict"*. He also instructed Hempel to refer to Germany's wide sympathy for *"Ireland and the national aspirations of the Irish people"*, but without mentioning Northern Ireland. Dr. Eduard Hempel called to see Dev on 31 August to so inform him[1]. Dev wrote immediately to Neville Chamberlain, *"The German Minister called on me today. He informed me of the friendly attitude of the German Government to Ireland and of their intention to respect Ireland's neutrality, should Germany be engaged in a European conflict. I replied that the Irish Government wished to remain at peace with Germany, as with all other powers and I referred to my statement published in the press of 20 February, that the aim of the Irish Government's policy was to maintain and preserve Ireland's neutrality in the event of war. This information will probably appear in the press on Saturday morning"*[2].

The very next day saw Germany invade Poland. Dev summoned the Dáil and Senate on 2 September. He told them that he was declaring neutrality, "as the guardian of the interests of our people and not as representing the sentiment or feelings of our people". In this policy, Brian Girvin asserts that Dev was supporting a Partitioned Ireland because that essentially is what neutrality meant[3]. Dev's policy was motivated by a fear of fomenting Civil War from the IRA, the self interest of the country, the inevitable result of Partition and the realisation that the country had already suffered enough as a colony of Britain.

On 14 September, the British sent Sir John Maffey, a diplomatic representative, on a secret mission to meet Dev. He assured Maffey that though in the past, *"I would have done anything in my power to help destroy the British Empire. But now my position is changed"*. He believed that Chamberlain had established a moral position, which would tell. He told Maffey that while most Irish people were pro-British, a very small minority opposed any cooperation with Britain due to Partition. He said that some of his friends in America suggested that he *"take a leaf out of Hitler's handiwork on the Sudeten-Deutsch trick in Northern Ireland?"*.

Hermann Goertz

Dr. Eduard Hempel

Sir John Maffey

Joachim von Ribbentrop

DeValera said that all war aeroplanes, submarines and warships would have to be banned. He, however, remained very conscious that neutrality was at the outer limits of independence for a small country. Dev impressed Maffey, who reported back that Dev intended *"to maintain neutrality and to help us within the limits of that neutrality to the fullest extent possible"*[4]. Maffey was correct, as the Irish State assisted Britain in very many ways right throughout the war.

Dev had sought to get the British to raise the status of their representation in Dublin. Neville Chamberlain replied, *"Your suggestion that the United Kingdom representative in Dublin should have the name and status of Minister, would raise the most contentious issues for us here and is one, which it would not be one for me to accept"*. He asked Dev to understand his position at this grave time for Britain and himself[5]. Dev replied, *"My colleagues and I, in the circumstances, are prepared to accept the 'representative' you propose"*.

GERMAN SPY GOERTZ

When Belgium and Holland were invaded in May 1940 DeValera protested, though without naming Germany, saying, *"Today these two small nations are fighting for their lives, and I think it would be unworthy of this small nation if, on an occasion like this, I did not utter our protest against the cruel wrong which has been done them"*[7]. This drew a protest from the German Minister in Dublin.

The German spy Hermann Goertz had been parachuted into Ireland on 5 May and established a close liaison with Iseult Stuart, the daughter of Maud Gonne, at Laragh Castle. He later escaped capture at the house of Stephen Carroll Held, in Templeogue County Dublin, where a radio transmitter, £20,000 and a codebook were discovered. Among his papers were maps of Irish defences and German plans for an invasion of Ireland at Donegal Bay. Germany intended to allow all Irish nationalists to join them in liberating the North. Though Held was immediately arrested, Goertz remained free for nearly a year with the assistance of various supporters.

When the fact that a German spy was operating in the country leaked out, Dev feared Britain would retake the Irish ports immediately. On the very next day, 23 May 1940, Dev despatched Joseph P Walsh and Liam Archer, head of G2 Military Intelligence, to London. They told the British that if Germany invaded they would be resisted and the British would be invited to assist. Irish defences were fortified and hundreds of suspected German collaborators were then interned. Herr Hempel well realised that Dev had a "friendly understanding" with Britain "even in the face of the threatening danger of Ireland becoming involved in the war"[8]. Dev consulted the Opposition asking for their support in the crisis. He offered to include them in a new Defence Council. Ristard Mulcahy responded that the Opposition had been ignored since the war started and it was a bit late offering a Defence Council[9].

Poster of DeValera and Lord Craig Avon, facing each other down.

Poster read. "God bless Eire's neutrality - until the Fuhrer gets there".

It was fortunate, that with Dev's approval, a good working relationship existed between British Intelligence and Irish Military Intelligence since 1938. MI5's assessment of the link was, *"The Dublin link was, therefore, established at the request of the Éire Government and operated with the full knowledge and approval of the British and Éire Governments. From the outset, the personal relations between the British and Irish intelligence officers immediately concerned, were extremely friendly and this mutual confidence was, it is believed, maintained and developed during the war"*[10].

Dev broadcast to the people on 1 June saying, *"When great powers are locked in mortal combat, the only thing that counts is how one may secure an advantage over the other, and if the violation of our territories promises such advantage, then our territory will be violated, our country will be made a cockpit, our homes will be levelled and our people slaughtered"*[11].

When Churchill took over from Neville Chamberlain as Prime Minister in early 1940, Dev wrote a well earned letter to Chamberlain, saying, *"I hope you will not resent a personal note to tell you how much we have admired your dignity and patriotism in recent events...I would like to testify that you did more than any former British Statesman to make a true friendship between the peoples of out two countries possible... P.S. This was written before the disquieting news of the surrender of Holland reached me"*[12].

Churchill became Prime Minister on 11 May and sent a message to Dev, *"I look forward with confidence to continued friendship between our two countries and you may rely on me to do my utmost to ensure this"*. Dev, who well realised Churchill's attitude to himself and Ireland, replied, *"I thank you for your message of greeting, which I cordially reciprocate"*[13].

In a six-month period, 700 Allied ships had been torpedoed in the North Atlantic, as Britain stood alone against Hitler. Churchill saw Irish neutrality as a threat, fearing that Hitler might invade Ireland. He wanted the strategic unity of the two islands recognised and naval units put into the Irish ports in the south.

UNION OF IRELAND 'OFFERED'

Dev feared a possible invasion from both sides, as the British pressurised him to allow them access to the ports. Malcolm MacDonald, who had known Dev well from earlier contacts, visited Dublin on 17 June as Churchill's emissary. He found Dev, *"depressed and tired, and I felt that he had neither the mental nor the physical vigour that he possessed two years ago"*. MacDonald told Dev that Éire was too weak to resist a German invasion and to enter a joint defence arrangement with the North. Dev felt that, for a variety of reasons, he had no option but to remain neutral.

MacDonald returned to see Dev again to explore whether he would change his stance, if the end of Partition were offered. The British cabinet felt that their national security had to be paramount, though they accepted that it would, of course, have to be put to Lord Craig Avon.

WAR NEWS

ISSUED BY IRISH REPUBLICAN PUBLICITY BUREAU

Spread The Truth!   FEBRUARY 1941   Read Pass It On

A Message from the Army

The Chief of Staff has issued the following:—

CITIZEN SOLDIERS OF THE REPUBLIC; The Army Council, impressed by your loyalty, courage and discipline, thanks you in the name of the Irish people for the help you have given the cause of freedom.

Your task as individual citizens and soldiers has been a hard one: you have had to face imprisonment or death that Ireland may live; you have had to endure in silence the calumny of those who justify their own cowardice or indifference by attacking courage, devotion, and national faith.

You have had to exercise the most severe self-restraint in not answering in arms the assassinations, the judicial murders, illegal imprisonments, midnight searches and assaults, that have always as now characterised the Government policy of men who have been easily perverted from the national faith.

You have been still more self sacrificing in restraining your active resentment and indignation at the evils inflicted upon the mass of the people by selfish and unscrupulous men.

You have seen most sacred principles of humanity as well as of nationality sold or debauched.

You have heard the very language of truth and patriotism debased until the vocabulary of political currency is a denial of the truth —rather an assertion that all truth is a lie.

You have seen institution after institution, public body after public body, corrupted until most of our organised social life is a brazen pretence, a putrefying carcass.

You see a British army of occupation in your country and two competing hordes of Ministers and officials living on the substance of the people, luxuriating in the common people's misery and despair.

You see—you whose sole thought is to fight for Ireland—the make-believe of the brown uniforms; the ancient ammunition-less rifles; the million useless gas masks (ordered to give British trade a filip); the proclaimed neutrality directed by five British slavelings; the scandal of the Judiciary; the shameless graft of officials; the muddle of education; the betrayal of the language.

You see poverty, unemployment, hardship and suffering everywhere.

In the face of all these things you, Soldier-Citizens have kept steady and kept the faith, knowing that a premature attempt to right them would have caused still more suffering to the plain people of the country.

You had to submit to the current of events around you but the time is almost upon us when we shall shape the course of events and direct the resistless torrent of the will to freedom. Soon Ireland will give us the word—Forward, March!

Yours,
          STEPHEN HAYES, Chief of Staff.

Message from the IRA to Irish Citizens in 1941.

Dev's response was, *"If there was not only a declaration of a United Ireland in principle, but also agreement upon its Constitution, then the Government of Éire might agree to enter the war at once. But the Constitution would have to be fixed first"*. The British cabinet agreed to explore the idea on 25 June, but Churchill insisted that the offer of a United Éire would be conditional on its acceptance by Northern Ireland. MacDonald brought a six-point offer to Dev and read it for him.

The points were:

1. *A declaration to be issued by the United Kingdom government forthwith accepting the principle of a United Ireland.*

2. *A joint body including representatives of the government of Éire and the government of Northern Ireland to be set up at once to explore the constitutional and other practical details of the Union of Ireland. The United Kingdom government to give such assistance towards the work of this body as may be required.*

3. *A joint defence representative of Éire and Northern Ireland to be set up immediately.*

4. *Éire to enter the war on the side of the United Kingdom and her allies forthwith, and, for the purposed of the defence of Éire, the government of Éire to invite British naval vessels to have the use of the ports in Éire and British troops and sea planes to cooperate with the Éire forces and to be stationed in such positions in Éire as may be agreed between the two Governments.*

5. *The Government of Éire to intern all German and Italian aliens in the country and to take any further steps necessary to suppress Fifth Column activities.*

6. *The United Kingdom government to provide military equipment to the government of Éire[14].*

At this very time, Dev received advice from his secretary at External Affairs Joseph Walshe headed, *'Britain's Inevitable Defeat'*. It said, "Britain's defeat has been placed beyond all doubt. France has capitulated...neither time nor gold can defeat Germany"[15]. At this time too, confidential documents in the Department of External Affairs, which outlined the extent of cooperation of Ireland with the Allies, were being destroyed.

Walshe advised Dev on the British offer on a United Ireland writing, *"There is not any guarantee, that having accepted the vague half-boiled proposals for a Union of Ireland, the Northern Government would be under any obligation to accept our view as to what the Union should be."*[16].

Dev felt that the document was not definitive but rather "a pious hope", dependent on British goodwill and the Northern Unionists. Unknown to Dev, Chamberlain had sent a copy of the proposals to Craigavon who replied, "Am profoundly shocked and disgusted making suggestions so far-reaching behind my back. To such treachery to loyal Ulster I will never be a party"[17]. Dev told MacDonald, *"If we have a United Ireland, it will be neutral for at least 24 hours. We will then call a meeting of our assembly and it will decide if we -as an independent nation- will come into the war"*[18].

Dev brought the offer to cabinet next morning where it was rejected. While most ministers supported Britain, others felt that Germany would win the war and they did not wish to antagonise the Germans.

Dev's official response on 5 July said;

"We are unable to accept the plan outlined, which we note is purely tentative and has not been submitted to Lord Craigavon and his colleagues. The plan would involve our entry to the war. This is a course for which we could not accept responsibility. Our people would be quite unprepared for it and Dáil Éireann would certainly reject it.

The only way in which the unity which is needed, can, in our view, be secured, is by the immediate establishment of a single sovereign All-Ireland Parliament, free to decide all matters of national policy, internal and external – the government which it would elect being responsible for taking the most effective measures for national defence..."[19].

It appeared that remaining out of the war was the Dev's top priority, as he feared another Civil War within his own party and the country, if he pursued the British proposal. Chamberlain was correct when he wrote, *"The real basic fact is that it is not Partition, which stands in the way at this moment but the fear of Dev and his friends that we shall be beaten. They don't want to be on the losing side and if that is numeric, one can only say that it is very much the attitude of the world from the USA to Romania and from Japan to Ireland"*[20]. Dev later explained his refusal by way of the boyhood practice in Bruree of 'equal holds'; each boy was to have a firm grip on what he was to receive, before he loosened his grip on that with which he was parting. The offer, which he knew came from Churchill, did not meet that measure. Chamberlain in fact was seriously ill and he died in November. Dev wrote to his widow, *"Mr. Chamberlain will always be remembered by the Irish people for his noble efforts in the cause of peace and friendship between the two nations"*[21]. Dev was later represented by the Irish Ambassador at the funeral of Mrs Chamberlain in Birmingham[22].

Paul Bew has written that for Dev, *"neutrality was the goal, not unity, and he was hostile to any attempt, whether from Downing Street or Nationalists in the six counties, to raise the unity issue"*[23].

Churchill had used Dev's supposed friendship with Malcolm MacDonald to entice Dev to allow the British access to the ports. In reality, Churchill regarded MacDonald as "rat-poison on account of his connection with the (Éire) ports"[24]. When MacDonald failed, Churchill sacked him from the cabinet and made him High Commissioner in Canada[25]. As the war situation became more intense, Churchill warned Roosevelt that he might have to change policy on Éire. Dev appealed to American public opinion saying that he intended to remain neutral[26]. The British realised that Irish-American public opinion was important to Roosevelt. The American Secretary of State Cordell Hull warned the British off, and was reassured that Britain would not invade Éire unless the Germans moved first.

Ribbentrop repeated his earlier assurances to Dev on 11 July that as long "as Ireland conducts herself in a neutral fashion it can be counted on with absolute certainty that Germany will respect her neutrality unconditionally"[27]. Churchill never gave any such guarantee to Dev; rather did he talk about the large German and Italian legations based in Dublin and reports of U-boats off the west coast.

Sir John Maffey succeeded in persuading his Government to supply Dev with arms for the Irish army. The British had feared that Éire might attack the North, but Dev reassured Maffey, "we will never do that. No solution can come there by force. There, we must now wait and let the solution come with time and patience"[28].

Dev attended the All Ireland hurling final at Croke Park on 2 September 1940 with Maffey and David Gray, the American representative. The next day the *Irish Press* carried a front-page picture of the three men together. A few days later two IRA men, who had been involved in an incident where two detectives had been shot dead, were executed. Dev was demonstrating that he was capable of being as forthright as WT Cosgrave in earlier years. David Gray was a graduate of Harvard and aged 70. He was married to an aunt of Eleanor Roosevelt's and was a close friend of the President.

DEALING WITH THE OPPOSITION 1940

Fine Gael favoured a National Government to steer the country through the war. Fianna Fáil rejected this saying that a Coalition Government would lead to instability. It feared that some of the smaller parties, especially Clann na Talmhan, would make inroads into its own vote should it get into any form of Government. Dev believed in single party Government with himself at the head, as the best way of ensuring the future for Fianna Fáil and the country. He did agree to set up a National Defence Conference composed of James Dillon, TF O'Higgins, Richard Mulcahy of Fine Gael; William Norton and William Davin of Labour; Frank Aiken, Gerry Boland and Oscar Traynor of Fianna Fáil. Mulcahy described the attempts of the Opposition members to elicit basic information as akin to "hens scratching" for facts. The Conference, however, gave a public image of national solidarity, which was all Dev wanted from it.

When finally informed of the British proposal, Ristard Mulcahy offered Fine Gael support. He wrote, *"If DeValera tried to carry the country for abandoning neutrality on the strength of the present British promises, he would be beaten; doubted that the Dáil or the country would support it"*[29]. Richard Mulcahy was most unhappy with Chairman of Defence Council Frank Aiken, accusing him of restricting proceedings narrowly and using it as a means to persuade the country that the main political parties were united behind its policies. On 9 July WT Cosgrave himself wrote to Dev concerned that if an invasion took place from Germany, the Irish defence would be so poor that Britain would also invade and Ireland could become the location for a major war, which would devastate the country for years to come. He wanted the defence forces bolstered immediately, with help from Britain. He agreed with Dev that a change in neutrality could only occur when national unity was obtained and was supported by the people.

North Strand Dublin, aftermath of German bombing raid, May 1940.

DeValera and Ministers visit the scene of the German air attack.

Cosgrave agreed that the recent British offer on unity did not meet those criteria. He called on Dev to allow the all-Party Defence Conference to discuss policy matters, writing, "Our representatives on the Defence Conference discuss with you the imminence and the extent of the danger and the steps necessary to defend the country". Dev replied on 13 July 1940 that the continuing policy was to "maintain our neutrality and give no pretext to either side for violating our territory"[30]. Though Dev promised that the Defence Conference would consider policy, Aiken did not allow this[31].

Later that year, after Churchill's diatribe on the refusal of access to the ports, Cosgrave wrote again to Dev, "Neither my colleagues on the front bench, nor I, have any information regarding the problems likely to arise or what measures have been taken or are under consideration for dealing with them". Cosgrave had only heard of Dev's reply to Churchill through the press. Dev realised that he had Cosgrave cornered, as officially he was in total support of the government policy and could not afford to break with that publicly. At the same time Dev was not prepared to allow Cosgrave any input to national policy, being suspicious that Fine Gael continued to be too pro-British. David Gray, the American representative in Dublin was critical of the calibre of the Irish Government when it did not "consult the Opposition over the emergency"[32]. As well as external attacks, the Government also feared a possible internal rising by the IRA with ex-Chief of Staff, Seán MacBride in particular having close contacts with German activities[33].

The defence measures taken in Ireland to guard against an invasion included securing the docks, airports, and oil installations by the military. The British laid a minefield off the Waterford coast to push any German invasion into the Atlantic, where the British navy could deal with them. The Irish army had 8,000 troops with another 110,000 in reserve to repel an invasion. It was composed almost entirely of infantry, with minimum transport facilities. It was hamstrung by a lack of modern equipment and a noted reluctance for males to join up. Most young adventurous men appeared to join the British forces instead. The head of the Irish army, General McKenna, did an excellent job with the material at his disposal. While Chamberlain was British Prime Minister, requests for arms and ammunition were well received, but when Churchill took over that diminished greatly. An ongoing problem the Irish army faced was the possibility of a British invasion from the North and a German one from the South.

On the night of 15 April, Germany bombed Belfast killing 750 people. Dev responded to a request from John MacDermott, the North's Security Minister for fire engines, after consulting Cardinal MacRory first. Thirteen units of Dublin's fire brigade went north immediately, to help put out the ensuing fires. This may have been a technical breach of neutrality and the fire engines were recalled on the following night.

Speaking in Castlebar some days later, Dev said, "*I know you will wish me to express on your behalf, and on behalf of the Government, our sympathy with the people who are suffering - they are all our people. We are one and the same people – and their sorrow in the present instance are also our sorrows and I want to say that any help we can give them in the present time, we will give to them wholeheartedly, believing that were the circumstances reversed they would also give us their help wholeheartedly*"[34].

The following month of May saw Dublin bombed at the Phoenix Park and at the North Strand, where 34 people died, 90 were injured and 300 houses were damaged or destroyed. Brian Girvin writes, *"It is likely that this and other attacks by the Germans were intended to terrorize the Irish population and to emphasise the costs of giving up neutrality. If so they were clearly successful"*[35]. On that same night however the Germans had also bombed Liverpool and Bristol, so it is more likely that Dublin was mistaken for a British city. In 1956 Germany paid £327,00 in compensation for the Dublin bombings. During the *'Battle of Britain'* Germany blitzed Britain and 43,000 civilians were killed.

When Churchill spoke in Parliament in November 1940, he had to face growing disenchantment and defend his Government. He choose to attack the lack of facilities at the Irish ports, saying that if they had been available "our losses would have been far less". This attack on Irish neutrality caused great anger in Ireland. But as Brian Girvin points out, Churchill was seeking a suitable scapegoat to overcome a fraught domestic political situation. Girvin goes so far as to say that in fact, "Churchill was diffusing the issue of neutrality"[36]. A submarine had just sunk the liner The Empress of Britain.

President Douglas Hyde, with Sinéad and Eamon DeValera.

CHAPTER 20

DEALING WITH THE USA

David Gray, the American representative in Dublin, was seventy years of age and as tall a man as DeValera himself. Many of his private letters to President Roosevelt carried detailed commentaries on his work in Ireland. He was a most unorthodox diplomat and was to cause Dev great grief during his seven years stay in Ireland, from April 1940. Gray was anxious that Dev would give up neutrality and join in the effort to defeat Germany. He warned Dev that a German victory would be a disaster for Ireland. Dev wanted an American statement that it would defend Ireland from invasion. If this was forthcoming he told Gray that he would consult the Dáil on neutrality. Dev also sought arms. Roosevelt refused in June 1940 to make any offer, as Germany was being victorious in Europe. Churchill was also in contact with Roosevelt, trying to get access to the Irish ports but also in the hope of getting America to drop its neutrality and enter the War.

It became apparent that both Britain and Germany acknowledged that America had become a global power. Roosevelt, while favouring Britain, could not understand why Dev would not give the British access to the ports, but he was acting carefully in public for domestic political tactics. Dev had replied, *"There can be no question of leasing these ports. They are ours. They are within our sovereignty. Any attempt to bring pressure to bear on us by any side can only lead to bloodshed"*[1]. Gray reported to Washington following this statement that, *"Dev's whole power is based on his genius engendering and utilizing anti-British sentiment...He has the qualities of a martyr, fanatic and Machievelli. No one can outwit him, frighten or blandish him. Remember that he is not pro-German, nor personally anti-British, but only pro-DeValera. My view is that he will do business only on his own terms or must be overcome by force"*[2].

The American Association for the Recognition of the Irish Republic was isolationist and resisted Roosevelt's pressures on Dev, who had urged the AARIR to *"Request your members and all friends of Ireland to organise and put Ireland's case including Partition and the condition of the Nationalist Minority in the Partition area clearly before the American people. To force into this war a people relatively defenceless against air attack would be an inhuman outrage. The Irish people have a right to keep out of it as Americans have"*[3]. When Roosevelt was returned as President in November 1940, David Gray reported that no member of Fianna Fáil offered congratulations[4]. He told Roosevelt in Feb 1941, that it was difficult to get the Irish to realise that the American people had little understanding or sympathy with Mr DeValera's academic contentions[5]. Britain had powerful friends within Roosevelt's administration who were pushing towards assisting Britain in a war for democracy against dictatorship.

Sir John Maffey, who was on good terms with Dev, nevertheless warned London, *"Dev is still the chosen tribal leader for their feuds…. Éire is a bog with a petty leader raking over old muck heaps. He has in the past enjoyed world prestige, he is vain and ambitious, but the task he has followed without looking either to right or left, is now leading to insignificance"*[6]. Churchill's view of Irish neutrality in January 1941 was, *"I do not personally recognise Irish neutrality as a legal act. Southern Ireland having repudiated the Treaty, and we not having recognised Southern Ireland as a Sovereign State, that country is now in an anomalous position. Should the danger to our war effort through the denial of Irish bases threaten to become mortal, which is not the case at present, we should have to act in accordance with our own self-preservation and that of our Cause"*[7].

Wendell Wilkie, whom Roosevelt had defeated for the Presidency in 1940, came to Britain in early 1941, as his personal representative. Wilkie also came to Dublin, where he spoke frankly to Dev about the bigger war picture. Dev told him that he wanted Britain to win the war and Wilkie said that he should help the British cause. In February, Dev again sought arms from the Americans. Gray demanded an assurance that such arms would not be used against the British. Dev responded that they would not be, unless the British invaded. Gray did not support the request and reported that many Fianna Fáil politicians and people were expecting that Germany would win the war.

The legal status of an Irish minister in the United States influenced the State Department. It told Joe McGarrity in 1939, *"The Irish minister to the USA bears letters of credence from King George, which are countersigned by the Prime Minister of Ireland"*[8]. This attitude made the Irish suspect that the State Department still regarded Éire as part of the British Empire and the British Ambassador had precedence over the Irish representative. The Irish view that their neutrality was the essence of their independence, was not comprehended by the USA or Britain, and most likely would not be understood by a victorious Germany. Dev stood on this principle for the long-term, when others had to think in the short term of defeating Hitler at all costs.

In early 1941, Churchill told Roosevelt that Britain could not *"undertake to carry any longer the 400,000 tons of feeding-stuffs and fertilisers which have hitherto conveyed to Éire through all the attacks of the enemy. We need this tonnage for our own supply and we do not need the food that Éire has been sending us…our merchant seamen and the public take it much amiss that we should have to carry Irish supplies through air and U-boat attacks and subsidise them handsomely, when DeValera is quite content to sit happily and see us strangled"*[9].

Roosevelt said publicly that American arms were only available to those resisting aggression and prepared to do so. He added that there was no specific aid programme in train for Ireland. Dev broadcast as usual to America for St Patrick's Day saying that blockading from both sides was challenging Ireland's neutrality. Gray accused Dev of hypocrisy, as Britain and Ireland had for the previous 18 months been adopting mutually advantageous arrangements on which Ireland depended for her supplies. Gray told Roosevelt that Ireland was not in any position to defend itself against "any third power unless it was British policy to help". He also told the President that Dev "cannot get out of his self-centred dream world and realize that the Irish will be goose stepping if Britain goes down".

Gray developed a pessimistic view of Dev as using neutrality and anti-British sentiment for his own domestic political success. He saw this as scuppering any possibility of ending Partition in the long run[10].

When Frank Aiken saw Roosevelt in April, they did not have a meeting of minds. As Aiken pressed him for an assurance that Britain would not attack Ireland, Roosevelt replied, *"You don't fear an attack from England. England is not going to attack you. It's a preposterous suggestion. It is absurd nonsense, ridiculous nonsense. Why, Churchill would never do anything of that kind. I wouldn't mind saying it to him myself"*[11].

Irish Americans remained firmly of the view that Ireland was under mortal danger of being invaded. On Sunday 11 May 1941 the Rosary was said throughout America to invoke the Divine aid to preserve Ireland from invasion. As Irish-Americans pressurised Roosevelt, he responded, *"When will you Irishmen ever get over hating England? Remember if England goes down, Ireland goes down too. Ireland has a better chance for complete independence if democracy survives in the world than if Hitlerism supersedes it"*[12]. After meeting Churchill in August 1941 and edging towards manoeuvring American participation in the war, Roosevelt hoped that his meeting "may make a few more people in Ireland see the light…People are, frankly getting pretty fed up with my old friend Dev".

When Gray challenged Dev at a meeting in Dublin on the allegation that Britain was blockading Ireland, Dev exploded, shouting, *"This is an impertinence to question the statement of the Head of State"*. Dev's official biography confirms this exchange but says Dev's own note, *"does not record the anger"*[13]. Gray did admire Dev, telling Eleanor Roosevelt, *"I like him very much, though I despair of coping with him. The great thing DeValera's Government has done and is doing, is to govern in the interests of the under-privileged. They have a real New Deal here"*. Sinéad and Dev attended one dinner party the Grays gave, but they were not at ease together in social situations, and asked not to be invited again. DeValera himself came to dislike Gray intensely[14].

CENSORSHIP

Censorship was being so strictly applied in Ireland that the only version of events made public was that of the Governments and the public knew nothing of these battles with the USA. Gray told Roosevelt that he believed that DeValera never even told his own Cabinet of the rows he had with him[15]. The censorship regime under Frank Aiken, Joseph Connolly, TJ Coyne and Michael Knightley acted like zealots in their devotion to their work. Their censorship was total in preventing the people from knowing what was going on in Ireland and the greater world. But they also made themselves and the country look ridiculous, as they extended their writ to ban books and films.

George Bernard Shaw

James Joyce

Seán O'Casey

Frank Aiken

James Joyce, Frank O'Connor, Seán O'Faolain, GB Shaw and Seán O'Casey had their work banned. It was forbidden to play the records of Bing Crosby least his 'crooning' destroy the morals of the youth.

Dev even asserted that criticism of him could be against the national interest, and should be censored as he was faithfully carrying out the policy of the State. The Fianna Fáil party, the nation and the State were treated as one and the same by Dev and coalesced in his own person. The Irish State was solidly established, but the cultural domain, in whose name the whole separatist agitation had been mounted, remained largely marginal, even tokenistic[15a].

Radio Éireann was an under-financed section of the Department of Posts and Telegraphs with news broadcast three times daily. National news relied heavily on Dáil Debates and Government bulletins. Opposition politicians complained that the station might as well be called 'Radio Fianna Fáil', given its tendency to broadcast DeValera's speeches[16].

CONSCRIPTION

On 22 May 1941, the Irish High Commissioner in London, John Dulanty, met Churchill, who told him that he was being pressurised by Lord Craigavon in Northern Ireland to introduce conscription there. Churchill said that all the people there would be treated equally but "no obstruction would be put in the way of those people who wanted to run away". Churchill was very hostile saying that he had no sympathy with Ireland since the Treaty[17]. Dev consulted all the Opposition party leaders on the threat. Cardinal MacRory, based in Armagh, condemned the idea[18]. Gray contacted *Washington condemning the threat, adding, "It will seriously hamper the Opposition on which we must rely"*. Gray reported that they predicted, *"draft riots, the escape of draft dodgers to Southern Ireland who will be acclaimed as hero-martyrs by ¾ of the population and the fomenting of trouble by Republicans and 5th Column Communists"*.

Dev told Churchill officially, *"the imposition of conscription in any form would provoke the bitterest resentment among Irishmen and would have the most disastrous consequences for our two peoples. The conscription of the people of one nation by another, revolts the human conscience...The Six-counties have towards the rest of Ireland, a status and a relationship which no Act of Parliament can change, They are part of Ireland. They have always been part of Ireland, and their people, Catholic and Protestant, are our people"*[18a].

Churchill replied in fury to Dulanty, denouncing the Irish as breaking faith on the Treaty and losing her soul. He invoked Irishmen like the Redmond brothers and Tom Kettle, who had demonstrated courage and valour. He threw Dulanty's note aside and ranted in his Victorian attitude to Ireland as an integral part of the Commonwealth, and Dublin as the second city of Empire. He said he would put Dev's case before the Cabinet and let the matter be decided there[19].

DeValera called a special meeting of the Dáil on 26 May, where the party leaders spoke cautiously on the threat[20]. James Dillon, who believed that Ireland's duty was with the Allies, annoyed his own party colleagues by asserting that "the Government's present policy of indifferent neutrality" was wrong. The next day Churchill said that conscription in the North would be more trouble that it was worth. Dev thanked God for the decision[21].

PEARL HARBOUR

David Gray well realised that Roosevelt was intent on joining the war, though Dev believed that this was unlikely, as it would necessitate getting authorisation from the Houses of Congress. Gray predicted that Japan would attack America. He wrote to Roosevelt on 21 October 1941, *"Japan may have touched things off. You have handled the situation as miraculously, as every other, as far as I can see"*. On 7 December the Japanese attacked Pearl Harbour, which it was felt certain, would herald the entry of the USA into the war. Churchill was euphoric and later that night called his amanuensis Mrs Hill to take a telegram. Dev was awakened in the early hours of the morning to receive the British representative carrying an important message. Dev alerted his military chiefs, unsure as to what the communication might contain. Dev received the note directly from Sir John Maffey. It read: "Now is your chance. Now or never. *'A Nation once again'*. Am very ready to meet you at any time". The fact that Churchill chose to quote what had been the official anthem for the old Irish Parliamentary Party was not lost on Dev.

Churchill was elated at the time over Pearl Harbour, which he saw as leading to his own long-term aim of bringing the USA into the war. Dev was relieved that the message contained no threat and decided to take a few days grace before he replied. He did not feel it wise to accept the invitation to visit London. He was astute enough not to accept Churchill's inference that the ending of Partition was then likely nor did he wish to compromise neutrality. He replied in a very low key, *"Thanks for your message. Perhaps a visit from Lord Cranbourne would be the best way towards a fuller understanding of our position here"*[22].

Cranbourne came to Dublin in secret very shortly and had a full discussion with Dev. Cranbourne told Dev that if Éire did not enter the war, it would not be represented at the post war peace conference. Dev entertained Cranbourne and Maffey to lunch at Iveagh House. Maffey at times was envious of how frankly Gray felt able to speak to Dev. He reported, *"An American minister had the temerity to make it plain to Irish nationalists that that they were no longer the darling Playboys of the Western World, and to point out that the audience were bored"*. Gray could afford to be aggressive with Dev, as he knew that he had the full backing of Roosevelt, who told to him on 2 August 1941, *"Praise the Lord, you have got the number of certain persons in the emerald Isle! People are, frankly, getting pretty fed up with my old friend Dev"*. Dev made inquiries and suggested that Gray be moved but was rebuffed[23]. Gray was not privy to the extent of the secret cooperation between Ireland and Britain, and went along with the public hostility of Churchill, who appeared not to know either.

The British Secret Intelligence Service Agent in Dublin, Capt. Collinson, added to their file on DeValera in 1943, which had originally been opened in 1919, *"The legendary DeValera desires to appear a Simon Pure Patriot with a single idea. He is conceived as a 20th century democratic leader whose record has never been spoiled by deviation from First Principles. Fanatical but honest is another view. So skilfully has this fiction been fostered that to many, it would be considered a travesty of the ideal to hold him up as he really is – a peculiarly astute politician with a strict economy of the truth, who by no stretch of the imagination is a democrat"*[24]. This file was operative until 1975.

The entry of America into the war meant that very many Irish-Americans would be directly involved in the combat. Dev acknowledged this on 14 December when he spoke in Cork. He said that the people of Ireland would naturally feel sympathetic to the people of the USA. He reiterated however, that Ireland could only be a friendly neutral in the war. "Any other policy would have divided our people, and for a divided people to fling itself into this war would be to commit suicide". The American Friends of Irish Neutrality went out of existence shortly after America entered the war. Paul O'Dwyer, its main sponsor, had to bow to practical politics and cease his anti-British agitation. Neutrality had become a badge of dis-honour in America.

Maffey sounded out Dev in December 1941 about the possibility of facilitating American bases. Dev refused. Roosevelt met Churchill in Washington in January 1942 and decided to station American troops in Northern Ireland. Very soon Irish Coastwatchers from Mayo to Donegal reported American aircraft coming in from the Atlantic flying towards Northern Ireland[24a]. When the troops landed on 26 January, Maffey requested Dev not to object. Dev was anxious not to antagonise American opinion, but however issued a statement reiterating his view that, "The Irish people's claim for the union of the national territory, and for the expression of jurisdiction over it, will remain unabated"[25]. The value of the strategic position of the South quickly became obsolete as American ships patrolled the North Atlantic. Ireland was left alone and isolated.

Dev made representations directly to the USA. The State Department assured him that the American presence in the North meant no change in principle on Partition. Roosevelt told Dev in February 1942 that there was no question of the American forces invading Irish territory or of attacking the Irish army. When Eleanor Roosevelt made a visit to Belfast, she pointedly did not travel to Dublin.

On Easter Sunday 1942, the IRA had shot a policeman in Belfast. The IRA group were given the death penalty in July 1942. Dev feared that a mass execution would revivify the IRA. He appealed to Churchill and the Americans to avoid executions. Five sentences were repealed but despite Dev's personal appeal to Churchill. Tom Williams was hanged on 1 September 1942[26].

*Identification signs were painted along the Irish coastline in many places,
to warn off both Allied and German Aircraft.*

*The Irish Pine though it had clear markings on its hull showing it was a neutral ship,
was still sunk by the German U-Boat 608 on 16 November 1942, with no survivors.*

Gray was only made aware of the extent of the Irish-British military and civilian cooperation in March 1942. He described the extent of this cooperation as, *"beyond what might reasonably have been believed possible"*. This cooperation was then extended to the Americans. Gray embarrassed and annoyed Dev when he sought to discuss this cooperation with him. Dev did not wish to discuss such matters on a diplomatic level, rather believing they were matters for the military and civil servants. Dev met representatives of the Allies on a regular basis and was fearful that their reports could be intercepted. He kept his own meetings with the Axis diplomats to a minimum. The reports of these diplomats to their own countries were being intercepted throughout the war, often causing consternation to the Allies.

Herr Hempel complained about the term, 'friendly neutrality' but due to the capture of the German spy in Ireland, he was not in a very strong position to press it. Goertz had been at large in Ireland and in contact with the IRA. Hempel wanted this incident kept secret. The Irish warned Hempel that the use of a radio transmitter at the German Legation could attract enemy attention and should not be used. In February 1942, the Irish threatened to impound the transmitter if it was used again. As the Germans continued to parachute spies into Ireland, the transmitter was eventually deposited in a bank vault for the duration of the war, by mutual consent, on 21 December 1943.

COOPERATION WITH THE ALLIES

Hitherto both German and British military personnel, who were captured in Ireland, were interned. After the arrival of the Americans this was changed to release all military personnel who made forced landings during non-operational flights. This naturally favoured the Allies, as the Germans were unlikely to fly over Ireland on training flights. Hempel protested. This was but one example of very many, where *de facto,* Dev favoured the Allies during the war. This was recognised as such with Randolph Churchill, describing 'non-operational' as a 'convenient fiction'. The Canadian High Commissioner reported that the term "non-operational has sometimes been stretched almost beyond recognition". Of the 142 Allied planes involved, 47 were refuelled and left immediately; 27 damaged planes were returned by road to the North. Of the 538 men involved, 493 left shortly and 45 were interned briefly for show purposes.

Of the 55 Germans who landed, all were interned until the end of the war. The Irish did not detain any Allied sailors, though 214 German were interned. Captured spies were similarly treated, while intelligence cooperation continued to a large extent. This included radar stations on the south coast and wireless equipment at Malin Head and Valentia Island. Most of the Allied internees were secretly released, after being moved away from where the Germans were being interned. A strong case could be made that Dev's official policy of neutrality helped the Allied war effort against Hitler, rather than hindered it.

COZY HOMESTEADS SPEECH 17/3/1943

The 50th anniversary of the founding of the Gaelic League was celebrated around the country in 1943. Dev participated in many ceremonies. On St. Patrick's Day he broadcast live on Radio Éireann on his vision for the ideal Ireland. He nominated the revival of Irish as the most vital task for the nation saying: *"It is our very own. It is an essential part of our nationhood. It has been moulded by the thought of a hundred generations of our forebears.. for many the pursuit of the material is a necessity. Man, to express himself fully and to make the best use of the talents God has given him, needs a certain minimum of comfort and leisure. A section of our people have not yet this minimum...that Ireland which we dreamed of would be the home of a people who were satisfied with frugal comfort and devoted their leisure to the pursuit of the things of the spirit – a land whose countryside would be bright with cosy homesteads, whose fields and villages would be joyous with sounds of industry, and the romping of sturdy children, the contests of athletic youths and the laughter of comely maidens, whose firesides would be forums for the wisdom of serene old age. It would, in word, be the home of a people living the life that God desires that man should live"*[26a].

That speech has been mocked and derided extensively in succeeding years. But in the context of the closed, puritan controlled society, it was not at all so ridiculous as it appears to modern ears. It was a kind of a *Tir Na n-Og*, a kind of land of milk and honey where Irish Catholics could live *en route* to heaven. Of course nobody knew better than Dev himself that it was pie in the sky, but that did not detract from its political value for him. He was entitled to look into his own heart and speak to his people.

Ironically in the wider context of where Ireland is in the globalisation of the 21st century, that speech takes on an insurrectionary anti-colonial intensity. Declan Kiberd; writing in the *Irish Times* of 29 September 2001 asks why did most artists and journalists treat Dev's ideas with such hostility?. He suggests that the exclusion of intellectuals, under conditions of censorship from the national project, may after the 1920's, may be the real explanation. If they had been included they might have further developed the Yeats/DeValera themes of decolonisation and of a reclaimed national landscape. Censorship, in the midst of the horrors of war and the tribulations of the Emergency, ensured that any contrary voice was not heard.

Clare Willis writes, *"Certainly the viability of an independent, sovereign Ireland had taken root during the war, as DeValera's independent foreign policy built on political freedoms established in the 1937 constitution. But by 1943 most other pieces of the Republican dream looked to be in tatters, with the collapse of rural Ireland one of its greatest failures. The small farmer class was either buried alive by rural poverty or gone to England. And along with the vanishing Irish went the vanishing Irish language"*[27].

☙❦❧

David Gray wrote to President Roosevelt that Dev was not in touch with reality:

"Mr DeValera is living in a dream Ireland and still shutting out the rest of the world. Ireland is a puritanical country with a clergy, many of whom have never been away from the island and whose reading and general culture is limited. It is honestly believed by these elements of the clergy, that the Irish people must be protected from what in America seems innocent and amusing fun".

"Your friend Mr. DeValera is continuing to ignore those little events of history, which in spite of him keep occurring. He is in fact too busy attending meetings celebrating the revival of the Gaelic language to give his attention to such matters...Douglas Hyde who founded the Gaelic League has his reward in being the paralysed, dummy President of an Éire, which would have seen Britain overrun by Hitler with a degree of satisfaction and without lifting a finger to prevent it".

"Meanwhile the Censor is loose again. The American flag was recently cut out of a film called 'Good Luck Mr. Yates'...Meanwhile I am surrounded by mountains of turf, some two hundred and fifty thousand tons, all brought from the interior with American gasoline. If I go nuts can you blame me?"[28].

GENERAL ELECTION JUNE 1943

At the beginning of the war, the country united to a great extent behind Fianna Fáil and Dev. But as the economic effects in particular and social restrictors in general became prolonged, the tide of public opinion began to shift. Dev realised this and postponed the upcoming election until the last possible occasion in June 1943. A farmer's party called Clann na Talmhan had been founded in the west in 1938 and gave a focus to the grievances of small farmers in particular. Within urban areas there was great poverty and the Labour Party was critical of the Government's failings.

The elections results were as expected, a close run affair.

Fianna Fáil	67
Fine Gael	32
Labour Party	17
Clann na Talmhan	13
Independents	8

Though Fianna Fáil lost ten seats, it also gained 9 seats more than it was entitled to under a strictly proportionality basis. The new party Clan Na Talmhan did very well in the west, part of Fianna Fáil's traditional heartland. Labour made remarkable headway gaining nine seats. Fine Gael was in a state of drift and did poorly.

Dev ruled in a minority Government because the Opposition parties could not join together to form a government. The omens looked bad for Fianna Fáil continuing for a full term. But luck was on their side as a vicious split occurred in the Labour Party, between William O'Brien and Big Jim Larkin. The Labour Party was accused of being Communistic by O'Brien and Fianna Fáil was happy to join in, particularly in the case of that political street fighter, Seán MacEntee. A new National Labour Party emerged, which was friendly to Fianna Fáil. WT Cosgrave retired from the Dáil and as leader of Fine Gael in January 1944. The new leader Ristard Mulcahy did not have a Dáil seat.

ALLIES WORKING TOWARDS VICTORY

In May 1943, David Gray suggested to the State Department that it demand the lease of air and shipping facilities for the Allies, the removal of the Axis diplomats from Dublin, and clarification on Ireland's position on the British Commonwealth. A refusal of facilities could lead to cutting off of supplies and conscription in the North. But the American military and the British government doubted the importance of the military facilities. Gray did not put these demands to Dev until Feb 1944. Dev read the Note and said "Of course, the answer will be, as long as I am here; it will be no". Then he asked, "Is this an ultimatum?" Gray demurred. But the next day Maffey arrived with a similar demand. The American Note dated 7 March 1944, went into details about the possibilities for espionage by the Axis diplomats. It ended by demanding *"You will, of course, understand the compelling reasons why we ask as an absolute minimum the removal of these Axis representatives…It is hardly necessary to point out that time is of extreme importance, and that we trust, Your Excellency (Eamon DeValera) will favour us with your reply at your early convenience"*.

Cardinal Spellman of New York had visited Ireland in1943 to encourage Irish support for the war effort. At a dinner in his honour, attended by DeValera, Archbishop McQuaid, Seán T. O'Kelly and Sir John Maffey, the Cardinal made a toast to *"the President of the United States and the cause he serves"*[29].

Though Dev knew at that stage that the war was nearing its end and that the Allies would be victorious, he was determined to preserve neutrality. A draft of his reply said; *"The request was one to which it must have been known by the American Minister here, the Irish Government could not possibly accede…it seemed designed therefore to put the Irish people in the wrong before the American public, in the case of certain contingencies occurring…"*. Dev was aware of the bad publicity that a refusal could engender. The revelation of the details of the cooperation between the Irish military and those of Britain and America, could be used to demonstrate that Ireland had been cooperating extensively with Britain all along, but Dev did not favour this. He approached both the Canadians and Australians to have the Note withdrawn, without success. Dev had received the Note on a Monday and waited until the Friday to inform the Opposition parties.

Brian Girvin writes, *"This reflected his usual contemptuous attitude to them on matters he considered the Government's responsibility"*[30]. Dev got the support of Labour and Clann Na Talmhan, with the Clann's leader Mick Donnellan advising that if the Axis Legations were to be expelled, then so should those of the Allies. Fine Gael procrastinated and asked to see his reply to the Note[31]. Gray assured Dev that no matter what the reply was, there would not be an American invasion. Dev's reply of 10 March spoke about safeguarding the interests of the USA but reiterated, *"The Irish Government must in all circumstances protect the neutrality of the Irish State"*.

The American Note and the Irish reply were both published, to the embarrassment of Dev. For the next two weeks, the American press portrayed Dev as being indifferent to the presence of Axis spies, who were a threat to the lives of US soldiers. Churchill reacted angrily and took measures to isolate Ireland by restricting all trade least any information about the Second Front leak out. Churchill commented, *"No one, I think can reproach us for precipitancy. No nation in the world would have been so patient"*[32]. He advised Roosevelt on 19 March that he felt it was too soon to offer Dev any reassurances. He wrote, *"To keep them guessing for a while would be better in my opinion. I think that we should let fear work its healthy process, rather than to allay alarm in DeValera's circles"*.

The reality was quite different, as Sir John Maffey wrote, *"The case against Éire on the score of the Axis Legation is not so strong as we have to make out. The German Legation is the symbol and if I could say to Mr DeValera, 'Keep your symbol but put it in the zoo' he would say: 'Now you are talking'. We would be sure in fact, that Germany would be not much more effectively represented in Dublin by Hempel than Greenland is by the Polar Bear"*. As T. Ryle Dwyer has pointed out so clearly, the intelligence forces of Britain and the US were very happy with the assistance that Dev was giving them. Robert Brennan, the Irish Minister in Washington, asked permission to reveal the latter, but Dev who felt that such a disclosure would have made a mockery of Ireland's supposed neutrality, refused this. Dev did not do 'losing face', for himself or Ireland. Instead he sent Joseph P Walshe to London to offer to implement whatever security measures the American and British wanted, short of expelling the Axis representatives. Russell Forgan acting head of the European operations for American Security said after the war, *"The Irish provided some 'very useful' cooperation on intelligence matters. In general, despite the American news media, the Irish worked with us on intelligence matters almost as if they were our allies. They have never received the credit due them"*. In fact the American military were reluctant to have Ireland join the Allies, as they believed that Irish bases would be a liability to the Allied war effort. The American note was more a political matter than a security one. As T. Ryle Dwyer writes, *"In the last analysis, DeValera gave the Allies all the help he could, while at the same time keeping Ireland out of the war. It was a magnificent achievement"*[33].

Despite DeValera's admirably adroit handling of the delicate situation, he paid a high and unwarranted price. James Reston of the *New York Times* wrote that DeValera would not enjoy, "quite the same political support from the USA that he has always counted on in his battles with the British"[34]. Thus, in fact, was a large part of Gray's strategic diplomatic aim achieved. Dev would never again have the stature of an international statesman that he had in the 1930's at the League of Nations. This undermined whatever slight possibility there might ever have been of doing anything about Partition. It strengthened Britain's hand, and that of Northern Ireland, as having stepped up to the mark in the defeat of Hitler and all he stood for. Dev's Éire had stood aside, been recalcitrant. It never even received the credit due for its truly very effective pro-Allies neutrality.

Undeterred by his international isolation, Dev issued an appeal to all the armies fighting in Italy to spare the city of Rome from any bombing. After consulting with the Papal Nuncio Paschal Robinson, he said, *"As the head of the government of a state whose citizens in a great majority, belong to the Holy Catholic Apostolic and Roman Church, I think it my duty to express, on their behalf, the deep distress which they feel, a distress shared by the three hundred million Catholics throughout the world...Future generations will forget the military considerations should the city be destroyed...So, too, should the city be spared, future generations will remember..."*[35].

This appeal to Herr Hempel elicited a reply on 15 April, that Germany had instructed all its soldiers to bypass Rome. In May 1944 an address of thanks, signed by hundreds of artists from Rome thanked Dev. It said: *"Rome is for us the reason of life. And it is easy to understand our emotion when we think that a son of such a far away country, had tried to keep it from being harmed, just as if he himself felt himself to be a son of Rome. We Italians feel you to be a brother, and the attachments of affection and thanks between Italy and Ireland will never weaken. The memory of this noble gesture on the part of Ireland's Prime Minister will pass on to future generations"*[36].

GENERAL ELECTION MAY 1944

On 9 May 1944, Dev's minority Government was defeated by one vote in the Dáil on a Transport Bill. He could have called a vote of confidence the next day and continued in government. Dev however saw an opportunity for electoral success and advised the President that same night, that he was dissolving the Dáil, and calling a snap General Election for 30 May. The Opposition were furious as the cross-party unity during the war years was sacrificed for electoral success. James Dillon said to Dev in the Dáil, *"There you are; the old warhorse is pawing the ground and sniffing the air. He thinks he is going to secure political advantage in a snap General Election"*[37].

The General election was a triumph for Dev, as Fianna Fáil won 76 seats, fourteen more than the combined opposition. Labour was reduced to 9 seats while Fine Gael got 30 and Clan Na Talmhan held on to 11 seats. Ironically Dillon, acting in his own idiosyncratic fashion, did not vote against Dev for Taoiseach in the new Dáil, arguing that the people had given him a clear majority.

Dev's defence of Irish neutrality contributed to and was bolstered by this electoral success. In September 1944 when it was clear than the Allies were being victorious, Gray demanded from Dev an assurance that Ireland would not give asylum to "Axis war criminals". This was refused.

Roosevelt died on 12 April 1945; Dev adjourned the Dáil saying, *"President Roosevelt will go down in history as one of the greatest of a long line of American Presidents, with the unparalleled distinction of having been elected four times as head of the United States. Personally I regard his death as a loss to the world"*[38].

Gray wrote to Eleanor Roosevelt about the Government ministers and their wives calling to offer condolences. He added, *"Mr. DeValera made a very moving tribute in the Dáil this morning and moved adjournment till tomorrow. I thought I knew this country and its people, but this was something new. There was a great deal of genuine feeling"*[39].

On 30 April, Gray demanded that he be allowed to seize the German Legation in Dublin. Gray was informed that when the Germans formally surrendered, Hempel would be ordered to hand over the keys of the Legation. Dev told Gray, "I do what I think is right"[40]. Hitler had committed suicide that same day of 30 April 1945. DeValera, accompanied by Joseph Walshe paid a formal visit to offer condolences to the German Minister.

While this visit caused outrage around the entire world, DeValera wrote to Robert Brennan in the USA saying, *"I expected this. I could have had a diplomatic illness, but as you know I scorn that sort of thing. So long as we retained our diplomatic relations with Germany, to fail to have called upon the German representative would have been an act of unpardonable discourtesy to the German nation and to Dr. Hempel himself. During the whole of the war, Dr. Hempel's conduct was irreproachable. He was always friendly and invariably correct - in marked contrast with Gray. I certainly was not going to add to his humiliation in the hour of defeat. It would establish a bad precedent. It is of considerable importance that the formal acts of courtesy on such occasions as the death of a Head of State, should not have attached to them any further special significance, such as connoting approval or disapproval of the policies of the State in question, or of its Head. It is important that it should never be inferred that these formal acts imply the passing of any judgements, good or bad"*. Brennan replied, *"Personally I am glad you did the right thing concerning Hempel, but the atmosphere created here because of that is still bad. For instance, not one of our old friends in Congress offered to put your speech on the Record"*[41].

DeValera did not offer any explanation of his action in public, as it might have been interpreted as an excuse, an admission that he had acted wrongly. He remained adamant that he had acted correctly and wisely. James Dillon, who was a one-time admirer of Dev but latterly a critic, especially on neutrality, said that Dev, *"never did anything which at the time of doing he believed to be wrong. When he acted, he would act ruthlessly and inflexibly and never look back"*[42].

HIGH COMMISSIONER
FOR IRELAND

Secret Report No. 9.

ÉIRE

55-57 REGENT St
LONDON S.W.I

15th May, 1945.

The Secretary,
Department of External Affairs,
Dublin.

C. O'9.

A mutual friend of ours asked me on the telephone, somewhat peremptorily, whether I would be lunching that day at a certain place which we both frequent. When I met him he showed a rather violent reaction to the visit of the Taoiseach and yourself to Hempel.

He was appalled at what struck him as the diplomatic unwisdom of the Irish Government's action in regard to the death of Hitler.

Whether neutrality was a good or a bad thing, whether Hitler was an agreeable or disagreeable character, or even whether it was a good thing or not for Ireland that the United Kingdom had won the war, were questions not relevant to his present point. His point, which he put vehemently, was that England _had_ won the war, that she now had it in her power to make conditions more easy or more difficult for Ireland in the future and that, consequently, it should be one of the first objects of the Irish Government to please English opinion so far as it was consistent with its own interests.

I said we were probably the best judges of what was consistent with our own interests. We had been neutral throughout the war; we had merely followed diplomatic usage and our own dignity required Ireland in the last act to conform to the protocol. Surely he must have known that the question of Hitler, the man - as distinct from the Head of a State - whatever his real character might, or might not have been, never arose. Our friend's own experience, I should have thought, would have shown him repeatedly that what was morally indefensible nearly always turned out to be politically inept. He rejoined that in the case in point, there was no moral issue at all and no principle that mattered a damn. Protocol was not principle. It was made for man, not man for it. Nor could he see that any question of dignity arose. Even if it did, the practical disadvantages of doing what our Government

had/

A portion of a letter condemning DeValera's visit to German Minister Hempel, written by the Irish High Commissioner John Dulanty to Joseph Walshe, Secretary at the Department of External Affairs Dublin, expressing strong negative views.

Paul Bew writes, *"The moral myopia associated with the state's promotion of neutrality was most flagrantly exposed in DeValera's infamous visit to the German Minister in Dublin to present his condolences on the death of Hitler"*[43].
Germany surrendered on 7 May 1945. That same day saw disturbances in Dublin as a mob of university students burnt a British flag at Trinity College. The students attacked American and British businesses. The Government had to apologise the following day.
The scale and nature of the Nazi atrocities in some of the concentration camps was already known widely. Buchenwald had already been liberated.

DEV REPLIES TO CHURCHILL'S ATTACK

On 13 May 1945 Churchill, in a victory broadcast, attacked Dev, saying, *"Had it been necessary, we should have been forced to come to close quarters with Mr. DeValera. With a restraint and poise, to which I venture to say, history will find few parallels, His Majesty's Government never laid a violent hand upon them, though at times it would have been quite easy and quite natural, and we left the DeValera Government to frolic with the German and later the Japanese representatives to their hearts' content".*

On 16 May DeValera replied in a famous carefully crafted radio broadcast to Churchill saying, *"Mr. Churchill makes it clear that, in certain circumstances, he would have violated our neutrality and that he would have justified his action by Britain's necessity. It seems strange to me that Mr. Churchill does not see that this, if it be accepted, would mean that Britain's necessity would become a moral code and that, when this necessity became sufficiently great, other people's rights were not to count. It is quite true that other great powers believe in the same code -in their own regard - and have behaved in accordance with it. That is precisely why we have the disastrous succession of wars - World War No. 1 and World War No. 2 - and shall it be World War No. 3? By resisting his temptation in this instance Mr. Churchill instead of adding another horrid chapter to the already bloodstained record of the relations between England and this country, has advanced the cause of international morality an important step. Could he not find it in his heart the generosity to acknowledge that there is a small nation that stood alone not for one year or two, but for several hundred years against aggression; a small nation that could never be got to accept defeat and has never surrendered her soul?"*[43a].
DeValera's reply was a masterpiece and was seen by Irish people all over the world as absolving him from any opprobrium over his actions during the war, including his visit to Hempel to offer sympathy on Hitler's death. On the international stage, it did not merit such understanding as to take away from the incredulity and outrage at Dev's visit and condolences. Neither did Dev's praise for Churchill's predecessor, Neville Chamberlain, endear him to many British ears. Of Chamberlain he said, *"I believe he will yet find the honourable place in British history which is due to him, as certainly he will find it in any fair record of the relations between Britain and us".*

Professor Eunan O h'Alpin wrote, *"Ireland had been completely dependent on Britain in economic and strategic terms; she could not import or export a single item without British agreement...Hitler could do nothing to help the Irish State against Britain even had he wished to...Irish-Allied cooperation can equally be read simply as sheer pragmatics, if not outright cynicism, rather than proof of a principled unvoiced attachment to the Allies and the associated democratic and humanitarian values with which their cause was retro-fitted...Circumstances, not free choice, determined most states' involvement in or avoidance of the war"*[47b].

When Harry Truman became President, Dev assumed that it would be easy to have Gray moved out of Dublin. This did not happen and it was wrongly assumed that his relationship with Eleanor Roosevelt meant that he still had undue influence in Washington. The new Secretary of State, however, wished to improve relations with Ireland and agreed that Gray was an obstacle. Gray was aware of these diplomatic manoeuvrings. During their last meeting on 25 June in Leinster House, Dev told Gray that he hoped their difficulties would be forgotten. Gray replied that that it had not been helpful to seek to use Irish-American organisations to influence and to pressurise the American Administration. On Partition he told Dev that if he wanted it ended peacefully, *"The only other course is in your own hands; that is to make conditions so desirable in Éire that the North will wish to join you"*. Eventually Gray did leave Ireland on 28 June 1947. Dev held an official reception for him, at which both men indicated how much they had respected each other in difficult times. Dev did Gray the honour of providing a navy Corvette to take him out from Cobh to the *SS America*. Gray summarised Dev thus:

"He believes that his mission is to save Ireland. Believing this, it is essential that he should remain in power. To continue in power, the Nationalist issue of Partition is essential. To achieve the ending of Partition would be equivalent to relinquishing power, since 36 Protestant members would represent the Northern counties in the Dáil" [44].

Dr. Adolph Mahr, a Nazi, had been Director of the National Museum before the war. He went to Germany for the duration of the war and sought reinstatement in his position in Dublin subsequently. This was refused after Dev received advice from MI5 and James Dillon, with Mahr pensioned off against his wishes[45]. There is little doubt that many Irish people, with some justification, favoured Germany in the war. As RM Douglas reports in Vol 17 No. 5 of *History Ireland* (September-October 2009), Freddie Boland found *"the vast majority of nationalists in the six-county area are absolutely pro-German"*. Dev himself confided to an American journalist that 'the people were pro-German'. Many felt that Ireland owed Germany a debt for her support in Easter 1916 and expected Germany to win the war and the end of Partition. The Sudetenland was regarded as Germany's 'six-counties', since the Versailles Treaty. The material success of the Axis countries was admired. Within Ireland some of these feelings formed the basis for the relative success of '*Ailtiri na hAiseirghe*', a new political party established in June 1942 by Gearoid O'Cuinneagain, which was clearly pro-Axis.

The power struggle within the Department of External Affairs where Secretary Joseph Walshe was pro-Fascist and Freddie Boland was pro-Allies, meant that Ireland was ready diplomatically to go either way, depending who won the war.

In 1957, Dev explained why Ireland kept out of the war, *"the terms on which the war would be ended would not be the terms we would have wished for, but the terms which would suit the interests of the large powers engaged in the war"*[46].

NUMBERS IN WAR

DeValera's achievement in keeping Ireland neutral, thus reinforcing its independent status, was almost universally popular in Ireland and further enhanced his stature within the country. For this reason the extensive cooperation with the Allies, right throughout the war, was little dwelt upon by Dev or the Fianna Fáil party in the aftermath.

One element of this assistance from Ireland, North and South, concerned the fact that all the Irishmen who participated in the war in the British forces were volunteers. So many of their graves can be seen in the various Commonwealth Cemeteries throughout Europe. Indeed the large American War Cemetery at Nettuno, outside Rome, contains soldiers with names such as Linehan, McBride, McGovern, McCarthy, McCauley, McNally and Murphy. The numbers of Irish in the British forces however, became a matter of controversy over the years. One fact appeared to be that nationalists in the North were proportionately much higher involved than were Unionists. Another fact was that, remarkably, eight men from the South received Victoria Crosses, while one Catholic from the North, James Magennis, was so honoured[47]. While the estimated numbers involved vary considerably, it is likely that over 120,00 volunteers came from Ireland as a whole, with 80,000 of them from the South[48]. Nearly 5,000 Irish died in the British forces, according to Yvonne McEwen, 2,302 from the South and 2,241 from the North[49]. The very day I write this, I read that Dr. McEwen from the University of Edinburgh's Centre for the Study of the Two World Wars, has been in Dublin to present a copy of the *Roll of Honour for Irish World War 2 Veterans* to Dr. Charles Benson, Keeper of Early Printed Books and Special Collections at Trinity College Dublin. Dr. McEwen said, *"Men from North and South fought together on the battlefield with no distinction as to who was who, and they need to be commemorated together"*[50].

Strict censorship was applied to death notices for these volunteers in the Irish newspapers. There was a tendency in official Éire to suggest that many of the volunteers were mere mercenaries, despite the fact that work in the war factories in Britain paid better than work in the armed forces.

Dev's Government treated those deserters from the Irish defence forces, who did not join the British forces but remained at home, less harshly than it subsequently treated members of the Irish defence forces, who deserted and joined the British forces[51]. When Irish volunteers in the British forces returned home on leave in 1945, they were not allowed to wear their uniforms publicly, though visiting American soldiers were allowed to do so.

The annual British Legion's march to the Irish National War Memorial at Islandbridge was banned in November 1945. The Government did not want to risk a major display of public support by its citizens for the war effort.

Nearly six thousand personnel of the Defence Forces were dismissed for desertion in time of National Emergency pursuant to the terms of the Emergency Powers Order 1945 or of the Defence Forces Act 1946.

JEWISH QUESTION

In 1995, I visited the Anne Frank House in Amsterdam. There was a large map on the wall, with the numbers of Jewish refugees taken in by each country attached. I was shocked to see no number beside Ireland. Had it been that bad?.

Ireland had a representative in Berlin since 1929. When Hitler came to power in 1933, the Nazis soon launched a terror campaign, which instituted a dictatorship. On 15 March 1933 the Department of External Affairs was informed that anti-Semitism was *"the principal plank in the Nazi platform"*[52]. Jewish communities around the world were horrified and demanded counter measures internationally. Ireland was not immune to anti-Semitism, fuelled no doubt by Christianity and sheer envy of Jewish industriousness and wealth. On 4 May 1933 DeValera publicly received Robert Briscoe TD the only Jewish member of Dáil Éireann, to express sympathy for the Jewish suffering in Germany[53]. DeValera also received the President of the *World Zionist Organisation*, Dr. Sokolow. He asked Dev, due to Ireland's close friendship with Germany, to intervene on its persecution of Jews and to assist with Jews immigrating to Palestine. Dev promised to do his best[54]. Non-German Jews in particular sought visas to escape to Ireland from Germany, but were discouraged, being regarded as *"only refugees"*[55]. This remained the official position of the Departments of External Affairs, Justice and Industry and Commerce throughout the period. The *Irish Catholic* newspaper reported in 1937, *"Hitler has many admirers among Irish Catholics"*[56].

The Irish reaction to Kristallnacht, when a pogrom was carried out against Jews and their property, was to establish the non–governmental *Irish Coordinating Committee for Refugees* in November 1938. This body monitored and processed applications for visas and helped to obviate the vicious anti-Semitic views of the Irish representative in Berlin, Charles Bewley. This is most clearly seen in a long report, from Bewley to Joseph Walshe, on the anti-Semitic movement in Germany, dated 8 September 1938. It reads like a justification for the anti-Semitism rife in Germany and other countries. It is a disgraceful document[57]. The Coordinating Committee facilitated the settlement of German and Austrian refugees, but ruled practising Jews ineligible for aid from Ireland, except for Jewish converts to Catholicism. Mervynn O'Driscoll writes, *"Except for the foundation of the ICCR and a few individual cases in which he had a personal interest, DeValera was content to allow the relevant authorities to deal with such applications"*[58].

When Charles Bewley read in the *Irish Press* on 26 November 1938 that 50 Jews were to be allowed into Ireland for training purposes, he was irritated that he had not been contacted on the matter. He wrote to the Department of External Affairs on 25 January 1939, *"It is my duty to make the following comments. It is a notorious fact that in the last few months, thousands of Jews have been baptised for the purposes of avoiding other inconveniences, to which they were exposed by membership of the Jewish religion"*[59]. In fairness to the secretary of the Department and the Minister Eamon DeValera, the Department soon issued what can only be seen as a sideways reprimand to Bewley. It wrote, *"The Minister will be glad to receive a comprehensive report on the European situation, so far as Germany is concerned, and what we consider to be the prospects of peace or war in the near future. The Minister is disappointed that no report on the international situation has been received from you since July 1938, notwithstanding the gravity of the September crisis and the predominant part which is being played by the German government, which might at any moment bring our Government face to face with issues of vital importance to the Irish people"*[60].

Early in 1939, the German *Charge d'Affaires*, Herr Thomsen, sought an urgent meeting with JP Walshe, Secretary of the Department of External Affairs. It is clear from Walshe's subsequent report to his Minister, Dev, that the character of the Nazis was clearly understood. Walshe wrote that Herr Thomsen complained about a press report of a pastoral letter from Bishop Browne of Galway, which "accused Germany of violence, lying, murders. The condemning of other races and peoples...". Walshe added, *"Herr Thomsen is insolent, bombastic. He is the first German I have met who seems to combine in himself all the worst ideas behind the Nazi regime..."*. Walshe then contrasts the cultured and diplomatic Herr Hempel with Herr Thomsen. He makes reference to a situation, which has received little enough subsequent attention in Ireland, *"I suggested to him the existence of a Nazi organisation in Dublin having its chief member and organiser an employee of our State, was not calculated to improve relations between our two governments"*[61].

As late as 1946, the Department of External Affairs official policy was that, *"our practice has been to discourage any substantial increase in the Jewish population. They do not assimilate with our people, but remain a sort of colony of a worldwide Jewish community. This makes them a potential irritant in the body politic and has led to disastrous results from time to time in other countries"*[62].

Donald Akenson writes of Ireland's attitude, *"The unbending self-interest is clearly shown in the government of Ireland's response to the Jewish refugee situation. The Irish were well informed of what was happening to the Jews in Europe, especially from 1938 onwards. Yet its response was to permit virtually no Jewish immigration...Ireland maintained a neutral stance between the perpetrators of the Holocaust and its victims"*[63].

In the 1960's the Irish-Jewish community organised the planting of an *'Eamon DeValera Forest'* in central Galilee. In April 1973 six pine trees were transplanted to Áras an Uachtaráin in a ceremony to honour Dev[64].

Taoiseach John Bruton, speaking at the National War Memorial at Island Bridge in 1995, apologised for Ireland's restrictive policy on the admission of Jews during the war. President Mary McAleese also expressed unhappiness on the issue some ten years later[65].

POST-WAR EMERGENCY LEGISLATION

At the end of the war in 1945, the Government introduced a Bill, which purported to drop the emergency legislation introduced in 1939. It was a complicated piece of legislation and many Deputies had difficulty dissecting it. James Dillon questioned DeValera on precisely what powers were being retained and what powers were being dropped. DeValera asserted that most of the emergency legislation would disappear. He admitted that since the end of the war, the Government had discovered that the IRA was continuing with its illegal activities and the Government had decided not to release its leaders. Dillon was not happy with DeValera's reply and said, "*I hope Deputy Costello will be more illuminating*". John A Costello said, jocosely, that he hoped to illuminate the darkness of Dillon's mind in a very short and simple sentence on the subject; "*The residue remaining in the Act when the Bill passes into law will be everything in the 1939 Act as amended, with the sole exception of censorship. All other powers could be introduced by the Government*". The Taoiseach exclaimed, "*Oh, no*". Costello continued saying that the Constitution would remain in abeyance. The Government could, by order, do anything they like. They could repeal Acts of Parliament. Dev interjected "*If it were only correct*", to which Costello retorted, "*I challenge the Taoiseach or any of his legal advisors to say it is incorrect. The Government, if this Bill is passed, may pass any particular legislation, by Order, about any matter they like, except censorship, and it cannot be questioned in the courts. That is the position we have to face here*".

Costello maintained that the emergency powers had strangled the business operations in the country. While Dev maintained that the Emergency was not over, Costello said, "*I say with confidence that the Emergency is over. I recognise that the country is still faced with difficulties, but they are not the type that enabled this House unanimously to grant these drastic measures to the Government in the 1939 Act*"[66]. The Act was passed.

DeValera had his greatest achievements completed after the war and might have exited from active politics at the zenith of his career, as he approached his 66th birthday. A successor who understood economics would have proved timely. Brian Girvin writes that his continuing leadership extended many of the illiberal and negative features of Irish society. Girvin accepts that these features were indeed embedded in society and that conservative Catholic Ireland, would have required a radical potential to change, a possibility that was not apparent anywhere at the time[67].

CHAPTER 21

POST WAR DEFEAT

ECONOMIC PLANNING VERSUS LAND DIVISION

The land policy was fundamental to the type of society Irish Governments wished to foster; an egalitarian rural self-sufficient and protectionist one espoused by DeValera, or the pursuit of economic development, increasing the national output and earnings from exports, as Seán Lemass and others favoured. Lemass had sought to have economic planning discussed as early as 1942. The secretary of his Department, Joseph Leyden, spoke to Dev about setting up a powerful committee to discuss it. Dev blocked this idea by setting up a 'shadow' committee consisting of Seán T. O'Kelly, himself and Lemass[1]. Later as the end of the war loomed, Lemass foresaw a huge influx of returned Irish emigrants from Britain. He sought to set up a Ministry of Labour to plan for that situation. Dev also stymied this proposal[2]. In 1944 the British produced a paper on full employment. This inspired Lemass to do likewise. He argued that a full employment policy was practical and was in line with economic thought, that "it involved no departure from principles".

Lemass must have shaken many of his Cabinet colleagues, particularly Dev, when following the principles of Michael Davitt, he told the Cabinet in January 1945 that private ownership of unproductive farmland should not be tolerated. He favoured large viable holdings. Seán Moylan had been an early advocate of querying the advisability of continuing land division, which had been a long-time policy of all governments. Seán T. O'Kelly, as Minister of Finance, had argued likewise. Lemass and Joseph Connolly criticised Dev for not instituting the policy of sustainable farms, promised since 1932. As late as 1957, Erskine Childers, Minister of Lands, said that land division was contributing to congestion rather than diminishing it, by creating too many small and uneconomic holdings[3].

The abandonment of land division would have negative electoral implications for Fianna Fáil. Dev would not tolerate this and he continued to urge greater progress in land division. Thus was the opportunity of 'creating a comprehensive and integrated programme' for economic development lost for over a decade as stagnation won out[4]. The essential policy of Dev was to retain political control and to achieve this he was willing to act in ways inimical to the economic interests of the people. This mirrored Catholic Church Leaders' actions in areas of education and health, where successive governments had allowed them extensive control[5]. Garret Fitzgerald terms Dev's attempts to make our part of this small island economically self-sufficient as *"futile and destructive"*[6].

Seán T. O'Kelly was elected President in June 1945 and moved off the political stage. This and the post war situation created room for change within the hierarchy of Fianna Fáil. Aiken, whose level of intelligence was questionable, and who had endured a disastrous visit to the USA during the war, was made Minister of Finance. Dev had earlier told Gray, *"We don't pay any attention to Frank's ideas about finance"*[7].

Seán Lemass also favoured radical social welfare changes, akin to the Beveridge Report of 1932 in Britain. Seán MacEntee, who was very conservative, regarded Lemass as a dangerous ideologue and akin to creeping Communism. Dev's main aim was to preserve his own record on the national and constitutional areas, which he adopted since the Treaty and which had been reinforced by his successful policy during the war years. The crucial appointment he made in Fianna Fáil was to appoint Lemass as Tánaiste. This appeared to place Lemass in the position of heir-apparent, though Dev certainly had no intention of handing over to any successor for many years to come. Paddy Hillery reported that Dev confessed to him that he had not had such a hard life in politics, as he never had to contend with any intrigue within the Fianna Fáil Party[8].

Dev remained Minister of External Affairs and wished to resume his involvement in international affairs. Ireland was very isolated diplomatically after the war. Her position within the British Commonwealth was somewhat vague. Technically it was still a member, though Dev described it as a Republic and did not attend Commonwealth meetings. He was content to leave the State's status "undefined". Dev did not occupy his office in the Department of External Affairs at Iveagh House and as Maire Cruise O'Brien writes, *"there was a certain sense of saturnalia about his absence. On the other hand, it meant that we were never in any doubt as to what government policy was on any issue"*[9]. All changed in 1948 when Seán MacBride became 'a resident minister'. Ms. O'Brien described herself as a *"dyed-in-the wool Fianna supporter who went around in a not unpleasurable state of moral indignation"*, at the defeat of Dev[10]. She writes that her father, Seán MacEntee, disliked and distrusted MacBride and his mother, Maud Gonne, believing them both and all their circle to have been double agents during the Civil War, and to have accepted both British and German money to destabilise the DeValera Government[11].

Dev raised the question of applying to join the United Nations in the Dáil and received backing there for his initiative. He declared, "However imperfect this Charter, I think it is our duty to play our part in this organisation"[12]. In November 1947 Dev had told Commonwealth Secretary Phillip Noel-Baker that Éire would soon be admitted to the UN, that she would then take part in a Western Regional Defence System[13]. Later in September 1949 the Soviet Foreign Minister Andrei Gromyko vetoed the application. He said that Éire had maintained relations with Fascist countries during the war and refused to open diplomatic ties with his country. *"Her behaviour is hardly calculated to help her admission to the United Nations"* he added[14].

DEV DEFEATED IN 1948

Dev tried to urge restraint in the country after the war. But several issues arose which made his attempts impossible. The Irish National Teachers Organisation had a major grievance over pay since 1939. They met Dev in September 1945 and got little encouragement from him. He did not think that primary teachers should be paid as much as secondary teachers. The Minister of Education, Tom Derrig, treated the teachers insensitively. Archbishop McQuaid offered to mediate but was rebuffed by Derrig. A long and acrimonious strike in the national schools in Dublin lasted from 20 March to 28 October 1946. The strike was eventually ended by the intervention of Dr. McQuaid, who "persuaded the INTO to capitulate"[15]. This left a huge well of bitterness towards Fianna Fáil, from a once traditional base[16].

One of the matters, which the Irish public had not been aware of during the war, due to censorship, was the plight of IRA prisoners interned by Dev. This became a major issue just after the war when censorship was ended. A Republican Prisoners Release Association became active, seeking to free the IRA men still interned. This culminated in the person of Seán McCaughey, who had been held in solitary confinement for four years. In April 1946 McCaughey went on hunger and thirst strike in protest at his imprisonment. He died on 11 May 1946. Con Lehane, a lawyer, contacted the prison governor immediately saying that he wanted to be present at the inquest. Lehane, accompanied by Seán MacBride and Noel Hartnett, who both appeared in full court costume, attended at Portlaoise prison. MacBride was allowed to question the prison doctor. The questioning was:

MacBride: Are you aware that during the four and a half years he was in prison here, he was never out in the fresh air or sunlight?

Dr. Duane: As far as I am aware he was not.

MacBride: Would I be right in saying that up to twelve or thirteen months ago, he was kept in solitary confinement and not allowed to speak or associate with any other person?

Duane: That is right.

MacBride: Would you treat a dog in that fashion?

Mr. McLoughlin (for the authorities) that is not a proper question.

MacBride: If you had a dog would you treat it in this fashion?

Duane: (after a pause) No[17].

No further questions were allowed. When the interchange was published, it caused a massive outcry as the Government sought to defend itself from the ensuing opprobrium. When MacEntee fielded Clann Na Talmhan's Mick Donnellan's twelve questions in the Dáil, Dev complained about 'trick questions'.

Of course the question on every ones mind, was how could Dev have continued to allow such horror to take place under his regime, with the war long since over? Earlier he had interceded with the British and Northern authorities to be merciful to other IRA men. Dev's response was given in the Dáil on 29 May when he said, *"If we gave way on the matter of clothes, then it was going to be another matter and another matter until the prisoner got exactly what he wanted – immunity"*[18].

CLANN NA POBLACHTA

On 6 July 1946, a new Republican party was founded at a meeting in Barry's Hotel, Dublin. It was called Clann an Poblachta. Much of its membership consisted of well-known republicans, with Seán MacBride as leader. Another ex-Chief of Staff of the IRA, Michael Fitzpatrick together with two former Adjutants General, Donal O'Donoghue and Jim Killeen, sat on the Executive. The new party also had another tier of socially conscious legal people like Noel Hartnett, Con Lehane and Peadar Cowan. Some, like Noel Hartnett who had once been on the Fianna Fáil National Executive, had political experience. Many national teachers joined the party. It got good press coverage and the Special Branch duly attended the launch, noting the names of all those present. It was a good time to form a new political party, with much unease felt by so many segments of society. The new party created great uneasiness within Fianna Fáil, as it was so obviously intent on challenging Dev's mantra about Partition, as mere shadow boxing. In the Mansion House on 5 February, MacBride said:

"If there is any reality to any attempt to end Partition, we must throw open the door to elected representatives of Northern Ireland. In the Constitution it is claimed that the Dáil is the parliament of the whole country. Yet Mr. DeValera's Government refused to allow elected representatives of Northern Ireland to sit in Leinster House We must face realities and we must realise that if we get a Republic in name, it would mean nothing, unless it ensured economic and social freedom for all the people of the country. We have to ensure that no section of the people will be exploited by another section"[19].

Three by-elections were scheduled for October 1947, and the new party felt confident enough to contest all three. Fianna Fáil warned that if it did not do well in the by-elections, a General Election would follow. The new party caused a political sensation by winning two of the three seats involved, with MacBride elected in Dublin. They took their Dáil seats on 5 November. Two days later the Dáil set up a *Tribunal of Inquiry* into the sale of Locke's Distillery in Kilbeggan. Oliver Flanagan TD had accused Dev, Seán Lemass and Gerard Boland, of bribery and corruption in the matter. Dev realised the imminent electoral danger posed by the Clann to Fianna Fáil. He was determined not to allow it time to organise properly around the country, where it might seriously damage Fianna Fáil. The Dáil constituencies had been redrawn, with the number of three seaters increased from 15 to 21. This would favour the largest party. The number of Dáil seats was increased from 138 to 147[20]. The *Locke Tribunal* reported on 19 December that there was no foundation to the allegations made.

Two days later, and 15 months before it was necessary, Dev announced the dissolution of the Dáil with the General Election to be held on 4 February. Some of Dev's senior colleagues were against this strategy, wishing to hold on until more favourable conditions prevailed[21]. The opposition catch cry, which was personally hurtful to Dev, was 'put them out'[22]. Fianna Fáil had used the same slogan against WT Cosgrave in 1932. John Maguire writes, *"In many respects Clann Na Poblachta possessed an appeal similar to that of Fianna Fáil in 1932"*[23].

The election resulted in Fianna Fáil getting the lowest number of first preference votes since 1927. It had no overall majority. The result was:

Fianna Fáil	68
Fine Gael	31
Labour	14
Clann Na Poblachta	10
Clann Na Talún	7
National Labour	5
Independents	12

Fianna Fáil however, had won more seats than all the Opposition parties combined. It appeared that Dev would be returned as Taoiseach again, especially as National Labour were aligned to Fianna Fáil. General Richard Mulcahy, the leader of the much weakened Fine Gael party, decided to issue an invitation to all the other party leaders to meet. He said that they should seek to agree a common platform to oust Dev. Such a course appeared very unlikely, but the very next day the unlikely was challenged when Seán MacBride responded positively to Mulcahy's invitation. There appeared a chasm between MacBride and Mulcahy, one the ex-IRA Chief of Staff, the other head of the army during the Civil War, a man held responsible by Republicans for the execution of many of their colleagues. Was it possible that their detestation of Dev could bring them into a political alliance?

All the Opposition party leaders, and representatives of the Independents, except for National Labour, met and agreed a common programme. The idea of Richard Mulcahy possibly becoming leader of 'their' Government was a step too far. When this was made clear to Mulcahy, he magnanimously stood aside as the name of John A Costello of Fine Gael, found common agreement. Mulcahy then had to approach Costello with the offer. Costello was reluctant at first but after some prevarication, agreed and attended the meeting to finalise matters, including the allocation of Cabinet portfolios[24].

Dev continued to believe, however, that he would be re-elected as Taoiseach again. The Congress of Trade Unions met and instructed the five National Labour TD's to vote for him. Costello met with James Everett and Dan Spring of National Labour.

Costello was completely forthright with them. There was a Cabinet seat available for Everett, and Costello promised them a fair deal all round. Despite the pressure on Spring and Everett, they agreed to support Costello's nomination. On the very day the Dáil met, Dev still expected to be victorious but shortly before the vote he heard of National Labour's intention. There was a major task in clearing his office of personal papers and preparing it for his successor. Dev was defeated by 75 to 70 votes, with Costello being elected by 75 votes to 68. Costello had a brief meeting with Dev in the Taoiseach's office before he left to meet the President, Seán T. O'Kelly.

This must have been a devastating outcome for Dev, in continuous power for sixteen years. Kathleen O'Connell retired from the civil service to continue to act as his devoted secretary. John Horgan writes, *"For a time after the election, Dev virtually disappeared from view and Lemass took his place. This was partly because Dev chose to absent himself on a number of tours abroad – to the United States, Australia, New Zealand and India – to publicise Ireland's case on Partition. It was a decision that in any case spared him the undoubted difficulty of having to continue to make an impact on national policies from the seat of leader of the Opposition, without notes and civil servant service support and afflicted by deteriorating eye sight"*[25]. The disposition engendered in Fianna Fáil, due to the shock of being in Opposition after sixteen years of being in government, created what John Healy described as, *"The mood was such that the Party would have opposed the Ten Commandments had they been introduced by a coalitionist Moses"*[26].

In America, DeValera was greeted rapturously by many thousands of supporters. He remained there for a month, meeting high officials of Church and State. In Washington President Truman and General George Marshall met him at the White House. He made an hour's broadcast from Chicago on the evils of Partition. In Los Angeles he attended the enthronement of Cardinal MacIntyre. He then visited India, where Pandit Nehru welcomed him in New Delhi. He was the guest of Viceroy Lord Mountbatten on the night before Indian independence. In Australia, his good friend Cardinal Daniel Mannix of Melbourne greeted him. He was honoured at the Federal Parliament in Canberra.

When Dev returned from America in April 1948 several thousand people greeted him at a meeting in College Green. These international anti-Partition publicity tours by Dev, increased pressure on the new Government to be seen to do something on Partition. Much of the rhetoric by Dev on the matter did not please the Unionists in the North. Lord Brookborough declared that he was confident the tour "would not influence the course of events in the slightest degree" as the US administration was opposed to any step which would whip up – as Mr. DeValera's tour was intended to do - anti-British feeling, particularly at a time when the UK was so much dependent on Marshall Aid...the whole constitutional structure of Northern Ireland was being assailed from every angle and it was an elementary duty of the Government to answer any attacks"[27].

That summer, Clement Atlee the British Minister, holidayed in West Mayo and met Seán MacBride, Minister for External Affairs, who lobbied him unsuccessfully on Partition.

DECLARATION OF REPUBLIC

On 11 July 1945, James Dillon asked Dev in the Dáil, *"Are we a Republic or are we not, for nobody seems to know?"* Dev replied, *"We are, if that is all the Deputy wants to know"*. Some days later, on 17 July, Dev famously quoted passages from a variety of dictionaries on the definition of the word 'Republic'. He told James Dillon, that the material for a conclusive answer on whether we are or are not a member of the British Commonwealth, is not fully available".

Though John A Costello was a compromise Taoiseach of an Inter-Party Government, he had an impressive political and legal background. He had been WT Cosgrave's Attorney General from 1926-1932 during a period of huge constitutional development. He had been a frontbench spokesman for Fine Gael for nearly fifteen years. He had ideas of his own as he settled in as 'Chairman' at the Cabinet table, rather than as a 'Chief', as Dev had been. Costello had long argued that the External Relations Act of 1936 was a sham. He intended to repeal the Act and take the country out of the British Commonwealth. Some have seen this as Costello 'stealing the Long Fellow's clothes'. Dev had long talked about the Republic but never taken the formal step. A Fine Gael Taoiseach would outmanoeuvre Dev and the Republican Party.

Costello said, *"I made up my mind to repeal the External Relations Act 1936, as soon as possible. I reached this conclusion entirely on my own and never at any time did Seán MacBride try to force me on the matter"*[28].

On 28 July 1948, Peadar Cowan TD asked Costello in the Dáil exactly how Ireland had ceased to be a member of the Commonwealth. Costello replied that it was a gradual development and though Ireland was *"sovereign, independent and democratic, it was still associated with the Commonwealth"*. Because that association was a free one, it *"can be terminated by unilateral action"*, he added. William Norton of the Labour Party said, *"It would do our national self-respect good, both at home and abroad, if we were to proceed without delay to abolish the External Relations Act"*. DeValera added *"Go ahead; you will get no opposition from us"*[29]. This was a very important intervention from Dev, for it committed him to accepting what Costello was to propose. The Government then made a unanimous decision to introduce legislation to repeal the Act, when the Dáil reassembled after the summer recess

Costello was due to travel to North America to speak at the Bar Association of Canada. At the last Cabinet meeting before the summer recess on 19 August, his speech was, unusually, read and approved. That same meeting agreed an *aide memoire* to the British Government recommending that the title of Irish envoys to Commonwealth countries be that of 'Ambassador' rather than 'High Commissioner'. The Cabinet also decided that Ireland would not be represented at the proposed meeting of 'Commonwealth Prime Ministers', but postponed a decision to attend otherwise than as a member of the Commonwealth.

L to R: Cardinal Spellman, Eamon DeValera, and Mayor Impellitteri
at a dinner in New York USA, March 1948.

Clement Atlee (centre) with American President Harry Truman (left)
and Canadian President William Lyon Makenzie King (right).

The circumstances that led to Costello making a public announcement about the repeal of the External Relations Act in Canada, on foot of a story in the *Sunday Independent*, have given rise to many conspiracy theories[30]. Seán MacBride's reaction in the Department of External Affairs was, *"There was complete consternation when they realised that we were going to repeal the Act, because it was exposing Fianna Fáil policy. This could have been done at any time, but we were doing it and showing that it could be done without any repercussion. Most officials in the Department were strongly Fianna Fáil"*[31].

When The Republic of Ireland Bill came before the Dáil in November 1948, Dev, despite barely suppressed fury from many Fianna Fáil Deputies, spoke positively about the measure. He regarded it as a natural follow on from his 1937 Constitution and the general acceptance of the Republican status of the country. He welcomed Costello's action but doubted that if he had proposed the measure, he would *"have got unanimity. But you will get unanimity from us because we have been in public life not to retard, not to put barriers to the outward march of the nation. This Bill does not purport to be establishing a new State. We are simply giving a name to what exists – that is a Republican State"*.

DeValera then added a word of warning. He said, *"I want the country and every representative here to see that we are, by doing this, burning our boats. I do not say it is a bad thing to do. There are times, but rare times, when it should be done. I hope there is to be no further disestablishment of the Republic... It must be on the basis of that Republic, existing as a State, that the relationship and the association, whatever it may be, whatever its form, with the states of the British Commonwealth will be founded"*[32].

Fianna Fáil and its leader, however, refused to participate in the ceremonies to celebrate the coming into operation of the Republic Act on Easter Sunday 1949. It was left to the President Seán T. O'Kelly and the Government Ministers, to represent the State at the ceremonies. The Minister for External Affairs, Seán MacBride was strangely absent also, being abroad on business. Noel Browne, who has asserted that MacBride was miffed that Costello had taken personal control of the whole episode and ignored him, represented his party colleague.

Costello explained that as a student of international law many years earlier, he had seen that it was difficult for any State to gain international recognition as a member of the Community of Nations. He declared, *"We now stand alone, as a nation on our own...We are a great mother country"*. He thanked the contributions made by Canada, Australia, New Zealand, South Africa and the USA. That night the President and Costello attended a Ceilidhe in St. Patrick's Hall, Dublin Castle. The Austin Stack Ceilidhe Band played the music.

The British Government under Clement Atlee responded robustly by enacting in law, the Ireland Act 1949 which said, *"in no event will Northern Ireland or any part thereof cease to be part of His Majesty's Dominions and of the United Kingdom without the consent of the Parliament of Northern Ireland"*. This caused great anger in the Republic and the Taoiseach introduced a resolution in the Dáil, condemning the move.

Costello said that the British Government had learned nothing from the last 169 years, or the last 35 years, of the consequences of their actions to the Irish people. He bemoaned the fact that their Act had secured that hundreds of thousands of Irish men and women, in the territories of Tyrone, Fermanagh, Derry, South Armagh and South Down, had to remain under the North Eastern Parliament against their will, by the creation of an artificial entity created by the British Act of Parliament 1920. He ended his speech in anger saying, *"That part of our country has been taken from us and is being annexed. We wanted to get the unity of our country on the basis of friendliness with the North and with Great Britain. We no longer need to play the role of the wounded Samson. We can hit the British Government in their prestige and in their pride and in their pocket"*[33].

DeValera supported all that the Taoiseach had said, deploring the fact that the power of veto had been given to a Parliament created specially to frustrate the will of the whole Irish people. He said they were a minority in Ireland, about one fifth of the population and not a fiftieth of the population of Britain. To that minority he said, *"We are not going to support you in your claim for privilege. We are not going to permit this small minority of the two peoples, to continue to set the two peoples by the ears and to stir up and continue the old antagonisms between them. The British had the power to undo the injustice, which they had perpetrated. If you had properly informed public opinion in Britain and a Parliament that responded to the feelings of the fair-minded people of Britain, we would have reached the stage when this would be done"*[34].

Costello then chaired an Anti-Partition Conference in which Dev participated. When Pandit Nehru visited Ireland in 1949, Costello and Dev led him to a seat of honour in the Dáil In 1950, the Holy Year, Dev attended the commemorations in honour of St. Columbanus at Luxeil in France. He travelled on to Rome for the ceremonies there. He then went on to the Holy Land, where he stayed in Jerusalem and was received by the Israeli Government. He always regretted that circumstances then did not allow him to visit Nazareth.

DeValera got an opportunity to get involved at an international level when he was a delegate to the Council of Europe at Strasbourg in 1949. Churchill was also there. Dev avoided him, lest his wartime adversary snub him[35]. Dev said that Ireland would not join any European federation as long as Partition remained[36].

COALITION GOVERNMENT FALLS

The major Church/State controversy on the *Mother & Child Scheme* had its origins in a Fianna Fáil Draft Health Bill of 1947. When James Ryan, Health Minister, showed it to Dev, he immediately saw difficulties, writing *"Confidential. I would not transmit this as it stands. It requires considerable revision"*[37]. When revised, it was shown to Archbishop McQuaid on 24 December 1947.

ଈଛ ଛଈ

Costello's Government inherited the Draft Bill and the new Minister of Health, Dr. Noel Browne, became embroiled in bitter disagreement with the bishops, the medical doctors and lastly his Cabinet colleagues. This was eventually played out in the media and the Dáil. Dev wisely steered clear and as the final bitter debate took place in the Dáil, he famously commented, *"I think we have heard enough"*.

When the Inter-Party Government did fall, Dev, who was then 69 years old and almost blind for several years, *"was still the hardiest of the campaigners. So long as he had the use of a microphone, three or even four meetings a day seemed to impose no real strain on him, and even at midnight he will still not hesitate to travel as far as 100 or 150 miles to the nearest city, have a meal before getting to bed about 3 a.m. and be on the move again at 8 a.m."*[38]. He was returned again to power, though in a minority Government.

Dev was a believer in strong majority rule government as best for the country and saw proportional representation, as enabling small parties to gain Dáil representation at the expense of the larger parties. He had warned in 1948 that this form of government "had led to dictatorship in certain European countries", as he called on his opponents to "have this bargain now in the open, and not to let the people be asked to vote in the dark. That is what they are doing and they know it"[39]. After victory in 1951, Dev did not retain the portfolio of External Affairs but put his long time friend and colleague, Frank Aiken, into Iveagh House.

Dev had major problems with his sight for very many years and was operated on at several junctures. At the age of 70 he again had an operation and spent his birthday in hospital in Utrecht. Among the messages he received there was one from Winston Churchill. A few of his close friends remained in Utrecht during his hospital stay. These included Kathleen O'Connell[40]. As he awoke after his operation, he could detect hospital staff surrounding his bed and they appeared to be chanting. He wondered whether they thought he was dead and then realised that they were singing 'happy birthday'. Dev spoke in the Dáil on 23 July 1952 and appeared as well as ever, in managing affairs of state.

MOTHER AND CHILD DEBACLE AGAIN

Archbishop McQuaid had experienced a major change between the Cabinets of John A Costello's and that of Dev's. He had found dealing with Costello's Cabinet, apart from Seán MacBride and Noel Browne, *"a very pleasant experience"*. He wrote in 1952 that the new policy with Fianna Fáil was one of, *"distance as far as the Church is concerned. That policy is seen as in the failure to consult any bishop on the provisions of a Health Scheme. All the present difficulty results from that failure. In assessing the attitude of Fianna Fáil Government, one may never forget the revolutionary past of that Party. On so many occasions the Party was on the side opposed to Episcopal directions. While, then, the outward courtesies will be accorded, the inner spirit of sympathetic and open collaboration with the Hierarchy will be missing"*[41].

Archbishop John Charles McQuaid (left) and Cardinal Dalton with DeValera.

Roger Casement's grave in Glasnevin Cemetery Dublin.

McQuaid was probably remembering the occasions in 1937 when he did not get all his preferred way on the Constitution, and in 1943 when as Chair of the *Commission on Unemployment*, he differed with Seán Lemass. McQuaid wanted answers concerning the spiritual and religious welfare of Protestants, to be directed to the Commission through the Government. Lemass demurred and suggested that such questions be omitted altogether. McQuaid approached Dev directly and was indignant with the reply telling him, *"The Commission itself is essentially a lay body"* which could not be involved in any religious discrimination. Though McQuaid protested to the upstanding Catholic Dev, the ruling stood[42].

In 1953, the aftermath of the 'Mother & Child' saga returned to cause Dev some difficulty. The Catholic hierarchy resurrected their objection to the Health Scheme that the Government was introducing, by sending a critical letter to the papers. Dev was determined that there would not be a repeat of the earlier public Church-State debacle. He contacted his old school friend, whom he had recommended for elevation to be a Prince of the Church, Cardinal d'Alton, and immediately went to meet him in Drogheda. They had an amicable discussion and the earlier letter to the media was withdrawn. The public were none the wiser that Dev's government bowed to the wishes of the hierarchy on the new Bill. For safety sake Dev did not participate in the Dáil debates on the matter[43].

Noel Browne described what happened, *"In May 1953 the Episcopal committee, which dealt with health matters, met Eamon DeValera and Dr. James Ryan in Cashel Co. Tipperary. The detailed notes of this fascinating meeting are at last available. DeValera and Ryan outlined the new amendment demanded by the bishops and already accepted, but the hierarchy now reconsidered the earlier amendment. Once again reshaped to their joint requirements, they were in turn accepted meekly by DeValera. All pretence at being independent members of the Cabinet of a sovereign parliament had been abandoned"*[44].

Dev was still feeling diplomatically isolated after the war, and was happy to accept invitations from foreign governments. He had recently visited two rather autocratic if not dictatorial leaders, General Franco of Spain and Antonio Salazar of Portugal, when a very welcome invitation came to visit his old adversary, Winston Churchill at Downing St. Churchill was also back in office as Prime Minister, since his post-war electoral defeat. There had been several earlier formal communications between the pair and this was a cordial occasion. The event had not been publicised, but a crowd of about one hundred had gathered and "cheered the Irish party lustily, though a police Inspector protested at the display"[45]. Churchill emerged from Downing Street to greet Dev and pose for photographs. FH Boland, who accompanied Dev reported, *"Churchill met us at the door. He greeted DeValera warmly, took him by the arm and said, "if you shout I shall be able to hear what you say. Now I will lead the way because I can see a little better"*. This brought a general bout of laughter. The two men talked privately for about 25 minutes before taking lunch". Dev did not let the occasion pass without raising Partition but Churchill stuck to the official policy of the Ireland Act 1949.

On the question of the repatriation of Roger Casement's body, Churchill was more forthcoming and promised to consult his Cabinet, though he did advert to the possibility that the people of Northern Ireland might not favour such a move. Churchill later told Dev that legal difficulties forbade the transfer of Casement's body to Ireland and that there was no need to reawaken *"the bitter memories of old differences"*[46].

In 1965, DeValera rose from his sick bed at the age of 83, to honour the arrival of Casement's body back to Ireland, for burial at Glasnevin. At the graveside, Dev recalled how when the prisoners were being released in 1917, they were held in Pentonville for a couple of days. He remembered them finding their way to Casement's grave and as they knelt to pray, seeing Eoin MacNeill, who knew Casement from the early days of the Gaelic League, pick up a few blades of grass to keep in memory. Dev referred to Casement's great humanitarian work in the Congo and Putamayo. He continued, *"This grave, like the graves of the other patriots who lie in this cemetery, like the graves in Arbour Hill, like the grave in Bodenstown, the grave at Downpatrick, the grave in Templepatrick, and the grave at Greyabbey – this grave, like these others, will become a place of pilgrimage, to which our young people will come and get renewed inspiration, to make this land worthy of all the sacrifices that have been made for it in the past"*[46a].

In the Dáil, when Dev refused to protest about a solidarity message Churchill had sent to the Prime Minister of Northern Ireland, Oliver J Flanagan of Fine Gael mocked him, saying *"Has the Taoiseach ceased to send such protests since he was given the latchkey to and hospitality at number ten Downing St…wining and dining with the British. Does the Taoiseach remember his charges of 20 years ago?"*[47].

When Churchill died in 1965 DeValera, who was then President, said, *"Sir Winston Churchill was a great Englishman, one of the greatest of his time, a tower of strength to his own people and to their allies in their hour of need. For this he will be acclaimed throughout the world. But we in Ireland had to regard Sir Winston over a long period as a dangerous enemy. The fact that he did not violate our neutrality during the war must always stand to his credit…"*[48].

The 1951-1954 Government of Dev's, was in power at a most difficult economic period and did little to ease matters. Dev did not understand economics and Seán Lemass had not been given his head to make any fundamental changes in a stagnant economy, where emigration saw massive numbers continue to leave the country. At the end of 1953, Fianna Fáil lost two by-elections placing it in a very precarious situation in the Dáil. A very mild budget was introduced in April 1954, proposing to free up to 40,000 people from the tax net; lowering stamp duty to 1% on houses up to £1,000 and a maximum of 3% on houses up to £32,500; reducing the price of bread, and flour, cutting entertainment tax and fixing the price of a box of matches at one and a half pence. John A Costello objected to an outgoing Government bringing in such a budget saying, "many of the provisions, due to statutory provision, fail to have any real effect and could hamper an incoming Government and its policy and operation". Three days later the Dáil was dissolved[49].

The General Election of 1954 saw Dev lose office again, as John A Costello returned to lead a second Inter-Party Government until 1957. Clan Na Poblachta, which had earlier imploded as a political party, was not part of this government. The IRA began a military campaign in the North, which Costello, despite the official rhetoric of the injustice of Partition, was forced to resist by charging and jailing IRA activists. Some of the IRA met Dev in 1956, in the expectation of getting his support or at least connivance in their campaign. He rebuffed them saying that Partition could not be ended by force of arms. Dev generally supported Costello's efforts to contain and defeat the IRA during this period. In 1956 Dev suffered a great personal loss with the death of Kathleen O'Connell, who had been his personal secretary for 38 years. Her niece Marie O'Kelly succeeded her.

It was during Costello's second government that eventually the Gordian knot of governmental economic planning was broken. Costello and his Minister of Finance, Paddy McGilligan, had been converted to Keynesian economics by Costello's economic advisor Paddy Lynch, during the 1ˢᵗ Inter-Party Government. During the 2ⁿᵈ Government the international financial crisis of 1956 forced a radical appraisement of economic planning and development. Costello outlined this on 5 October 1956 in a major speech. The plan had six principles:

To favour investment in Agriculture over all forms of investment.

To favour and encourage private investment to supplement and relieve the pressure on public investment.

To favour home investment rather than foreign investment.

To favour higher investment in Ireland based on Irish savings.

To encourage all kinds of exports.

To achieve the results desired by cooperation rather than by compulsion.

All kinds of initiatives were planned to achieve the targets, which were outlined in detail. The *Irish Times wrote, "The plan that Mr. Costello announced yesterday is the one that ought to have been put before the country thirty years ago. The pity is that we have had to wait for a moment of crisis, when the spending which it necessarily involves, looks more formidable than it would have appeared in more normal times"*[50].

The plan was generally welcomed, but Dev reacted by saying, *"The Taoiseach has treated us to another of his coalition blueprints for prosperity tomorrow...If promises, programmes and promises with commissions, councils and consultations were a cure for our ills, or a substitute for decisions and effective action, this country should never be in bad health"*[51].

Towards the end of 1956, Dev attended the centenary commemoration of John Redmond's birth in Wexford. He did so as Chancellor of the National University, which was established in 1908, through the efforts of Redmond and his Party. He declared that he was also attending for another reason. He outlined how he had opposed Redmond's attempts to take over the Volunteers and encourage Irishmen to fight in the First World

War. *"If we are worthy of the fight made for our nationality, whether made by John Redmond, Parnell or anyone else, we have the grit to triumph over the difficulties that beset us in the present time. I am happy to play my part in doing honour to a great Wexford man, to whom we are quite ready to give credit for having worked unselfishly, according to his views, for the welfare of this country"*[51a]

The General Election of 1957 returned DeValera to office with an overall majority of nine. This was the first occasion that this had happened since 1944. Dev was aged 75 and many of his Cabinet had been Ministers going back to1932. On 20 March Dev was proposed as Taoiseach by Seán Lemass and seconded by Seán MacEntee. He introduced some new blood into cabinet in the persons of Neil Blaney, Kevin Boland and Jack Lynch. His cabinet was; Seán Lemass at Industry and Commerce, Jim Ryan at Finance, Frank Aiken at Foreign Affairs and Agriculture (temporarily), Oscar Traynor at Justice, Paddy Smith at Local Government & Social Welfare, Erskine Childers at Lands, Jack Lynch at Education & the Gaeltacht, Neil Blaney at Posts & Telegraphs, Kevin Boland at Defence and Seán Moylan at Agriculture.

The May budget was a harsh one, with huge cuts introduced into the housing programme and the removal of food subsidies, attracting the name of the 'Famine Budget'[52].

It was during this government that a settlement was being worked on between the British and the Irish on the long running controversy over the Hugh Lane Paintings. When Dev was returned to office he collaborated closely with Costello on the matter, until the latter agreed, writing reluctantly, *"I appreciate your courtesy in keeping me informed of the progress of these events...I have read the documents and I am sure it comprises the best that could be done in all the circumstances"*[53].

Crucially, Dev allowed the Secretary at the Department of Finance, appointed by Costello's Government and working organically from its new policies, to publish his *First Programme for Economic Expansion* on 21 November 1958. It was this plan, which formed the basis for the economic success of the country under Taoiseach Seán Lemass. Of course in allowing the publication, uniquely, under Ken Whitaker's own name, the author felt the Government *"thought they could get away with the total reversal of policy, if they ascribed it to the advice of independent civil servants"*. He felt that the longer sighted members of the Government, like Lemass and Jim Ryan, backed it and Dev went along with it too. Whitaker described Lemass as the 'arch-protectionist' following Frederick List, who realised that in the grim days of the 1950's *"something needed to be done or else the future might see a request to return to the union with Great Britain"*. Whitaker said that no one asked him to write the Programme and it was a *"self-imposed task"*. He said that Lemass was the one in Dev's governments who looked after the practical aspect of economic policies, while Dev looked after the spiritual. Dev never discussed economics with Whitaker. Despite all this, Dev insisted that the Programme was following his own long-standing policies since 1926[54].

CHAPTER 22

PARTITION AND OTHER ISSUES

Dev was fundamentally unsure of how to best approach the problem of Partition and the Unionists in general. In 1917 he favoured the expulsion or coercion of Northern Unionists. In America he advocated their assimilation, and by 1921 he advocated accommodating them in a federal Ireland within the Commonwealth[1]. Later in 1921, he declared that violence could not be justified as it would not work, and would be equivalent to what England had done in Ireland. By 1939, he said in the Senate, that he was ready to use force if it would be successful to, *"rescue the people of Tyrone and Fermanagh, South Down and South Armagh and Derry City from the coercion they are suffering"*[2].

On 12 July 1955, while speaking on External Affairs in Dáil Éireann, Dev said that the fact of Partition never meant the country was isolationist. It had participated in the League of Nations and had applied for admission to the United Nations. He claimed that Ireland's strength was more spiritual than physical. He was sure that the country was right in remaining neutral during the recent war. The fight against Germany was declared on the basis of good and moral reasons, but in every war such reasons were put. Small nations were not consulted on how wars were started and the great powers decided on the terms on which they ended. Military alliances are fraught with danger for small countries. While accepting that there was much scope for economic cooperation, he said it would have been most unwise, for instance, in the Council of Europe, to enter into a political federation, which would mean that you had a European Parliament deciding the economic circumstances of life in Ireland. In such an assembly, Dev said Ireland would be outvoted by 30 or 40 to one. He said that we did not escape from domination by outside forces, to go into a worse situation. He saw clearly at the Council of Europe an attempt to provide a full-blooded political constitution, with members divided into political parties, just like a national parliament. He noted that Britain itself was sceptical of such developments.

Dev agreed with the then Minister of External Affairs, Liam Cosgrave, that Partition would not be solved by force, and that the best line to pursue was the line of cooperation, to the utmost extent. He commended the offer of the Taoiseach to meet the Prime Minster of the Six County area and regretted that the latter wished to impose unacceptable conditions.

Dev said that numbers of Irishmen were induced to fight in the First World War, believing that it would bring unity between North and South. But Britain and the United States, which pledged self-determination, then failed to deliver. He said that similar inducements were made in the last war and were considered by him.

The phrase 'Ulster must not be coerced' was a recurrent theme, which was never reciprocated to the substantial numbers in Ulster, who never wished to be included in that entity. Dev concluded that the old phrase would be used again to break any pledges given for becoming militarily aligned. He felt that there was great scope for smaller states to work closely together at Strasbourg[3].

Dev sought to wean the IRA away from its campaigns in the North but without success. He reintroduced internment on 5 July 1957 and the following day saw the arrest of 63 well-known republicans. He was heavily criticised by many Irish-Americans who expected a different strategy from him to end Partition[4].

Though Dev always made the ending of Partition one of his two main goals in political life, he always found it difficult to be constructive in seeking to influence Northern Nationalists or Unionists. His aim of a Gaelic speaking Ireland and the Catholicisation of the State ensured that Unionists were entirely hostile to the notion of any unity with the South. Though his 1937 Constitution was for a 32 county country, he rebuffed Northern Nationalists requesting representation in the Parliament. When others proposed moves to influence Northern Unionists, Dev was cautious and negative. John A Costello's second Government had instituted the consideration of the 'practical problems arising on re-integration of the national territory'[5]. On becoming Taoiseach, Dev ordered the work to continue[6]. On 1 August 1957 he got a report on the matter. Most Ministers were against any further work on the issue[7]. Senator Stanford proposed in the Senate on 29 January 1958, *"That Seánad Éireann requests the Government to set up a commission or to take other energetic or decisive steps to consider and report on the best means of promoting social, economic and cultural cooperation between the 26 Counties and Six Counties"*[8]. Dev outwitted Stanford in getting him to agree to Dev's own proposal for a Joint Commission from both jurisdictions. Dev said, *"The Government is duty-bound - certainly in my opinion and in the opinion of the present government – to do everything in its power to foster economic, social and cultural relations...it was the duty of the Departments of State."*[9]. When Maurice Moynihan kept reminding Dev of progressing the matter, Dev finally responded, *"it is not necessary to raise the matter at a Government meeting. It may be presumed that Departments will keep the matter in mind without any explicit directions"*[10].

During his tenure at Áras an Uachtaráin, Dev confessed to Tom O'Neill and Ken Whitaker, that he had never understood the North. He told the family of Erskine Childers that their father had written to him before being executed saying, that Dev's greatest challenge would be Northern Ireland. Childers had said that the Northern Protestants could not be coerced[11].

ॐ ॐ

CENSORSHIP

A controversy arose in 1957 over the censorship of books. Professor JJ Piggott chaired the Censorship Board with two fellow conservatives and two liberals as members. Costello's Government had unusually not replaced a Catholic priest on the Board by another priest, thereby lessening conservative influence. Under the Censorship Act, books could only be banned when there were three votes in favour and not more than one against. Thus Costello shattered the status quo. Piggott protested and refused to convene the Board. He later resigned together with his two conservative colleagues. Their replacements were all Catholics but none were priests. Catholic institutions mounted a concerted lobbying campaign and the hierarchy wrote to the Government on 30 Jan 1958. Dev responded in a finely crafted letter to Bishop Mac Neely, effectively rejecting a request for hierarchical representation on the Censorship Board[12].

FETHARD-ON-SEA BOYCOTT

The Fethard on Sea conflict over the rights of the education of children in a mixed religious marriage, and the subsequent boycott during 1957-8, also saw Dev intervene in a positive way and standing up to hierarchical pressures. A Protestant mother, named Sheila Cloney, married to a Catholic husband, had taken her children to the North and later to the Orkney Islands, to escape their being brought up as Catholics, as demanded by local curate, Fr. William Stafford. The couple had been married in a Catholic church in London in 1949 and she had apparently undertaken to accept the 1908 Papal decree *Ne Temere*, which stipulated that children of a mixed marriage would be raised as Catholics. Fr. Stafford called for a boycott of Protestant-owned local business in a retaliatory measure, claiming that the removal of the children had been done with the support and connivance of the local Protestant community. Bishop Browne of Galway preached an inflammatory sermon at a High Mass in Wexford, in the presence of Cardinal d'Alton. Archbishop McQuaid also spoke trenchantly on the matter and posed the question, *"Do non-Catholics never use this weapon of boycott in the North? Here in the South, do we never hear of them supporting only their own co-religionists in business and the professions? Those who seek the mote in their neighbour's eye, but not the beam in their own, are hypocrites and Pharisees"*. Brendan Corish T. D. of the Labour party supported the boycott, asking Dev in the Dáil, *"Will the Taoiseach endeavour to ensure that certain people will not conspire in this part of the country to kidnap Catholic children?"*[13].

Dev was forced to enter the matter publicly, when Noel Browne put down a Dáil Question on 4 July 1957. Dev had taken the precaution of discussing the situation earlier with Archbishop McQuaid and ascertained that McQuaid was not happy. Dev also showed McQuaid both Browne's Question and his own answer, before speaking in the Dáil. Dev replied, *"Certain representations have been made to me. I have made no public statement because I have clung to the hope that good sense and decent neighbourliness would, of themselves, bring this business to an end. I cannot say that I*

Sheila Cloney of Fethard on Sea Wexford,
with her children Eileen and Mary.

Brendan Corish T. D. of the Labour party,
who supported the Fethard on Sea boycott.

Meeting village children,
Spain, 1957.

Greeting Archbishop John Charles McQuaid.
Frank Aiken is on extreme left.

know every fact, but, if, as Head of Government, I must speak, I can only say, from what has appeared in public that I regard this boycott as ill-conceived, ill-considered and futile for the achievement of the purpose for which it seems to have been intended; that I regard it as unjust and cruel to confound the innocent with the guilty; that I repudiate any suggestion that this boycott is typical of the attitude or conduct of our people; that I am convinced that 90% of them look on this matter as I do; and that I beg of all who have regard for the fair name and good repute of our nation, to use their influence to bring this deplorable affair to a speedy end. I would like to appeal also to any who might have influence with the absent wife, to urge on her to respect her troth and her promise to return with her children to her husband and her home"[14].

Dev's own followers in Wexford, who had been part of the boycott favoured by the clergy, were in a quandary. Should they follow their Church or their political master? After Dev had spoken, the Bishops remained quiet and the boycott fizzled out. Mrs. Cloney returned home at the end of the year and educated her two girls at home. Seán Cloney told the *Irish Times* in 1957, *"I totally rejected the boycott. It caused a lot of trouble for me. My main support in breaking the boycott came from Old IRA men, who themselves had fallen out with the clergy during the War of Independence"*. Though Tim Pat Coogan argues that this episode, which Dev effectively brought to an end, illustrates that Dev was essentially a Catholic Head of Government, I think rather the shallowness of Irish Catholicism is illustrated by the episode[15]. Dev, as Joe Lee writes, certainly emerges with great credit in the matter. While Dev was a genuine practising Catholic, his adherence was to that particular form of Irish Catholicism, which allows its adherents their own *a la carte* version, as the occasion suits. Irish Catholics can disregard their religion, as the occasion demands with impunity, and do what needs to be done, and return to the fold immediately afterwards. They can ignore the admonitions of doctrine, biblical, Papal, or Episcopal and be automatically forgiven by Mother Church, through a simple formula. It does not automatically follow that in doing so they are objectively doing any wrong, for Irish Catholicism has not always distinguished itself in its moral or conscientious teaching to its flock. Dev, as supreme pragmatist, was never in awe of any clerical authority. Seán Cloney died in 1999 and his wife died on 28 June 2001.

EMIGRATION

The levels of emigration from the Twenty-Six counties to Britain, rose rapidly during the war. John A Costello's first Inter-Party Government set up a *'Commission on Emigration and other Population Problems'* in April 1948. The Report was not published until May 1954. In the meantime in 1951, an Irish social worker named Foley, had compiled a survey on the appalling conditions in which Irish workers lived in, in Birmingham, contributing to a high level of alcoholism among them. Dev felt he had to be seen to do something on foot of the survey being read to him. He sent a copy to the Bishops and to the Secretary of State for Commonwealth Relations. He also decided to speak on emigration at a Fianna Fáil function in Galway on 29 August. He outlined the enormity of the scale of emigration, an average of forty thousand per annum. Then he added, almost unbelievably, *"The saddest part of all this is that work is available at home, and in conditions infinitely better from the point of both health and morale. In many occupations, the rates of wages are higher at home than they are in Britain...an Irish worker's conditions are so unattractive that he prefers unduly long hours of overtime to a leisure which he cannot enjoy. There is no doubt that many of those who emigrate could find employment at home as good, or better, wages- and with living conditions far better – than they find in Britain"[16].*

Many Irish emigrants were outraged by Dev's speech, and it was also criticised at home. Dev defended himself arrogantly, Diarmaid Ferriter judges, as he explained, *"I made this statement because I believed that a public statement was the quickest and most effective way of getting proper attention paid to the situation, and of ensuing that a remedy will be provided"[17].*

Little action followed and later, Irish emigrants sought Irish Government action to help alleviate their plight in Britain[18]. A petition signed by 20,000 of them asked the Government to establish an emigrant information office in Birmingham. This request was rejected. The Government stated, *"It could not accept any responsibility for the financing of such a project"[19].* All it promised was to assist, if a collection was properly organised, for funds to help the emigrants. In January 1955 Cardinal Griffin of Westminster, launched a collection to build an Irish Centre in Camden Town, and contributed £1,000 himself. Archbishop McQuaid gave £500 and Cardinal d'Alton £200. The centre was opened on 27 September 1955. Around 60,000 people emigrated during 1957 alone.

EDUCATION

It is one of the paradoxes relating to Dev, who had such a wide experience of educational matters, that he did not appear to regard it as a radical means to improve the lot of the people. Educational opportunity could have immeasurably improved peoples' lives at home and abroad, as well as contributing to the well being of the economy. Dev shares the political responsibility with the Cumann na nGael governments for allowing the Catholic Church to continue to retain control over primary and post-primary education, health and social services, after independence. The Church had been singularly successful in thwarting efforts by the British to have a non-denominational education system, open to all, established. It even opposed the idea of compulsory education at primary level, as an infringement on parental rights, thus depriving the introduction of poorer children into the system. The Church's control became almost absolute after independence, and at secondary level, was used first and foremost as a recruiting ground for religious vocations. I have shown in my autobiography, *The Good Samaritans – Memoir of a Biographer*, that this policy was used in an immoral way in Ballyhaunis County Mayo, to hinder access to secondary education for innumerable boys, over many decades[20].

DeValera's Government declined to increase the school leaving age from 14 to 16 in1936. He refused to go along with the Bishops advice to remove the ban on married women teachers in primary schools until 1958[21]. The non-denominational State system of vocational education, which was in theory, controlled by local Vocational Education Committees, often had priests on their committees and the ethos of undue deference to the clergy, meant that as often as not, they were elected to Chair the committees. In the 1950's, priests chaired 22 of the 27 Vocational Education Committees.

The current dilapidated state of many of our primary schools arises from the Church's resistance to State subvention. It had appeared that in 1952, the Minister of Education, Seán Moylan, was about to respond to pressure from the Irish National Teachers Organisation for the State to accept responsibility for the maintenance and construction of primary schools. The hierarchy, in the person of Eugene O'Callaghan, Bishop of Clogher, attacked the move as *"an intolerable state of affairs whereby civil servants from Dublin might come down and attempt to take control of the primary school"*. The Government allowed the *status quo* to continue, shirking its responsibility to the well being of school children. The Catholic Church's belief that original sin inclined children towards badness was the basis of society's espousal of severe corporal punishment both in school and in the home. Successive national governments were unable to counter or control excesses in this regard.

The *Ryan Report* from the *Commission on Child Abuse*, published in May 2009, has shown that most vulnerable children, under the jurisdiction of the State, were often cruelly abused, as the Church's remit usually ran in health and social service areas[22]. It says that Peter Tyrell, who spent the years 1924-32 in Letterfrack Industrial School, had written in the 1960's to President DeValera, Taoiseach Seán Lemass, Archbishop John Charles McQuaid and Bishop Michael Browne of Galway, concerning the abuse he had suffered there, but received no replies. He later burned himself to death in London in 1967[23]. Seán O'Faolain wrote that Dev had never really tried to radically help the poor help themselves but rather, *"he has kept the poor afloat by every kind of state charity"*[24].

Dev's attitude to the detention of boys can be seen from an exchange between himself and James Dillon in the Dáil in 1940, on a debate on a financial resolution for Reformatory and Industrial Schools. His attitude reflected the general attitude of Irish society of the times.

Dillon questioned Dev on his attitude to boys detained or remanded in the facility at Glasthule, which he wanted closed, along with the remand centre at Summerhill, which he described as no place for the incarceration of 8-12 years olds. Dillon added that the children of the poor were vulnerable as were their parents, who could not challenge the law. The 'public man' should be a trustee of the poor. "The children were not criminals and needed help from the Minister of Education, rather than police and magistrates. The institutions were run largely by Christian Brothers and orders of priests, who do their very best, very often with deplorably inadequate equipment. That is no fault of theirs, but these institutions are not adequate substitutes for good family surroundings", Dillon said. He asked Dev if he would allow a son of his, to be so treated?

In response, Dev said, *"I think that is a very fair test and a proper way to look at it. In my opinion, if taking him to Summerhill was going to cure him—and he was guilty, I would be sorry for him—I am sure all parents would be—but in the long run, I could not say that I had any complaint"*. Dev presumed that an investigation would be carried out to ascertain that the child was normal and what the child had done, was the child's fault, before being sanctioned in the courts. He said that if Summerhill was made too attractive, instead of having it as a deterrent, it might be rather an inducement. He had visited it, and found it scrupulously clean with a small number of boys there. Dev added, *"If it is certain, that boys have committed a certain offence, it may be better for the boys to let them appreciate the difference between being in their own homes and conducting themselves there, and being taken away. That may act as a deterrent and cure them of their desire to do certain things. I think you have to have things simple there. It is a mistake to try to accustom them to conditions, which they will not be able to reproduce, when they come out afterwards to earn their living. They must be conditions, which will not lead them to feel, when they come out, that there is a very big and violent change. I went prepared to find something very much worse than anything I did find"*.

When Dillon asked, did Dev notice the decrepitude of the locality the remand house was in, Dev replied, *"I did not see anything like that, in the part of it I visited, anyhow."* Dillon commented, *"You are an innocent poor man"*[25].

Another story from the past that is current as I write, in November 2009, concerns schemes which saw large numbers of very young 'destitute' children, sent from Britain to the colonies, including Australia. This was a long-standing practice. In a two-year period between 1848-1850, some 4,114 young Irish girls, handpicked by Government officials from workhouses, were sent to Australia. These are remembered in Hyde Park Barracks Museum, in Sydney. Their fate was very harsh. Currently, both Britain and Australia are in the process of apologising and 'rectifying' the lives of those sent from Britain in the late 1930's.

According to the seminal historian on child migration, Alan Gill, a similar scheme was mooted from Ireland in the late 1930's. Brother Louis Conlon, the head of the Christian Brothers in Australia, approached the Irish Government in 1938. His proposal was considered by the Cabinet and was "not approved". This was most likely down to Dev's own personal view, as he did not approve of child migration or indeed migration in general, as a solution to the problems of the country[25a].

Diarmaid Ferriter criticises Tim Pat Coogan for appearing to have a personal dislike for Dev and holding him personally responsible for many of the ills in Irish society[26]. Ferriter himself may counterbalance this, when for instance he writes, *"and when DeValera pressed for plans for 'educational reconstruction' in the aftermath of the Second World War, he received little in return from the Department of Education"*[27]. The truth naturally is somewhere in between, within that most complex and fascinating personage, juggling so many balls in the air contemporaneously, as James Dillon may have been inferring above.

DEV AS 'STRAIGHT MAN'

Conor Cruise O'Brien has written perceptively and wittily on Dev. He recounted an incident that he witnessed. A visiting Australian politician, named Cauldwell, had lunch with Dev. Though Cauldwell used bad language in ridiculing some fellow Australian politicians, Dev, who was the model of courtesy at all times, showed no signs of distress at what sounded to him like personal rudeness. Dev did not laugh. The Cauldwell doctrine may have been close enough to his own political philosophy, but he clearly didn't care for the way it was put. His expression, habitually sombre, darkened frostily. He looked, Cruise O'Brien wrote, *"I thought, a bit, as he must have looked on that December day in 1921, when, while presiding over a Dante Commemoration, he heard that his plenipotentiaries had just concluded a Treaty of which he had not personally approved the content. In both cases, there was an impropriety involved, and impropriety was something Dev could not abide. Cauldwell further explained to Dev that when a political statement fails to meet with a fellow Australian's political approval, the latter doesn't do the equivalent of writing a letter to The Times. He sends the speaker a dead cat. Cauldwell told Dev that he personally received many dead cats in his time. This impressed Dev"*, O'Brien continued: *"He too had aroused ferocious animosity in his time, and was inclined to take someone seriously who could establish a national record in that line, even though the unit of measurement in this case might seem repellently exotic. The comedian in Cauldwell found the perfect foil in Eamon deValera – of all the straight men in the world, the King"*[28].

GAA AND DEV

Dev's links with Blackrock and Rockwell Colleges introduced him to the game of rugby. He was no mean player himself, with his height a key attribute for catching the high ball. He loved rugby and remained true to it, despite it being somewhat politically incorrect. He once said, *"for Irishmen, there is no football game to match rugby and if all our young men played rugby, not only would we beat England and Wales, but France and the whole lot of them together"*[29]. He opposed the GAA ban on 'foreign games' and was not afraid to say so publicly. This naturally caused controversy and Dev explained himself to the head of the GAA, writing;

"My views are simple. I am in favour of all outdoor games. I think they make for the health and vigour of our young people. The one thing that is wrong, in my opinion, is that the GAA should continue to maintain the ban...If Ireland is to match herself in football and play with the national teams from England, Wales, Scotland and from France, it must be in rugby or soccer, as at present... I do not think that under the present conditions, there need be any fear that the national spirit of the GAA players, who would also play rugby would be lessened by contact with those who play rugby alone"[30]. In 1967 Dev told the British Ambassador, *"For my part I have always preferred Rugby"*[31].

Dr. Brendan O'Regan of Shannon Development with DeValera.

Meeting the American film actor Cary Grant.

CHAPTER 23

'RETIRED' TO PRESIDENCY IN 1959

Fianna Fáil was worried that in the event of Dev's retirement, it might never again succeed in gaining an overall majority victory in a General Election, under proportional representation, as it facilitated smaller parties to gain a foothold in the Dáil. Even Dev himself, had only succeeded in winning an overall majority in four out of 12 General Elections. Though some TD's, who were elected on the coat tails of more successful candidates, were quite happy with the voting system, it was decided that the future success of the Party, would be best secured by dropping proportional representation.

This would demand an amendment to the Constitution, a measure Dev introduced in the Dáil on 2 November 1958. On the Second stage on 26 November, he said, *"the main feature of a straight vote is that it is an integrating influence, whereas the other is a disintegrating influence. We have reason enough, goodness knows, for forming groups and parties without, so to speak, being encouraged by our fundamental system to do so"*. Some prominent members within Fine Gael, agreed with Dev's argument, and could never envisage a Fine Gael Government under proportional representation.

IRISH PRESS CONTROVERSY AND RESIGNATION

Noel Browne T.D. put down a Dáil question about Dev's control of the *Irish Press*, and subsequently believed that this controversy was a contributory factor in Dev's *retirement. On 12 December 1958, Browne proposed a Dáil motion, "In continuing to hold the post of Controlling Director of the Irish Press Ltd while acting as Taoiseach, Mr. DeValera has rendered a serious disservice to the principle of integrity in a parliamentary government and derogated from the dignity and respect due to his rank and office as Taoiseach"*. Browne, who had earlier been given a present of one share in the *Irish Press*, had been able to investigate the dealing in shares of the paper.

Though Dev had earlier declared, *"I have no financial interest"*[1], Browne was able to demonstrate that since 1929, Dev and his son Vivion had been buying shares to the number of 150,000 at a "grossly deflated under valuation". Because the shares were not allowed to be quoted on the Stock Exchange, this prevented the true value of the shares being established and enabled the DeValeras to buy them cheaply. Browne also spoke of the political value that the *Irish Press* had been to Dev, down the years, and included the fact that Dev had obtained public money to maintain the paper. Browne said the paper was, a DeValera family business.

Much of the money collected by Dev in America in 1919 remained there. He deemed the attempt of the Free State Government to get it as *"audacious and altogether untenable...as the monies had been subscribed for the purposes of a Republican Government only"*[2]. Dave Hannigan writes of the background to this episode: *"The battle for the bonds eventually wound its way through the New York Courts for several years, before a ruling in 1927, disallowing the various claims to the funds and appointing receivers, to begin the process of returning the cash to the purchasers of bond-certificates"*.

In December of that year, DeValera was back in America running a rather gauche campaign trying to persuade bond-certificate holders, to turn over their return to him, in order to help with the establishment of the *Irish Press* newspaper in Dublin. In this way, he may have received as much as £100,000 from original subscribers. Nine years after that DeValera was in power himself when the Irish Government took over from the receivers, the task of ensuring, where humanly possible, that the original subscribers received $1.25 for every dollar paid to the fund. Opposition politicians were quick to label the Government's Bill authorising this, as the *'Irish Press Bill, second edition'* given the obvious impact it would have on the fledgling paper's fortunes"[3].

Dev responded to Noel Browne's Dáil motion: *"I am quite satisfied in my conscience, and I believe that any fair minded person will be similarly satisfied, that in the circumstances, knowing the position in which I was placed with regard to the Irish Press before I came here, there was nothing to suggest that I had been acting all these years, in a manner which was inconsistent with the dignity of the office which I hold"*[4]. Browne accepted that Dev's position with the *Press* was widely known, but what was not known, was that he did not adopt the usual practice in this type of case, of either resigning or asking for leave of absence without pay from these posts, while acting in his capacity as Taoiseach.

Dev responded, *"Over the period in which I have been acting, I have not found at any time, that my duties conflicted in any way with the full and proper exercise of my duties as Taoiseach. There is such a thing as delegation. I was one of a Board. It was not necessary for me always to be there. I had to see that the work was properly delegated, and I felt it was right that I should retain the reserve powers given me by the Articles of Association. Had it been necessary at any time to exercise any of these powers, I would have been entitled to do so, but the suggestion that whilst I was Taoiseach, I was part-time Taoiseach, is not correct. I have therefore discharged my duty, both to the people who subscribed the money, by retaining that ultimate power, and I have discharged my duties to the State by giving it my whole time. It is true that if there was a very important development in the Irish Press, if there was some new departure, or, something of that kind, I would expect to be consulted and that if it was a departure which I considered wrong, and not for the purpose for which the money was subscribed, I would intervene"*[5].

When Seán MacEntee spoke on behalf of Dev, on the last two days of the debate, matters deteriorated, with much interruption. MacEntee essentially said that the people knew Dev was the controlling shareholder in the Press Group, and returned him in successive elections. Both the leaders of Fine Gael and Labour said that what Dev had done was wrong. Oliver J. Flanagan was quite vociferous, making such contributions as, *"Fianna Fáil were making a racket out of it"*; "And he wants to be President on top of it all"; *"This is very interesting"*. Flanagan was shouted down as he tried to make a point of order, before eventually getting the chance to ask, *"May I enquire if, in view of the fact that the Taoiseach is offering himself for the Presidency—"*. More interruptions followed before Flanagan added, *"Surely the Minister for Justice should take action, if Deputy Browne's statement that Mr. DeValera is robbing the shareholders of the Irish Press—"*. At this juncture the Ceann Comhairle told the Deputy that he *"has been grossly disorderly in disobeying the instructions of the Chair. He will leave the House"*. Flanagan replied, " *I most certainly will"*. Mr. O'Sullivan asked, *"What will the Irish Press say tomorrow?"* The motion was defeated by 71 votes to 49[6].

The next days *Irish Press* contained a short statement from Dev, saying that he had not the opportunity in the Dáil on the previous night to respond to Dr. Browne. He made a full rebuttal of all the allegations. The main headline in the paper that day, announced the fact that Dev was to stand for the Presidency[6a].

Diarmaid Ferriter writes of this controversy, *"Browne claimed that DeValera had systematically over a number of years become a majority shareholder, paying only a nominal price to ordinary shareholders, and maintained DeValera's continuing role as Controlling Director was incompatible with his role as Taoiseach, particularly given that as far back as 1932, he had announced that no members of his Cabinet could continue to hold directorships in any commercial concern. It was an embarrassing charge that was not answered adequately, by the soon to retire DeValera, who insisted his position did not bring significant personal reward"*[7]. Ferriter adds that the announcement that Dev was to seek the presidency, knocked the story off the news headlines and that *"accusations that he had compromised the office of Taoiseach, by continuing to hold his post as Controlling Director of the Irish Press, were not enough to cause his resignation"* and that *"It was an unconvincing defence"*[8].

T Ryle Dwyer writes that when he (Dev) turned over the company to his son Vivion, a number of loyal Fianna Fáil supporters questioned the propriety of the move, but it never developed into any kind of scandal, probably because few people would give any credence to the idea that "The Chief" would be involved in any kind of financial scandal. He had always been willing to live in the frugal comfort he espoused[9].

Dev's actions and even his own defence in the Dáil, however, left a bad example for future politicians and public servants, who might have acted unethically or even illegally, to admit any wrongdoing and resist pressures to resign. William Gladstone had expected that once the Irish had their own Parliament under Home Rule, their *"eagerness to plunder the public purse"* would come to an end. Stephen Collins, political correspondent of the *Irish Times*, writes, *"Sadly, the history of independent Ireland has proved that his confidence was misplaced. The dominating feature of Irish politics has been a short-sighted scramble to placate vested interests with public spending programmes, that have regularly undermined national policy on almost every front, from health policy to industrial development"*[10].

Another disquieting feature of political life in Ireland has been, where on occasion it was clear that particular politicians have behaved unethically, or even illegally, they have generally been supported unequivocally at subsequent polls by their constituents.

Declan Kiberd writes, *"DeValera, for all his talk of frugal self-sufficiency and his success in clearing some of the slums, had no macroeconomic strategy to meet the needs of a new age. He was by nature a cautious politician, ever ready to agree with the guarded advice of a British-trained Department of Finance, whose addiction to economic orthodoxies was at least as great as the Department of Education's commitment to the curricular study of the Edwardian canons. Only when DeValera retired to become President in 1959, was the way open for the entrepreneurial and meritocracy successor, Seán Lemass"*[10a].

Oscar Traynor and other very senior ministers had often discussed the future of the Fianna Fáil Party, without Dev. They foresaw an opportunity for his natural retirement and election as President in 1959, when Seán T. O'Kelly finished his two terms as President and could not stand again. Traynor talked Dev into accepting the wisdom of this strategy. At a Fianna Fáil parliamentary party meeting in January 1959, Dev announced his imminent retirement. This shocked some who thought their 'Chief' would go on forever.

Diarmaid Ferriter writes, *"The consensus is that he stayed too long and in doing so, hindered the embrace of the policies that were finally to achieve some prosperity for the country".* As usual however, Ferriter is reluctant to allow even his own criticism of Dev go unqualified, adding rather obliquely, *"What is often overlooked in this assessment, is that the Irish electorate returned him to office continually and that he was surrounded by strong and able politicians and the majority of loyal Fianna Fáil voters"*[11].

The Constitutional Bill on Proportional Representation had been passed in the Dáil, after a stormy passage in which Dev, though blind, played a vital and robust role. It was rejected in the Senate on 19 March by one vote. Dev re-introduced the Bill in the Dáil some six weeks later, proposing that if it passed in the Dáil again, it would be deemed to have passed in both Houses under the Constitution. Another debate ensued, as it became clear that the coming election of a new President would occur on the same day as the Amendment Bill to the Constitution. As Dev put it, in the Dáil, *"When two decisions have to be made, the public conveniences is best met, by having the two on the one day".* An Opposition Deputy added, *"And you will be in the scales".*

✆✖ ✖✆

DeValera's opponent in the Presidential election campaign was the man who had proposed him as President of the Irish Republic in 1921, General Seán MacEoin of Fine Gael. Dev resigned as Taoiseach on Election Day 19 May 1959. He was elected President by a comfortable margin and lost the battle to amend the Constitution by a slender margin. The electorate had exercised a sophisticated choice: a pro-Dev vote and an anti-Dev vote. Seán Lemass, who had been Dev's Deputy for fourteen years succeeded him as leader of Fianna Fáil and *"preferred to say nothing about Northern Ireland"*, in contrast to his predecessor[12]. Dev resigned as Controlling Director of the *Irish Press* to be succeeded by his son Vivion.

Dev was inaugurated as President in Dublin Castle on 25 June 1959, aged seventy-seven. Sinéad DeValera only moved into Áras an Uachtaráin very reluctantly. The presidential salary had remained at the £5,000 per annum figure fixed in 1937 with an expense account of £6,500.

Dev fulfilled all the duties of the Presidency in a fastidious manner. Though his functions were limited, he entered the public arena on occasion when the constitutionality of new Bills was tested.

One other occasion, on which Dev took the opportunity to take a look back, occurred on the 50th anniversary of the founding of the Irish Volunteers in November 1963. He said, *"their foundation came as a result of Irish people being robbed of the fruits of decades of patient constitutional endeavour, by an arrogant defiance of constitution and law. Some saw the opportunity to repair the mistake made, when the Volunteer organisation of 1782, a guarantee of civil rights and national freedom, was allowed to lapse. Some thought fondly that the Volunteers of the North, would one day stand with their brothers of the South, in common defence of their motherland and of their liberties as freemen. They believed that the English Tories and the feudal lords, who instigated and directed the arming of the North, would find the 'wage earners and rent-payers' of the North, would not remain for long as subservient tools. Others, like him, believed the occasion should be seized to establish a disciplined armed force to strike a blow for Ireland's freedom…. It is to their devotion and sacrifice that we are most indebted for that freedom, which we here enjoy today"*[12a].

Dev met foreign dignitaries and made official visits abroad. The visits to Ireland of ex-President de Gaulle and President John F Kennedy, were among the two most prominent visitors. Dev's visit to the USA on a State visit at the age of 83, was a most nostalgic visit, where he addressed Congress. He spoke about his earlier visit in 1919 -1920 when seeking American assistance. He referred to the recent visit of President Kennedy to Ireland, and the enthusiastic welcome he received. Dev acknowledged that part of that welcome was due to the President being of Irish blood, but insisted that *"in honouring him, they felt they were in some small measure expressing their gratitude to the people of the United States, for the aid that had been given to them"*[13].

ᏜᏜ ᏜᏜ

*DeValera was inaugurated as President in Dublin Castle
on 25 June 1959, aged seventy-seven.*

Opening Mainie Jellett Art Exihibition at the National Gallery.

Though DeValera had been very close to WT Cosgrave in early life, they had taken opposing paths since the Treaty. Whether they ever became in any way reconciled remains doubtful. The importance of that relationship to Dev can be gaged by a passage in Dev's official biography which reads: *"During his presidency the last of his colleagues in the Cabinet of the First Dáil , WT Cosgrave, died. His death brought a special pang, for the division over the treaty had kept them apart for more than forty years. DeValera had wished to restore the relations which had been broken. The divide was deep and the friendly meeting he had hoped for was long delayed. Eventually, however, Cosgrave accepted an invitation to meet the Papal Nuncio (Dr. Riberi) under the Presidents' roof. The two statesmen, at a certain point, were observed to be standing apart and chatting amicably - a matter of much satisfaction to so many who admired them both"*[14].

Unlike Cosgrave, who died in 1965, DeValera was able to participate in the 50th anniversary of the 1916 Rising in 1966, and derive enormous publicity through the coverage by RTE. For the commemoration, Dev again returned to his theme, *"Language is a chief characteristic of nationhood – the embodiment of the nation's personality and the closest bond between its people. No nation with a language of its own would willingly abandon it, their native language, the language of their ancestors, the language which enshrines all the memories of their past. To avoid such a fate, we of this generation must see to it, that our language lives. That would be the resolve of the young men and women of 1916"*[14a].

As Dev's first term as President ended in 1966, many people thought that as with Seán T. O'Kelly, he might be returned unanimously, but this was not to be. As his official biographers wrote, *"DeValera, however, was still too controversial a figure to be allowed this honour"*[15].

There had been reluctance within Fine Gael to contest the election and also a difficulty in finding a candidate willing to run. John A Costello was suggested, but Gerry Sweetman deemed him unacceptable, due to his absence from the revolution of 1916. Seán MacEoin insisted that to honour the memory of Michael Collins they had to oppose Dev. Tom O'Higgins, a nephew of Kevin O'Higgins, accepted the nomination[16]. Dev did not canvass at all during the campaign. Because of this the RTE News felt obliged not to give much coverage to O'Higgins, who ran a vigorous campaign, ably assisted by Michael Sweetman. Fianna Fáil appointees controlled the RTE Authority and senior staff there recognised what was expected of them. Government Ministers used their positions to garner publicity through RTE for Dev's re-election[17]. Despite this, 'a short head' saw Dev returned. He was quoted as saying, *"it is better to win by a short head than lose it"*. In his second inauguration address, he spoke of his double goals, both still unrealised, the end of Partition and the restoration of the Irish language.

With American President Ronald Reagan and his wife Nancy.

With Bart Bok, the Astronomer (left), and Dr. Eric Lindsay of Armagh Observatory.

The fiftieth anniversary of the First Dáil occurred on 21 January 1969. The two Houses of the Oireachtas assembled in the Mansion House. Twelve of the original Deputies, entitled to have attended the First Dáil were still alive, with eleven of those attending in 1969. Dev addressed the gathering; *"On that day Cathal Brugha stood up and read the Declaration of Independence, speaking in Irish. Others then read the Proclamation in French and in English. This made it known to the whole world that our desire was to be free and independent and that the form of government we would have was a republic...Nowadays there are some people who think that the ideals of nationhood which inspired the leaders of fifty years ago have become old-fashioned and out of date...We are not thought of as a province now; the whole world knows that we are a nation...The old nations will not lose their own qualities and culture; they will not set them aside...Now I pray, as you all prayed at the beginning, that the Holy Spirit will guide you and all of us in our work, and I ask for the blessing of God on all your actions".*[17a]

In 1969, the Fianna Fáil Government, under Jack Lynch, was in crisis over repercussions from the outbreak of the Troubles in the North. One of the Ministers, Kevin Boland, was about to resign when DeValera invited him to Áras an Uachtaráin. Boland's account of what transpired says, *"The President talked of the constitutional crisis that would be caused by my resignation – particularly on this issue. He foresaw a change to a Fine Gael controlled government and pointed out the seriousness of this in the circumstances that existed".* Boland agreed to attend the next government meeting, but did resign some months later during the Arms Crisis of May 1970[18].

DeValera himself became directly involved in the Arms Crisis, when on 5 May 1970, Peter Berry, Secretary at the Department of Justice, phoned Dev at Áras an Uachtaráin. Berry had received security information that an illegal attempt was in train to import arms through Dublin airport. He did not have confidence that if he informed his Minister, Micheal O'Morain, that the information would be brought to the attention of the Government. Berry told Dev, *"I have come into knowledge of matters of National concern and I am afraid that if I follow the normal course, the information might not reach the Government. Does my duty end with informing the Minister or am I responsible to the Government by whom I was appointed?"* Dev asked Berry was he absolutely sure of his information to which Berry replied that he was. Dev then said, *"You have a clear duty to the Government. You must speak to the Taoiseach"*[19].

Later, in November, there was an attempt from within Fianna Fáil to put pressure on Taoiseach Jack Lynch while he was in the USA. On arrival back in Ireland there was a show of support for Lynch by the solid hard-core of the foundation establishment of Fianna Fáil including, Frank Aiken, Seán MacEntee, Paddy Smith and Mick Hilliard. Among this group was Mairtin O'Flaithearthaigh, the representative of Dev himself[20].

❧❦❧

FREEMEN OF DUBLIN

One of the few honours, which Dev had not received, was that of Freeman of Dublin. When this was mooted in the City Council, it became evident that unless there was some reciprocity, it would not be agreed. This resulted in both Dev and John A Costello being honoured in a joint ceremony. Tom O'Higgins was a guest of Costello's on the occasion. After the formal ceremony all the guests were invited to the Lord Mayor's drawing room. Tom O'Higgins was prevailed upon by Seán MacEntee to meet Dev. As O'Higgins sat beside Dev, MacEntee introduced him as the Chief Justice. Dev exclaimed, *"Oh, you opposed me"*. *"Yes Sir, I did"* he replied. Dev then said, *"You have to admit that had I been able to campaign, the result would have been quite different"*. *"I'm sure you are right"*, O'Higgins answered tactfully." *I'm very glad to hear you say so"*, Dev answered. O'Higgins commented afterwards that he had made Dev happy and *"no harm had been done"*[21].

1973 COALITION GOVERNMENT

One of DeValera's last official functions as President, was to surprisingly host a formal dinner in Áras an Uachtaráin for the new Ministers of a Coalition Government. As ever Dev did his own thing. His health was poor and the fact that a Coalition Government was elected did not please him. Towards the end of the dinner Dev stood up, carefully holding on to the back of his chair for support. He spoke slowly, *"I have long had reservations about the system of vote, the system of voting called proportional representation, because I forewarned that if persisted in, this system was bound to lead eventually to Coalition Government"*. The shock of such a statement on such an occasion led the new Taoiseach Liam Cosgrave, son of WT Cosgrave, to laugh aloud and to be joined by several of his Ministers. Dev continued to play the straight man, as was his wont, ignored the laughter, and carried on with his homily on coalition government, ending with, *"You must make it work. The only way it will work is for you all to put loyalty to the Taoiseach before every consideration of party advantage"*[22].

After leaving the presidency, Dev and Sinéad retired to a nursing home, Talbot Lodge in Blackrock, run by the Sisters of Charity. His last years saw him worry about his health and old age and that he did not have enough money to care for Sinéad. In 1973 Bryan Alton, Dev's family doctor, told Jack Lynch, *"Mentally he is tending to develop a depression. The main basis for this appears to be financial"*[23].

Sinéad died within a year of them leaving the Áras, on 7 January 1975. Shortly afterwards Dev questioned one of his daughters as to whether Sinéad had felt she was neglected in any way since the troubled years? He told his daughter how when he was released from prison in 1917, he was shocked to find Sinéad and their son Brian looking so wasted and frail. Dev himself died on 29 August 1975, just six weeks short of his 93rd birthday. John A Costello spoke on RTE that same evening, in a fashion that hurt members of DeValera's family, saying, *"In my opinion he left nothing of permanent value, although he did a tremendous service of practical demonstrations of what his policy was during his lifetime; in particular I would emphasise on his keeping the country out of the war. Mr. DeValera was undoubtedly a most controversial figure; he impressed his personality and his ideals into practical effect upon the people of the country; he navigated the ship of State in the direction he wished it to go and formed the basis of the building up of the State, which we have now. He was a man who was capable of creating in other people tremendous loyalty and even excessive devotion. On the other hand he created in other people great distress, very practical hatred, almost certainly undue hatred, which in the people who formed it in the days from 1922 onwards, now exists and exists even in their children's children…. He was undoubtedly a forceful personality. He had strong views. In my opinion, one of the worst characteristics of his personality was his pertinacity in adhering to principles or ideals, which he had convinced himself, were the proper principles or ideals…. He thought very deeply and for a very long time, changed his mind frequently, but if he eventually came to the conclusion that what his view was the proper one, nothing could convince him that he was wrong or get him to change…. To that extent he was a difficult man to argue with in the course say a Committee stage in the Dáil, and in particular, on the Committee stage of the discussion of the Draft Constitution in the pre-1935 period. I have never been able to understand how he so firmly and fully and comprehensively, adopted the principles of the British Government and the British people in Parliamentary democracy. He adhered in every single respect and I believe quite illogically"*[24].

Ken Whitaker described Dev thus; *"He was the quintessential Christian Brothers' boy. He had enormous courtesy, but no social graces. His early upbringing told all through his life. He'd been brought up the hard way. He was an ideologue, not like Seán Lemass who was a pragmatic patriot, but quite a simple man really…but he had leadership qualities. He wasn't Irish in his manner. He had the strange name, 1916, the mathematics. It all inspired awe"*[25].

Shortly after Dev's death, Seán MacEntee, one of his longest friends and co-workers, wrote to Dev's grieving secretary, painting a moving picture of Dev that most had not witnessed, *"I firmly believe that our Chief was among the best and godliest of men. I cannot recall one unjust thing, not even an unkind one that he consciously did. He was rectitude and integrity personified; and he evoked, though maybe not in an equal intensity, those qualities in others. He set a standard in public conduct and private behaviour that those around him were led by his example to emulate. And with it, he was so simple, so human, so merry and full of fun…a human being who was infinitely lovable"*[26].

Professor Michael Fitzgerald of Trinity College Dublin diagnosed DeValera retrospectively, as appearing to have had autism and Asperger's Syndrome. He wrote in summary that this, *"seriously limited his political contribution. His narrow autistic outlook seriously damaged the development of Ireland. He lived 'in his head', and showed lack of empathy with the underprivileged. He devoted his life to personal power and control. DeValera would also meet the criteria for narcissistic personality disorder.*

DeValera State Funeral passes City Hall Dublin, August 1975.

The DeValera family plot in Glasnevin Cemetery, Dublin.

He had a grandiose sense of his own self-importance, was arrogant, believed that he was special and unique, and had a tremendous sense of entitlement. He was interpersonally exploitative and lacked empathy"[27]. I feel that this is unfair to Dev and apparently based, to a large extent, on selected quotes from biographies, which are in the main unfavourably disposed to Dev.

In the same vein, though much more destructive of the memory of Dev for a younger generation, was Neil Jordan's 1996 film, *Michael Collins,* which portrayed Dev in an extremely negative way in comparison to Collins[27a]. It is often the case that works of fiction, which films are, bear a stronger witness for many, than a written biographical or historical treatment.

Malcolm MacDonald described Dev as, *"the most consistent and finest statesman in his adherence to policies and principles whom I had known in any part of the world; he is not an international giant, only a national one"*[28].

SUMMARY

Eamon DeValera was very much a traditional Irish Catholic, wholeheartedly adopting its values and mores and rituals. The practice of Irish Catholicism offered its adherents the repeated private facility of forgiveness for any wrongs they might have committed, in the rite of confession. This sometimes encouraged an habitual attitude of doubtful behaviour, which could be later confessed and forgiven. It also encouraged the innate ability of rationalising ones actions to suit current needs. This general facility is common to most Irish Catholics, who were never encouraged to exercise their own consciences, but rather accept the Church's teaching including the facility of mental reservation and absolution for any wrongdoing. DeValera was no more or no less a creature of Irish Catholicism than most people. It appears to me that in a very few instances in his public life, he rationalised wrong doing.

The most outstanding of these were his speeches inciting violence on the outbreak of the Civil War, his taking/not taking the Oath of Allegiance on entering the Dáil and his involvement in the *Irish Press.* Because of his great influence on so many people, his example may have facilitated low standards in public life, including business practises. Elaine Byrne of the *Irish Times* wrote, *"A positive correlation exists between Catholicism and corruption. The Catholic Church places great emphasis on the inherent weakness of and shortcomings of human beings, their inability to escape sin and the consequent need for the church to be forgiving and protecting. Catholicism is a hierarchical religion while Protestantism is generally more egalitarian".* She quotes Daniel Treisman's, of the University of California, 2000 cross-national study where in his comparison between Denmark and Ireland, he suggests that *"if Ireland had an additional 5-10 per cent Protestant population, our corruption rating would be that of Denmark's, which has consistently been in the top five least corrupt countries in the world since polling began".* She notes that *"Ireland, Italy, Portugal and Spain have traditionally been distinguished by clannish catch-all parties and entrenched centre-*

periphery politics. Religion and society share comparative hierarchical predilections. These personages of authority, moulded by absolute deference stretched across a generation are now crashing down around us"[29]. Dev was able to instil these hierarchical values onto his own followers, as far as he was concerned. If the occasion demanded, as it did in the Wexford Case of 1957/8, he could overrule the loyalty which they as Catholics normally gave to their own canonically consecrated. priests/bishops. At the same time Dev could also be the loyal and observant Catholic, except when he deemed it politically or personally necessary to act otherwise.

Eamon DeValera participated unconditionally in the glorious revolution of Easter 1916. He emerged as the natural leader of the Provisional Government and played crucial roles there. He gradually accepted majority democratic parliamentary representation and remained steadfast to those principles after he assumed power. He instituted important constitutional changes. He kept the State out of the horrors of the Second World War. He projected a transcendental image of immaculate idealism, which convinced his followers that the *Promised Land* lay safely just beyond the next horizon. He was an exceptional man by any standards.

Commemoration Plaque, Kilmainham Jail Dublin.

SELECT BIBLIOGRAPHY

Barton Brian, *From Behind a Closed Door, Secret Court Martial Records of 1916*, The History Press 2010.

Bew Paul, *Ireland Since 1939*, Penguin Ireland 2006.

Boland Kevin, *We won't stand (idly) by, Dublin* 1972.

Boyer Bell J. *The Secret Army A History of the IRA 1916-1979*. Dublin 1980.

Bowman John, *DeValera and the Ulster Question 1917-1973 Oxford* 1982.

Bromage Mary, *DeValera and the March of a Nation*, Hutchinson 1956.

Brady Conor, *Guardians of the Peace* Dublin 1974.

Browne Noel, *Against the Tide*, Dublin 1986.

Caulfield Max, *The Easter Rebellion*, Gill & MacMillan 1995.

Colum Padraig, *Arthur Griffith*, Browne & Nolan Dublin1959.

Commission on Emigration and Other population Problems, Reports Dublin 1954.

Coogan Tim Pat, *DeValera Long Fellow Long Shadow, Hutchinson* 1993 p. 679.

Cooney John, John *Charles McQuaid – Ruler of Catholic Ireland*, Dublin 1999.

Cronin S. Ed. *McGarrity Papers,* Tralee Co. Kerry. 1972.

Cruise O'Brien. Conor, *States of Ireland*, Panther 1974.

Cruise O'Brien Conor, *Passion & Cunning*, Paladin 1990.

Duggan JP, *Herr Hempel at the German Legation in Dublin 1937-1945*, Dublin 2003.

Dwyer. Ryle, *Irish Neutrality and the USA; 1939-1947*, Dublin 1977.

Earl of Longford & Thomas P. O'Neill, E*amon DeValera*, Gill & Mac 1970.

DeValera, Terry *A Memoir*, Currach Press 2004.

De Wiel Jerome Aaan, *The Catholic Church in Ireland 1914-1918*, Irish Academic Press 2003.

Doherty Richard, *Irish Men and Women In the Second World War,* Four Courts 1999.

Dwyer T. Ryle, *DeValera The Man & The Myths*, Poolbeg 1991.

Farragher Seán P. CSSp., *Dev and his alma Mater,* Paraclete Press 1984.

Ferriter Diarmaid, *The Transformation of Ireland*, Profile Books 2004.

Ferriter Diarmaid, *Judging Dev*, Royal Irish Academy 2007.

Foley Conor, *Legion of the Rearguard The IRA and the Modern Irish State*, Pluto Press 1992.

Garvin Tom, *1922; The birth of Irish Democracy*, Dublin 1996.

Garvin Tom, *Preventing the Future* Gill & Macmillan 2004.

Gaughan Anthony Ed. *Memoirs of Senator James Douglas & Senate* Debates, 1983.

Girvin Brian, *The Emergency Neutral Ireland 1939-45*, Macmillan 2006.

Hannigan Dave, *DeValera In America*, O'Brien 2008.

Harkness D. *The Restless Dominion*, London 1969.

Hart Peter. *Mick*, Pan 2005.

Hogan Gerard, *1937 Constitution* Irish Jurist 2007.

Horgan John, *Seán Lemass*, Gill & Macmillan 1997.

Keatinge Patrick, *The Formulation of Irish Foreign Policy* IPA 1973.

Kennedy Michael, *Irish Foreign Policy 1919-1966; From Independence to Internationalism*, Dublin 2000.

Kennedy Michael, *Ireland and the League of Nations*, Irish Academic Press, 1996.

Kennedy Michael, *Guarding Neutral Ireland*, Four Courts 2008.

Keogh Dermot, *20th Century Ireland; Nation and State*, Dublin 1994.

Keogh Dermot, *Church and State in Modern Ireland 1923-1970*. Dublin 1971.

Keogh Dermot, *The Vatican, the Bishops and Irish Politics 1919-1939*, Cambridge 1986.

Keogh Dermot & O'Driscoll M. (eds), *Ireland in World War Two; Neutrality and Survival*, Cork 2004.

Kiberd Declan, *Inventing Ireland*, Vintage 1996.
Lee Joe, *Ireland 1912-1970 Politics and Society*, Cambridge 1989.
Lee & O'Tuathaigh G. *The Age of DeValera*, Dublin 1982.
Longford Earl of & O'Neill Thomas P. *Eamon DeValera*, Gill & Macmillan 1970.
Jordan Anthony, *WT Cosgrave – Founder of Modern Ireland*, Westport Books 2006.
Jordan Anthony, *John A Costello, Compromise Taoiseach*, Westport Books 2007.
Jordan Anthony, *Churchill- a Founder of Modern Ireland*, Westport Books 1995.
Jordan Anthony, Seán – *A Biography of Seán MacBride*, Blackwater Press 1993.
Macardle The *Irish Republic* London 1968.
MacMahon Deirdre, *Republicans and Imperialists*, Yale 1984.
Manning Maurice, *The Blueshirts*, Gill & Macmillan 1987.
Manning Maurice, James *Dillon*, Gill & Macmillan 1998.
Mansergh Nicolas, *The Irish Free State*, London 1934.
McCartan Patrick, *With DeValera in America*, 1932.
McCullagh D. *A Makeshift Majority: The First Interparty Government 1948-1951*, Dublin 1998.
McGarry Ferghal, *Eoin O'Duffy*, Oxford 2005.
McGarry Ferghal, *the Rising Ireland: Easter 1916*, Oxford University Press 2010.
Morrissey SJ. *William O'Brien*, Four Courts Press 2007.
Moynihan Maurice (ed), *Speeches & Statements by Eamon DeValera 1917-73*, Dublin 1980.
Murray Patrick, 'Obsessive Historian: Eamon DeValera and the Policing of his Reputation' in *Proceedings of the Royal Irish Academy*, Vol 101C 2001. pp. 37-65.
O'Brien William, *Forth the Banners Go*.
O'Broin Leon, *WE Wylie and the Irish Revolution*. 1989.
O'Connor Emmet. *A Labour History of Ireland*, Dublin 1992.
O'Driscoll Mervyn, *Ireland, Germany and the Nazis*, Four Courts Press 2004.
O'Faolain Seán, *Eamon DeValera*, Penguin 1939.
O'Halpin Eunan, *Defending Ireland*, Oxford 1999.
O'Halpin Eunan. (Ed), *MI5 and Ireland, 1939-45; The Official History*, Dublin 2003.
O'Malley Ernie, *On Another Man's Wound*, Anvil 2002
O'Sullivan Donal, *Irish Free State and its Senate*, London 1940.
Regan John. *The Irish Counter Revolution 1921-1936*. Dublin 1999.
Ryan D. *Unique Dictator- A Study of Eamon DeValera*, London 1936.
Sinnott Richard, *Irish Voters Decide*, Manchester 1995.
Titley Alan. *Church, State and the Control of Schools in Ireland, 1900-1944*, Kingston & Montreal 1983.
Townshend Charles, *Easter Rising*, London 2005.
Valiulis MG. " *The Man They Could Never Forgive" – The View of the Opposition; Eamon DeValera and the Civil War*' in JP O'Carroll, and JA Murphy (eds) *DeValera and His Times, Cork*, 1983, pp. 92-100.
Valulis MG *Richard Mulcahy* Dublin 1992.
Walsh Dick, *The Party: Inside Fianna Fáil*, Dublin 1986.
Whyte JH, *Church and State in Modern Ireland 1923-1970*, Dublin 1971.
Willis Clair, *That Neutral Island; a cultural history of Ireland during the Second World War*. London 2007.
Younger Carlton, *Ireland's Civil War*, London 1970.
Younger Carlton, *Arthur Griffith*, Gill & Macmillan 1981.

FOOTNOTES

INTRODUCTION

[1] . Farragher Seán P. CSSp., *Dev and his alma Mater* Paraclete Press 1984.

[2] . DeValera Papers UCD Archives, P 150/657 Letter to Mary MacSweeney 11/9/1922.

[3] . RTE Television Programme on DeValera *Hidden History Series* 2007.

[4] *Irish Times* 13/10/2007.

[5] . Murray Patrick, *Obsessive Historian Eamon DeValera and the policing of his Reputation,* Royal Irish Academy p. 23.

[6] . Coogan Tim Pat, *DeValera Long Fellow Long Shadow* Hutchinson 1993 p. 679. + History Ireland May-June 2008.

[7] . Ryle-Dwyer T. *DeValera The Man and the Myths* Poolbeg 1991. p. 317.

[8] . Bowman John, *DeValera and the Ulster Question Oxford 1982* p. 190.

[9] . Ferriter Diarmaid, *Judging Dev* Royal Irish Academt 2007 p. 13.

[10] . DeValera Eamon, *National discussion & Majority Rule* Dublin 1936 pp. 25-6.

[11] . Farragher. P. 155 & in interview with Fr. Farragher on 18 March 2010.
Eugene Hynes in his book, *Knock The Virgin's Apparition in Nineteen-Century Ireland,* published by Cork University Press in 2008, p. 172, says, "Social scientists are in no position to answer whether or not supernatural personages really appear in this world,; what is beyond doubt is that at different times and in different places people have claimed to have *encountered* the supernatural in unusually 'real' ways and that these claims are given more or less credence at difference times and places".

[12] . DeValera Papers, P/1/150/2260. 2 March 1934.

[13] . Dáil Debates, Vol 50. col. 2514 2 March 1934.

[14] . *Catholic Bulletin XXV,* 4 April 1935.

[14a] . O'Brien Cruise Conor, *States of Ireland* Panther 1974 p. 117.

[14b] . Crawford Heather C. *Outside the Glow: Protestants and Irishness in Independent Ireland.* UCD Press 2010.

[15] . DeValera Terry *A Memoir,* Currach 2005 p. 92.

[16] . Farragher. P. 166

[17] . ibid. p. 222-3.

[18] . Longford & O'Neill, p. 435

[19] . ibid. p. 423

[20] . Cooney John, *John Charles McQuaid, Ruler of Catholic Ireland* O'Brien Press, 1999, P. 335.

[21] . Longford & O'Neill, p. 463.

[22] . Cruise O'Brien. *States of Ireland,* Panther 1974 p. 33.

[23] . Dwyer Ryle T. *DeValera the Man & The Myths,* Poolbeg 1991. p. 311.

[24] . *Irish Press,* 14 October 1982..

CHAPTER 1

[1] . DeValera Terry, *A Memoir* Currach Press 2005 p. 161

[2] . Coogan op. cit. pp. 8-9.

[3] . TG4 Programme: *Uachtarain - A Profile of Eamon DeValera* 23 May 2010.

[4] . Farragher op. cit p. 9.

[5] . RTE programme on Dev.

[6] . DeValera Terry, op. cit. p. 168.

[7] . Longford Earl of & O'Neill, Thomas p. *Eamon DeValera* Gill & MacMillan 1970 p. 5.

[8] . Cruise O'Brien Conor, *Passion & Cunning* Paladin 1990 p. 67.

[9] . Longford & O'Neill, p 6..

[10] . ibid.

[11] . TG4 Programme on Dev.
[12] . Farragher p. 13.
[13] . ibid. p16.
[14] . Longford & O'Neill, p. 6.
[15] . Gallagher Papers, NLI.
[16] . Farragher p. 54.
[17] . ibid. p. 34.
[18] . Blackrock College Minutes, College Library.
[19] . Farragher, p. 83.
[19a] .O'Neill Tomas & O'Fiannachta Padraig, *DeValera,* Clo Morainn 1968. p. 25.
[20] . Dublin Archdiocesan Archives.
[21] . Farragher pp. 97-8.

CHAPTER 2

[1] Farragher, p. 98.
[2] . ibid. p. 100.
[3] . ibid. p. 101.
[4] . Memoir, p. 106.
[5] . Longford & O'Neill, p. 19.
[6] . ibid. pp. 17-18.
[7] . Ristard Mulcahy, 4/3/25 Comisiun na Gaelige Report Dublin Stationary Office 1926 .p. 3
[8] . *Times Educational Supplement,* 13/8/21
[9] . Farragher, p.101.
[10] . ibid p. 103.

CHAPTER 3

[1] . RTE Programme on Dev.
[2] . Longford & O'Neill, p. 21.
[2a] . Connell Joseph, *Where's Where in Dublin; A Dictionary of Historical Locations.* Dublin 2006.p. 158.
[2b] . BMH Witness Statement 129. Seán O'Shea.
[3] ibid. p 23.
[4] . O'Neill Tomas & O'Fiannachta, *DeValera,* Clo Morainn 1968. p. 45.
In 1953 Dev agreed to become a patron of the Irish Brigade Memorial Fund 1899-1902 being set up in Johannesburg to honour the memory of Major MacBride and those other Irish people who fought in the Boer Commandos and the Irish Transvaal Brigade. In 1963 Dev unveiled a Plaque on the house at the Quay in Westport Co. Mayo, where MacBride had been born in 1868. (DeValera papers UCD P150/494).
[5] . O'Neill Tomas & O'Fiannachta, *DeValera,* Clo Morainn 1968 p.70-71.

CHAPTER 4

[1] . Longford & O'Neill, p. 27 & Coogan p. 61
[1a] . McGarry Ferghal. *the Rising Ireland: Easter 1916,* Oxford University Press 2010 p. 113c, quoting statement by Joseph O'Connor to Bureau of Military History.
[1b] . O'Neill Tomas & O'Fiannachta Padraig, *DeValera,* Clo Morainn 1968. pp 70-71.
[1c] . Michael Staines: Witness Statement 284.
[2] . Memoir.
[4] . Kiberd Declan. *Inventing Ireland,* Vintage 1996 p. 389
[5] . The Easter Rebellion, Max Caulfield, Gill & MacMillan 1995 p. 147.

[5a] .Townshend Charles. *Easter 1916; The Irish Rebellion* London 2005, pp. 184-6.

[6] . ibid. p. 216.

[7] . Coogan. p. 251.

[8.] . RTE Documentary on Dev.

[9] . DeValera Papers, P150/507

[10] . Thou Shall not Pass - Ireland's Challenge to the British forces at Mount St Bridge, Easter 1916. IMA CD 62/3/57

[11] . Mulcahy Papers, P7D/23 6 April 1964.

[12] . Townshend Charles. *Easter Rising 2006* p. 200

[13] . Jordan Anthony. *Major John MacBride,* Westport Historical Society 2001 p.

[13a] .*The Catholic Bulletin* Events of Easter Week *p. 456.*

[14.] . *The Catholic Bulletin* Events of Easter Week p 330-1.

[15] . Caulfield Max p. 281.

[16] . O'Brien William Forth the Banners Go p.123-4

[17] . ibid pp.134-5.

[18] . Barton Brian. From Behind a Closed Door, Secret Court Martial Records of 1916 Rising. Blackstaff 2002 pp. 75-77.

[18a] .O'Broin Leon. *WE Wylie and the Irish Revolution* 1989 p. 32..

[18b] .*Irish Press* Interview 15 July 1961: as quoted in Brian Barton's *From Behind A Closed Door, Secret Courtmartial Records of the Easter Rising 1916.* p. 322 note 116 and pp. 92-93. Blackstaff 2002.

[18c] .O'Neill Tomas & O'Fiannachta Padraig, Clo Morainn 1968

[19] . Memoir p. 124.

[20] . ibid. p. 113.

[21] . UCDA p/150/524 3July 1969.

[21a] .Townshend Charles. *Easter 1916 the Irish Rebellion,* Penguin 2006. p. 283.

[21b] .Turi John J. *England's Greatest Spy Eamon DeValera,* Stacey Information 2009.

[22] . Barton p. 231

[23] . ibid.

[24] . Farragher p. 67

[25] . Jordan Anthony. *WT Cosgrave Founder of Modern Ireland,* Westport Books 2006 pp. 23-38.

[26]. McGarry Ferghal p. 289.

[27] . McGarry Ferghal. p. 157.

[28] . BMH Witness Statement 203. James Walsh.

[29] . BMH Witness Statement 258 Maeve McDowell.

[30] . Hansard HC Debates. Vth series. Vol. 8, Cols.935-51.

[31.] BMH Witness Statement 707. Michael Noyk.

[32] . O'Malley Ernie. *On Another Man's Wound,* Anvil 2002. p. 47.

[33] . De Wiel Jerome Aan. *The Catholic church in Ireland 1914-1918 War and Politics,* Irish Academic Press 2003. p. 106.

[34] . Liam O'Briain believed that Michael Staines, the Quartermaster General, was the 'senior surviving officer of Easter Week and not DeValera'. Witness Statement 6.

[35] . TG4 Programme on Dev.

CHAPTER 5

[1] . Younger Carlton. *Arthur Griffith,* Gill & MacMillan 1981 pp. 32-3.

[2] . Macardle Dorothy *The Irish Republic* London 1968 p. 190.

[3] . Longford & O'Neill, p. 66.

[3a] . *Freeman's Journal,* 20 August 1917.

[4] . Royal Irish Constabulary Reports CO 904 104.

[5] . Townshend p. 333.

[5a] .Coogan p. 388. Author reports Dev's claim in America in 1926 that he selected WT Cosgrave instead of Eoin MacNeill, as Countess Markievicz threatened to stand against the latter, whom she never forgave for countermanding the 1916 order.

[6] Feeney Brian *Sinn Féin* O'Brien 2002. p. 93.

[7] . O'Brien William. p. 144-5.

[8] . DeValera Papers Dr. Thomas Dillon folder

[9] . Morrissey SJ. *William O'Brien* Four Courts Press 2007. p. 133.

[10] . O'Malley Ernie. *On Another Man's Wound*, Anvil 2002 pp. 102-3.

[11] . Coogan p.72.

[12] . Ibid. p. 72.

[13] . O'Malley Ernie. p. 113 & p. 75

[14] . Capuchin Annual Vol 34. 1967 p. 408. "The Irish Volunteer Convention."

[15] . Conference on DeValera at UCD 2005, Maire Ni Cheallaigh.

[16] . Longford & O'Neill p. 71.

[16a] . De Wiel Jerome Aaan p.189.

[17] . Morrissey p. 146.

[17a] . Healy Tim, *Letters and Leaders of My Day,* vol. II, p.595.

[18] . O'Brien William. p. 166.

[19] . Coogan p. 19.

[20] . ibid. p. 110.

[21] . *The Times* 19 May 1918.

[22] . Feeney p. 103.

[23] . Memoir p. 125.

[24] . Colum Padraig. *Arthur Griffith,* Dublin 1959 p. 190.

[25] . Bromage Mary. DeValera and the March of a Nation, Dublin 1956 1956 p. 80.

[26] . Ryle Dwyer. p. 25.

[27] . Farrell Brian. *The Founding of Dáil Éireann, Parliament and Nation-building* Dublin 1971.

[28] . Letter to *Irish Press* by Tom Nelson, who was first asked to smuggle Dev on board his ship the SS Kilkenny, but advised that half the crew were English and suggested contacting Shemers Donoghue; information and letter from Paddy Murray grandson of Con's.

[29] . Valiulis Maryanne *Richard Mulcahy; Portrait of a Revolutionary Dublin* 1992. p. 36.

[30] . Minutes fo Proceedings of the First Parliament of the Republic of Ireland . p 151-2

[31] . ibid. p. 46-7.

[32] .Younger Carleton. p. 83.

CHAPTER 6

[1] . Longford & O'Neill p. 99.

[2] . NAI DE 2/245

[3] . Coogan. P. 166.

[4] . *New York Globe* 6 February 1920 & Moynihan Maurice (Ed.) *Speeches and Statements By Eamon DeValera 1917-1973,* Gill & MacMillan 1980.

[5] . MacEoin Uinsionn *Survivors* Dublin 1980 p. 45.

[6] . Dáil Debates, 27 April 1922.

[7] . Berg Papers New York Public Library 18 May 1920.

[8] . Memoir p. 144.

[9] . ibid. p. 131

[10] . Dwyer p. 52.

[11] . DeValera Papers. p/150/103(1) 2/10/1952

[12] . DeValera Papers. P150/248 7/4/1956.

[13] . DeValera Papers. P/150/727

[14] . Dwyer p. 44.

[15] . Tansill Charles. *America and the fight forIrish Freedom,* nu denvir-adair 1957 p. 394.

[16] . *New York Times,* 7 October 1920.

[17] . *Memoir* p. 148.

CHAPTER 7

[1] . Martin Gilbert. WS Churchill Vol iv 1917-1922, Heinmann 1975 p 450.

[2] . Farragher. p. 128.

[3] . Valiulis. p. 43.

[4] . ibid. p. 57.

[5] . McCartan Patrick. *With DeValera in America, 1932* p. 211.

[6] . Farragher Seán. *Dev and his alma Mater,* Paraclete Press 1984, p. 178.

[7] . Gallagher Frank Papers NLI 16 May 1952.

[8] . Coogan p. 284.

[9] . Jordan. *WT Cosgrave* p. 57.

[10] . O'Malley Ernie. Anvil 2002 p. 325-6.

[11] . ibid.

[12] . Coogan p. 205.

[13] . Hart Peter. *Mick The Real Michael Collins,* Pan 2005. p. 265.

[14] . Longford & O'Neill p. 148.

[15] . UCD Conference on DeValera, 8 September 2005. Contributions by John Regan & Peter Hart.

[16] . O'Brien William. p. 135.

[17] . Valiulis. p. 77.

[18] . No. 79 NAI DFA Box 14 File 96

[19] . Coogan p. 663.

[20] . NAI DE 2/144.

[20a] . DeValera Papers. 18 May 1921 p. 150/1902.

[21] . RTE 6/1/1978, Emmet d'Alton interview.

[22] . Harkness DW. *Northern Ireland since 1920,* Dublin 1983 pp18/-25.

[23] . DeValera Papers. 4 June 1921 P.150/1902.

[24] . NLI Diary. Sir Mark Sturgis, 26/6/1921

[25] . Dwyer p. 53.

[26] . Farragher. p. 129.

[27] . ibid.

[28] . Longford & O'Neill. p. 127.

[29] . Gallagher Frank. Papers NLI.

[29a] .Turi John J. *England's Greatest Spy Eamon DeValera,* Stacey Information 2009. pp. 191.
Leon O'Broin writes "That same night (22 June) DeValera was accidentally arrested in Dublin and released, though Greenwood found it illogical to let DeValera loose when Griffith was held as a prisoner". *WE Wylie & The Irish Revolutiom 1916-1921* Gill & MacMillan 1989 pp.135-6.

[30] . Gilbert. p. 665.

[31] . Dwyer p. 62.

[31a] .O'Broin Leon. *WE Wylie,* p. 137. O'Broin writes that on 22 July Churchill was so pleased with the developments in Ireland that he proposed to the Prime Minister that Andy Cope receive a knighthood.

[32] . Longford & O'Neill. p. 131.

[33] . Mulcahy Papers UCD. p.7/A/21.

[34] . Longford & O'Neill. p. 132.

[35] . Dwyer p. 55.

[36] . Gilbert p. 666.
[37] . NAI 2/244 15 July 1921.
[38] . Macardle p. 180.
[39] . *Manchester Guardian* 23 June & Longford & O'Neill pp. 355-6.
[40] . *Documents in Irish Foreign Policy.*
[41] . ibid.
[42] . Jee Joe. *Ireland 1912-1985 Politics and Society,* Cambridge 1990 p. 47.
[43] . O'Kelly JJ. *Stepping Stones* Irish Book Bureau Min of Education, Dublin pp. 15-16.
[44] . Longford & O'Neill p. 140.

CHAPTER 8

[1] . Dáil Debates, 23 August 1921.
[2] . Gaughan Anthony *Austin StackPortrait of a Separatist* 1977 Kingdom Books p. 158.
[3] . Pakenham. p.77-79.
[4] . Lee p. 49.
[5] . Dáil Private Session, 19 September 1921.
[6] . Collins Stephen *The Cosgrave Legacy* Blackwater Press p. 23.
[7] . Dáil Debates, 27 April 1922.
[8] . Ferriter. *Judging Dev* p. 62-9.
[9] . NAI DE 2/304/1.
[10.] Documents on Foreign Policy.
[11] . NAI De 2/304/1 No. 179.
[12] . ibid.
[13] . Longford & O'Neill, p. 157.
[14] . NAI DFA Es box 27 File 158 5 November 1921.
[15] . ibid.
[16] . O'Brien William. p. 231 & Morrissey pp. 199-200 & NAI Ms. 15,711.
[17.] NAI Ms. 15,711 (3).
[18] . Longford & O'Neill, p. 159.
[19] . Pakenham p. 210.
[20] . ibid p. 202.
[21] . ibid p. 202.
[22] . NAI DFA Box 27 File 158
[23] . Pakenham. p. 206.
[24] . ibid. p. 213.
[25] . Jordan. *Churchill*, p. 96.
[26] . Lyons FSL in Farrell, "*Parliamentary Traditions* pp. 251-3.
[27] . Pakenham. p. 239.
[28] . Jordan. *Churchill*, pp. 91-99.
[28a] . Colum Padraig *Arthur Griffith*, Browne & Nolan Dublin1959 p. xv.
[29] . Valiulis. p. 109.
[30] . Memoir. p. 135.
[31] . Pakenham. p. 263.
[32] . ibid. p. 264.
[33] . *Irish Times* Book Reviews, 1 October 2005.
[34] . Dwyer p. 64.
[35] . *Irish Times Man Behind the Myths,* 13 October 1997.
[36] . Jordan. *Churchill*, pp. 99-103.
[37] . Dwyer p. 87.
[38] . NAI DE No. 218 4/5/13.

[39] . Longford & O'Neill, p. 174 & Moynihan ob. cit pp.80-91.
[40] . ITUC Report, 1922.
[41] . Dáil Debates.
[42] *Freeman's Journal* 12 January 1922.
[43] . Dwyer p. 99.
[44] . NLI Ms. 9968.
[45] . Valiulis. p. 123.
[46] . Mulcahy Papers, p7/B/191.
[47] . Hagan Papers, Irish College Rome.
[48] . *Irish Catholic Directory,* 1923 p. 544.
[49] . *Irish Times* ,11 October 1922.
[50] . Keogh Dermot. *The Vatican, the bishops and Irish Politics* Cambridge 1986 6/11/1922 p. 96
[51] . *Irish Independent,* 17 March 1922.
[52] . ibid. 18 March 1922 & Moynihan pp.98-100..
[53] . Dáil Debates, 19 May 1922.
[54] . Bromage Mary pp. 165-6.
[55] . Longford & O'Neill p. 187.
[56] . Dwyer p. 104.
[57] . *Irish Independent,* 7 April 1922.
[58] . *Manchester Guardian,* 11 April 1922.
[59] . Longford & O'Neill, p. 187.
[60] . Macardle. p. 695.
[61] . Coogan p. 314.
[62] . ILP & TUC p. 30.
[63] . O'Brien. p. 219-220
[64] . *An Phoblacht,* 18 May 1922.
[65] . Jordan. *Churchill,* p. 109.
[66] . ibid. p. 120-1.
[67] . Gilbert p. 711
[67a] .Hart Peter, *Mick, The Real Michael Collins,* Pan 2005. p. 373.
[68] . Collins.
[69] . Gilbert. p. 711.
[70] . Harrington Niall. Kerry Landing, Anvil 1992 p. 25.
[71] . Dáil Debates, 8 June 1922.
[72] . 7 July 1922
[73] . Feeney. p. 139.

CHAPTER 9

[1] . Macardle. pp. 736-7.
[2] . RTE Hidden History Programme on Dev. 2007.
[3] . Longford & O'Neill p. 195.
[3a] .BMH Witness Statement 781. Patrick Kelly.
[4] . Archbishop's Byrne's Papers, Archdiocesan Archives, Drumcondra Dublin.
[5] . *Memoir* p. 150-1
[6] . Coogan. p. 330.
[7] . Bromage. Mary *DeValera and the March of a Nation,* Hutchinson 1956 p. 191. & Coogan p. 330.
[8] . NLI Ms.15,711. (3)
[9] . NLI Ms. 13,961.
[10] . NLI Ms. 15,711 (2).
[11] . Fitzpatrick David. *Harry Boland,* p. 197.

[12] . Mulcahy Papers P/155/139.

[13] . Longford & O'Neill, p. 199.

[13a] . Hart Peter. *Mick the Real Michael Collins*, MacMillan 2005. p. 410-412.

[14] . Coogan. p. 332.

[15] . Lee. p. 64.

[16] . *Irish Times* Report on release of Government files January 2009.

[17] . *Irish Times* Column 2009.

[18] . Gilbert. pp. 745-6.

[19] . *Memoir. p. 138.*

[20] . ibid. p. 136.

[21] . Ferriter. p. 69.

[22] . Keogh p. 95.

[23] . Valiulis. p. 174.

[24] . ibid. p. 175.

[25] . ibid. pp 175-6.

[26] . McGarrity Papers NLI Ms. 17,440 10 September 1922.

[27] . Valiulis p. 243.

[28] . ibid. p. 87.

[29] . *Memoir* p. 140.

[30] . Longford & O'Neill p. 200.

[31] . ibid. p. 203.

[32] . Bromage. p. 187 & McGarrity Papers 10 October 1922.

[33] . Coogan. p. 337.

[34] . *Irish Independent*, 6 November 1922.

[35] . McGarrity Papers NLI 28 November 1922.

[36] . Jordan. *WT Cosgrave*, p. 87.

[37] . Jordan. *Churchill*, p. 150.

[38] . Longford & O'Neill, p. 207.

[39] . Foley Conor. *Legion of the Rearguard*, Pluto press 1992. pp.29-30.

[40] . Jordan. *WT Cosgrave*, p. 88.

[41] . Longford & O'Neill, p. 208.

[42] . 5 December 1922.

[43] . Jordan. *WT Cosgrave*, p. 89.

[44] . Mulcahy Papers, UCDA P/7/b/2284.

[45] . ibid. 26 January 1923.

[46] . ibid. P/7/b/284

[47] . *O'Donovan* Papers, NLI Ms. 22,306.

[48] . *Irish Independent*, 10 March 1922 (letter written on 26 Febrauary 1922)

[49] . Longford & O'Neill, p. 212.

[50] . DeValera Papers, p/150/657.

[51] . *Irish Independent* 9 February 1923.

[52] . ibid. 12 March 1923.

[53] . DeValera Papers UCD, P.150/1813.

[54] . Jordan, *Seán, A Biography of Seán MacBride*, Blackwater 1994 p. 55.

[54a] . Hagan Papers, Irish College Rome, 7 february 1923.

[55] . Jordan. *WT Cosgrave*, p.91.

[55a] . DeValera Papers UCD. P.150/1826.

[56] . Keogh Dermot. *The Vatican*, 23 May 1923 p. 121.

[57] . ibid. pp. 108-121.

[58] . Macardle. pp. 851-3.

[59] . Gaughan Anthony Ed. *Memoirs of Senator James Doughlas* & Senate Debates 1923.

[60] . Hagan Papers Irish College Rome, 19 May 1923.

[61] . Macardle. p. 858.

[62.] Hagan Papers, 22 May 1923.

[63] . ibid.

[64] . Keogh Dermot. *The Vatican,* Letter to author 15 November 1983. p. 99.

CHAPTER 10

[1] . *Irish Independent,* 24 July 1923.

[2] . Longford & O'Neill, p. 228.

[3] . Dwyer p. 132.

[4] . O'Connell Papers UCDA.

[5.] Lee pp. 83-88.

[6] . Longford & O'Neill, p. 229 19 January 1924.

[7] . O'Connell Papers, UCDA p. 155.

[7a] . DeValera Papers, UCD P150/1833.

[8] . NLI 25 April 1924.

[9] . Feeney. p. 157.

[10] . Lee. p. 150.

[11] . Longford & O'Neill, p. 238.

[12] . *Irish Independent,* 18 March 1925.

[13] . ibid. 14 March 1925.

[14] . Macardle pp.893-4.

[15] . Jordan. *Seán MacBride,* p. 41.

[16] . Jordan. *WT Cosgrave,* p. 152.

[17] . Tom Johnson Papers Ms. 15,711 (2).

[17a] . Macardle. pp. 893-4.

[18] . Dwyer. p.138 4 December 1925.

[19] . Foley. p. 61.

[20] . Boyer Bell J. *Secret Army A History of the IRA , 1916-1979* Dublin 1980. p. 55.

[20a] . Moynihan. op. cit. P. 130.

[21] . Cronin S. Ed. *McGarrity Papers,* Tralee co. Kerry. 1972. pp. 140-1 11 March 1926.

[22] . Cruise O'Brien Maire. *The Same Age as the State,* O'Brien p. 73. 2003

[23] . *Irish Times* Interview with Seán Lemass 1974.

[24] . DeValera Papers p.150/2011, 17 April 1926.

[25] .Coogan. p. 397.

[26] . Macardle. p.898.

[27] . Longford & O'Neill, p. 249

[28] . McGarrity papers NLI.

[29] . Dáil Debates, January 1927.

[30] . Coogan. p. 398.

[31] . Boyer Bell, T*he Secret Army* pp 94-5 London 1972 & Brady Conor, *Guardians of the Peace,* Dublin 1974. p. 149-150.

[32] . Keogh Dermot. *20th Century Ireland; Nation and State,* Dublin 1994. p. 47.

[33] . Archbishop Byrne's Papers. Diocesan Archives Drumcondra Dublin.

[34] . Lee p. 154-5.

[35] . O'Connor Emmet. *A Labour History of Ireland 1824-11960,* Gill & MacMillan 1992. p. 123.

[36] . Tom Johnson Papers, NLI Ms. 17,168.

CHAPTER 11

[1] . Longford & O'Neill, p. 256.
[2] . ibid. p. 256.
[2a] . DeValera Papers UCD, p150/2110
[3] . *Irish Independent*, 10 September 1927.
[4] . DeValera Papers, P. 150/2110 6 October 1927.
[5] . Lee. p. 155.
[5a] . DeValera Papers, P150/2110.
[6] . Keogh Dermot. *20th Century Irelans* p. 133.
[7] . White Robert. W. *Ruairi O Bradaigh*, Indiana University Press 2006.
[8] . Jordan Anthony. *WT Cosgrave*, p. 154.
[9] . ibid. p. 155.
[10] . *Irish Independent* 12 September 1927.
[10a] . Moynihan op. cit p. 150-153.
[11] . Dáil Debates, 7 March 1927.
[12] . *Irish Press*, 24 January 1969.
[13] . *Irish Times*, 10 October 1978.
[13a] . Moynihan. op. cit. pp. 162-166.
[14] . Whyte JH. *Church & State in Modernn Ireland, 1923-1979* Gill & MacMillan 1981 p. 44.
[15] . NAI S 2547. A Cosgrave to O'Hegarty 10 January 1931.
[16] . Keogh Dermot. *20th Century Ireland*, p. 168.
[17] . Ferriter. p. 307.
[18] . Jordan Anthony., *WT Cosgrave*, p 143-8.
[19] . Jordan Anthony. *WT Cosgrave 1880-1965, Founder of Modern Ireland.*
  Westport Books 2006, pp. 143-148.

CHAPTER 12

[1] . Seánad Éireann, Vol. 15 col. 938 2 June 1932.
[2] . Fitzgerald Papers, UCDA p.80/5127.
[3] . Jordan. *WT Cosgrave*, p. 135.
[4] . Michael Kennedy. *Ireland and the League of Nations*, IAP 1996 p. 30.
[5] . *Irish Times*, 15 September 1923.
[6] . Kennedy Michael. p.p. 60-63.
[7] . Dáil Debates, Vol 33. col. 2050 & 2195-1330.
[8] . Jordan. *WT Cosgrave*, pp. 136-7.
[9] . Dáil Debates, Vol 28. col. 277-320.
[10] .O'Sullivan Donal. *Irish Free State and its Senate*, London 1940 pp. 251-2.
[11] . ibid. p. 252.
[12] . Hansard CYLIC COL 1193-4 & 1205.
[13] . Gilbert Martin. *Churchill*, Vol V Heinmann 1981 p. 375.
[14] . Jordan *WT Cosgrave* p. 141.
[15] . Jordan. Anthony, *Churchill a Founder of Modern Ireland*, Westport Books 1995 p. 162.
[16] . Pakenham. p. 273.
[17] . Ferriter p. 123.
[18] . Seánad Éireann Vol 15 col. 938. June 1932.

CHAPTER 13

[1] . Jordan. *Seán, A Biography of Seán MacBride* p.p. 50-53.
[2] . MacRory Papers, 9 October 1931.

[3] . Dáil Debates, Vol 40. Col. 235.

[4] . Foley Conor. *Legion of the Rearguard, The IRA and the Modern Irish State,* Pluto Press 1992. p. 92.

[5] . Dáil Debates, Vol Xl, Col 34-36. & 51 & 54.

[6] . *Irish Independent,* 19 October 1931.

[6a] . Murphy John A. The achievement of Eamon DeValera', in John A. Murphy & John P'O'Carroll (eds), *DeValera and His Times* Cork 1986. pp.1-17.

[7] . Keogh. *20th Century Ireland* p. 180.

[8] . Jordan. *Seán p. 56.*

[9] . Longford & O'Neill. p. 271.

[10] *.Irish Press* 18 February 1932.

CHAPTER 14

[1] . Dáil Debates,, 1931.

[2] . NAI DFA P 358/115 January 1932 Dulanty to Walsh.

[3] . *Irish Independent,* 7 February 1932.

[4] . *Irish Times,* 4 February 1932.

[4a] *.Irish Independent, 6 & 12 February 1932.*

[5] . *New York Times,* 12 February 1932.

[6] . *An Phoblacht,* January 1932.

[7] . Boyer Bell. *Secret Army,* Dublin 1980 p. 92.

[8] . ibid. p. 93.

[9] . Lehane Con *Hibernia* 12 April 1979.

[10] . Manning Maurice. *James Dillon,* Wolfhound 1999 p. 53.

[11] . Keogh Dermot. *20th Century Ireland,* p. 62.

[12] . ibid.

[13] . Jordan. *WT Cosgrave, P. 177.*

[14] . Brady Conor. *Guardians of the Peace,* Dublin 1974 pp. 167-8..

[15] . Regan John. *The Irish Counter Revolution 1921-1936,* Gill & MacMillan 1999. pp. 291-7.

[16] . *Irish Times* Interview, 1965.

[17] . *Irish Press* Interview, 24 January 1968.

[18] . Horgan John. *Seán Lemass,* Gill & MacMillan 1997. p. 59.

[19] . *New York Times,* 21 February 1932.

[20] . Lee. p. 174.

[21] . Ferriter. P. 185.

[22] . Longford & O'Neill, p. 275.

[23] . Farragher. P. 158.

[24] . Dáil Debates, 9 March 1932.

[25] . ibid. 15 March 1932.

[26] . Longford & O'Neill p. 276.

[27] . Farragher. p. 161.

[28] . *Irish Independent,* 15 March 1932.

[29] . Bromage. pp. 228-9.

[30] . Coogan. p. 464.

[31] . Jordan. *Seán.* p. 59.

[32] . Lindsay Patrick.*Memories* Blackwater 1992. p. 5.

CHAPTER 15

[1] . NAI DT S 2264 12 March 1932.
[2] . RTE Documentary Hidden History Series
[3] . Jordan. *WT Cosgrave*, p. 181.
[4] . Longford & O'Neill, p. 336.
[5] . Moynihan Maurice (ed). *Speeches and Statements by Eamon DeValera, 1917-1973.* Gill & MacMillan, 1990.pp. 219-233.
[5a] . Moynihan. op. cit. pp. 259-260.
[6] . ibid.
[7] . ibid.
[8] . ibid.
[9] . ibid.
[10] . ibid.
[11] . Foster Roy. *The Apprentice Mage*, Oxford 1998.
[12] . Dáil Debates, 27 April 1938.
[13] . *Irish Times,* 27 June 1932.
[14] . Keogh Dermot. *Church and State in Modern Ireland 1923-197o.* Dublin 1971. p. 47.
[15] . Keogh Dermot. *The Vatican, the Bishops and Irish Politics 1919-1939,* Cambridge 1986 p. 192.
[16] . Fianna Fáil Archives, 28 June 1933.
[17] . *Memoir.* P. 29.
[18] . Longford & O'Neill p. 288.
[19] . Memoir. P. 54.
[20] . Gearoid O'Tuathaigh, Finola Kennedy, and Diarmaid Ferriter in conversation, RTE Nov. 2007.
[21] . Memoir. P. 57.
[22] . DeValera Papers, p. 150/2329.
[22a] . Moynihan op. cit. pp. 300-302.
[23] . Longford & O'Neill, p. 266.
[24] . NAI DFA 7/55
[25] . MacMahon Deirdre. *Republicans and Imperialists,* Yale 1984. p. 104.
[26] . ibid. p. 104.
[27] . Foley Conor. *Legion of the RearGuard*, Pluto Press 1992. p. 146.
[28] . *The Times,* 5 August 1932.
[29] . NAU/DFA S, DeValera to JH Thomas 28 September 1934 Geneva.
[30] . Willis Claire. *That Neutral Island,* Faber 2007. p. 27.
[31] . *Irish Times,* 16 August 1932.
[32] . MacMahon Deirdre. ibid. p. 70.
[33] . NAI DFA 23 September 1932, JP Walshe to Seán Murphy.
[34] . PRO Ramsay MacDonald Papers. 30/69/678/782.
[35] . Coogan. P. 459.
[36] . Jordan. *WT Cosgrave,* p. 182.
[37] . NAI DFA 30 October 1932. Joe Walshe Memo.
[38] . Dáil Debates, xliv col. 141. 19 October 1932.
[39] . *Irish Independent,* 15 August 1932.
[40] . *New York Times,* 13 November 1932.
[41] . Wade Allan. *Letters of WB Yeats,* London 1954. p. 806.
[42] . NLI Yeats Papers Ms. 30,546 July 1933.

CHAPTER 16

[1] . Cruise O'Brien Conor. *Passion & Cunning,* Paladin 1990. pp. 54-5.
[2] . Carden Sheila. *The Alderman, Alderman Tom Kelly, 1868-1942 And Dublin Corporation.* Dublin City Council 2007, pp. 202-3.
[3] . Jordan Anthony. *John A Costello Compromise Taoiseach,* Westport 2007 pp. 36-7.
[4] *Memoir* p. 58.
[5] . Maguire John. *IRA Internments and the Irish Government – Subversives and the State 1939-'60.* Irish Academic Press p.16.
[6] . Girvin Brian. *The Emergency Neutral Ireland 1939-45.* MacMillan 2006   p.45.
[7] . Manning Maurice. *The Blueshirts,* Gill & MacMillan 1987 p. 115.
[8] . *Irish Independent, 21 December 1932.*
[9] . Dáil Debates, *Wearing of Uniforms Bill* Vol 50. Col. 2523-5.
[10] . ibid. col 2491
[11] . ibid.
[12] . ibid.
[13] . Cruise O'Brien Conor. *Magill no. 4* 14 June 1981 p. 25.
[14] . McGarry Fergal. *Eoin O'Duffy,* Oxford 2005 p. 348.
[15] . Dáil Debates, Vol 50. col. 2514 2 March 1934.
[16] . Willis Claire. *That Neutral Island,* Faber 2007. pp. 367-8.
[17] . For details of the Cenotaph cf. Jordan, *John A Costello* pp. 59-64.
[17a] . Moynihan. op. cit p.p. 268- 273.
[18] . Jordan Anthony. *Seán,* pp. 61-2.
[19] . McGarrity Papers, NLI. 2 October 1932.
[20] . Ryle Dwyer. p. 190.
[21] . McGarrity Papers, NLI. 31 January 1934.
[22] . *Evening Public Ledger* 16 September 1936.
[23] . Tarpey Veronica. *The Role of Joseph McGarrity in the Struggle for Irish Independence; Doctoral Thesis,* Arno New York 1976 (13 February 1942).
[24] . Dáil Debates, Vol 63. Col 112.
[25] . MacSweeney Papers, UCDA P48a/257(s)
[26] . Dáil Debates, 3 May 1935 col. 393.
[27] . ibid. 25 May 1935 col.1942.
[28] . ibid. 12 December 1935 col. 2630.
[29] . ibid. 10 April 1940 Vol. 79 col. 1090.
[30] . Dáil Debates, 23 June 1936.

CHAPTER 17

[1] . *Documents of Foreign Policy Vol. iv p. 252. NAI DFA Secretary Files.*
[2] . Longford & O'Neill, p. 292.
[3] . ibid. 293.
[4] . ibid. p. 294.
[5] . Dáil Debates, Vol 64. Col. 1293 ff. 11 December 1936.
[6] . ibid.
[7] . ibid. col 1277.
[8] . UCDA. P/150/2285.
[9] . Longford & O'Neill p. 290.
[10] . ibid. p. 290.
[11] . Dáil Debates, 14 May 1933. Col. 2752-4.
[12] . Manning Maurice. *James Dillon* Dublin 1999 p. 138.

[13]. Longford & O'Neill, p. 296.

[14]. NLI DT S 9880

[15]. *Prison Bars,* July 1937.

[15a]. Dáil Debates, 11 May 1937.

[16]. Jordan Anthony.*John A Costello- Compromise Taoiseach* Westport Books 2007. pp. 43-4.

[17]. Whyte J. *Church and State in Modern Ireland* Gill & MacMillan 1971. p. 49.

[18]. *Irish Press,* 17 May 1937.

[19]. NAI S 9852 4 May 1937. Jacob Slommer to Dev.

[20]. *Irish Times,* 1 July 1937.

[21]. ibid.

[22]. ibid.

[23]. Cruise O'Brien Conor. *Passion & Cunning* Paladin 1990. p. 67.

[24]. NAUK Do. 35/893/6 555/11/1938.

[25]. Coogan. p. 520.

[26]. Longford & O'Neill, p. 318. 25 January 1938.

[27]. PRO CAB 24, 171,CP, 128 (37) MacDonald memo 6 October 1937.

[28]. DeValera Papers, P/150/2836 22 April 1938 Dev to Roosveldt.

[29]. PEOGB DDO 35/893 17 March 1938 Chamberlain to Craig.

[30]. *Irish Times,* 27 June 2009.

[31]. DeValera Papers, P/150/2511. 23 April 1938.

[32]. DeValera Papers, P150/2517.

[33]. MacEntee Papers, UCDA P/67/179 & P/67/155 MacEntee to Dev. 17 February 1938; PDDE 71 c.38. 27 April 1938

[34]. Gilbert Martin. ibid p. 867.

[35]. ibid. p. 1049.

[36]. Longford & O'Neill, p. 332.

[37]. O'Connell JP. & Murphy John A (eds). *DeValera and his Times* Cork 1983 p. 35.

[38]. Dáil Debates, 19 October 1933. col. 141.

[39]. Coogan. P. 698.

CHAPTER 18

[1]. Foley Conor. *Legion of the Rearguard; The IRA and the Modern Irish State,* Pluto Press 1992. p. 187.

[2]. Seánad Debates, col. 982ff.. 7 February 1939.

[3]. ibid. col 1533.

[4]. ibid. col. 989ff.

[5]. Longford & O'Neill, p. 356-7.

[6]. Coogan. p. 525-6.

[7]. NAI/DFA A 113, 29 January 1940.

[8]. NAI/DFA S113, 2 February 1940. & Longford & O'Neill. p. 359.

[9]. Maguire John. p. 33.

[10]. *Irish Times,* 27 June 2009.

CHAPTER 19

[1]. Coogan. pp. 526-7.

[2]. NAUL Prem 1/341 £1 September 1939.

[3]. RTE Programme on DeValera.

[4]. PROGB,CAB 66/1, WP(39)34.

[5]. UCDA p/150/2548 19 September 1939.

[7]. *Irish Independent,* 12 May 1940.

[8] . 23 May 1940; to Foreign Ministry.
[9] . Mulcahy Papers, P7A/210 24 & 25 May 1940.
[10] . Girvin Brian. *The Emergency Neutral Ireland 1939-45*. MacMillan 2006. p. 100.
[11] . *Irish Press*, 3 June 1940.
[12] . DeValera Papers, P/150/2548 15 May 1940.
[13] . *The Times*, 17 May 1940.
[14] . PROGB Perm. 3/131/2 26 June 1940.
[15] . NAI DFA 21 June 1940. Joseph Walshe to DeValera.
[16] . NAI DFA 1 July 1940. p. 13.
[17] . Coogan. p. 553.
[18] . PROGB PREM 3/131/1 MacDonald's Report to Cabinet on conversations with DeValera.
[19] . Coogan p. 553.
[20] . Bowman John. *DeValera and the Ulster Question 1917-73*, Oxford 1972. p. 239.
[21] . *Irish Press*, 15 November 1940.
[22] . Longford & O'Neill p. 368.
[23] . Bew Paul. *Ireland Since 1939 2006*.p. 30.
[24] . Coogan. p. 520.
[25] . ibid.
[26] . *New York Times*, 5 July 1940.
[27] . Documents of German Foreign Policy, 10;184. 11 July 1940. Ribbentrop to Hempel.
[28] . PROGB CAB 66/9,WP(40)274. Maffey reporting on conversations with DeValera.
[29] . Mulcahy Papers, UCDA 5 July. 1940.
[30] . DeValera Papers, P/150/2597.
[31] . Girvin. pp. 142.
[32] . ibid. p. 187.
[33] . ibid. p. 180.
[34] . Moynihan Maurice. *Speeches and statements by Eamon DeValera 1917-73* Dublin 1980 p. 458.
[35] . Girvin. p. 180.
[36] . RTE documentary of DeValera.

CHAPTER 20

[1] . Dáil Debates, 7 November 1940. col. 583-6.
[2] . USA Diplomatic Papers, 1940. iii p. 169-170.
[3] . NAI DFA p/2 Telegram to AARIP New York.
[4] . Girvin. p. 186.
[5] . ibid.
[6] . PROGB DO 130/17 20 January 1941.
[7] . Churchill WS. *Second World War3: 611 17 January 1941.*
[8] . NAI DFA p. 35. 28 February 1941.
[9] . Churchill WS. *World War Finest Hour 11* p. 890.
[10] . Girvin. p. 206.
[11] . NAI DFA, Aiken Papers P/104/3585. p. 35. 7 April 1941.
[12] . Girvin. p. 214.
[13] . ibid. p. 381.
[14] . Franklin Delano Roosevelt, Public Library 10 February 1941.
[15] . ibid. 22 April 1941.
[15a] .Kiberd Declan. *After Ireland* in *Irish Times* 28 August 2009.
[16] . Willis Claire. *That Neutral Island*, Faber 2007. p. 190.
[17] . NAI DFA, JJ Walshe to DeValera 22 May 1941.
[18] . *Irish Press*, 23 & 24 May 1941.

[18a] . Moynihan. op. cit. p. 459.

[19] . NAI DFA. P/227. 26 May 1941 pp. 12-14

[20] . Dáil Debates, 26 April 1941 col. 971.

[21] . *Irish Independent,* 28 May 1941

[22] . Longford & O'Neill, p. 393. (10 December 1941).

[23] . FDRPL Gray Papers Box 5. 2 August 1941.

[24] . O'hAlpin Eunan. *MI5 and Ireland, 1939-45 The Official History* Dublin 2003. p. 185.

[24a] . Kennedy Michael. *Guarding Neutral Ireland Four Courts* 2008 p. 209.

[25] . Moynihan. p. 465.

[26] . Longford & O'Neill p. 359.

[26a] . Moynihan op. cit. pp.466-469.

[27] . Willis p. 333.

[28] . FDRPL Box 40. 9 November 1943.

[29] . Cooney John. *John Charles McQuaid Ruler of Ireland,* O'Brien 1999. pp. 150-1.

[30] . Girvin. p. 310.

[31] . DeValera Papers, P150/2658 February 1944.

[32] . Coogan. P. 605.

[33] . Dwyer Ryle T. 3 part series in *Irish Times.* 19xx

[34] . *New York Times,* 11 March 1944.

[35] . *Irish Independent,* 19 March 1944.

[36] . Longford & O'Neill, p. 409.

[37] . Dáil Debates, Vol 93. 10 May 1944. col 2482-4.

[38] . ibid. 12 April 1945.

[39] . FDRLPB Gray Papers 13 April 1945.

[40] . ibid. 30 April 1945

[41] . DeValera Papers, P150/2676 21 May 1945.

[42] . Fisk Robert. *Turning our backs on the fire of life,* 19 October 1999.

[43] . Bew Paul. *Ireland Since 1939,* Penguin Ireland 2006. p. 62.

[43a] .Moynihan. op. cit. p. 476.

[47b] .Irish Times 7 November 2009

[44] . Coogan. p. 615

[45] . O'Donoghue David. *History Ireland 2006.*

[46] . Akenson DH. *The YSA and Ireland* Cambridge Harvard Press 1973 p. 254.

[47] . *Irish Times,* 6 May 1946.

[48] . Doherty Richard. *Irish Men and Women in the Second World War* Four Courts 1999 p p. 21-6.

[49] . McEwen Yvonne. *Irish Volunteers and Volunteer Deaths in Irish Regiments 1939-45.*
University of Edinburgh MSC. thesis.

[50] . *Irish Times* 13 June 2009.

[51] . Girvin. P. 280.

[52] . NAI DFA 34/125 McCauley to Walshe 15 March 1933.

[53] . *Irish Press,* 5 May 1933.

[54] . ibid. 19 May 1933.

[55] . NAI DFA 102/ McCauley to Walshe.

[56] . *Irish Catholic,* 17 January 1937.

[57] . NAI DFA 202/63 9 December 1938 Bewley to Walshe.

[58] . O'Driscoll Mervyn. *Ireland, Germany and the Nazis,* Four Courts Press 2004 pp. 240-1.

[59] . NAI DFA 243/9 25 January 1939. Admission of Jews to Ireland.

[60] . NAI DFA 219/4 Joseph Walshe to Charles Bewley.

[61] . DeValera Papers, P150/2183 22 February 1939.

[62] . Keogh Dermot. *Ireland and Europe 1919-48,* Gill & MacMillan 1988 p. 110.

[63] . Akenson DH. *Conor, A Biography of Conor Cruise O'Brien, McGill Queens University 1994 p. 116.*
[64] . NAI DFA 97/6/563.
[65] . *Irish Times,* 7 February 2005.
[66] . Jordan Anthony, *John A Costello Compromise Taoiseach 1891-1976,* Westport Books 2007 p. 50.
[67] . Girvin. P. 329.

CHAPTER 21

[1] . Lee. p. 229.
[2] . NAI S 12882a
[3] . Dáil Debates, 24 April 1957. col 151, 166 & 250.
[4] . Lee. p. 232.
[5] . O'Toole Fintan. *Irish Times,* Lessons in the Power of the Church, 6 June 2009.
[6] . *Irish Times* 27 June 1009.
[7] . Gray To Secretary of State, 20 June 1945.
[8] . Seminar on Eamon DeValera, UCD, 8 September 2005.
[9] . Cruise O'Brien Maire. *The Same Age as the State,* O'Brien 2003. p. 186.
[10] . ibid. p. 187.
[11] . ibid. p. 187.
[12] . Dáil Debates, Vol 97. col. 2573.
[13] . PROGB DO/130/84 4 November 1947.
[14] . *Irish Press,* 8 November 1947.
[15] . Dwyer TR. p. 295.
[16] . *Irish Times,* 12 July 1947 & Lee p. 289.
[17] . *Irish Press Letter,* 20 May 1946.
[18] . Dáil Debates, Vol 101. Col. 134 & 159.
[19] . Jordan. *Seán,* p. 87.
[20] . *Irish Times, 20 October 1947.*
[21] . Longford & O'Neill, p. 430.
[22] . ibid. p. 431.
[23] . Maguire John. p. 60.
[24] . Jordan Anthony. *John A Costello,* pp. 9-16.
[25] . Horgan John. *Seán Lemass,* Gill & Macmillan 1997. p. 136.
[26] . Healy John, *Healy- Reporter- the Early Years.* Achill the House of Healy 1991 p. 69.
[27] . PRO NI. Cab. FO/123/11 29 April 1948.
[28] . Jordan. *John A Costello,* p. 74.
[29] . Dáil Debates, 6 August 1948 Col. 2440-1.
[30] . Jordan. *John A Costello,* pp. 75-80.
[31] . Lawlor Caitriona. *Seán MacBride,* Curragh 2007 p. 180.
[32] . Dáil Debates, 24 November 1948.
[33] . Jordan. *John A Costello,* p. 83.
[34] . Dáil Debates 10 May 1949.
[35] . Longford & O'Neill, p. 435-6.
[36] . *Irish Times,* 18 August 1949.
[37] . NAI S 142227.
[38] . *Irish Times,* 12 May 1951.
[39] . ibid. 6 January 1948.
[40] . Longford & O'Neill, p. 441.
[41] . Archdiocesan Archives Drumcondra, McQuaid to Apostolic Nuncio, 7 November 1952.
[42] . DeValera Papers, P/150/2652 17 December 1943.
[43] . Longford & O'Neill, p. 442.

[44] . Jordan. *John A Costello*, p.96.
[45] . Jordan Anthony. *Churchill – a Founder of Modern Ireland, Westport books 1995. p. 197.*
[46] . Longford & O'Neill, p. 443.
[46a] . Moynihan. op. cit. pp. 603-4. The executed leaders of 1916 are buried at Arbour Hill in Dublin. Wolfe Tone is buried at Bodenstown, County Kildare. Thomas Russell, founder of the United Irishmen, is buried in Downpatrick, County Down; he was executed in 1803. In Templepatrick lie the remains of William Orr, executed at Carrickfergus in 1797. The Rev. James Porter, who was executed in 1798, is buried at Greyabbey, County Down.
[47] . Dáil Debates, 25 October 1953.
[48] . *Irish Independent*, 25 January 1965.
[49] . Jordan. *John A Costello*, p. 102.
[50] . ibid. pp. 143-4.
[51] . McCarthy John F. *Planning Ireland's Future*, Glendale 1990. p. 29.
[51a] . Moynihan. op. cit. pp. 577-8.
[52] . O'Connor Emmet. *A Labour History of Ireland 1824-1960*, Gill 7 MacMillan 1992. p. 170.
[53] . Jordan. *John A Costello*, pp. 129-139.
[54] . Whitaker Ken, in interview with Vincent Browne TV3 News 8 October 2009.

CHAPTER 22

[1] . Bowman John. *DeValera and the Ulster Question, 1917-1973*, Oxford 1982, pp. 35-89.
[2] . Ferriter. p. 150.
[3] . Dáil Debates, 12 July 1955.
[4] . NAI S 16029.
[5] . NAI S 16220 16 April 1957.
[6] . ibid.
[7] . NAI S 1627a
[8] . Seánad Éireann, 29 January 1958 col 1411.
[9] . ibid. col 1412
[10] . NAI S Moynihan Minute 7 March 1958.
[11] . Coogan. pp. 682-3.
[12] . NAI S 2312B 8 March 1958.
[13] . Fanning Tim. *The Fethard-on-Sea Boycott*, Collins Press 2010, p. 146-147. & *Catholic Standard*, 21 June & 1 July 1957.
[14] . Dáil Debates, 4 July 1957.
[15] . Coogan. p. 658.
[16] . NAI S 11582C, 29 August 1951.
[17] . NAI S 11582C 30 August 1951.
[18] . *Irish Press*, 3 December 1953.
[19] . NAI S 11582D Irish Community Trust 30 January 1954.
[20] . Jordan Anthony. *The Good Samaritans –Memoir of a Biographer*, Westport Books 2008 pp. 71-2
[21] . Garvin Tom. *Preventing the Future*, Gill & MacMillan 2004. p. 145.
[22] . O'Toole Fintan. *Lessons in the Power of the Church, in Irish Times, 6 June 2009.*
[23] . *Ryan Report* Dublin 2009. cf. also Daire Keogh's *Peter Tyrrell, Letterfrack aand the Ryan Report* in Tony Flannery's (ed) *Responding to the Ryan Report* Columba Press 2009. Keogh reports that Senator Sheehy Skeffingfton, Fr. Derek Warlock, Fr. Robert Nash S. J. and the Irish Christian Brothers responded to Tyrrell's letters. The Brothers later referred Tyrrell to their solicitor. Tyrrell was identified one year after his self-immolation through a piece of paper, which survived in his clothes. It had the remnants of two words on it, 'Skeffington' and 'Dublin'.
[24] . O'Faolain Seán. *Eamon DeValera*, Penguin 1939 p. 18.
[25] . Dáil Debates, 29 February 1940 Col. 2217-2220.
[25a] . Gill Alan. *Orphans of the Empire* Vintage (Australia) 1998.

[26] . Ferriter. pp. 287-8.

[27] . ibid pp. 282-3.

[28] . *The Observer,* 3 February 1980.

[29] . *Irish Independent,* 29 April 1957.

[30] . DeValera Papers, P/1503110 12 May 1957.

[31] . Gilchrist Papers, 14B 27 February 1967. Churchill Archives Centre.

CHAPTER 23

[1] . Dáil Debates, 12 December 1958. Col 2182.

[2] . Coogan. P. 416.

[3] . Hannigan Dave. *DeValera in America,* O'Brien 2008. pp. 280-1.

[4] . Dáil Debates, Vol 171 Col.2170 ff. 12 December 1958.

[5] . ibid.

[6] . ibid. Col. 593. 7 January 1959.

[6a] .Burke Ray. *Press Delete The Decline and Fall of the Irish Press* Curragh 2005.

[7] . Ferriter Diarmaid. *The Transformation of Ireland,* Profile Books 2004. p. 229.

[8] . Ferriter, *Judging Dev.* pp. 280-1.

[9] . Dwyer TR. P. 312.

[10] . *Irish Times,* 8 August 2009.

[10a] . Kiberd Declan, *Inventing Ireland,* Vintage 1996. p. 479.

[11] . Ferriter. P. 6.

[12] . Maguire John. p. 194.

[12a] . Moynihan. op. cit. p. 598.

[13] . *Irish Press,* 29 March 1964.

[14] . Longford & O'Neill, p. 456.

[14a] . Moynihan. op. cit. p. 606.

[15] . ibid. p. 461.

[16] . Jordan. *John A Costello,* p. 169.

[17] . Coogan. P. 687.

[17a] .Moynihan op. cit . pp. 609-611. Those Deputies present in 1969, who were members of the first Dáil, were; James Ryan, Robert Barton, Richard Mulcahy, Joseph O'Doherty, Peter Ward, Eamon DeValera, Seán MacEntee, Ernest Blythe, Alec McCabe, B. Cusack and Patrick O'Keeffee. Joseph Sweeney was in America. The Proclamation was read in English by Eamon Duggan and in French by George Gavan Duffy.

[18] . Boland Kevin. *Up Dev,* pp.13.14.

[19] . Magill June 1981, *The Peter Berry Diaries* & *The Arms Conspiracy Trial Ireland,1970: The Prosecution of Charles Haughey, Captain Kelly and Others* by Angela Clifford. Arms Crisis Series No. 3. A Belfast Magazine 2009.

[20] . Keogh Dermot. *Jack Lynch A Biography* Gill & MacMillan 2008. p. 269.

[21] . Jordan. *John A Costello,* p.199.

[22] . *Irish Times,* 18 October 1981. Conor Cruise O'Brien interviewed by Muiris MacConghail.

[23] . NAI S2004/24/65.

[24] . Jordan. *John A Costello,* pp. 176-7.

[25] . Coogan. p. 703.

[26] . DeValera Papers, 3 September 1975 P/150/3559.

[27] . Fitzgerald Michael. *Autism and Creativity* Brunner-Routeledge 2004 p. 170.

[27a] . Lang Peter. *The Gun and Irish Politics;* examining national history in Neil Jordan's, *Michael Collins* Vol 11, Raita Merivita. 2010.

[28] . MacDonald Malcolm, *Titans and Others London 1972. p. 86.*

[29] . Byrne Elaine, *Irish Times,* 31 March 2009.

INDEX